Fodor's
Health &
Fitness
Vacations

Bernard Burt

Fodor's Travel Publications, Inc.
New York & London

First Edition

ISBN 0-679-01717-8

Fodor's Health & Fitness Vacations

Editor: Vernon Nahrgang
Associate Editor: Cherie Burns
Art Director: Fabrizio La Rocca
Cartographer: David Lindroth
Illustrator: Karl Tanner
Cover Photograph: Alec Pytlowany/Masterfile

Design: Vignelli Associates

About the Author

A resident of Washington, D.C., Bernard Burt has written two guidebooks to that city, contributed articles to *American Health, Second Wind,* and *SporTreks,* and is now preparing a World of Travel guide to Washington, D.C., and the Chesapeake. The State of Maryland honored him as Travel Writer of the Year in 1985.

Special Sales

MANUFACTURED IN THE UNITED STATES OF AMERICA
10 9 8 7 6 5 4 3 2 1

Contents

Foreword

The appeal of the fitness vacation—holiday time used for maintaining or achieving new levels of physical or mental well-being—continues to widen as new facilities, new programs, new technology, and new ideas attract health-conscious individuals.

Where yesterday's working men and women saw vacation time as an opportunity to escape and relax, today's traveler looks for opportunities to expend additional effort in pursuit of a stronger body, a better self-understanding, perhaps a new self-image. Those who invest vacation time to achieve health and fitness goals may groan about getting up before dawn to go on a hike, yet they tend to return home relishing the natural high it brings them.

Fodor's Health & Fitness Vacations surveys the entire range of fitness holiday opportunities in North America. In the pages of this guide, the in-depth profiles of 240 resorts and facilities and 12 cruise ships provide the detailed information anyone needs to begin to plan a vacation with a purpose.

The fees and prices quoted in the resort and cruise ship profiles are based on tariffs that were current in 1988 and early 1989 and are subject to change as costs rise and the contents of program and package offerings are reformulated. Where applicable, taxes and gratuities are additional. Deposits must usually be received in advance of the guest's arrival, and a cancellation charge applies to most bookings. Each resort makes its own policy with respect to accepting payment by personal check, traveler's check, money order, or credit card. The following abbreviations are used in the resort profiles in noting credit card acceptance: AE, American Express; CB, Carte Blanche; DC, Diners Club; MC, MasterCard; V, Visa.

Fees for medical services may be covered by health insurance and under some circumstances may be tax deductible; consult the resort's program director and/or your tax advisor for further information.

While every care has been taken to assure the accuracy of the information in this guide, the passage of time will always bring change, and consequently the publisher cannot accept responsibility for errors that may occur.

All prices and schedules quoted here are based on information available to us at press time. The availability of programs and facilities is subject to change, however, and the prudent fitness vacationer will confirm the details of resort or cruise line offerings before beginning to make serious plans.

Fodor's wants to hear about your travel experiences, both pleasant and unpleasant. When a resort or hotel fails to live up to its billing, let us know and we will investigate the complaint and revise our entries where the facts warrant it.

Send your letters to the editors of Fodor's Travel Publications, 201 East 50th Street, New York, NY 10022, or 30-32 Bedford Square, London WC1B 3SG, England.

Acknowledgments

The author is grateful for the assistance of Jeffrey Joseph of Spa Finders Travel Arrangements Ltd., Steven Trombetti of the American Hotel and Motel Association, Duncan Farrell and J. Reynolds of the Association of Retail Travel Agents cruise ship committee, Judith Singer of Health Fitness Dynamics, Inc., Liliana Sarda of the Canadian embassy's tourism division, and all the concerned professionals who worked out with him and contributed to the research and development of the original concept for this book.

The insights shared by T George Harris, the editor in chief of *American Health* and *Psychology Today* magazines, were a constant source of encouragement.

For personal support and encouragement, the author is indebted to Denise Austin, Jeffrey Burt, Nancy Love, and Lisa Rogak. Archana Kumar provided research assistance. Travel was facilitated by American Airlines, Eastern Airlines, Piedmont Airlines, and USAir.

Directory 1:
Alphabetical Listing of Resorts

Directory 2:
Listing of Resorts by Program

Life Enhancement

Weight Management

Preventive Medicine

Taking the Waters

Introduction

*by T George
Harris, editor in
chief of* American
Health *and*
Psychology Today
magazines

Americans are working harder than ever. In the last 15 years the leisure time of the average adult has shrunk by one-third to just 18 hours a week. The work week has grown longer by 20%, and for many working men and women it now approaches the 50-hour week once condemned in sweatshops.

This is not blue-collar sweat. The higher you rise in professional and executive ranks, the longer and harder you work. Then you labor still more hours learning new things, such as computer uses, that you need to do your job better. For many successful working men and women the stress of overload has become a badge of achievement: It comes with the territory. And those who in a previous generation might have been the idle rich often spend inherited wealth today on opportunities to try harder.

Stress has become the common cold of the busy classes. Fighting it, many strive to get into shape for peak performance. Fitness of body becomes the metaphor and means to fitness of mind. Gallup surveys for *American Health* magazine find that two out of three Americans now aim to do weekly exercise (though we don't always do as much as we intend). One in three of us considers health facilities in planning a vacation trip.

In fact the short, healthy trips become the turning point in many lives. When you go on vacation, it's foolish not to return in better shape than when you left. Travel is an investment in yourself, your productive capital. More and more people expect to get some good out of their trips. More people now take shorter and shorter vacations, and they vacation more often. Millions look for places where they will get the body back into motion, places where they will learn about fresh, tasty foods that are not larded down with fat, sugar, salt, and excessive calories.

That's the reason for this book. It fills the need for a detailed, easy-to-use guide to hundreds of places that now strive to provide meaningful recreation for the mind as well as the body. Moving far beyond the concept of the old European spa—those Marienbads where the elderly elite went to take the waters and be attended by doctors—some of the typically North American spots even offer specific programs to tone the brain and the spirit. The Golden Door in California invites a special few into "The Inner Door" to try the meditative lifestyle of serenity. Arizona's Canyon Ranch offers electronic feedback gear to help you tune in on your brain's alpha waves, long associated with meditation and creativity.

The Fodor's guides published by Random House have earned a reputation for practical, hard-to-get information. While other publishers bring out exotic volumes on "spas," this book provides the essential facts about healthy travel in a systematic way. *Fodor's Health & Fitness Vacations* not only gives you prices and the details of programs, it provides such down-to-earth specifics as the kind of workout gear available in the exercise room.

The purpose is simple: to help you find the kind of place you want, nearest where you want to be. You will probably be astonished to discover that among the 240 resorts profiled in this book, several are an easy drive from your home or workplace. Then there are the spas at sea, 12 cruise ships that sail in Caribbean and Pacific waters.

The resorts described in this guide are grouped by region; if you want to find a facility in a specific area, the *Table of Contents* will tell you where to look. If you already have the name of a resort and want to learn what it has to offer, look for it in the alphabetical listing in *Directory 1*. If you want to find a resort that offers a particular kind of program or treatment, turn to *Directory 2*, which lists resorts under 12 categories of fitness program:

- Luxury pampering
- Life enhancement
- Weight management
- Nutrition and diet
- Stress control
- Holistic health
- Spiritual awareness
- Preventive medicine
- Taking the waters
- Sports conditioning
- Youth camps for weight loss
- Non-program resort facilities

This book was conceived a couple of years ago at a dinner with Robert Bernstein, the lean and savvy president of Random House. To needle him, I asked why he didn't have a travel guide that tells people what they now want to know: how to take a trip that will turn one's life around. Bob heard the combative note in my voice, and he loves a fight, so he got a big grin on his face. He's the rare publisher who cares about what his books do and say. In fact, he was then about to take a personal journey to TV talk shows across the country to tell about the new unabridged *Random House Dictionary*; it has no single author, of course, so Bob was treating himself as the author and preparing to debate all comers on word selection and definitions. We soon found, however, that we had no argument. Used to working a fierce schedule himself, Bob quickly understood the need for a guide to spas, or retreats, or cruises, or health resorts, or whatever you might call them.

In the search for an author, it was clear that this book did not want a health-food zealot, a weight lifter, a spa devotee, or an exotic travel writer who loves only funky or pricey places. We needed someone who could represent the needs of the hard-working woman or man with a limited time to spend on vacation.

The ideal choice turned out to be Bernard Burt, a marketing consultant out of the University of Pennsylvania's Wharton School, a prizewinning travel writer and a practical-minded executive who had managed programs for Philadelphia's Civic

Center. Like many a manager who strives for health, Burt had quite a few naive ideas about health behaviors and healthy food—and found himself totally unprepared, as most executives do, when his doctor told him his life would be shorter than normal if he did not get his weight down. At 58, Burt was ready to study the kinds of places that might help him change his lifestyle, and he signed on to research the new Fodor's.

Burt began with a test run for the April 1988 issue of *American Health*, an article on the most innovative places then rising in the U.S. spa world. Eager to discover the ancestry of such places, Burt investigated one of Europe's great spas, Brenner's Park Hotel in Baden-Baden, West Germany. The historic Friedrichsbad, the emperor's bathhouse, had just been restored at great expense and was drawing Europe's and Japan's water-takers. Striding into the baths, Bernard paid little attention to the sign *Gemischt* (literally, "mixed"). Only when nude women and men appeared together did he realize the meaning of *Gemischt*. Being a gentleman of poise, he eased into the ancient European customs with hardly a blush.

Returned to the United States, Burt's poise underwent a more severe test at the Canyon Ranch in Arizona, one of the most innovative of American health centers. In addition to other programs, it offers a course called MindFitness. Mel Zuckerman, the founder and owner, has a missionary zeal about providing state-of-the-art programs, seminars, and nutrition. He and Dr. Bill Day, one of the fitness pioneers out of the national YMCA, have made Canyon Ranch the practical testing site for the newest biofeedback electronic devices that help us manage our brain waves and thus our state of mind.

Bernard Burt realized that the MindFitness program indicated a clear break between the European spa tradition and American ideas. In different ways, the American industry strives to serve the individual's strong need for the enhancement of physical and mental resources. For most Americans, health means being the best each of us can be at the things we care about, from work to parenting to spiritual growth.

So Burt signed up for five hours a day in the isolation booth with the biofeedback machines. But he had trouble coaxing his mind into the relaxed, creative state that produces alpha brain waves, those often generated by meditation. Worse yet, out in the anteroom the other guests watched the public indicator of his brain-wave pattern, hoping he'd score higher so that they could cheer. No luck; it's hard to make your mind loaf when you're a hardworking writer observing every detail even of your own activity in order to write effectively.

His luck on the alpha machine didn't change until his thoughts turned to one of his favorite operas, *Tristan and Isolde*. As one of Wagner's familiar themes raced through his mind, Bernard suddenly heard cheers from his friends in the anteroom. In thinking of the opera, he'd begun to generate alpha waves, his needle had jumped into the favorable zone, and soon he was taking bows as a fit-minded champ.

Burt found that other hardworking people seeking healthy turnarounds make wonderful companions. On his first dawn walks up a mountain, he learned that ordinary city clothes do not keep one warm in the desert. His feet seemed to be freezing until a companion executive dug out and passed on an extra pair of Brooks Brothers wool socks. In the supportive environment of the health resorts, guests as well as staff soon develop more than the customary concern for one another's welfare. The general feeling is, We're all in this together.

The most startling discovery Burt made concerned the cuisine. A gourmet who cares deeply about food, a wine lover and an honorary member of Washington's Sommelier Society, he expected to find tasteless brown things to eat, the bran-and-bean-sprout cuisine of the early health-food restaurants. Not so; in almost every resort he found the food so fresh "you don't need a lot of seasoning. And the beautiful presentation of the food always gets to me. Everything is low-fat. Part of the learning process is to find that you can enjoy these things without a lot of butter. All the intelligent and enthusiastic young people cooking in the resorts make it a pleasure to eat."

With help on his personal turnaround, Burt became even more faithful in his daily workouts at the Watergate Health Club in Washington, D.C. The grinding work of the writer does not often lead to exercise, but Burt got his cholesterol and his triglycerides under control. He dropped 30 pounds before he finished this book, and his doctor no longer threatens him. His single purpose now as a writer is to guide you toward the place you'll choose for your own turnaround.

1 Health & Fitness Programs

Planning a fitnesss vacation is a two-part process that involves determining one's personal fitness goals and finding the right program or resort. You can begin by setting very specific goals for yourself and then look for the program that best suits your needs. Or you can start by surveying the resort offerings to learn what's available and then decide what you want to achieve. This chapter will help in both parts of the planning process; it identifies and describes 12 categories of fitness program and explains what each attempts to do and what participants can hope to accomplish.

Never before have there been so many varied and challenging opportunities for exercising the mind, the spirit, and the body in a vacation with a purpose. The range of programs and facilities is wide, both for healthy men and women who want to stay in shape and for those who are determined to address a problem or improve a condition.

Some pleasure seekers may choose to relax amid the luxurious furnishings of a posh resort; others will find gratification in a weeklong hiking adventure or the rugged atmosphere of a ranch that resembles a boot camp. New Age retreats and yoga ashrams, naturopaths and natural healing ranches offer health and healing based on combinations of ancient therapies and the latest concepts in behavior modification. Some establishments preach preventive medicine, taking a holistic approach toward strengthening the body against illness through improved nutrition and an understanding of the relationship between mind and body. Others address such problems as the need to lose weight, to stop smoking, and to deal with stress; these programs educate participants, reinforce motivation, and provide the regime not for quick results but for effective long-term improvement.

Increasingly sophisticated and often specialized resorts offer programs to help guests change their lifestyles at home. The establishment of new eating and exercise habits is now considered preferable to crash courses and 700-calorie daily diets. Techniques such as biofeedback have advanced to patterning weeks called MindFitness that can have even longer term effects. Hydrotherapy equipment from Europe appears alongside mud, seaweed, or algae for body cleansing to accompany the latest in toning, shaping, and weight loss technique.

Computer technology is now applied at nearly all levels of fitness training and understanding. Interactive exercise machines analyze body fat content ratios; others report calories expended, adjust themselves to increase your effort, and calculate when your body is functioning best. These machines are a valuable aid to staff members in designing health regimens to suit individual goals and physiology. But they don't take the sweat out of conditioning; the results of a fitness vacation remain yours to achieve.

The costs of a fitness holiday vary widely throughout North America. Where luxury and personal attention are the formula and the staff outnumbers the guests, you can expect to pay premium prices. At the same time, the budget-conscious traveler will find options at $25 a day (including meals) and opportunities to use various resort facilities (without participating in a program) for a small daily fee. Many resorts will offer, for a set price, a package of services to complement the principal program you have chosen. In some areas the off-season brings markedly reduced rates and bargain packages.

Because rate policies differ widely among resorts, the wise traveler will want to have a clear understanding of precisely what features are included in a program rate and what taxes and tipping will be added to the rate quoted. The prices given in the resort profiles in this book were accurate at the time of writing, but they should be used only as a preliminary guide; they will vary throughout 1989 and 1990 as increases go into effect, new combinations of services are offered, and new programs and packages are formulated.

In the following pages, the descriptions of the 12 categories of fitness program explain in general terms what you can expect to find in the individual programs. Each description concludes with the Fodor's Choice of leading resorts that offer that program. Look up the leading resorts in *Directory 1* and turn to the profiles in the next section of this guide for details of the program offerings at each of the resorts. *Directory 2* gives the complete list of resorts for every program category and indicates the page on which each of the facilities is profiled.

Luxury Pampering

Usually found at resorts where the staff members outnumber the guests, **luxury pampering** is intended for those who long to be herbal wrapped, massaged, and soaked in bubbling pools fragrant with chamomile. The height of survival chic is lounging in an elegant robe and discussing a delicious spa meal; exercise classes and a weight loss diet can be part of the program, but there will be no activity to put too much strain on the body.

An abundance of options makes luxury pampering a highly personalized regimen, designed for men as well as women. The services include exotic body and skin care treatments and the latest image-enhancers at the beauty salon, among them thalassotherapy tubs, loofah body scrubs with sea salts and almond oil, and paraffin facial masks for dehydrated skin. Recent advances have joined European spa treatments with American fitness concepts, such as an underwater massage followed by a mud pack.

Deluxe accommodations and lots of amenities are basic to luxury pampering. Many resorts have Sunday-to-Sunday schedules, while some offer pampering à la carte. To those who say, "No pain, no gain," the pampered reply, "No frills, no thrills."

Luxury Pampering: Fodor's Choice
Cal-a-Vie Health Resort, California
Doral Saturnia International Spa Resort, Florida
The Golden Door, California
The Greenbrier, West Virginia
The Greenhouse, Texas
Maine Chance, Arizona
Norwich Inn and Spa, Connecticut
Charlie's Spa at the Sans Souci, Jamaica
Turnberry Isle Yacht and Country Club, Florida

Life Enhancement

The **life enhancement** program aims for long-term physical and psychological benefits. It involves a total assessment of one's condition, with medical tests and personal consultations on nutrition and fitness. Some programs have a spiritual element, others emphasize an educational approach through exercise, diet, and behavior modification.

Developed in many cases at specialized centers, life enhancement programs usually require complete commitment from participants. The size of the group is generally limited to about a dozen men and women, each working one-on-one with a team of health and behavioral specialists in an intensive experience that little resembles a resort-style program.

Life Enhancement: The Aerobics Center, Texas
Fodor's Choice Duke University Diet and Fitness Center, North Carolina
Esalen Institute, California
Hartland Health Center, Virginia
Hawaii Health & Wellness Vacation, Hawaii
Hilton Head Health Institute, South Carolina
Green Valley Health Resort, Utah
La Costa Hotel and Spa, California
Palm-Aire Spa Resort & Country Club, Florida
SunRise Springs Resort, New Mexico

Weight Management

Learning how to lose weight properly and how to maintain a healthy balance in body mass is the basis of a **weight management** program. This is not a course for a dramatic loss of weight; rather, it teaches proper eating habits, beginning with what to buy in the supermarket and how to prepare meals.

The weight management resort integrates motivational sessions with exercise, diet, and pampering, reeducation with recreation. Some programs involve fasting on juices and water. Some resorts are residential retreats for the seriously obese; some offer a full range of sports and outdoor activities.

Carefully controlled and supervised, the typical regimen is tailored to the individual's fitness level and health needs. A team of specialists—therapists and nutritionists—coaches you on the basics of beginning and maintaining a personal program. Additional motivation and support arise in the camaraderie of being with a group of like-minded dieters.

Weight Management: Fodor's Choice
Canyon Ranch Health and Fitness Resort, Arizona
The Kerr House, Ohio
L'Aqualigne, St. Maarten
Living Springs Lifestyle Center, New York
National Institute of Fitness, Utah
Pawling Health Manor, New York
Rocky Mountain Wellness Spa, Colorado
Sans Souci Health Resort, Ohio
Structure House, North Carolina
The Woods Fitness Institute, West Virginia

Nutrition and Diet

Nutrition and diet programs maintain that well-being begins in the kitchen, that understanding the relationship between nutrition and diet can enhance one's lifestyle and promote sound, healthy habits. Here you may learn to evaluate product labels ("high in fiber," "low in cholesterol") and to cope with the variety of advertising claims.

Participants, both vegetarians and newcomers to macrobiotics, gain a new perspective on nutrition through lectures and first-hand experience in food preparation. How foods affect your health, how to shop, how to choose from restaurant menus, how to plan and prepare meals are among the subjects covered. Classes are designed to generate menus and recipes for nutritious dining that participants will then take home with them.

Designed as an educational experience, with no attempt to provide a crash diet plan, the nutrition and diet program provides the fundamentals for following a regimen of eating healthy natural foods. And participants get to enjoy the meals prepared in class.

Nutrition and Diet: Fodor's Choice
Birdwing Spa, Minnesota
Bonaventure Resort & Spa, Florida
The Equinox, Vermont
Green Mountain at Fox Run, Vermont
Hippocrates Health Institute, Florida
The Kushi Macrobiotic Center, Massachusetts
New Life Spa, Vermont
The Oaks at Ojai, California
Pritikin Longevity Center, California
Pritikin Longevity Center, Pennsylvania
Southwind Health Resort, Georgia
Weight Watchers Camp New England, Massachusetts

Stress Control

Gaining control of the causes of stress is a basic element in the programs of most health and fitness resorts. The approaches to **stress control,** however, are varied; they include relaxation techniques, behavior modification, biofeedback, and meditation.

As a total experience, with a physical setting and food to lift one's spirits, stress control programs can create a strong feeling of well-being. Some are offered as an executive retreat within a resort, as an antidote for job burnout, or as a recipe for self-renewal. The opportunity to work one-on-one with advisors, away from the causes of stress, can enhance the individual's ability to cope with the stress factors of daily life.

Stress Control: Fodor's Choice
The Ashram Health Retreat, California
Bluegrass Spa, Kentucky
Canyon Ranch Health and Fitness Resort, Arizona
Heartland Health and Fitness Retreat, Illinois
The Himalayan Institute, Pennsylvania
Jane Fonda's Laurel Springs Retreat, California
Mohonk Mountain House, New York
The Option Institute, Massachusetts
Pualani Fitness Retreat, Hawaii
Rocky Mountain Health Ranch, Colorado

Holistic Health

The theme of **holistic health** programs is that, in order to be truly fit and healthy, you must develop your emotional, intellectual, and spiritual self as well as your body. The nontradional therapies seek to achieve a sense of wholeness with the world and oneself that will help the body to fend off illness.

Holistic health training can be vigorous or mellow; it is usually a combination of exercise, nutrition, stress control, and relaxation. Activities include walking, hiking, biking, cross-country skiing, tennis, swimming, and aerobics classes. A wide range of alternative healing therapies stretches from massage to yoga, and the body can be cleansed with herbs, enemas, or psychic diagnoses.

The credo of holistic health retreats is that illness results from a lack of balance within the body, whether caused by stress or physical conditions, and that the balance can be restored without the use of medicine. When secluded in places of great natural beauty, the healing process may draw on spiritual sources as well as natural energy to help participants find inner strength.

Holistic Health:
Fodor's Choice

Feathered Pipe Ranch, Montana
Foxhollow Wellness Spa, Massachusetts
Hawaiian Fitness Holiday, Hawaii
Hollyhock Farm, British Columbia
Instituto de Vida Natural, Puerto Rico
Kripalu Center for Yoga and Health, Massachusetts
Murrieta Hot Springs Resort, California
New Age Health Spa, New York
Northern Pines Health Resort, Maine
Omega Institute for Holistic Studies, New York

Spiritual Awareness

In celebrating the human potential, **spiritual awareness** programs strive to stretch the individual's limits both mentally and physically. They try to foster a process of personal growth and transformation through workouts that synchronize mind and body and make one aware of one's inner resources. Specializing in alternative education, vegetarian diets, and natural therapies, they offer psychic tools for living.

The experience may draw on any number of Eastern and Western philosophies, and it might focus on yogic training or sensory awareness. Body therapies, visualization, and shamanism are among the healing processes that can be explored. Private counseling and group sessions are usually available for both beginners and advanced meditators.

Retreats rather than resorts, these centers for spiritual training are situated in places where nature's beauty can be enjoyed without distraction or tension.

Spiritual
Awareness:
Fodor's Choice

Breitenbush Retreat Center, Oregon
The Center of the Light, Massachusetts
Esalen Institute, California
Kalani Honua, Hawaii
Kripalu Center for Yoga and Health, Massachusetts
Kripalu Yoga Ashram, Pennsylvania
The Last Resort, Utah
Maharishi Ayur-Ved Health Center, Massachusetts
Omega Institute for Holistic Studies, New York
Sivananda Ashram, Quebec
Sivananda Ashram Yoga Retreat, Bahamas

Preventive Medicine

Preventive medicine centers take a scientific approach to health and fitness by combining traditional medical services with advanced concepts for the prevention of illness. Designed for healthy people who want to stay that way, the programs involve medical and fitness testing, counseling on nutrition and stress control, and a range of sports and exercise activities along with massage and bodywork.

Conceived as a regenerative experience for healing and relaxation, the programs can also treat problems associated with obesity, aging, and cardiovascular disease. These programs, usually developed in consultation with your personal physician at home, are carefully structured, supervised at all times, and require full participation.

Participants work with a team of physiotherapists and doctors in learning new techniques for survival; they discover how to eliminate negative habits and modify a lifestyle. The one-on-one training with fitness instructors, nutritionists, and psychologists can reveal ways of accomplishing personal goals.

Along with hospital-related programs, specialized centers for preventive medicine can now be found at leading fitness resorts and at retreats under the auspices of Seventh-day Adventist medical services organizations. They bring together specialists in all fields of health and nutrition to provide a comprehensive prescription for healthy living.

Preventive Medicine: Fodor's Choice
Canyon Ranch in the Berkshires, Massachusetts
Four Seasons Fitness Resort, Texas
The Greenbrier, West Virginia
King Ranch, Ontario
Palm-Aire Spa Resort & Country Club, Florida
The Phoenix Fitness Resort, Texas
Poland Spring Health Institute, Maine
Pritikin Longevity Center, California
Weimar Institute, California
Wildwood Lifestyle Center, Georgia

Taking the Waters

The practice of bathing at hot springs gave rise to the fashionable spas of Europe and America, where people congregated as much for social as for therapeutic purposes. Today **taking the waters**—which may involve drinking six to eight glasses of mineral water daily—is a practice enjoyed for health and relaxation.

The introduction of water-based therapies and mud baths at American fitness resorts is a recent phenomenon. The cross-fertilization of European and American approaches to maintaining a healthy body and a glowing complexion has revived interest in bathing at grand old resorts where natural waters are available free for the asking. Related but different treatments that involve seaweed, algae, and seawater are offered at spas that specialize in thalassotherapy.

For the purist, a secluded hot spring promises the best kind of stress-reduction therapy. Others need the added stimulation of body scrubs with sea salts by a masseur armed with a loofah sponge—or a whirlpool bath bubbling with herbal essences.

Taking the Waters: Aqua-Mer Center, Quebec
Fodor's Choice The Arlington Resort Hotel & Spa, Arkansas
Centre Thermal Harry Hamousin, Guadeloupe
Glenwood Hot Springs Lodge, Colorado
Harrison Hot Springs Hotel, British Columbia
The Homestead, Virginia
Kah-Nee-Ta Resort, Oregon
Safety Harbor Spa and Fitness Center, Florida
Saratoga Spa State Park, New York
Spa Hotel and Mineral Springs, California

Sports Conditioning

For the active vacationer or the athlete seeking new challenges, **sports conditioning** programs offer advanced training in a variety of sports, workouts with experts, and high-tech training with the latest in exercise equipment.

The current buzzword is *cross-training*, which denotes a varied program that teaches the benefits of alternating sports such as tennis or swimming with exercises such as walking or weight lifting. Mountain hikes, beach runs, and cross-country skiing are programmed to stretch your endurance limits.

Mental training techniques can also be incorporated in sports conditioning programs. Following the lead of Olympic athletes and professional golfers, trainers are offering courses in guided relaxation, affirmations (positive statements), and visualization to improve the competitive edge. These practices are more than morale boosters; the visualization of successful performance may create neural patterns that the brain will use in telling the muscles what to do.

Therapy for sports-related injuries is a feature of some resorts. Others specialize in the mind-body relationship, with disciplines to promote both physical and spiritual development. Martial arts, yoga, and croquet are newly popular vehicles for integrating exercise and mental concentration.

Sports The Aspen Club, Colorado
Conditioning: Chateau Whistler Resort, British Columbia
Fodor's Choice Chukka Cove, Jamaica
Cliff Lodge at Snowbird, Utah
The Hard & the Soft, Montserrat
Le Sport, St. Lucia
The Maui Challenge, Hawaii
Mountain Biking at Winter Park, Colorado
PGA Sheraton Resort, Florida
Saddlebrook Golf and Tennis Resort, Florida

Youth Camps for Weight Loss

Youth camps for weight loss are summer camps without fast food; located on college campuses, at private schools, and at resorts, they combine instruction in healthy eating habits with a full regimen of fitness and fun.

Cooking classes and talks on health and nutrition emphasize the selection of foods that are tasty and healthy and the avoidance of fattening fad foods. Supervised workouts in high-tech weights rooms help campers shape up.

Designed for boys, girls, and young adults, the weight loss camps are managed by private organizations. In most cases the facilities are leased for the season and staffed with nutritionists and cooks who prepare calorie-controlled meals and snacks. A sports staff and use of campus facilities are usually added features.

Youth Camps for Weight Loss: Fodor's Choice

Camp Camelot, California
Camp Camelot, North Carolina
Camp Del Mar, California
Camp Murrieta, California
Canyon Ranch Health and Fitness Resort, Arizona
Castleview Camp, Rhode Island
Weight Watchers Camps (12 locations in the USA and Canada)

Non-program Resort Facilities

Non-program resort facilities—often a health club that adds the fitness element to a vacation resort—can be just the place for weekend getaways or family vacations. Some fill a gap in areas where fitness resorts are not available; others are close to cultural and historical attractions. Most offer outstanding facilities and special services geared to the fitness-oriented traveler.

Non-program Resort Facilities: Fodor's Choice

The Claremont Resort, California
The Kingsmill Resort, Virginia
Marriott's Desert Springs Resort, California
Marriott's Mountain Shadows Resort, Arizona
Rancho La Puerta, Mexico
The Royal Bahamian Hotel & Villas, Bahamas
Scottsdale Princess, Arizona
Sonesta Beach Hotel & Spa, Bermuda
Wheels Country Spa at Wheels Inn, Ontario
Woodstock Inn & Resort, Vermont

2 Health & Fitness Resorts

California

A trendsetter in food, fashion, and fitness, California has been luring health-conscious visitors since the Spanish explorers first landed in San Diego. The 150 miles of coastline between Los Angeles and Mexico boasts more varieties of health spa than will be found in any other part of the nation; mud treatments, mineral waters, vegetarian diets, luxury pampering, and spiritual retreats are widespread.

Northern Californians consider themselves residents of a different state, one with San Francisco at its center. For them the wine country to the north is a principal attraction, and taking mud baths at Calistoga ranks with visiting the vineyards of Napa and Sonoma counties to taste and select one's own private reserve. Inland, the natural grandeur of Yosemite National Park vies with the dry heat and luxury resorts of Palm Springs.

The Ashram Health Retreat

Life enhancement
Stress control
Weight management

California
Calabasas

Barbra Streisand called the Ashram "a boot camp without food." Others have found it a rite of passage to a new self-image; Shirley MacLaine described it in *Out on a Limb* as "a spiritually involved health camp."

The Ashram displaces old stresses with new ones. Most of the fairly affluent achievers who come here have high-pressure jobs, and by subjecting themselves to a week of enormous physical exertion and minimal meals, and meeting these challenges, they can experience what some speak of as a transcendent, positive change in attitude.

Living together in close quarters, 10 to a group, guests follow a routine of mountain hikes, exercise, and yoga. A daily massage and a few hours of relaxation are the only respite. Everyone joins in; participation in every activity is required.

Not everyone can handle the discipline. Defections will occur, yet group support and personal counseling work for most participants. There is considerable joking about deprivation training—and serious talk about loving yourself for what you are rather than pursuing a new image.

Turning the concept of a retreat (the original meaning of ashram) into the ultimate challenge was an idea tested in a Guatemalan jungle by the Ashram's owner, Anne-Marie Bennstrom. A cross-country skiing champion in her native Sweden, she tested her personal limits by spending five months alone in the jungle. The mystical clarity of life's essentials, as opposed to the nonessentials, is what she shares with her guests in this retreat high above the Pacific Ocean and the sybaritic life of Malibu Beach.

California

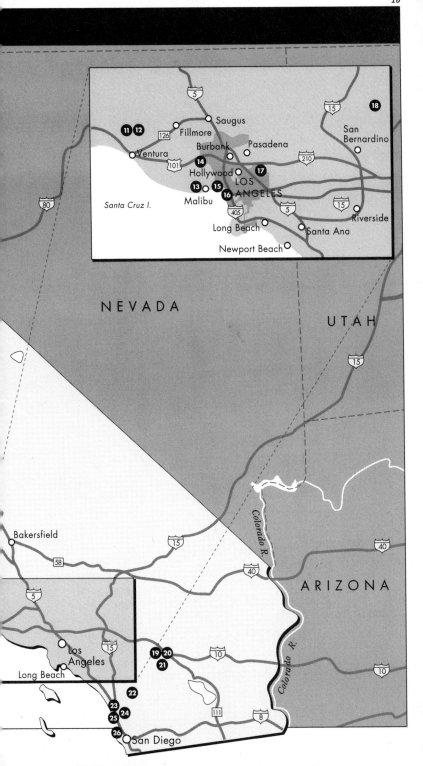

The unpaved entrance road winds uphill to a plain, two-story stucco house. Surrounded by towering eucalyptus trees, the garden contains a small heated swimming pool, a solarium for sunbathing, and a geodesic dome where yoga and meditation sessions take place.

The day begins at 6:30 AM with stretching and breathing exercises that help take the kinks out of sore muscles and build energy for a strenuous hike into the hills. Breakfast is a glass of orange juice. The morning schedule usually includes an hour of weight lifting followed by an hour of exercise in the pool; it winds down with a game of water volleyball.

During the afternoon each guest has a one-hour massage. Calisthenics and a two-hour walk complete the day. The personal traits and individual techniques of the program leaders enhance the experience and guarantee that each guest's physical and psychological needs are attended to.

The energy level rises each day as the hikes become increasingly difficult. For those who stay the course, a sense of ascetic purification is promised. Having stretched your limits, the world seems more manageable.

The Ashram Health Retreat
2025 McKain Rd.; Box 8, Calabasas, CA 91302
Tel. 818/888–0232

Administration	Owner-manager, Anne-Marie Bennstrom; program director, Catharina Hedberg
Season	Year-round, scheduled weeks.
Accommodations	Guests double up in 5 small bedrooms in the ranch house. Simply furnished, with shared bathroom facilities, library, lounge, and weights room. Sweat suits, shorts, T-shirts, and robe provided.
Rates	$1,700 per week, all-inclusive. $700 in advance. No credit cards.
Meal Plans	600 calories a day in fruit, vegetables, sprouts, seeds, and nuts, mostly raw or liquefied. Lunch can be a yogurt-and-cottage-cheese blend with fruit slices, dinner a green salad. Snacks of raw vegetables and juices throughout the day.
Services and Facilities	**Exercise Equipment:** Free weights. **Services:** Massage, nutritional counseling. **Swimming Facilities:** Outdoor pool. **Recreation Facilities:** Water volleyball. **Evening Programs:** Lectures on developing healthy habits, spirituality, energy centers of the body, sexuality.
Getting Here	One hour from Los Angeles. Not accessible by private car; all guests picked up by van at locations in the area. Free pickup to and from Los Angeles International Airport and local hotels.
Special Notes	No smoking.

Cal-a-Vie Health Resort

Life enhancement
Luxury pampering

California
Vista

Terraced into a Southern California hillside, the 24 country villas of Cal-a-Vie seem lifted from a scene in Provence. Yet the lavish outdoor pool, manicured gardens and streams, and wonderful food are all American. For luxury and weight loss, this is the ultimate escape.

European hydrotherapy and beauty treatments are the specialty of the house. Seaweed wraps to cleanse the pores, lymphatic massage for detoxification, and underwater-massage tubs are part of the sybaritic experience.

"Detoxify" and "cleanse" are terms that are spoken of daily. The program is designed to heal the body by restoring the balance of mind, body, and spirit. No intrusion from the outside world is allowed to disturb the peace and tranquillity of your week of hikes, aerobics classes, and calorie-controlled meals.

Guests surrender quickly to a world without computers and television and leave the thinking to those who run the resort with quiet but firm efficiency. Designed as a total environment for health and fitness, the 125-acre resort accepts only 24 guests a week; the all-inclusive Sunday-to-Sunday program offers diverse body and skin-care treatments for men and women.

Thalassotherapy based on European techniques was introduced here, a California first. During the procedure, you are cocooned in a mixture of algae and seawater, coated with clay, and gently scrubbed and massaged. Another popular treatment, the aromatherapy massage, is intended to fight tension and its consequences and is also geared to rid the body of cellulite. Essential oils from flowers and herbs are blended and applied to points of the body in varying combinations. As many as 25 oils can be combined for particular trouble spots. A loofah body scrub sloughs off old skin.

Guests soon learn to relax as they receive total care. A toothbrush and personal things are all you need to bring; sweat suits, robes, shorts, and T-shirts are provided. As you go on to another activity, a fresh set of clothes is supplied. The staff has raised mothering to a fine art, and its members do seem to care. With a ratio of four accredited staff members to each guest, little is left to chance.

The first step is your personal fitness evaluation. Your vital statistics and the results of a battery of tests to determine flexibility, cardiovascular capability, and upper and lower body strength are fed into a computer; your personal diet and exercise regimen will be based on the printout.

The options for a richer, more meaningful approach to fitness are here. For many guests the issue is maintaining a healthy schedule rather than losing weight. Meals by the Belgian chef Michel Stroot are an added attraction; his *cuisine fraîche* totals less than 1,000 calories per day.

The day begins with a prebreakfast hike into the hills—long or short depending on your preference—followed by cooling down exercises, and workouts with a group in the swimming pool or in the gym with a personal trainer. Yoga, tai chi chuan, and Dancercize are further options, and a golf course is just over the hill.

The peace of mind and well-being a guest achieves are contagious. With its freedom from stress, the experience takes on the aspect of joining a big, happy family. There are men-only, women-only, and couples weeks; the resort is for adults only.

Cal-a-Vie Health Resort
2249 Somerset Rd., Vista, CA 92084
Tel. 619/945-2055

Administration Manager, Gary Driver; program director, Deborah Stevenson

Season Year-round except mid-Dec.–Jan. 2.

Accommodations 24 private villas with heat, air conditioning, French provincial furnishings; beam ceilings, stone fireplaces, flowered chintzes, carved wooden armoires.

Rates $3,300 per person, all-inclusive, includes 10% service charge; $50.43 tax additional. $1,000 in advance. Credit cards: AE, MC, V.

Meal Plans 3 meals served to order daily, based on suggested calorie intake. Lunch can include a seafood salad, whole wheat pizza with *chèvre* cheese, sautéed tofu, and lentils. Dinner entrees can include turkey patties, sautéed free-range chicken with rosemary and roasted garlic, a pilaf of lentils and brown rice, and grilled swordfish. Fresh herbs from the garden; lemon and grapefruit juice enhance flavors without salt; breads, sorbets, and desserts are made from scratch. Special diets accommodated.

Services and Facilities **Exercise Equipment:** 12 Keiser Cam II pneumatic weight training units, Lifecycles, rowing machine, rebounders. **Services:** Massage (Swedish, shiatsu, aromatherapy), thalassotherapy, hydrotherapy, loofah body scrub, reflexology, pedicure, manicure; facial, hair and skin care. **Swimming Facilities:** Heated outdoor pool. **Spa Facilities:** Indoor sauna and steam room; recessed Roman whirlpool. **Recreation Facilities:** Tennis court, volleyball; golf, horseback riding nearby. **Evening Programs:** Lectures on current topics, fitness, and nutrition; cooking demonstrations; movies.

In the Area Morning hiking; San Diego museums, theaters, and waterfront; Sea World; herb farm; Mount Palomar Observatory.

Getting Here *From San Diego.* By car, Rte. 163 to I–15 to Vista (1 hr). Free pickup on Sunday to and from San Diego International Airport. Limousine, taxi, rental car available.

Special Notes Smoking and nonsmoking accommodations; tables for nonsmokers in the dining room; no smoking in the spa building.

Camp Camelot

Youth camps for weight loss

California Located on the Whittier College campus, sunny, palm-fringed
Whittier Camp Camelot is a coed slim 'n' trim down place that offers a
mixture of supervised diet, education, exercise, and fun making for an active vacation. There are facilities for physical,
creative, and cultural activities for campers age 8–12, 13–17,
18–21, and young women 21–29. The campus includes a main
gymnasium with a dance studio, racquetball court, weights
room, and a training room with whirlpool and locker rooms.
Campers also have access to a mini-gymnasium for exercise and
karate. Outdoor facilities include a jogging trail, tree-lined biking trails, multiple fields and courts for softball, basketball,
soccer, track, and six all-weather tennis courts.

The nearby beaches and lakes afford opportunities for
waterskiing, sailing, and boating under the supervision of instructors. Camelot also schedules optional day excursions to
Disneyland, Universal Studios, Dodger Stadium, Hollywood
Bowl, and the Los Angeles and San Diego zoos, among other
places.

The 1,200-calorie diet (1,500 for boys) is served in colorful dining halls provided with modern equipment for food preparation
and service. The menus are prepared under the supervision of a
nutritionist and include three meals daily, with two snacks of
assorted vegetables and fresh fruit.

Camp Camelot
Whittier College, Whittier, CA
(Office) 949 Northfield Rd., Woodmere, NY 11598
Tel. 516/374–0785 or 800/421–4321

Administration Program directors, Thelma Hurwitz, Bonnie and Elliot
Hurwitz, Michele Friedman

Season July–Aug.

Accommodations Fully equipped dorms with 24-hour security; separate lodging
for male and female campers. Lounges and recreation rooms for
social and evening activities. Modern baths.

Rates 7 weeks camp $3,650; 4 weeks $2,450; 3 weeks $1,925. $375 in
advance. Credit cards: MC, V.

Meal Plans 3 balanced meals a day. Diet takes into account each camper's
individual growth and nutritional needs. Lunch and dinner entrees include Polynesian chicken, veal scaloppine, broiled
steak, barbecued chicken, beef Stroganoff and turkey divan.

Services and **Exercise Equipment:** Universal weight training gym, free wei-
Facilities ghts, Exercycle, rowing machine, treadmills. **Swimming
Facilities:** Aquatic center; beaches and lakes. **Recreation Facilities:** Jogging, softball, basketball, soccer, 6 tennis courts,
racquetball; instruction in aerobics, modern and jazz dance; bicycle trips; waterskiing, sailing and boating. **Evening
Programs:** Game nights, dramatics, bowling, movies, dancing.

In the Area Nature walks and hikes; Disneyland, Marineland; Los Angeles
Music Center; museums and galleries.

Getting Here *From Los Angeles.* By car, Rte. 10 north, Hwy. 605 (1½ hr). Rental car, taxi available.

Special Notes No smoking indoors.

Camp Del Mar and Camp Murrieta

Youth camps for weight loss
Boys only (Camp Del Mar); Girls only (Camp Murrieta)

California Based at college campuses in the Mission Bay area, the summer
San Diego programs of Camp Del Mar and Camp Murrieta are designed to teach young people how to cope with food fads and to control their weight. Operated by a nutritionist and exercise specialist, the camps capitalize on the climate and the sunny lifestyle of San Diego, from the beaches to Balboa Park and Old Town.

The daily regimen includes exercise, walking, running, and counseling. Behavior modification techniques are used to improve the campers' self-image as they shed pounds. There are outings to local beaches and parks and at least one excursion per week.

The diet plan is a system that can be adapted at home by the campers. They learn how to balance calories from basic food groups, to eat smaller portions, and to avoid fats and high-sodium foods. Cooking classes are also offered.

The beautiful campus of the University of Point Loma is used for the boys' camp; the girls have full use of facilities at the University of San Diego. Campers range in age from 8 to 18, and they stay for four to six weeks.

Camp Murrieta
University of San Diego, Linda Vista Dr., San Diego
Camp Del Mar
*University of Point Loma, Lomaland Dr., San Diego
(Office) 6091 Charae St., San Diego, CA 92122
Tel. 619/460–3376*

Administration Program director, David Kempton

Season Late June–mid-Aug.

Accommodations Dormitory rooms with 4–8 beds, private closets. Shared bath and showers, laundry. Campers provide towels and bed linen.

Rates 4-week program $2,200, 6 weeks $3,200. $1,000 in advance. Credit cards: MC, V.

Meal Plans Daily diet of 1,000 calories. Breakfast is fruit, a roll or bagel, and skim milk. Lunch includes green salad, soup, and fruit. A typical dinner is broiled chicken, steamed broccoli, half a baked potato, and Jell-O. Diet soda or fruit snacks.

Services and **Exercise Equipment:** 12-station Universal weight training
Facilities gym. **Services:** Counseling, cooking instruction. **Swimming Facilities:** Indoor and outdoor pools. **Recreation Facilities:** Tennis,

hikes, badminton, volleyball. **Evening Programs:** Camp theatricals, outings to local shows.

In the Area Scheduled bus trips to Sea World, Balboa Park museums and zoo, San Diego State Historical Park; Water-slide park, animal park, beaches.

Getting Here *From San Diego.* Both campuses can be reached by public bus or car (30 min). Free pickup to and from San Diego International Airport or Amtrak station.

Special Notes No smoking in the dormitories. Remember to bring sheets, blankets, beach towel, bath towels.

The Claremont Resort

Luxury pampering
Non-program resort facilities

California
Oakland
The San Francisco Bay Area's new spa attraction is the Claremont Resort, which occupies a Victorian-style castle built in 1915. The white-turreted hotel presides over 22 acres of landscaped grounds in the hills of Oakland and Berkeley. Fitness programs and a new restaurant offering a low-calorie menu were added in the resort's recent major face-lift.

The spa programs include aerobics classes and circuit weight training, and the daily schedule of one-hour classes runs from 8 AM to 9 PM. A multipurpose aerobics gym, fully equipped weights room, outdoor exercise and lap pool, and 10 day/night tennis courts are ready for you.

Therapy treatments and massage are major features here. In the hydrotherapy area are rooms with specialized equipment for underwater massage, herbal wraps, and loofah body scrubs. Herbal and floral essences are used in baths and aromatherapy massage to detoxify the body. Separate locker rooms for men and women are equipped with steam room, sauna, and whirlpool; a full-service salon offers hair, nail, and skin care.

Weekend packages, focus weeks, and local membership privileges are further offerings; guests may undertake a total spa program or use some of the facilities as desired. Downtown San Francisco is just 20 minutes across the bay.

The Claremont Resort
Ashby and Domingo Aves.; Box 23363, Oakland, CA 94623
Tel. 415/843-3000 or 415/843-7924

Administration Manager, Henry Feldman; program director, Vicki Poth

Season Year-round.

Accommodations 239 spacious rooms with oversize beds (some are four-posters) and sitting areas; public rooms for art displays and social and business functions.

Rates 3-day spa package $708–$882 with meals, $524–$698 without meals, depending on the season; bay-view rooms $160–$190 single, $180–$210 double; junior suites $250. One night payable in advance or credit card guarantee. Credit cards: AE, CB, DC, MC, V.

Meal Plans A spa menu is planned for the hotel's Pavilion Room; the spa cafe's menu is calorie controlled, low in cholesterol and sodium. Specialties have included mesquite-grilled swordfish with papaya chutney, grilled and steamed vegetables, steamed wonton.

Services and Facilities **Exercise Equipment:** Computerized Lifecycles, rowing machines, treadmills; Nautilus weight training units. **Services:** Massage, hydrotherapy, facials; hair, nail, skin care; nutrition counseling; tennis and swimming lessons. **Swimming Facilities:** Olympic-size outdoor pool. **Recreation Facilities:** Water volleyball, 10 tennis courts; golf nearby.

In the Area Downtown San Francisco; Bay Area museums, beaches, water sports. Wine country tours. Oakland's Jack London Square (entertainment, shopping, arts).

Getting Here *From San Francisco.* By Bay Area Rapid Transit, Rockridge Station (20 min). By car, Bay Bridge to Rte. 24, Claremont Ave. exit (30 min). Taxi, rental car available.

Special Notes Specially equipped rooms, ramps, and elevators provide complete access to the spa for the disabled. Tennis and swimming clinics for children. No smoking in the spa; smoking permitted in some guest rooms and public areas.

Dr. Wilkinson's Hot Springs

Taking the waters
Stress control

California
Calistoga
Mud, mineral water, and massage, as offered in Dr. Wilkinson's Hot Springs resort, are the reasons for visiting this historic spa town at the northern end of the Napa Valley. Whether you suffer from arthritis or simply want to relax in the dark warmth of a mud bath, the therapy is reasonably priced.

Half a dozen downtown hotels advertise mud baths and mineral-spring water swimming pools. Their unpretentiousness makes them the antithesis of Southern California's most celebrated spas; neither The Golden Door nor La Costa can offer the combination of treatments found here.

Native Americans discovered the hot springs and considered them a miracle, but the town achieved its reputation as a resort in the 1860s when newspaperman/entrepreneur Sam Brannan built an elaborate bathhouse that attracted San Francisco society. Today, with all things natural back in favor, the crowd at the baths is younger and includes many European visitors. Compared with bathing in the mud at Ischia or Terme di Saturnia in Italy, Calistoga is a bargain.

What does mud bathing accomplish? The heat and the weight relax muscles and increase circulation. Joints loosen and the nervous system slows down. Between layers of mud and hot mineral water, you feel suspended and soothed. A healthy sweat follows your initial immersion in the primal ooze, and the body detoxifies as pores open and the skin softens.

In the mid-1940s, a chiropractor, Dr. John Wilkinson, developed mud-bath treatments for arthritis and bursitis; the regimen gained popularity in the '70s as interest in holistic health blossomed. Dr. Wilkinson's building still looks like an ordinary motel, but under the management of Wilkinson's son Mark, the services and treatments maintain a standard of excellence. Appointments must be made well in advance during summer months because the baths are open to the public.

Like most places in town, there are separate facilities for men and women (coed baths are available at the Golden Haven, 1713 Lake St.). After you disrobe and drape yourself with a towel, an attendant leads the way to a large, skylighted room that smells of sulfur. Two tiled tubs, each about four feet high, bubble with mud in one corner; showers and soaking tubs complete the scene. Sinking into the mud is easier than it looks, and the attendant gently pats it around your chin. A board under your neck keeps your head up.

Stuck in the mud, you commune with nature for about 12 minutes. The 105-degree mix of volcanic ash, peat, and mineral water works its magic soon enough (people with heart conditions or high blood pressure are advised to stay immersed only a few minutes). After a shower and cooling bath, you are swaddled in sheets and instructed to rest. A whirlpool or steam bath is suggested before your massage.

The final touch is a cool swim in the outdoor pool, filled with the same mineral water sold nationwide for drinking. Use of the swimming pool, large indoor whirlpool, and outdoor hot tub is restricted to motel guests. Health precautions at the baths are meticulous. The mud is drained nightly and sanitized with boiling water.

The bath routine can be varied, if you wish, with a treatment imported from Japan. Available only at the International Spa, 1300 Washington Street, it's a soak in a tub filled with cedar fibers (read "sawdust") and plant enzymes that give off natural heat as they ferment. The soothing process takes about 20 minutes and is followed by a similar cooling process.

Calistoga's other attractions are within a four-block downtown area on Lincoln Avenue. For the adventurous, there are balloon and glider trips. The Calistoga Bookstore is another attraction. Wine lovers can visit local vineyards.

Dr. Wilkinson's Hot Springs
1507 Lincoln Ave., Calistoga, CA 94515
Tel. 707/942-4102

Administration Manager, Mark Wilkinson

Season Year-round.

Accommodations 42 modern motel rooms facing a garden courtyard. Private bungalows with complete kitchens. Contemporary and Victorian furnishings, king- or queen-size beds, private baths. TV, telephone, air-conditioning, coffee maker, mini-refrigerator, bottled mineral water.

Rates $44–$55 single, $46–$65 for 2 persons. Larger rooms for up to 4 persons. Mid-week overnight "Healthy Getaway" package with treatments $90 per person, double occupancy. Spa services additional. 1 night payable in advance. Credit cards: MC, V.

Services and Facilities **Services:** Massage (Swedish, Esalen, shiatsu, acupressure, deep tissue), blanket wraps, facials. **Swimming Facilities:** Outdoor pool. **Spa Facilities:** Private tubs for mud and mineral water baths, whirlpools (indoors and out). **Recreation Facilities:** Hiking; nearby tennis courts, racquetball courts, golf course.

In the Area Balloon rides, glider trips, winery tours; the Sharpsteen Museum (local history), Sam Brannan Cottage (Victoriana), Robert Louis Stevenson House at the Silverado Mine, geysers.

Getting Here *From San Francisco.* By car, Rte. 101 to Novato, Rtes. 37, 121 to Napa, Rte. 29 to Calistoga (1½ hr). Taxi, rental car available.

Special Notes Limited access for the disabled. No smoking in the spa or pool areas.

Esalen Institute

Life enhancement

California
Big Sur
The "human potential" movement nurtured in these clifftop gardens and hot springs is alive and well after more than 25 years. Once considered a hippie haven, the Esalen Institute became an American utopia for seekers of ancient wisdom and new truths. Those gave birth to the Esalen style of sensuous massage and turned encounter therapy into an art form.

Secluded above the rocky surf of the Pacific Ocean, this idyllic retreat is surprisingly accessible. Seminars and workshops on holistic health, esoteric religions, and such emerging sciences as Gestalt therapy, psychosynthesis, shamanic healing, and neurolinguistics are offered throughout the year.

Many who come here simply want to unwind, and accommodations are available on a daily basis when rooms are not filled by program participants. Overnight guests can book a massage, hike in the Ventana wilderness, and soak in natural rock pools filled by hot mineral springs.

The Esalen catalog details various ways to experience learning and personal growth here. Introductory weekends, five-day workshops, work-study programs, and special events open to the public are listed. Private sessions are also available for neo-Reichian emotional release, vision improvement, and medical studies. The institute also offers a hiking trip to Tassajara Zen Mountain Center.

Esalen Institute
Big Sur, CA 93920
Tel. 408/667–3000 (408/667–3005 for reservations)

Administration Chairman, Michael Murphy; manager, Brian Lyke

Season Year-round.

Accommodations 100 beds in rustic cabins, comfortably casual furnishings with ocean views and the sound of the surf. No TV, radio, telephone, air conditioning. Guests share rooms and baths.

Rates Weekend workshops $295, 5-day seminar fee with lodging $575. Daily rate with meals about $75. $50 deposit for weekends, $100 for longer programs. Credit cards: AE, MC, V.

Meal Plans 3 meals daily, served buffet style; meat, fish, and poultry, salads and fresh vegetables grown on the property served at lunch and dinner, with a vegetarian entree such as spinach lasagna.

Services and Facilities **Services:** Massage, special studies. **Swimming Facilities:** Heated outdoor pool. **Recreation Facilities:** Walks, hiking, tai chi chuan, morning exercise class, hot mineral baths. **Evening Programs:** Lectures, concerts.

In the Area Wilderness experiences (5 days or more); Hearst Castle at San Simeon, Mission of San Antonio de Padua (1771), Tassajara Zen Center in Los Padres National Forest (May 1–Labor Day), Big Sur State Park.

Getting Here *From San Francisco.* By bus, Greyhound via Monterey connecting with Esalen limo (3 hr). By car, Rte. 101 south to Monterey, Rte. 156, Hwy. 1 (2½ hr). Limousine service Fri. and Sun.

Special Notes Limited access for the disabled. Special activities and dining plan for children; limited child care facilities. Nonsmoking cabins, nonsmoking areas in dining room.

The Golden Door

Life enhancement
Luxury pampering
Nutrition and diet
Spiritual awareness

California
Escondido

The doyen of fitness resorts in Southern California, the Golden Door opened in 1958 a mile from its present location, which now encompasses 177 acres of canyon and orchard. Beyond the ornate brass gate lies an enchanted realm of oriental gardens and inns. Guests in standard issue sweat suits and *yukata* robes step peacefully to aerobics classes or massage appointments. The setting and the incredibly thoughtful staff create an air of calm order. The experience is restorative and regenerative.

The process of transforming yourself from sloth to sylph begins on your arrival Sunday afternoon with an interview about your fitness level, diet, and preferences. Do you prefer tennis, instruction in lap-swimming techniques, or a cooking class? A massage with a therapist, who gets to know every muscle in your body, is scheduled every day at the same time.

On the orientation tour for first-time guests (repeaters make up a large percentage of the 36 Doorites in residence), one can't help but be impressed by the attention to detail and devotion to comfort that have been incorporated into the spa's impressive design, a cross between a first-class resort and a Japanese country inn. The four spacious gyms have sliding glass walls that open to fresh air and the beauty of the lush gardens. A graceful bathhouse, tiled and topped with gray oriental carving, contains a modern sauna, steam room, Swiss shower, and whirlpool large enough for several people.

Each day begins at 6 AM with a brisk mountain hike led by staff members who, Sherpa-like, supply flasks of cool water and fruit to sustain you until you are served breakfast. On the beautifully laid wooden tray is a paper fan with your schedule for the day. All decisions have been made for you, so it is simpler to go with the flow. If you miss an appointment, a kimono-clad woman will come searching for you.

Camaraderie grows as new friends discuss their dance routines with a diminutive Japanese choreographer and do Dynamic Dumbbells together with a weight lifter. Personal trainers are assigned to help you improve both form and content in the workouts so you can take home an exercise plan tailored to fit your needs. Classes are designed for three fitness levels.

The 50-minute exercise periods fill most of the morning; afternoons are for pampering and personal pursuits. You can have lunch by the pool, in the dining room, or in the privacy of your room. Massages can be alfresco or in your room, with a choice of shiatsu, traditional Swedish, deep-tissue, or aromatherapy. Daily beauty treatments are included in the program cost; men in particular enjoy the facials and pedicure.

There might be a final session of yoga in the garden, or aquaerobics in the pool. A social hour with nonalcoholic cocktails precedes dinner. Interesting talks are scheduled in the evening, but for some guests the prospect of a massage by moonlight is an excuse for going to bed early.

For fit guests who return whenever they need to recharge, there is now an Inner Door program. It is an advanced course for a small group in problem solving, meditation, and body movement. For four days there are two-hour sessions for exploration of spiritual and inner forces, even tai chi chuan, designed for inner serenity.

Most guests are middle-aged and success oriented; about half are in their 30s and 40s. Eight weeks are reserved for men only, five for couples; the rest of the time is for women only.

The Golden Door
Deer Springs Rd., Escondido;
(Office) Box 1567, Escondido, CA 92025
Tel. 619/744-5777

Administration Manager, Rachel Caldwell; program director, Juanita Hayes

Season Year-round except Christmas week.

Accommodations Single rooms for 36 guests in buildings patterned after old Japanese honjin inns. 1-story ocher stucco buildings have 2 to 14 bed-sitting rooms overlooking private gardens. Decorated with muted colors and Japanese wood-block prints. Parquet floors with carpets, sliding shoji screens and jalousie windows. Private baths stocked with Golden Door skin-care products. Guest units cluster on courtyards, a short walk from the main building. One private cottage.

Rates $3,500 weekly. $1,000 with reservation, balance due before arrival. No credit cards.

Meal Plans Three meals plus snacks served daily. 1,000 calories per day calculated for maximum energy with weight loss, 1,200 for maintenance. Low-cholesterol meals, rich in fiber and whole grains, low in salt, sugar, and fat, served with oriental flair. Lunch can include miso soup, stir-fry vegetables with tofu, or fresh Pacific shrimp sautéed with orange and ginger. Dinner entrees include boneless breast of chicken with wild mushrooms; whole wheat crepes filled with a mixture of spinach, mushrooms, and ricotta cheese; or cabbage rolls stuffed with bulgur pilaf and vegetables. Options: decaffeinated coffee, herbal tea; ulcer diet, diabetic diet, hypoglycemic diet, vegetarian or lacto-ovo vegetarian diet. Mid-morning juice or broth, veggie snacks, and nonalcoholic cocktails served.

Services and Facilities

Exercise Equipment: 12 Hoggan Camstar weight training units, 6 Trotter treadmills, 2 Bosch stationary bikes, StairMaster, PTS/Turbo bike, rowing machine, free weights. **Services:** Massage (Swedish, Trager, shiatsu, and others), aromatherapy, FANGO, herbal wrap, body scrub, daily skin care, facials, manicure, pedicure, hair styling. Instruction in tai chi chuan, yoga, swimming, circuit training; fitness evaluations and submaximal stress test. **Swimming Facilities:** 2 outdoor pools. **Recreation Facilities:** 2 tennis courts, hiking, classes in flower arranging, crafts, gardening. **Evening Programs:** Lectures on nutrition, stress management, sports medicine, other health-related topics; movies.

In the Area

Meditation hiking; mountain trails, beaches.

Getting Here

From San Diego. By car, Hwy. 163 to I–15, north to Deer Springs Rd. exit (40 min). Free pickup to and from San Diego Airport.

Special Notes

Ramps and one-story structures make the entire complex accessible to the disabled. No smoking in public areas. Remember to bring appropriate shoes for hiking, walking, sports (checklist provided).

Jane Fonda's Laurel Springs Retreat

Life enhancement
Nutrition and diet
Stress control

California
Santa Barbara

As you soak in a redwood hot tub perched high above the Pacific Ocean, you can see the Channel Islands and the red-tile roofs of Santa Barbara from Jane Fonda's Laurel Springs Retreat. Silence, clean air, and relaxation are your reward after a day devoted to hiking, biking, and aerobic dance. Such an ideal scene usually exists only on television.

The gymnasium is strictly Beverly Hills posh, mirrored and with stunning views. In addition, there's a personal trainer. Because nine guests is the limit, each gets a personalized exercise program that includes working out on the latest equipment. There's also a swimming pool for aquaerobics and stretching exercises, and the sun deck, cantilevered on a cliff, is perfect for yoga and meditation.

Exercise physiologist Daniel Kosich custom designs the daily regime of specific exercises, outdoor recreation, and nutritious meals for each guest. Adding an hour-long massage costs $50; otherwise everything is included, even daily laundry service.

Rigidly programmed, the week is planned to motivate changes that you can adapt permanently. After tasting the cook's gourmet creations, you get firsthand experience in the kitchen. A recognized authority on nutrition comes by to discuss weight loss and meal planning. And there are outings to the beach and other attractions, with bikes supplied.

The process begins with a complete physical examination, either at the Jane Fonda Workout Studio in Beverly Hills or on arrival Sunday afternoon at the retreat. All participants submit to a battery of cardiovascular, strength, flexibility, and body composition tests. If special diets are requested, the cook will be consulted. Allergies are taken into account.

The mountain setting distinguishes this retreat. On a ranch 3,500 feet above sea level in the Santa Ynez Mountains, the redwood lodge is surrounded by an oak grove. Wood and fieldstone are used throughout the buildings, and the two-story lounge with its 17-foot fireplace impresses. The library and game room have a full supply of videotapes, from workouts with you-know-who to feature films. There's also an aerobics studio with coed sauna and steam room.

The concept of moving people from their daily environment to this high-energy retreat pays off. Air-conditioning isn't needed, and you sleep like a baby. Part of the tuition supports research on health and fitness by the Temescal Foundation, part goes to a performing arts camp for children, which is also on the ranch. Jane Fonda has a place here, but don't count on seeing her; her house is well up the road.

Jane Fonda's Laurel Springs Retreat
Star Route, Santa Barbara, CA 93105
(Office) 373 S. Robertson Blvd., Beverly Hills, CA 90211
Tel. 213/964–9646 or 805/964–9646
Fax 805/638–8861

Administration Manager, Karen Averitt; program director, Daniel Kosich

Season Year-round.

Accommodations 3 bedrooms, each with a distinctive personality, decorated by Jane with folk art, including an Appalachian four-poster bed with a canopy of woven twigs, hand-sewn quilts, and throw rugs. Modern private baths with a view.

Rates $2,500 per week single, $1,500 for an additional person sharing the room. All inclusive. $1,000 due one month in advance. No credit cards.

Meal Plans 3 meals daily, 1,000–1,200 calories per day. Whole-grain cereal or homemade muffins, skim milk or yogurt for breakfast; a Cobb salad or fresh vegetables, whole-grain bread, and fruit for lunch; broiled swordfish, roasted game hens for dinner. Snacks mid-morning and afternoon, "fruit smoothie" drinks, and 6–8 glasses of water.

Services and Facilities **Exercise Equipment:** 10-station bodybuilding equipment, 8 weight machine units, free weights, stationary bikes, rowing machine. **Services:** Massage, nutritional counseling, exercise counseling. Fitness and medical tests. **Swimming Facilities:** Outdoor pool. **Recreation Facilities:** Sunbathing, reading. **Evening Programs:** Discussions on nutrition, exercise, stress management, change of lifestyle.

In the Area Excursions: Escorted hiking and biking trips; Santa Barbara art galleries and boutiques, Santa Barbara Museum of Art, Mission Santa Barbara (1786), Solveig (Scandinavian arts and crafts).

Getting Here *From Los Angeles:* By train, Amtrak service twice daily (1 hr).
By car, Rte. 101 (45 min). Free pickup to and from Los Angeles
International Airport or from hotels in Los Angeles.

Special Notes No smoking indoors. Remember to bring shoes for hiking and
running, clothing for aerobics and outdoor activity.

La Costa Hotel & Spa

Luxury pampering
Life enhancement
Weight management
Nutrition and diet

California A megaresort for the fun and fitness crowd, La Costa Hotel &
Carlsbad Spa has a serious program for change of lifestyle. Neverthe-
less, the country club ambience is more suited to pampering
than to preventive medicine.

When the 1,000-acre complex was renovated several years ago,
the idea was to be able to offer something for every taste. The
result was overcrowding in the spa building, which was not expanded. That the attractive dining room for dieters can be
reached only by a challenge course through Mexican, Chinese,
and French restaurants and several bars seems further evidence of poor planning.

The Life Fitness Center's one-week package is designed to educate and motivate guests to adopt healthy habits. Each day
begins with a brisk walk around the golf course. Power walking
has now become the preferred exercise, for the fit and the not
so fit, because it has none of the stress associated with running
and jogging. Mornings are devoted to exercise at the gym, or
therapy and massage, followed by workshops and lectures. Optional periods allow opportunities for golf, tennis, or personal
counseling.

The lifestyle center across from the spa building has its own
demonstration kitchen and discussion area. The casual surroundings feel more like a home than a classroom. A
nutritionist and the spa's medical director teach how to cook
and to eat better. Everyone learns to make omelets without
egg yolk.

Medical and physical evaluations are included in the program.
An Aeriel computerized exerciser tests your strength, flexibility, and pulmonary function. Nutritional and body composition
analysis determine your diet and measure the percentages of
fat and muscle in your body. A take-home program, provided at
the end of the week, facilitates follow-up.

Between learning to read labels in a supermarket and practicing stress-reduction techniques, guests are treated to plenty of
pampering. Personal attention from a skilled staff of physical
therapists, many of whom have spent a lifetime in their field,
makes up for the assembly-line atmosphere of the spa. Attention is paid to appearance; facials and hair styling are part of
the package for both men and women.

Camaraderie exists within the small group of Life Fitness program participants, but most of the time you're surrounded by
golf and tennis buffs or the fit-looking local club members. It's

wise to schedule early appointments at the spa, especially when a large group is meeting at the convention center across the way.

La Costa can be enjoyed simply as a luxury getaway without adhering to a program. Packages are available for two to seven nights, with a choice of eating in the spa or in the other dining rooms. Gourmets may find their downfall in the sinfully delicious desserts in the Champagne Room. Lunch can be served poolside on a terrace near your room if you would rather avoid the gamut of temptations.

Another option—for women only—is the noon-to-noon makeover, a concentrated course in beauty and fitness. Golf and tennis packages are always available, and they can be combined with a fitness program. Anyone can drop in for an aerobics class without prior registration.

The true luxury of La Costa consists of the personal attention guests receive, even though the place is crowded. Locker-room attendants remember your name and slipper size and hand out fresh towels and robes without being asked; they deserve handsome tips. The separate facilities for men and women add to the clublike atmosphere. Included are a eucalyptus-scented inhalation room, steam room, sauna, Swiss multihead showers, hot and cold plunge pools, and an outdoor Jacuzzi. The gym and salon are coed.

Conceived on a grand scale, with two golf courses, a tennis center, waterfalls, and rambling mission-style lodges, La Costa dotes on you while encouraging healthy habits. The new owner, a Japanese conglomerate, may bring changes.

La Costa Hotel & Spa
Costa del Mar Rd., Carlsbad, CA 92009
Tel. 619/438–9111 or 800/854–5000
(Life Fitness Center 800/ 426–5483)
Telex 697946, Fax 619/438–5866

Administration Life Fitness Center director, Jonelle Simpson; medical director, Gordon Reynolds, M.D.

Season Year-round.

Accommodations 482 deluxe rooms and suites in Spanish-style buildings and a motellike spa complex. Newer rooms overlook the golf course. Fine furnishings. Fitness and spa program guests stay in bed-sitting rooms by the pool, unless they request otherwise. Six private residences.

Rates Fitness programs $460 a day single; $340 per person for couples sharing a room. 2-night spa package $230 single, $115 double; 7-night Life Fitness program $3,220 single, $2,380 double; 6% tax in addition. Spa and salon service charges included. One night payable on booking. Credit cards: AE, CB, DC, MC, V.

Meal Plans You select from daily menus of 600, 800, 1,000, or 1,200 calories. Breakfast options include fruit, muffins, an egg-white omelet with salsa, and an energy mix of grains, apple butter, and raisins. For lunch, cheese blintzes, papaya stuffed with crab, and beef Stroganoff. Chicken stuffed with foie gras, fettucini primavera, salmon fillet with horseradish sauce, and veal with artichoke sauce are dinner entrees, with fresh fruit, sherbet, or custard for dessert; coffee (regular or decaffeinated), tea (herbal or regular), nonfat milk, and Swiss Valser water. Special diets accommodated.

Services and Facilities
Exercise Equipment: Eagle weights, Lifecycles, computerized treadmills, aerobic trainer, rowing machines, free weights, rebounders. **Services:** Massage (Swedish, shiatsu, sports, reflexology), herbal wraps, loofah body scrub, spot toning, facials. Salon for hair, nail, and skin care. Nutrition counseling, medical and fitness evaluations. Personal trainer for exercise, swimming, golf, and tennis. **Swimming Facilities:** 5 outdoor pools. **Recreation Facilities:** 23 tennis courts (8 lighted), 2 18-hole golf courses, driving range, horseback riding. Bike rental. **Evening Programs:** Lectures on health and fitness, stress management; movie theater and resort cabaret. Cooking demonstration.

In the Area
Bus or limousine trips to Sea World, San Diego Zoo, Disneyland; Coronado beaches, San Diego museums and Horton Plaza shops, Laguna Nigel (The Ritz Carlton).

Getting Here
From San Diego. By car, I–5 to Carlsbad, La Costa Ave. exit (40 min). By train, Amtrak to Oceanside (30 min). Limousine, taxi, rental car available.

Special Notes
Access available for the disabled. Tennis and golf clinics and summer day-camp programs for children. No smoking in the spa building or the dining room.

Lake Arrowhead Hilton Lodge & Spa

Luxury pampering

California
Lake Arrowhead
A Bavarian health spa in the scenic San Bernardino Mountains is a surprising discovery. A mix of California lifestyle and European therapy, the Lake Arrowhead Hilton Lodge is an ideal getaway for the healthy, active person in need of pampering and exercise. It offers a one-day program without accommodations on weekdays, packages for weekends and up to seven days, and a two-week session devoted to body purification and weight loss.

The program is based on techniques perfected at the Kurhotel Barbarossa, a health resort in the Bavarian alps, by Hans and Christa Stompler. Using hydrotherapy equipment, conditioning creams, and herbal combinations, the Stomplers and their staff work closely with guests. The program includes aerobics classes, hiking the lakeside trails, and a series of European body wraps that draw toxins and other impurities from the skin while tranquilizing the nervous system. A sauna, steam room, and whirlpool are available.

Beginning with a brisk morning walk, your day can include yoga, tennis, or racquetball and a fango pack to ease muscle fatigue. Sports injuries such as tennis elbow, as well as rheumatism and arthritis, are treated with this mix of volcanic ash in paraffin to remove pain-causing metabolic acids stored in tissues and joints. A relaxing Swedish massage or deep-penetrating underwater massage caps the day.

Diet plays a special role in the Stompler Method. If losing weight is your goal, they will design a daily diet based on maintaining your energy for exercise. They will also schedule shaping and toning sessions, including cellulite treatments according to your needs.

The alpine atmosphere and the view of Lake Arrowhead from the weights room enhance the experience.

Lake Arrowhead Hilton Lodge & Spa
Lake Arrowhead, CA 92352
Tel. 714/336–1511 (800/223–3307 in CA)

Administration Spa director, Hans Stompler

Season Year-round.

Accommodations 264 guest rooms, suites, and condominium apartments in the three-story alpine lodge. Manor suites equipped with fireplaces and complete kitchens enjoy lake views and quiet. Modern furnishings.

Rates 1-day spa program with lunch and lodging $190; 2-night programs $450 per person double occupancy; $550 single on weekends, $350–$450 during the week. 1-week package $1,250 per person double occupancy, $1,550 single; 2-week weight-loss program $2,750 single, $2,250 double. Tax and 15% service charge in addition. 50% nonrefundable deposit to confirm. Credit cards: AE, CB, DC, MC, V.

Meal Plans Three low-cal meals served daily in the main dining room. Breakfast choices include fresh muesli cereal, fruits, whole grain rolls. Carrot soup with chives, salad of Belgian endive with sunflower sprouts, or vegetables Stroganoff for lunch. Salmon rolled with Dover sole, spinach gratin and potato balls, and fresh pear with orange sauce for dinner. Coffee and tea.

Services and Facilities **Exercise Equipment:** 13 Nautilus units, Universal gym, 4 Lifecycles, 2 Liferowers, StairMaster, Star Trak treadmill, Turbo 1,000 recumbent bike, cross-country ski machine, Cateye ergocizer. **Services:** Massage, hydrotherapy baths, fango packs, herbal wrap, cellulite wrap, facial, makeup consultation, hair and skin care. Nutrition classes, aquatics, yoga instruction. Body purification treatments. **Swimming Facilities:** Outdoor pool. **Recreation Facilities:** Walking, hiking, boating, biking, tennis and racquetball courts. Golf and horseback riding nearby. Cross-country skiing. **Evening Programs:** Guest speakers on health-related topics.

In the Area Los Angeles (2 hr) museums and sightseeing; Palm Springs (1½ hr) mineral spring baths, desert museum.

Getting Here *From Los Angeles.* By bus, Trailways or Greyhound to San Bernardino (3 hr). By car, I–10 to San Bernardino, I–215 or Rte. 30 and Hwy. 18 (2 hr). By plane, regional and commuter flights to Ontario International Airport (20 min). Limousine service to and from Ontario airport and bus station on request (fee); taxi, rental car available.

Special Notes Elevator connects all floors. No smoking in the spa; nonsmoking area in the dining room. Remember to bring gym shoes (non-black sole), medium-weight jacket, warmup suit or sweats.

Malibu Mountain Retreat

Weight management

California
Malibu Beach

Rugged and challenging, this week-long program for 16 participants offered by the Malibu Mountain Retreat emphasizes weight loss. Intense exercise is combined with a minimum-calorie diet. Working under the direction of a nutritionist and physical therapist, the group hikes and bikes in the Santa Monica Mountains and along the Malibu beaches, taking in spectacular scenery while burning off fat.

Based at an old mountain lodge with a southwestern look, the retreat is tightly organized. Guests are expected to participate in all activities, and their personal needs—from sweat suits and T-shirts to robes, caftans, and sunscreen—are provided. Participants need to bring only lightweight hiking boots, running shoes, swimsuit, and toothbrush.

The program is designed for maximum weight loss and greater fitness. Stretching, shaping, toning, aquaerobics, and workouts with free weights and professional exercise equipment help to achieve results. Mountain bikes are provided for outings, a Jacuzzi for relaxation.

Tailored to the needs and fitness level of each participant, the exercise schedule is closely supervised. As you progress to more challenging workouts and climb that extra mile, a sense of well-being and accomplishment is your best reward.

Malibu Mountain Retreat
Malibu Beach, CA
(Office) 23901 W. Civic Center Way, Malibu, CA 90265
Tel. 213/456–7056

Administration Director, Kristina Hurrell; nutritionist, Jesse Hanley, M.D.

Season Year-round.

Accommodations 9 guest rooms in the main house, furnished with Southwest Indian artifacts, pine dressers, and lodgepole beds. No TV or air-conditioning. Clean and airy baths are shared.

Rates $1,800 per person, one week, all-inclusive. $800 30 days in advance. No credit cards.

Meal Plans Vegetarian meals served family style 3 times daily. Whole grains, legumes, fresh fruits, vegetables, sprouts, nuts, seeds, and tofu form the basis of casseroles and steamed dishes. Special diets and food allergies are accommodated.

Services and Facilities **Exercise Equipment:** Universal weight training units, free weights, rebounders. Fat-tired mountain bikes for outings. **Services:** Swedish massage, acupressure, aromatherapy, herbal wrap, body scrub, skin care. Body composition test, motion analysis. **Swimming Facilities:** 40-foot outdoor pool. **Recreation Facilities:** Volleyball in the pool, croquet, hiking. **Evening Programs:** Lectures on nutrition, weight control.

In the Area Daily hiking along Chumach Indian trails, exploring caves and waterfalls; state and national parks, beaches. Hollywood and Los Angeles are 1 hour by freeway.

Getting Here *From Los Angeles.* By car, Rte. 1 (1 hr). Free transfers on arrival from Los Angeles airport, Santa Monica, and Malibu.

Special Notes No smoking.

Marriott's Desert Springs Resort

Luxury pampering

California
Palm Desert

The Desert Springs Resort, the elaborate flagship resort created in the desert by the Marriott Corporation, literally floats you away. Gondolas glide from the main lobby to the health spa, an island oasis surrounded by lagoons and a golf course.

Water is involved in the treatments and services offered, from hydrotherapy pools to hot and cold plunges, a Turkish steam room, and a private aromatherapy whirlpool bath. A 30-minute calisthenics class in the outdoor pool, called "waterworks," is designed to tone up the body with water resistance. A vigorous White Water Workout aims to increase muscular endurance.

Separate facilities for men and women provide privacy while guests pursue a rejuvenation regimen. Entrusted to a personal trainer, guests have a choice of fitness consultations and beauty treatments, including underwater massage, acupressure, and facials. Extended-stay packages are available, from a four-day sampler to the deluxe seven-day program. Or you can pay the daily admission of $18, which includes workout clothing and robe. The fee is waived when you book a one-day package that includes lunch, treatments, and two exercise classes for $163 or $225, plus service charges.

Guests at this airy 325-acre retreat find its elegance and desert views relaxing. Escape the midday sun at the juice bar or the spa cafe. The dry flotation unit, a space-age capsule with its own environment, is extremely efficient in helping you unwind.

Skin-care products by Kerstin, featured in the spa salon, are formulated with natural ingredients that include lavender, chamomile, vitamins, collagen, seaweed, and proteins. Applied by shiatsu acupressure technique, the ointments, gels, and sprays are intended to help prevent sun damage and aging. Treatments can be booked as part of a half-day pampering package or on a separate basis.

Natural light floods the indoor gym and aerobics studios, where yoga, stretching, and rigorous calisthenics are scheduled throughout the day. The weights training room nearby allows you to work out with a view.

Although it was designed for conferences and sales meetings, the resort caters to vacationers as well. The self-contained spa, open from 7 AM to 6:30 PM daily, has saunas, steam rooms, and an Olympic-size lap pool. Private training and fitness consultations are available. A morning walk or jog around the manicured lawns in the hot, dry climate is a great way to begin a day of work or play. Desert hiking is a popular resort feature. To end the day, try a 30-minute session of oriental stretching exercises as the sun sets on the Santa Rosa Mountains.

Marriott's Desert Springs Resort
74855 Country Club Dr., Palm Desert, CA 92260
Tel. 619/341–2211, 800/255–0848, or 800/228–9290
Telex 6712074, Fax 619/341–1872

Administration	Manager, John Ceriale; spa director, Janet Denyer
Season	Year-round.
Accommodations	892 rooms, including executive suites, with oversize beds, private baths. Refrigerator mini-bar, balcony with view, and TV with feature movies.
Rates	$215–$359 Jan.–May. 4-day spa sampler $836–$1,236 single, $656–$886, double occupancy, depending on season. Deluxe spa program, 4–7 days, including medical screening and additional services, $1,036–$2,513 single, $860–$1,900 double occupancy. One night payable in advance. Credit cards: AE, CB, DC, MC, V.
Meal Plans	Three spa meals totaling 900 calories a day included in package rates. Lunch can be a salad or cold poached salmon. Main dining room dinner entrees include grilled loin of veal, broiled chicken, pasta primavera. Coffee, herbal tea, dairy products. Special diets on request.
Services and Facilities	**Exercise Equipment:** 11-station Universal weight training gym, 6 Lifecycles, 3 treadmills, 3 Monark bikes, rowing machine, dumbbells and 2–50 lb. free weights with 5 benches. **Services:** Massage (Swedish, shiatsu, sports, aromatherapy), facials, herbal wraps, loofah body scrub. Nutrition counseling, computerized fitness and body-composition analysis. Beauty salon. **Swimming Facilities:** Outdoor pool. **Recreation Facilities:** 2 18-hole golf courses, 16 tennis courts, walking, croquet, water volleyball. Bike rental, horseback riding, skiing. **Evening Programs:** Resort entertainment.
In the Area	Guided mountain hikes, sightseeing tours; aerial tramway to Mt. San Jacinto, ballooning, Desert Fashion Plaza (shopping), Bob Hope Cultural Center, Palm Springs Desert Museum (art), Living Desert Reserve (nature studies), Polo Club.
Getting Here	*From Los Angeles.* By bus, Greyhound (4 hr). By car, I–10 to Hwy. 111 (2½ hr). By train, Amtrak to Indio (2 hr). Airport van shuttle service, limousine, taxi, rental car available.
Special Notes	Limited access for the disabled. Supervised games, movies, tennis lessons for children. No smoking in the spa; nonsmoking areas in restaurants.

Murrieta Hot Springs Resort

Taking the waters
Holistic health

California *Murrieta*	A spa in the Old World style, the Murrieta Hot Springs Resort is a place to soak your body in a vat of mud, get a great massage, and enjoy vegetarian meals. The new ownership has given the rooms a face-lift and added a second dining room that features chicken, fish, and wines from local vineyards. The atmosphere remains pleasantly laid-back.

New fitness programs have come with the renovations; low-impact aerobics, exercise classes in the water, weights, and a holistic health course are now offered. Meanwhile, the resort's former owner, the nonprofit Murrieta Foundation, continues its four-to-six-week sessions of "Total Health in Mind/Body" and weekend seminars in fitness, stress management, personal relationships, and polarity bodywork.

Stretching across 47 acres of landscaped grounds, the tranquil resort was once roamed by the Temecula Indians, more recently by the Teamster Union executives who had the mission-style lodges built for their retreats. Hot springs from the Elsinor fault provide the mineral water of varying temperatures that fills the Olympic-size swimming pool and two smaller baths.

Mud baths, body work, and skin care using natural products come with several spa packages and can be ordered à la carte. The arthritis treatments attract large numbers of seniors, while many guests simply like to mellow out in the cleansing mud, a mineral-rich mixture of fine Betonite clay, sea kelp, and peat moss. The bathhouse, a 1920s-style Spanish villa with mosaics and tiled tubs, has private rooms for soaking with essential oils and Bach flower mixes, Finnish saunas for men and women, and a full range of massage.

This is not a luxury facility, and the prices reflect that. A 90-minute treatment with mud bath, herbal wrap, and private soak in mineral water costs $32.

A full schedule of aerobics classes, tennis, and workshops in body awareness and makeup design allow you to be as busy as you choose. Special weeks focus on art appreciation, vegetarian cooking, and hiking and jogging. A staff nutritionist will recommend a regimen of vegetables, fruit, tofu, sprouts, and grains for those seeking to shed some weight, and the regular Fit and Trim program begins every Sunday.

Murrieta Hot Springs Resort
39405 Murrieta Hot Springs Rd., Murrieta, CA 92362
Tel. 714/677–7451 or 800/322–4542 (800/458–4393 in CA)
The Murrieta Foundation
28779 Via Las Flores, Murrieta, CA 92362
Tel. 714/677–9661 or 800/322–4542

Administration Spa director, Gary Peterson; program director, John Chitty

Season Year-round.

Accommodations 240 guest rooms in private cottages and terraced stone lodges furnished with old oak dressers and new oversize beds. New suites with white wicker furniture, brass fixtures and two queen-size beds. All with private bath, TV, and telephone. Air-conditioning by request.

Rates $60 a day, single or double. Full American Plan with 3 vegetarian meals daily $67–$77 single, $94–$104 double. 2-night special package with baths and massages $161.44 per person double occupancy; stress-management weekend with classes and one indoor bath $325 single, $279 double. Fit and Trim weekends, midweek specials, and golf and tennis packages. Full-week fitness program with all meals, treatments, and classes $1,099 single, $935 double. One-day admission $10. Taxes additional. One night payable in advance, 25% for packages. Credit cards: AE, MC, V.

Meal Plans Vegetarian buffet, fish, or chicken dishes. Entrees include tofu-cauliflower curry, pasta, vegetarian enchiladas, bean burritos, Mexican-style salad. Mesquite-grilled fish and barbecue chicken served in a separate dining room. Coffee, tea, wine; no eggs but fresh dairy products and cereals at breakfast.

Services and Facilities **Exercise Equipment:** Planned for 1989. **Services:** Massage (Swedish, polarity, lymph drainage), herbal wrap, mud bath, loofah body scrub, back scrub, foot care, facial. Self-awareness counseling. Beauty salon. **Swimming Facilities:** Outdoor pool. **Spa Facilities:** Outdoor pools, indoor Roman-style pools, and private baths, some with mud mixture. **Recreation Facilities:** 14 tennis courts (4 lighted), badminton, shuffleboard. Hiking, walking, jogging trails. Golf at the nearby Rancho California Country Club's par-72 course. Horseback riding, lake fishing. **Evening Programs:** Workshops on holistic health, body polarity, nutrition; dinner-theater productions, concerts.

In the Area Temecula's old-town district, antique shops, wine tours, ballooning.

Getting Here *From San Diego.* By bus, Greyhound to Temecula (90 min). By car, Hwy. 163 to I–15 past Temecula, Hot Springs Rd. exit (70 min).

Special Notes Limited access for the disabled. Children are welcome to bathe with parents and participate in some workshops. No smoking in public areas.

The Oaks at Ojai

Nutrition and diet
Weight management

California
Ojai

At The Oaks at Ojai, fitness and weight-control programs are the main attractions for men and women who want to unwind or work out without fancy lodging or physical therapy. When you stick to the basics—up to 17 exercise classes and activities daily and a diet of fresh, natural foods that totals only 750 calories—the Oaks promises that you can lose up to a pound a day safely.

The program operates on an all-inclusive American plan, and guests are welcome to stay a few days or weeks and take part in as many of the activities as they please. A number of special packages are available, including a spa-cooking week, mother-daughter days, and a five-day course to quit smoking.

Ojai is an art center and a favorite of the practitioners of several healing faiths. The Oaks is located on the main square of the town, and appointments can be made with psychics, astrologers, pyramid enthusiasts, members of the Theosophy movement, or the Krishnamurti Foundation. All are attracted by the natural beauty of a fertile valley near the Los Padres National Forest, little more than an hour's drive north of Los Angeles.

Built as a country inn in 1918, the dignified wood-and-stone structure gained a new lease on life in the 1970s when Sheila Cluff became its owner. A former professional ice skater and physical fitness instructor, Cluff drew together a team of exercise physiologists and spruced up the tiny guest rooms with country antiques. A sister spa in Palm Springs, the Palms, offers a similar no-frills program.

Concerned more with teaching and motivating exercise habits than with pampering or bodywork (available at additional cost), the program includes workouts in the pool, body contouring, intense aerobics, and progressive stretches. There are morning hikes into the hills, brisk walks along country roads, and yoga at the end of the day.

Most activities are held in the main lodge and garden. The complex includes saunas, an aerobics studio, a large swimming pool, and a cluster of guest bungalows. Classes, rated according to the guests' fitness level, last from 45 minutes to an hour. A nurse is on staff to help plan each person's appropriate schedule.

The day begins with a challenging aerobic workout at 6 AM (repeated at 5:15 PM). Fruits, muffins, and vitamins are set out at the Winners Circle, a juice bar in the lodge. Lunch can be eaten by the pool or in the dining room. There is a midmorning broth break, and vegetable snacks are served in the afternoon. The program is aimed at burning calories, conditioning the heart and lungs, and toning the body. Guests here are diverse, ranging from young professionals to grandmothers; film industry folk, TV actresses, and housewives drop in to shape up or relax.

The Oaks at Ojai
122 E. Ojai Ave., Ojai, CA 93023
Tel. 805/646–5573

Administration Manager, Mary T. Lins; program director, Bill Henrich

Season Year-round.

Accommodations 46 guest rooms in the main lodge and cottages, from small singles to a cottage for 3. Simply furnished with modern beds, all have private bath, color TV, telephone, air conditioning.

Rates From $99 per person, small double lodge room with shower only; $125 in a cottage. Private rooms $145–$155 per day. One night payable in advance. Credit cards: MC, V.

Meal Plans 3 meals daily. Natural foods, no additives, salt, white flour, or sugar. Lunch can be soup, tuna salad with egg, mushrooms, and cheese, or vegetable crepes. Dinner entrees: vegetarian lasagna, baked chicken, broiled fish, or pasta salad.

Services and Facilities **Exercise Equipment:** 10-station Paramount weight training gym, hand and ankle weights, stretch bands. **Swimming Facilities:** Outdoor pool. **Recreation Facilities:** Hiking, nature walks; tennis, golf, and horseback riding nearby. **Services:** Massage, facials; salon for hair, skin, and nail care; computerized body analysis. **Evening Programs:** Talks on health and fitness.

In the Area Group hiking and walking every morning; bicycle tours, boating and fishing at Lake Casitas, annual music and dance festivals; crafts boutiques; Bart's Corners book and sheet-music shop.

Getting Here *From Los Angeles.* By bus, Greyhound to Ventura (2 hr). By car, Hwy. 101 (Ventura Freeway) to Ventura, Hwy. 33 to Ojai, Hwy. 150 to center of town (80 min). Taxi, rental car available.

Special Notes No smoking in public areas.

The Palms

Nutrition and diet
Weight management

California
Palm Springs

Finding an informal place to exercise and diet in the center of Palm Springs resort life is quite a feat. The Palms is a "come as you are" place, one with few frills, plenty of options, and no attendance requirements.

Activity centers on a large swimming pool, and additional classes are held indoors in a small aerobics studio and outdoors under the palms. With up to 16 activities offered daily, guests are encouraged to take part in as many or as few as they please. Special weeks feature high-powered speakers on health, nutrition, and fitness; a seminar on women in management; and a 21-day course on quitting smoking.

The program operates on an all-inclusive American Plan, regardless of how long you stay, and guests may arrive on any day (unless a workshop is scheduled). The flexibility allows you to enjoy the attractions of the Palm Springs area, some within walking distance.

The regimen emphasizes aerobics and body conditioning. Workouts strive to increase flexibility, burn calories, strengthen the heart, and increase lung capacity. The desert climate, a low-calorie diet, and rigorous exercise work together to build power and energy.

Owned by Sheila Cluff, a former professional ice skater and physical fitness instructor, this is the kind of place that appeals to women and their devoted spouses. Most of the guests are in their middle 50s; many are already in good shape but want to lose a few pounds.

The converted manor house and cluster of private bungalows exude a Spanish-colonial ambience and sit handsomely beneath the dramatic starkness of mountains. Although there is no hydrotherapy, a sauna and whirlpool are tucked into the complex, and a massage or facial is available for a fee.

The Palms
572 N. Indian Ave., Palm Springs, CA 92262
Tel. 619/325–1111

Administration Manager, Barbara Nos; fitness director, Marilu Rogers Horst

Season Year-round.

Accommodations 37 rooms in the manor and bungalows, most on the ground floor with private patio. Motel-style furniture, double beds, generous closets. All rooms with private or shared bath, air-conditioning. Facilities comfortable but dated.

Rates $125 per person, double occupancy, private bath, on a daily program basis; $99 with shared bath. Single rooms $145–$165. Taxes and service charge additional. One night's lodging in advance. Credit cards: MC, V.

Meal Plans Three meals totaling 750 calories served daily in the dining room. Breakfast is fresh fruit, diet muffin, and a vitamin supplement. Lunch includes soup, choice of chicken tostada seasoned with chili and cumin, or vegetable crepes. Veal loaf, broiled red snapper in tomato sauce, turkey divan, or vegetarian lasagna for dinner. No salt, sugar, or chemical additives. Coffee and hot or iced herbal tea all day. Midmorning broth break, afternoon vegetables.

Services and Facilities **Exercise Equipment:** 2 Universal weight training gym units, hand and ankle weights, stretch bands. **Services:** Massage, facials; salon for hair, skin, and nail care. Consultation on fitness, body composition analysis. **Swimming Facilities:** Outdoor pool. **Recreation Facilities:** Hiking. Bike rental, horseback riding, tennis, and golf nearby. Downhill and cross-country skiing in the mountains. **Evening Programs:** Talks on dressing for success, the history of Palm Springs, other subjects.

In the Area Local sightseeing tours; aerial tram ride, Desert Museum, art museum; ballooning, baths at nearby hot springs; Living Desert Reserve.

Getting Here *From Los Angeles.* By bus, Greyhound (4 hr). By car, I–10 to Hwy. 111 (2½ hr). By train, Amtrak to Indio (2 hr). Airport van shuttle service, taxi, rental car available.

Special Notes Limited access for the disabled. No smoking in designated areas.

Pritikin Longevity Center

Nutrition and diet
Weight management

California
Santa Monica

The Pritikin Longevity Center, which occupies an entire beachfront hotel, is dedicated to the diet and exercise regime espoused in the 1970s by the late Nathan Pritikin. It is the development center for programs offered elsewhere around the country, and since 1978 it has offered a vacation that combines the elements essential to preventing degenerative disease and improving the quality of one's life.

The medically supervised programs last for 13 and 26 days. The core curriculum includes daily exercise, nutrition and health education, stress-management counseling, and medical services. The two-week program is recommended for persons afflicted with physical problems such as heart disease, insulin-dependent diabetes, obesity, or high blood pressure. The full course offers increased individual attention, counseling, and supervision.

Healthy people, too, come here to maintain their health, learn to control their diet, cook and eat Pritikin-style, and exercise. A free hot line is included for those who need continuing support after they leave the program.

The daily schedule includes cooking classes, lectures, and three exercise sessions. A full physical examination is a major part of the program; it includes a treadmill stress test and a complete blood-chemistry analysis. Depending on your personal history and fitness level, you will be assigned to a specialist in either cardiology or internal medicine who will monitor your progress on the prescribed diet and exercise program.

Ocean views from the dining room are a pleasure at mealtimes. The chefs cook without added fat, salt, or sugar, and no coffee or tea is served. Meals are largely vegetarian, although fish and chicken are served several times a week; there are many fresh fruits and whole grains. (The Pritikin diet is 5% to 10% fat, 10% to 15% protein, and 80% high complex carbohydrates.)

Some nutritionists and doctors consider the diet unnecessarily austere, but the results attained by a loyal legion of followers may be convincing evidence that the concept works. The beachfront location is another attraction. If your spouse or partner is not a participant in the program (you are encouraged to bring a support person and work together), there are plenty of diversions at hand. Treading the boardwalk is exercise everyone enjoys.

However, the strict regimen demands concentration, so don't expect a purely fun-in-the-sun holiday. Between lectures and classes you'll work out in a well-equipped gym, in the pool, and perhaps on the beach. If you enjoy swimming in the ocean, it can be made part of your exercise routine. (All exercises are subject to your doctor's approval.)

Pritikin Longevity Center
1910 Ocean Front Walk, Santa Monica, CA 90405
Tel. 213/450–5433 or 800/421–9911 (800/421–0981 in CA)

Administration Director, Robert Pritikin; program director, John Hall

Season Year-round.

Accommodations 128 newly renovated rooms, from singles to suites, with desk, reading chair, tiled bath and glass-enclosed shower. Better rooms include a Jacuzzi ($450–$550 supplement for a 13-day program) and ocean views. Air-conditioning, and just enough quiet comfort to make it feel like a resort.

Rates 13-day program $5,175 single, $2,325 for a participating partner; 26-day program $8,938 single, $4,338 for partner. (Medical costs may be covered by health insurance.) $500 in advance, 13-day program; $1,000 in advance, 26-day program. Credit cards: MC, V.

Meal Plans 3 meals plus 3 snacks daily. Luncheon buffets include vegetarian lasagna, chili relleno, and salad bar. Mostly vegetarian dinners include seafood crepe or salmon teriyaki.

Services and Facilities **Exercise Equipment:** 44 Trotter treadmills, 3 Lifecycles, 8 Schwinn Air-Dyne bikes, 3 Bodyguard computerized bikes, 3 ergometers, 4 recumbent bikes, 4 Precor rowing machines, 5-station Muscle Dynamics weights system, dumbbells (3–30 lbs.), hand weights. **Services:** Medical, fitness, and nutrition counseling; massage, acupressure, and beauty salon appointments. **Swimming Facilities:** Outdoor pool, ocean beach. **Recreation Facilities:** Tennis, golf, fishing nearby; boardwalk along beach. **Evening Programs:** Lectures and films on health-related topics.

In the Area Shopping centers, museums, guided food shopping, and restaurant dining; J. Paul Getty Museum, Norton Simon Museum, Venice Beach, Santa Monica center (artist colony); concierge service for show and concert tickets.

Getting Here *From Los Angeles.* By bus, Santa Monica Blue Bus from downtown (tel. 213/451–5444) takes about 45 min. By car, San Diego Freeway (I–405) north, Santa Monica Freeway (Rte. 10) to 4th St. exit, Pico Blvd. (20 min). Taxi, limousine, rental car available. Parking on site.

Special Notes Elevator connects all floors. No smoking indoors.

Pro Muscle Camp

Sports conditioning

California Anyone who is at all interested in bodybuilding or has looked
Los Angeles through a copy of *Muscle & Fitness* magazine probably knows that top professionals train at Pro Muscle Camp. Some are involved in all aspects of the camp, hanging out in the dorms and eating with campers; others show up only for scheduled sessions, to the dismay of envious guests.

Set on the Marymount College campus on the outskirts of the city, this isn't your typical summer camp. Nor are most of the campers bodybuilders but rather men and women who have learned that weight training gets them in shape quicker than other sports. So don't worry about being outclassed if you're not in top form.

The day begins with breakfast at 7:30, followed by a seminar with a celebrity bodybuilder such as Rachel McLish *(Pumping Iron II)*, who demonstrates how she works the upper and lower body. An hour of aerobics is scheduled before lunch, a high-energy class of running, swimming, or using weights in the gym.

During the discussions on training that follow lunch, the stars offer tips and answer questions. After that comes three hours of nonstop training in the gym, and the pros walk about and give advice.

Workout facilities are extensive: You can train to your heart's content. According to Lisa Rogak, the publisher of the *SporTreks* newsletter, the quality of instruction given by the stars varies greatly, but the counselors, all competitive amateur bodybuilders, are consistently good teachers who have sound advice.

Campers lodge in college dormitories and tend to be rowdy. There is much gossip in this fishbowl environment but few gripes about the meals. For someone who loves working with iron, a week here is like being a kid in a candy store.

Pro Muscle Management
202 Main St. (#8), Venice, CA 90291
Tel. 213/396–6568 (800/648–2267 in CA)

Administration Program director, David Zelon

Season 7 one-week sessions.

Accommodations 4 persons share on-campus apartments; each 2-bedroom unit has bath with shower, kitchen, air conditioning.

Rates $635 per person, one week, includes meals. Credit cards: MC, V.

Meal Plans	3 cafeteria meals daily. Salad bar with lunch and dinner. Entrees include broiled chicken, vegetable lasagna, steamed vegetables. High fiber, balanced menus low in fat, salt, and sugar.
Services and Facilities	**Exercise Equipment:** 3 units each of all bodybuilding equipment, plus Lifecycles, Liferowers, VersaClimbers, and the Bally Lifecircuit computerized weight training system. **Services:** Classes and private instruction, consultation on health and fitness. **Swimming Facilities:** Indoor Olympic-size swimming pool, ocean beach nearby. **Recreation Facilities:** Tennis, hiking, jogging, sunbathing. **Evening Programs:** Training sessions.
In the Area	Hollywood, Disneyland, Santa Monica waterfront.
Getting Here	Located minutes from the Los Angeles International Airport, the campus is reached via the Santa Monica Freeway. Supershuttle van service at the airport.
Special Notes	For the disabled there are access ramps to all facilities. No smoking indoors.

St. Helena Hospital Health Center

Life enhancement
Weight management
Spiritual awareness

California
Deer Park

Napa Valley vineyards spread for miles around the St. Helena Hospital Health Center complex run by the Seventh-day Adventists. Nondenominational and nonsectarian, the medically oriented programs are designed to teach self-management.

Disease prevention is emphasized here. Following a physical examination and analysis of your diet, doctors prescribe a course of action intended to help you achieve a healtheir lifestyle. Their specific recommendations for diet take into account your physical condition, nutritional requirements, and weight-loss goals. Together you devise an exercise schedule and discuss hydrotherapy treatments.

The health center's association with St. Helena Hospital enables it to draw on sophisticated medical facilities and medical consultants appropriate to your special problems. The center treats asthma, chronic bronchitis, emphysema, bronchiectasis, and pain disorders. A pulmonary rehabilitation program and a seven-day smoking treatment are also available. Seniors get special attention in a three-day program on aging.

The 12-day McDougall nutrition and diet program includes group therapy and relaxation techniques, vegetarian cooking classes in a teaching kitchen, and bodywork—massage plus use of the steam baths, sauna, and whirlpool. Also available are a gymnasium, exercise track, swimming pool, and biofeedback equipment.

Like other Adventist health centers across the country, St. Helena is known for its emphasis on nutrition. Its "Vegan" diet of fruits, vegetables, and legumes, plus modest amounts of high-fat natural foods such as nuts, avocados, and olives, is taught in cooking class.

The balanced diet is complemented by lectures, exercise in the open air, sunbathing, and increased water intake. You even have the option of bathing in mineral water or mud at nearby Calistoga Springs.

The center supplies you with a fresh new perspective on the state of your health in one of California's most scenic and historic areas.

St. Helena Hospital Health Center
650 Sanitarium Rd., Deer Park, CA 94576
Tel. 707/963–6200

Administration Medical director, John Hodgkin, M.D.

Season Year-round.

Accommodations 22 rooms with private bath, air conditioning, and balconies with views of Napa Valley; 2 beds and reading chair in motel-modern style.

Rates 7-day stop-smoking program $1,795 single, $1,595 double; 12-day diet and nutrition program $3,795 single, $3,295 double. Meals included. (Medical insurance may cover part of the cost.) $100 nonrefundable deposit; $200 for the stop-smoking program. Credit cards: MC, V.

Meal Plans 3 vegetarian meals daily, buffet style. No tea, coffee, or condiments. Cooking without butter and oil; vegetables sautéed in water. Specialties include vegetarian lasagna with mock cheese topping, baked tofu loaf, and eggplant "Parmesan" without cheese. Whole-grain breads baked without dairy products or eggs, fresh daily. Fresh fruit at most meals.

Services and Facilities **Exercise Equipment:** Weights room with treadmill, stationary bikes, rowing machines. **Services:** Massage, exercise instruction, private medical counseling. **Swimming Facilities:** Indoor pool. **Recreation Facilities:** Nature walks, hiking, cycling, tennis, golf, aerobic dancing; horseback riding and glider rides nearby. **Evening Programs:** Informal lectures on health-related topics.

In the Area Antiques, shops, mineral baths in Calistoga, winery tours, Jack London Park.

Getting Here *From San Francisco.* By car, Hwy. 80 north past Vallejo to Hwy. 37 going west, Hwy. 29 through St. Helena to Deer Park Rd., cross the Silverado Rd. and turn left on Sanitarium Rd. (90 min). By bus, free pickup at San Francisco airport. Airport shuttle service at fixed prices.

Special Notes No smoking in guest rooms or health center facilities.

Sivananda Ashram Yoga Farm

Spiritual awareness

California
Grass Valley

The Sivananda Ashram Yoga Farm follows the yogic disciplines of Swami Vishnu Devananda. Located in a peaceful valley north of Sacramento, the simple farmhouse provides lodging and space for two daily sessions of traditional postures (*asanas*), breathing techniques, and meditation. The intensive regimen of self-discipline is designed to foster a better understanding of the body-mind connection.

Meditation at 6 begins the morning session, brunch is served at 10, and then your schedule is open until 4 PM. Attendance at classes and meditations is mandatory.

The teachings of Swami Sivananda have been widely documented as promoting both physical and spiritual development. His followers and new students join in practicing the 12 asana positions, from a headstand to a spinal twist, each believed to have specific benefits for the body. Participants learn that the proper breathing (*pranayama*) in each position is essential for energy control.

The 60-acre farm attracts a diverse group, families as well as senior citizens. Guests are asked to share bedrooms and to contribute time to communal activities. You may arrive on any day and stay as long as you wish.

With its clear mountain air, fresh spring water, and unspoiled surroundings, the farm is said to suggest the rural paradise of Lord Krishna, called Vrindavan. Spiritual as well as physical, this is karmic yoga at its best.

Sivananda Ashram Yoga Farm
14651 Ballantree Lane, Grass Valley, CA 95949
Tel. 916/272–9322

Administration	Manager, Avoram
Season	Year-round.
Accommodations	8 guest rooms have 3 beds each, minimal furnishings. Showers and toilets shared. Tent space on the grounds. Private rooms on request.
Rates	$25 per person per day includes lodging, program, meals; campers pay $20. $25 in advance. No credit cards.
Meal Plans	2 lacto-vegetarian meals daily, buffet style. Morning meal of hot grain cereal, granola, yogurt, fruit. Stir-fry and steamed vegetables, rice, and scrambled tofu for dinner. Homemade soups, whole-wheat breads, green salads.
Services and Facilities	**Services:** Massage. **Swimming Facilities:** None. **Recreation Facilities:** Walking, meditation; skiing at nearby resorts. **Evening Programs:** Lectures on Hindu philosophy, concerts.
In the Area	Lake Tahoe, historic gold-mining towns of Nevada City, Grass Valley, old-town Sacramento.
Getting Here	*From Sacramento.* By bus, Greyhound to Grass Valley (2 hr). By car, I–80 to Auburn, Rte. 49 (1½ hr). Pickup in the farm van $5 at Grass Valley, $30 at Sacramento.
Special Notes	Limited access for the disabled. Children are welcome to participate with parents. No smoking.

Sonoma Mission Inn and Spa

Luxury pampering

California
Boyes Hot
Springs   San Franciscans have been "taking the cure" at the Sonoma Mission Inn since the turn of the century, but fitness training and pampering are modern attractions. The sparkling mineral water, bottled for drinking, is supplied to guests' rooms daily.

The high-tech spa is a favorite escape for young couples from the city as well as a popular stopover on wine-country tours. Its first consideration is health maintenance rather than weight loss, and a few days here can do wonders for your spirits.

Several wings of deluxe rooms and mini-suites have been added to the big pink stucco palace since its new owners restored this grand old hotel in 1980. An old-fashioned country market and restaurant are on the grounds. The resort accepts bookings for corporate conferences and sales meetings and, as a result, can be packed one day, quiet the next. Avoid weekends if you yearn for peace and seclusion.

Midweek spa packages are the best buy; weekend rates are strictly à la carte. All adult guests are allowed free access to the bathhouse, which includes twin exercise rooms (one with Keiser Cam II weight equipment, the other with Dynavit units), sauna, steam room, and indoor whirlpools beside a flower-bordered outdoor exercise pool. Scheduled daily are coed aerobics classes, aquacize groups, and hydrotherapy sessions.

Driving up to the main lobby is like arriving for a party at Jay Gatsby's. Juice, coffee, muffins, and a bowl of apples for early risers sit on a buffet near the great fireplace. The baronial reception hall, awash in pastel pinks and peach against bleached wood, sets the mood of casual elegance. The inn and its fashionable dining room and wine bar seem far removed from the rigors of calorie counting.

Down a path through gardens abloom with camellia and jasmine is the spa building, sandwiched between a conference center and tennis courts. After you check in with the spa director and schedule massage and beauty treatments, you are left pretty much on your own.

An airy, two-story atrium that belies the building's origins as a Quonset hut is the setting for most of the activities. The glass-walled exercise room faces a sunlit marble fountain. Try the Keiser Cam II pneumatic resistance machine that tones muscles while you pump air instead of iron, or pedal a Dynavit exercise cycle outfitted with a biofeedback computer that monitors calorie expenditure and pulse rate while charting your cardiovascular response.

Report for treatments upstairs in a rather somber room, where you can sip herbal tea and watch TV while you wait to be summoned.

Hydrotherapy is an important aspect of the spa program. The corrosive nature of the mineral water has caused it to be eliminated from the course of treatments; however, the inn has imported equipment that includes a full-length tub for underwater massage in which 30 bubbling jets and a high-pressure hose work to invigorate you. Then an herbal wrap is applied to relax muscles, soften the skin, and draw out toxins. A young attendant explains how each step increases circulation, stimulates heart and lungs, and eliminates toxins.

Serious swimmers will find the spa's pool too small for laps and often crowded with aquacize groups. The large pool for inn guests is unheated.

Sonoma Mission Inn and Spa

18140 Sonoma Hwy. 12, Boyes Hot Springs, CA 95416
(Reservations) Box 1447, Sonoma, CA 95476
Tel. 707/938–9000 or 800/358–9022 (800/862–4945 in CA)

Administration	Manager, Peter Henry; program director, Nancy Natemeyer
Season	Year-round.
Accommodations	170 rooms in the main building and garden units. Plantation shutters, canopied beds, and ceiling fans; king, queen, and twin beds. Fireplaces, sun deck, and marble baths in the new Wine Country rooms.
Rates	1-night mini-package during the week $235–$340 single, $200–$267 per person double occupancy; 5-night Sun.–Fri. deluxe spa program $1,650–$2,122 single, $1,350–$1,720 double. Tax and gratuities included. One night in advance, $500 for package. Credit cards: AE, CB, DC, MC, V.
Meal Plans	Spa menu with calorie counts in main dining room. Choices at 1,000–1,200 calories per day include salmon poached in Chardonnay with tarragon, breast of free-range chicken and steamed vegetables, grilled veal loin with leeks, whole-wheat pizza topped with wild mushrooms, goat cheese, and tomatoes. Decaffeinated coffee, herbal tea, nonfat milk.
Services and Facilities	**Exercise Equipment:** 9 Keiser Cam II pneumatic weight units, 2 Monark bikes, Lifecycle, Schwinn Aero-Dyne bike, Concept II rowing machine, StairMaster, recumbent bike. **Services:** Massage (Swedish, Esalen), fango clay body pack, herbal and seaweed body wraps, loofah scrub, facials, manicures, pedicures. Aromatherapy massage, underwater hydrotherapy massage. **Swimming Facilities:** 2 outdoor pools for exercise; unheated 40-foot pool. **Recreation Facilities:** 2 tennis courts, hiking. Horseback riding, golf nearby.
In the Area	Guided group hiking daily; ballooning and gliding; winery tours, Sonoma Mission historic area, antique shops, specialty food shops, Calistoga mud baths.
Getting Here	*From San Francisco.* By bus, Greyhound to Sonoma (90 min). By car, Golden Gate Bridge, Rte. 101, Hwy. 37 to Sonoma, Hwy. 12 (45 min). Public bus at door; Sonoma Airporter scheduled van service to San Francisco airport; limousine, taxi, rental car.
Special Notes	Limited access for the disabled. No smoking in the spa or in designated areas of the dining room.

Spa Hotel and Mineral Springs

Luxury pampering
Taking the waters

California *Palm Springs*	Here is one alternative to rustic resorts with geothermal pools. The Spa Hotel and Mineral Springs boasts marble floors in the bathroom, lush gardens, and lavishly decorated rooms. The spa, which bases its fitness program on European hydrotherapy, is built on the site of hot mineral springs used by Native Americans for centuries. The Agua Caliente tribe owns the land and leases it to the resort.

Decked out in white slippers and oversize terrycloth towels, guests attend sessions of eucalyptus inhalation and use the sauna or the steam room. After a shower, they are escorted along a palm-tree-lined corridor to sunken marble tubs. The "magical water" of the springs soon disposes of tension and promotes relaxation.

Herbal tea or ice water is served in the cooling rooms while guests, wrapped in sheets, wait for the masseur or masseuse. The one-hour treatment helps prepare you for a swim in the Olympic-size outdoor pool or a sunbath in the rooftop solarium (clothes optional). Aerobics classes and aquatic exercise in the mineral-water pool are other options.

The completely private recently renovated spa hotel is in the center of Palm Springs, close to the shops, restaurants, and recreational attractions this desert resort is famous for. Programs are tailored to your needs and interests, allowing you plenty of time to enjoy the area.

Spa Hotel and Mineral Springs
100 N. Indian Ave., Palm Springs, CA 92262
Tel. 619/325–1461 or 800/854–1279 (800/472–4371 in CA)

Administration Manager, Scott Bullock; spa director, Faye Antaky

Season Year-round.

Accommodations 230 rooms (20 suites) in a contemporary 5-story hotel. Fashionable rooms with rattan furnishing, oversize bed, dressing area and bath. Balcony, TV, air-conditioning, and morning paper.

Rates Daily European plan $105–$155 in summer, $155–$185 in winter. Spa packages: 3-day/2-night $399 single, $299 double; 6-day/5-night $970 single $730 double. One night payable in advance. Credit cards: AE, CB, DC, MC, V.

Meal Plans 3 meals a day total 1,000 calories. Fresh fruit and yogurt at breakfast, cold salmon for lunch, choice of lamb medallions, whole-wheat pasta, or grilled shrimp and vegetables for dinner. Coffee, tea, and regular menu are available.

Services and Facilities **Exercise Equipment:** 12-station Paramount weight training gym, 3 Lifecycles, Liferower, treadmill, free weights. **Services:** Massage (Swedish, sports, shiatsu), aromatherapy, herbal wrap, body scrub, facial; salon for hair, nail, and skin care. **Bathing Facilities:** 34 private Jacuzzis with mineral water. **Swimming Facilities:** Outdoor pool. **Recreation Facilities:** 3 tennis courts. Golf and horseback riding nearby. Desert hiking, cross-country skiing nearby.

In the Area Sightseeing tours, bicycle rental (38 mi of trails), ballooning; aerial tramway, Living Desert Museum (nature and art exhibits, concerts), Botanical Gardens, Polo Club.

Getting Here *From Los Angeles.* By bus, Greyhound (4 hr). By car, I–10 to Rte. 111 (2½ hr). By train, Amtrak to Indio (2 hr). Limousine, taxi, airport van service, rental car available.

Special Notes No smoking in the spa and in designated areas of the dining room.

Weight Watchers Camp California

Youth camps for weight loss

California
Santa Ynez Valley

The Weight Watchers Camp California, a summer coed camp, is located on the Dunn School campus in the Santa Ynez Valley, ringed by the San Rafael Mountains. Its program focuses on diet, exercise, and health education. Campers have exclusive use of playing fields, a swimming pool, and a gymnasium. Activities and living quarters are assigned according to age groups; campers range from 10 to 21 years old.

The meals feature Weight Watchers recipes; cooking classes and lectures on nutrition teach campers to eat properly. The dining room serves as the center of special activities.

Accredited counselors supervise workouts with Nautilus equipment, slimnastics and aerobics classes, and sports. Those who complete the course are guaranteed to lose weight or get a refund.

Weight Watchers Camp California
Box 98, Los Olivos, CA 93441
Tel. 805/688–6181
Weight Watchers Camps
183 Madison Ave., New York, NY 10016
Tel. 212/889–9500 or 800/223–5600 (800/251–4141 in Canada)

Administration Program director, Anthony Sparber

Season June–Aug.

Accommodations Cabins with lounges, linen service, modern laundry facilities.

Rates Sessions of 2–7 weeks from $1,450. $100 in advance. Credit cards: AE, DC, MC, V.

Meal Plans 3 balanced meals daily in the cafeteria; 2 snacks.

Services and Facilities **Exercise Equipment:** Weights room with Nautilus equipment; gymnasium equipment. **Swimming Facilities:** Outdoor pool, beach nearby. **Recreation Facilities:** Softball, soccer, football, tennis, volleyball, basketball; jogging and track. **Evening Programs:** Fashion shows, dancing, musicals, talent shows, campfires.

In the Area Hiking, country walks.

Getting Here Pickup at Santa Barbara airport. Taxi, rental car available.

Special Notes No smoking indoors.

Weight Watchers Camp Golden Gate

Youth camps for weight loss

California
Portola Valley

The San Francisco Bay Area is the setting for a summer of fitness, diet, and nutrition education for campers age 10–21. The Weight Watchers Camp Golden Gate, on the campus of the Woodside Priory School, has been operated by Weight Watchers for the past 17 years.

Campers enjoy outdoor sports, use of a fully equipped gymnasium, and a theater for shows and movies. Facilities also include an arts and crafts building, a library, and modern two-story dormitories. Accredited counselors supervise aerobics, calisthenics, and slimnastics classes.

Meals feature Weight Watchers recipes, and cooking and nutrition classes explain proper eating habits. Those who complete the course are guaranteed to lose weight or get a refund.

Weight Watchers Camp Golden Gate
302 Portola Rd., Portola Valley, CA 94025
Tel. 415/851–0638
Weight Watchers Camps
183 Madison Ave., New York, NY 10016.
Tel. 212/889–9500 or 800/223–5600 (800/251–4141 in Canada)

Administration	Program director, Anthony Sparber
Season	June–Aug.
Accommodations	Dorm rooms shared by campers of the same age. Lounge facilities with TV, VCR, and Ping-Pong tables. Modern baths; coin-operated laundry facility.
Rates	Sessions of 2–7 weeks from $1,450. $100 in advance. Credit Cards: AE, DC, MC, V.
Meal Plans	3 balanced meals daily in the cafeteria; 2 snacks.
Services and Facilities	**Exercise Equipment:** Gymnasium with free weights, Universal equipment, stationary bikes. **Swimming Facilities:** Heated outdoor pool. **Recreation Facilities:** Soccer, basketball, softball, jogging, track, aerobics, calisthenics, slimnastics; 4 tennis courts. **Evening Programs:** Disco, skit nights, camp shows.
In the Area	Hiking, nature walks.
Getting Here	Pickup at San Jose airport. Taxi, rental car available.
Special Notes	No smoking indoors.

Weight Watchers Camp Ojai

Youth camps for weight loss

California
Ojai

Located at the western end of the picturesque Ojai valley on the Villanova Preparatory School campus near Santa Barbara, the Weight Watchers Camp Ojai, a summer coed camp for 10- to 21-year-olds, offers a weight-loss program consisting of diet, education, and exercise. Campers have exclusive use of outdoor sports facilities, outdoor swimming pool, and a gymnasium with modern equipment. Horseback riding is available for an additional fee. Living quarters are in large, modern dormitories.

The meals feature Weight Watchers recipes. Campers learn proper eating habits in classes on cooking and nutrition, as well as in the dining room, which serves as a social center.

Accredited counselors supervise full weeks of workouts with Nautilus equipment, slimnastics and aerobics classes, and sports. Those who complete the course are guaranteed to lose weight or get a refund.

Weight Watchers Camp Ojai
12096 Ventura Ave., Ojai, CA 93023
Tel. 805/646–1464
Weight Watchers Camps
183 Madison Ave., New York, NY 10016
Tel. 212/889–9500 or 800/223–5600 (800/251–4141 in Canada)

Administration Program director, Anthony Sparber

Season June–Aug.

Accommodations 2 large modern dormitories; carpeted rooms with built-in desks and closets; modern baths, TV rooms, and coin-operated laundries.

Rates Sessions of 2–7 weeks from $1,450. $100 in advance. Credit cards: AE, DC, MC, V.

Meal Plans 3 balanced meals daily in the cafeteria; 2 snacks.

Services and Facilities **Exercise Equipment:** Weights room with Nautilus equipment; gymnasium equipment. **Swimming Facilities:** Outdoor pool. **Recreation Facilities:** Soccer, volleyball, basketball, tennis, touch or flag football; aerobics; swimnastics; horseback riding (additional fee). **Evening Programs:** Songfests, campfires, dramatics, talent shows, fashion shows.

In the Area Hiking, bicycling, nature walks.

Getting Here Pickup at Santa Barbara airport. Taxi, rental car available.

Special Notes No smoking indoors.

Weimar Institute

Life enhancement
Preventive medicine
Weight management

California
Weimar
A diabetic housewife, a stressed-out doctor, and an overweight retiree are representative of the older generation of fitness converts who come to the Weimar Institute to learn healthy habits. Medically oriented yet devoted to education and exercise, the 19-day Newstart program teaches guests to help themselves through a combination of physical, mental, and spiritual healing.

The doctors and staff, all Seventh-day Adventists, see prevention as the best medicine. With the help of computers, the staff makes specific recommendations for diet based on assessments of your physical condition, nutritional requirements, and weight-loss goals. After you undergo a complete physical, your personal schedule will be set by a physician who continues to monitor your progress throughout the three-week program.

Hydrotherapy and massage are part of the program. Included are a 16-head enclosure of contrasting hot and cold showers, Russian-style steam baths, and whirlpools. Those afflicted with neuromuscular problems learn to relieve themselves of pain.

The Adventists, long known for their interest in health and nutrition, accept anyone willing to adhere to a strictly vegetarian diet and exercise regimen at home. The physicians and educators here encourage patients to get off medication as soon as is safely possible. They believe modern technology has overshadowed simple cures for common ailments. Their programs help participants to quit smoking, control weight, and cope with degenerative diseases such as arthritis, diabetes, cancer, and cardiovascular problems.

The first activity of the day is calisthenics. Everyone is encouraged to walk and enjoy the miles of woodland trail on the 457-acre campus. "Stretchercise" classes that won't strain bodies unaccustomed to exercise are scheduled between cooking classes and private counseling or therapy sessions.

Newstart shares resources with Weimar College, a training institution for health related ministries that offers an intensive, outpatient type of program with live-in accommodations. Weekend seminars are often scheduled for those who want a refresher course in health cooking or controlling stress. Others come simply to relax at the new Weimar Inn, which also has a weights room.

Located in the Sierra Nevada foothills between Sacramento and Reno, Weimar is a nondenominational and nonsectarian place that renews body and spirit.

Weimar Institute
Box 486, 20601 W. Paoli Lane, Weimar, CA 95736
Tel. 916/637–4111 or 800/525–9191

Administration	President, Herbert Douglass; medical director, Hubert F. Sturges, M.D.
Season	Newstart program June–mid-Dec.; weekend seminars year-round.
Accommodations	29-room country lodge without frills. Large rooms with sitting area and private bath, single or king-size beds. Informal social gatherings around the fireplace in the lobby; self-service laundry. 23 rooms with cherry furnishings, quilted bedspreads, mirrored closet doors, and flowered wallpaper at the Weimar Inn.
Rates	19-day live-in Newstart program $3,670; $3,125 for participating spouse or partners, $1,840 for accommodations only. $32 per night for two, $28 single, without meals, at the Weimar Inn. Newstart program $500 per person in advance; inn accommodations 50% in advance. Credit cards: MC, V.
Meal Plans	3 vegetarian meals daily in the Weimar Country Cafeteria. Specialties include a "haystack" of chili, rice, sprouts, lettuce, and tomato on corn chips, vegetarian lasagna, steamed vegetables on rice with oriental sauce. Breads baked daily. Whole and sprouted grains. No eggs, cheese, or dairy products.
Services and Facilities	**Exercise Equipment:** 3 Exercycles, Schwinn Air-Dyne bike, 2 rowing machines, 2 treadmills, cross-country ski machine, tiltboard, free weights. **Services:** Newstart program includes complete physical and medical history evaluation, blood tests, treadmill stress tests, consultation with physician; hydrotherapy and massage; cooking classes; 24-hour nursing staff. **Swimming Facilities:** River bathing and wading. **Recreation Fa-**

cilities: Volleyball; golf course nearby. **Evening Programs:** Music, video presentations, and talks on inspirational and health-related topics.

In the Area Weekend outings to the Empire State gold mine, the California State Capitol, and the Railroad Museum in Sacramento; sightseeing and shopping in the Lake Tahoe area; Yosemite National Park, the Nevada casinos, Old Sacramento.

Getting Here *From Sacramento.* By car, I–80 north to Weimar, exit on W. Paoli Lane (60 min). By bus, Greyhound to Weimar (60 min. By train, Amtrak to Colfax (45 min). Weimar Institute provides service from the train and bus station (fee); taxi and rental car available.

Special Notes One room at the lodge and the inn has access for the disabled. No smoking.

The Southwest

Health resorts are the new bonanza in the Old West. Ranches and lodges in the desert offer the latest in diet, nutrition, and exercise programs, and fitness can be combined with skiing, trail rides, and hiking. Two hours north of the Las Vegas casinos, near the pioneer settlement of St. George, in an area of intense development commonly referred to as Utah's Banana Belt or the Other Palm Springs, are modern, palm-studded oases where stress control and weight-management courses are the major attraction.

The trendsetters among fitness resorts in the Southwest are the Canyon Ranch and Maine Chance in Arizona and SunRise Springs in New Mexico, each with its own programs and ambience, each offering sophisticated yet refreshingly personal service. In the Rocky Mountain states, Colorado has taken the lead as a center for holistic health and sports conditioning, and summer music festivals in Aspen and Vail bring a further dimension to holidays for healthy bodies and minds.

Buckhorn Mineral Wells Spa

Taking the waters

Arizona
Mesa
Locals and sufferers from arthritis and skin problems know Buckhorn Mineral Wells Spa, a small resort in the desert near Phoenix that offers treatments on an à la carte basis to guests and day visitors. Bathers enjoy private rooms with tiled tubs into which hot mineral water flows continuously; a whirlpool unit enhances the effect, and a licensed masseur or masseuse is on hand from 9 AM to 5 PM.

Surrounded by cactus and palm trees, the motel-style lodge looks like a combination of hacienda and gymnasium. Separate men's and women's entrances lead to the cement bathing cubicles. The mineral water, unchlorinated and naturally heated at 106 degrees, flows at the rate of 7,000 gallons per hour. Cooler water can be added, but the nurse in attendance recommends the high temperature to relieve sore muscles and aching bones. Tubs are drained, cleaned, and refilled after each use.

The hot, dry desert climate compounds the effect of the bath. Aside from solariums for nude sunbathing, no other health facility is available. Game areas and a museum displaying mounted native birds and animals are on the grounds.

Built in the 1940s, the Buckhorn Spa was expanded by the owner and operator, and now guests can stay in adobe cottages equipped for housekeeping. There are no restaurants, however, and no planned activities.

Buckhorn Mineral Wells Spa
5900 E. Main St., Mesa, AZ 85205
Tel. 602/832–1111

The Southwest

Administration   Manager, Alice A. Sliger

Season   Year-round.

Accommodations   25 cottages with twin beds, private [...] and linens provided. Units have Spa[...] air conditioning, daily maid service.

Rates $35 a day for 2, Jan.–Mar.; $225 we[...] mer. One night payable in advance. No credit cards.

Services and Facilities   **Exercise Equipment:** None available. **Services:** Whirlpool mineral baths ($10), Swedish-type massage with vibrator ($15). Series rates and combination treatments. **Swimming Facilities:** Nearby lake. **Spa Facilities:** Hot mineral well water in 27 private rooms. **Recreation Facilities:** Golf courses, horseback riding nearby; fishing, picnic areas, parks, water sports.

In the Area   Scottsdale resorts and restaurants; Phoenix; the Heard Museum (Indian art); Paolo Soleri's Arcosanti village.

Getting Here   *From Phoenix.* By Car, Hwys. 60, 80, 89, Recker Rd. (30 min). Rental car available.

Special Notes   No smoking in the bathhouse.

Canyon Ranch Health and Fitness Resort

Life enhancement
Weight management
Holistic health

Arizona
Tucson   A 60-acre spread in the foothills of the Santa Catalina Mountains, the Canyon Ranch Health and Fitness Resort is a high-tech emporium of good health that positively radiates energy. From the moment you are welcomed in the big hacienda and shown to your casita, the nonstop pursuit of health and well-being seems to put everyone in a happy, optimistic mood. Even the most stressed-out Type A personalities tend to find the extensive schedule of exercise classes, hiking, bike trips, and bodywork to their liking.

The prebreakfast walk requires rising before dawn. On a typical morning, about 50 men and women dressed for the predawn chill warm up on a playing field. The exercise leader sets a brisk pace on paths through the desert landscape of cacti, mesquite, acacia, and palo verde trees. Conversations come naturally with fellow ranchers, and newcomers quickly learn the lay of the land. Later, over a breakfast of Spanish omelet (made of egg whites), orange juice, and freshly brewed decaf coffee, intense debates on the merits of shiatsu and Swedish massage can develop. (The old hands seem to have pronounced opinions on every method of exercise and diet.)

The scope and scale of the sprawling ranch will probably be bewildering until you familiarize yourself with the various activity centers and residential clusters. Unlike more rigidly programmed resorts, the ranch allows you to select your activities, and it may take some time for you to establish your priorities. Reservation clerks who computerize appointment schedules in the big exercise and spa building can offer suggestions, but be sure to attend the briefing held by the fitness staff members. Many activities require signing up in advance to lim-

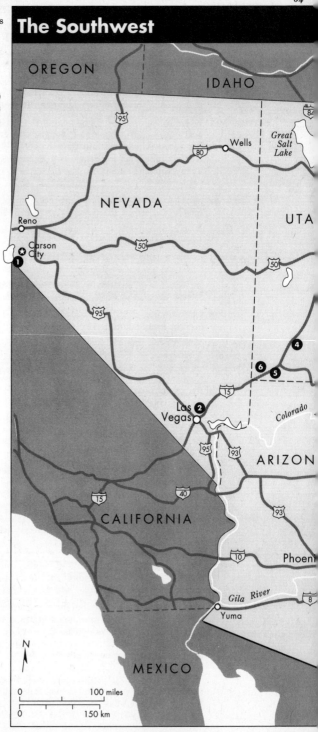

al Wells

...nch Health
...ess Resort, **24**
...e Chance, **19**
...rriott's Mountain
...adows Resort, **21**
Scottsdale Princess, **20**
Spring Creek Ranch, **18**
Tucson National Resort
& Spa, **23**

Colorado

The Aspen Club, **15**
The Cascade Club at
The Westin Hotel, **12**
Eden Valley Lifestyle
Center, **8**
Glenwood Hot Springs
Lodge, **9**
Indian Springs
Resort, **11**
Mountain Biking at
Winter Park, **10**
Rocky Mountain Health
Ranch, **14**
Rocky Mountain
Wellness Spa, **7**
Waunita Hot Springs
Ranch, **16**
Weight Watchers Camp
Rocky Mountain, **13**
Wiesbaden Hot Springs
Lodge, **17**

Nevada

Desert Inn Hotel &
Casino, **2**
Walley's Hot Springs
Resort, **1**

New Mexico

SunRise Springs
Resort, **25**
Truth or
Consequences, **26**

Utah

Cliff Lodge at
Snowbird, **3**
Green Valley Health
Resort, **5**
The Last Resort, **4**
National Institute of
Fitness, **6**

The Southwest

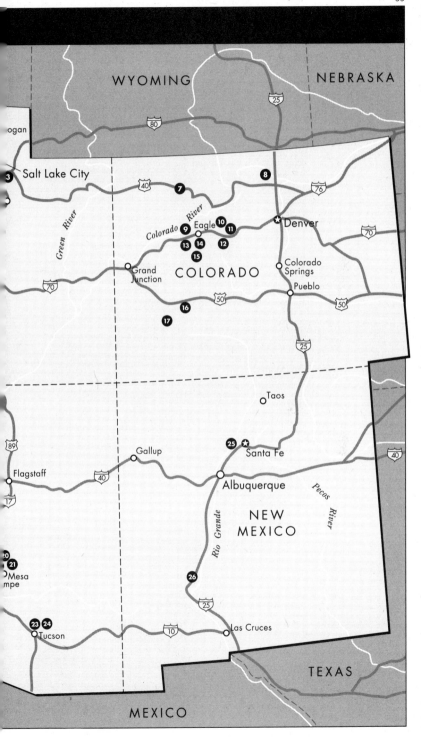

it the size of the group, and you may find that your appointments clash with outings or classes.

Group psychodynamics, a shared experience that builds synergy as you experience many kinds of exercise and health services, is the philosophy that has guided the ranch's development. Options include holistic healing, a computerized evaluation of your fitness level, hiking the canyon country, and high-impact aerobics. There are also men's aerobics, low-impact aerobics for beginning and advanced groups, water aerobics, and batteries of treadmills and stair-climbers. If the choices prove overwhelming, you can retreat to the privacy of the men's and women's hydrotherapy areas to soak in hot and cold whirlpools and sunbathe in the nude. The saunas, steam rooms, inhalation rooms, and swimming pools are open 14 hours a day.

Preventive medicine plays a major role here. Some people return several times a year to combat job burnout or to work on special problems. Programs are scheduled for quitting smoking, weight loss, relief from arthritis, and physical rehabilitation. The resort has expanded recently, adding a medical/wellness complex with behavioral health professionals and medical services staff, larger gyms, padded aerobics studios, an indoor swimming pool, and a rest and meditation room in a glass-walled tower with a panoramic view of the mountains.

Canyon Ranch uses biofeedback to enhance relaxation techniques. The newly installed MindFitness program takes five half days (and is booked months in advance). Research into post-surgery life enhancement is supported by an outside foundation.

Once your juices get going, you may find that the meals seem suspiciously gourmet. The secret is all-natural ingredients low in salt and saturated fat, high in fiber, and prepared without refined flour or sugar. The cheerful staff will bring seconds and even pack fruit for you to take back to your room. Herbal teas and decaf and regular coffee are available throughout the day; at night there's popcorn in the movie room—unsalted and unbuttered.

Casual in every way, Canyon Ranch attracts an interesting cross section of people, from young executives to grandmothers, from all parts of the Americas and Europe. Up to 30% of the 250 guests in residence at any one time are men. For those who are already fit, there's the Ultimate Challenge week; if weight loss is your goal, the Life Enhancement Center shows how one can take off 30 pounds or more, here and at home.

Canyon Ranch Health and Fitness Resort
8600 East Rockcliff Rd., Tucson, AZ 85715
Tel. 602/749–9000 or 800/742–9000 (800/327–9690 in Canada)

Administration Managers, Enid and Mel Zuckerman; fitness director, Karma Kientzler; health services director, Daniel Baker

Season Year-round.

Accommodations 140 rooms in luxury casitas with rooms and suites, and private condominium cottages with kitchen, living room, and laundry. A new building for special programs has quarters for 25. All in desert colors with modern, southwestern furnishings, large beds, TV/radio, and private baths. Year-round air conditioning.

Rates Minimum 4-day stay in standard rooms $1,310 single, $1,050 per person double occupancy; 7-night program $2,290 single, $1,870 double. Casita rooms: 4 days $1,650–$2,270; 7 nights $2,840–$3,850; 13-night weight-loss program $2,454 single, $2,012 double. Two days payable in advance. Credit cards: MC, V.

Meal Plans 10-day cycle of calorie-controlled meals (1,000 calories a day for women, 1,200 calories for men). Breakfast selections are french toast, bran muffins, rye cereal, 7-grain waffle; lunch selections are curried chicken salad, Mexican spaghetti, bean burrito, stir-fry vegetables, meatless chili; dinner entrees include barbecued chicken breast, cioppino, tomato-basil ravioli, lamb chops, fresh fish. Fresh fruit sorbet, berries in season, blueberry cheesecake are desserts. Fruit-flavored nutrition shakes, crudités, and nonalcoholic drinks served daily. Tea and decaf coffee always available. Vitamin supplement at breakfast; alternative vegetarian menu daily.

Services and Facilities **Exercise Equipment:** Full line of Cam II pneumatic training units, 8 Lifecycles, 6 recumbent bikes, 13 Trotter treadmills, Pacer treadmill, 2 rowing machines, 2 NordicTrack cross-country ski machines, mini-trampolines, free weights. **Services:** 9 types of massage, aromatherapy, herbal wraps, body scrub with crushed pearl; hair salon, nail and skin care. Consultation on nutrition and diet, holistic health, body composition, and fitness level. MindFitness biofeedback program (advance registration). Cooking class. **Swimming Facilities:** Indoor pool, outdoor pools. **Recreation Facilities:** 8 tennis courts, basketball, volleyball, parcourse; 15-speed mountain bikes; golf and horseback riding nearby. **Evening Programs:** Talks by psychologists, authors, naturalists, and other specialists.

In the Area Daily hikes, biking trips in Sabino Canyon, tours to local museums and shopping malls; Sonoran Desert Museum, crafts market in Nogales, Mt. Lemmon. Tucson's old-town arts district, Mission San Xavier del Bac in Santa Cruz Valley.

Getting Here *From Tucson.* By car, Speedway Blvd. east to Kolb Rd., Tanque Verde to Sabino Canyon Rd., Snyder Rd. to Rockcliff (30 min). Free transfer from Tucson airport on arrival and departure and to golf courses; rental car, taxi service available.

Special Notes Limited access for the disabled. Summer camp programs for teenagers (15–18); minimum age of guests is 14. Smoking permitted on patios of guest rooms, discouraged elsewhere. Remember to bring completed medical questionnaire, hiking shoes, walking shoes, clothing for warmth, and sun protection.

Maine Chance

Luxury pampering   *Women only*

Arizona Maine Chance is Elizabeth Arden's sunbelt showplace, a health
Phoenix retreat for the woman who wants to get away from it all in comfort. Set on a 105-acre estate, the old-world mansion with its

views of Camelback Mountain gives guests a sense of being in the middle of a rose garden. The staff of 130 extends lots of personal service to the guests, whose number is limited to 56.

The Sunday–Sunday program is tailored to the individual's needs and fitness level. The full schedule of exercise classes includes workouts in the swimming pool and yoga. Treatments such as the Ardena Wax Bath, manicures, pedicures, and makeup sessions—all using Arden products—require appointments. Focus can be on weight loss or gain, relaxation, or a complete head-to-toe makeover.

Guests are free to do as much or as little as they please. The all-inclusive fee encourages you to try underwater massage as well as the popular Swedish-style soother. Rigorous activities from advanced aerobics to tai chi chuan are also available. You can do laps without exposing sensitive skin to the sun in the newly constructed indoor pool.

Your exercise can consist of jogging between the manicurist and the hairstylist, or you can participate in the light 30-minute workouts and sessions in the steam cabinets, sauna, and whirlpool.

Maine Chance
5830 E. Jean Ave., Phoenix, AZ 85018
Tel. 602/947–6365

Administration General manager, Frederick Quirk

Season Oct.–May.

Accommodations Elegant rooms, single or double occupancy, suites in 7 "cottages," French antique furnishings and modern baths; hair dryer, cosmetics, daily change of wardrobe for spa workouts supplied.

Rates One week $2,350–$2,800 per person double occupancy, $2,550–$3,100 single, all services included. 50% payable in advance. No credit cards.

Meal Plans 3 meals daily begin with breakfast in bed; the 950-calorie daily diet includes fresh fruit and vegetables, lean meat, fish, coffee or tea. Shrimp mixed salads, cheese soufflés, angelhair pasta with pesto sauce, and filet mignon are among the offerings.

Services and Facilities **Services:** Massage, facials, skin and nail care, hairstyling, hydrotherapy. **Swimming Facilities:** Indoor pool. **Recreation Facilities:** Tennis, golf, horseback riding nearby. **Evening Programs:** Talks on health, nutrition, fashion.

In the Area Shopping trips to local boutiques; museum tours on request; the Heard Museum (American Indian), Scottsdale, the Desert Museum (natural history).

Getting Here Skyport International Airport 15 min away by car or taxi. Limousine service on arrival and departure.

Special Notes All activities take place on the ground floor. No smoking indoors.

Marriott's Mountain Shadows Resort

Non-program resort facilities

Arizona
Scottsdale

Getting the couch potatoes at the swimming pool to participate in aquaerobics was the first step. Then a trek up Camelback Mountain was promised to all who came to a "peak energy" breakfast on Sunday morning. Suddenly the new fitness center at Marriott's Mountain Shadows, a long-established golf resort, was making news.

Introduced during the winter season of 1987–1988, the $125,000 state-of-the-art facility offers 30–35 exercise classes a week, including yoga and aerobics, and circuit weight training on computerized equipment. Guests at the resort are invited to use the equipment at no charge, and they pay only $5 per class. Other services—massage, hair and nail care—and meals are à la carte.

Pleasantly informal, the weights room and aerobics studio are sandwiched between a snack bar and the pro shop, with a view of the putting green. To make a massage appointment, it's necessary to find the locker room past the club members' bar. The masseur, a professional trained in Scandinavia, is worth the effort.

Aiming for fitness has given the aging resort a new lease on life. It has introduced programs for a family vacation that won't dent the pocketbook. Thanks to a general manager who is a fitness buff, the main dining room now has calorie-counted items on the menu alongside steak and omelets. The chefs at its flagship restaurant, Shells, have gotten into the game, too, with fresh-from-the-sea entrees. A disco accommodates those who want to exercise after dinner.

Such pleasures aren't news to a health-conscious person, but in the fast-paced tourism industry around Phoenix there haven't been many options in the budget category. Executives staying at Mountain Shadows during sales meetings and conventions now drop in for a morning energizer or a late-afternoon relaxer. The opening of a full-scale European spa down the road at Marriott's Camelback Inn makes it possible to combine a bit of pampering with golf, tennis, and aerobics at bargain rates.

The new status symbol here is a T-shirt that declares, "I conquered Camelback." It's not for sale, and you'll have to sign up early for that Sunday trek to get one.

Marriott's Mountain Shadows Resort
5641 E. Lincoln Dr., Scottsdale, AZ 85253
Tel. 602/948–7111 or 800/228–9290
Fax 602/948–7111, ext. 1898

Administration Manager, James Rose; activities director, Jill Eisenhut

Season Activities Jan.–Apr., club open year-round.

Accommodations 339 recently refurbished rooms in single-story units have private bath, patio, and parking nearby.

Rates $185–$240 a day in winter. Children under 18 stay free with parents. Golf and tennis packages. Advance confirmation with credit card. Credit cards: AE, CB, DC, MC, V.

Meal Plans No special diet plan. Shells offers seafood selections from the grill, and its steamed vegetables with tomato pesto sauce won the "Heart Smart Award." Low-calorie menu items in the Cactus Flower Cafe.

Services and Facilities **Exercise Equipment:** 8-station Universal weight training gym, bench and dumbbells, computerized VCR bicycles. **Services:** Swedish and sports massage; beauty salon for hair, nail, and skin care. Tennis and golf instruction. **Swimming Facilities:** 3 outdoor pools include a double Olympic-size pool with lap lanes. **Spa Facilities:** Coed whirlpools, separate saunas. **Recreation Facilities:** 18-hole executive golf course, 8 lighted tennis courts. Shuffleboard, volleyball, table tennis, bicycle rental. Horseback riding, ballooning nearby. **Evening Programs:** Movies, bingo.

In the Area Guided climb up Camelback Mountain with breakfast, walks, greenhouse tour. Gray Line tours of local attractions. The Heard Museum in Phoenix, Cosanti Foundation sculpture garden, Paolo Soleri's Arcosanti, Buckhorn hot mineral water baths, Sedona spiritual energy tour, Mexican crafts market in Nogales, Big Surf water theme park; sports, racing, and performing-arts centers.

Getting Here *From Phoenix.* By car, north on 44th St. to Lincoln Dr. (30 min). Shuttle bus service from Skyharbor Airport; hotel provides pickup service on request. Taxi and rental car available.

Special Notes Limited access for the disabled; all facilities on ground floor. Organized activities for children 5 and older include games, dinner, movies, tennis clinic, tennis day camp. No smoking in the Fitness Club; nonsmoking areas in restaurants.

Scottsdale Princess

Non-program resort facilities

Arizona *Scottsdale* Rising from the Sonoran Desert like a mirage, the rose-colored towers and velvet green golf course of the Scottsdale Princess beckon you to a world of luxury. The 450-acre resort, member of a hotel chain noted for striking architecture in Mexico and Bermuda, has a king-size health club that enhances the burgeoning Phoenix–Scottsdale area. Use of the exercise equipment here and participation in the five daily aerobics classes are free to registered guests.

A fitness staff member sets the pace on a 45-minute 3-mile walk in the crisp desert air at 7 AM along the grounds and golf course. The rest of the day is your own to schedule with bodywork and a bit of luxury pampering, including European hydrotherapy treatments, a rarity in Arizona.

With a choice of three outdoor swimming pools, an air-conditioned aerobics studio, and an array of exercise equipment, there's no need to broil in the desert sun. Other options include nearby hiking trails in the McDowell Mountains and an equestrian center.

Designed for conventions and sales meetings, the Princess stays full on weekends by offering special packages. It also organizes a fitness fair and three hours of Olympic-style competition for corporate groups.

Scottsdale Princess
7575 E. Princess Dr., Scottsdale, AZ 85255
Tel. 602/585–4848 or 800/223–1818

Administration Manager, Gratien Kruczek; fitness director, Ron Adamson

Season Year-round.

Accommodations 525 new guest rooms and suites range in style from Mexican colonial to contemporary high-rise. Condominium units. All with living and work areas, terraces, wet bars, and large baths. Casitas with wood-burning fireplaces near the tennis courts.

Rates $100–$260 per person, double occupancy, Jan.–May 14; $45–$110 mid-May–mid-Sept.; $90–$220 mid-Sept.–mid-Dec. Packages with the health spa, tennis lessons, and golf (3 days, 2 nights) $109–$282 per person, double occupancy, high season. One night payable in advance. Credit cards: AE, CB, DC, MC, V.

Meal Plans Champions Bar & Grill (golf clubhouse) and Las Ventanas (garden atrium and golf-course view) feature grilled seafood and chicken and salads. La Hacienda serves Mexican specialties for lunch and dinner.

Services and **Exercise Equipment:** 12-station Universal weight training
Facilities gym, 2 computerized Aerobicycles, 2 rowing machines, 2 treadmills, free weights, and suspended hardwood floor for 5 daily aerobic classes. **Services:** Herbal wrap, loofah body scrub, salt-glow treatment; beauty salon for facials, hair and nail care; massage. **Swimming Facilities:** 3 outdoor pools, 1 (75 ft) for swimming laps and aquatic exercise. **Recreation Facilities:** 9 tennis courts, 2 18-hole golf courses, racquet and squash courts; nearby equestrian center offers riding, shows, and polo. **Evening Programs:** Resort entertainment.

In the Area Desert tours by jeep; Sedona arts and spiritual center; hiking trails in the McDowell Mountains.

Getting Here *From Phoenix.* By car, north on 44th St. to Camelback Rd., turn right to Scottsdale Rd., then left to Bell Rd. (45 min). By bus, scheduled service from Sky Harbor International Airport.

Special Notes Some rooms specially equipped for the disabled; ramps and elevators to all areas. No smoking in the health club.

Spring Creek Ranch

Life enhancement
Weight management
Spiritual awareness

Arizona Nestled in a cactus valley near Sedona, Spring Creek Ranch
Cornville provides a residental program for a small number of guests that emphasizes hiking and personal counseling rather than group exercise. Staying here is like being a houseguest of Dr. and Mrs. Sterling Ryerson, whose home this is.

The Spring Creek program is based on the Seventh-day Adventist philosophy of spiritual, mental, and physical health. Medical and nutritional counseling are provided to persons learning to cope with degenerative disease, obesity, and un-healthful habits.

Hiking is the principal exercise here, and there are pre-breakfast walks every day. Picnics are a part of the excursions to nearby canyons, where the Arizona sunshine and crisp air assist in the therapy.

The one-on-one treatment is especially helpful for those who require a great deal of personal attention or need the guidance of a senior counselor. A typical day includes lectures, cooking classes, gardening, and bread-baking. A special program for stopping smoking lasts from one to three weeks. Three weeks seems to get the best results.

Spring Creek Ranch
HC 66, Box 2269, Cornville, AZ 86325
Tel. 602/634–4988

Administration	Director, Sterling J. Ryerson, M.D.
Season	Year-round.
Accommodations	8 guest rooms with private bath in the single-level ranch house. Southwestern and Mexican accents. Twin beds.
Rates	$600 per week includes meals and program. 50% payable in advance. No credit cards.
Meal Plans	3 vegetarian meals daily, served family style. The diet features fruit, vegetables, legumes, nuts, and avocados. Lunch and dinner include a green salad and water-steamed garden vegetables. Typical entrees are a Mexican-style vegetarian enchilada and whole-wheat pizza with fresh vegetables. The homemade whole-grain bread contains no eggs or dairy products. No coffee, tea, or condiments.
Services and Facilities	**Services:** Cooking and stopping smoking classes, medical consultation. **Swimming Facilities:** A creek on the property is refreshing but is not for serious exercise. **Recreation Facilities:** Hiking, gardening.
In the Area	Guided walks through Sedona, hiking in Oak Creek Canyon; Flagstaff museums of American Indian culture, Frank Lloyd Wright architecture center, Indian ruins.
Getting Here	*From Phoenix.* By car, I–17 north, Rte. 289 to 89A (2 hr).
Special Notes	No smoking.

Tucson National Resort & Spa

Luxury pampering

Arizona
Tucson

Pleasure pure and simple is the reason to come to the Tucson National Resort & Spa. Set in the desert foothills of the Santa Catalina Mountains, the resort spreads across acres of cultivated gardens and golf courses. Designed on a lavish scale as a country-club community, it has the best little spa in the west.

Hidden within a spectacular clubhouse, the facilities include an Orthion multitherapy stretching system, hydrotherapy rooms for Scotch douches and loofah body scrubs, and a Russian steam bath. The usual collection of saunas and whirlpools for men and women and a weights room are housed here in elegantly tiled and decorated salons, but the special feature is a rooftop deck for alfresco massage that has a spectacular view of the desert.

Mornings begin with a prebreakfast walk along a three-mile path that leads through part of the golf course and over an arroyo. The daily schedule of classes in the aerobics studio is designed for an older clientele, with gentle stretching rather than high-impact aerobics. The spa is small and the staff-to-visitor ratio is high. When you want to work out with weights or exercise bikes, someone is always on hand to check your form. There is no required program, and a practical approach to fitness for fun and relaxation prevails.

The resort atmosphere and conference-center activities are not conducive to dieting unless you stick to the daily menu, listed at 1,200 calories. Meals are served in a restaurant with glass walls that overlooks the greens of the former Tucson National Golf Club. It is open to members and guests. There's no special seating, and you're free to order from the regular menu.

The luxurious resort contrasts sharply with the wasteland that surrounds it. Hiking into nearby Sabino Canyon is an added attraction, opening up a wonderland of boulders, waterfalls, and giant saguaro cacti. The sun-bleached hills take on shades of purple and gold in the early morning.

The trek from your room to the spa building to collect your daily change of shorts and robe is a minor inconvenience. Shower scuffs and towels are also provided. After your workout, try a Swiss shower for a 16-jet water massage, followed by a cold plunge. The women's locker room also has steam cabinets and a recessed Roman-style whirlpool. Both sides have inhalation rooms to clear your sinuses.

Among the treatments in spa packages or à la carte are a vigorous rubdown with sea salts or grated walnuts in sesame seed oil, herbal wraps, and facials. Only at the nearby Canyon Ranch can you find this level of desert-style sophistication.

Tucson National Resort & Spa

2727 West Club Dr., Tucson, AZ 85741
Tel. 602/297–2271 or 800/528–4856
Telex 510–601–5043, Fax 602/297–7544

Administration Spa director, Steven J. Waguespack; program director, Billie Wright

Season Year-round.

Accommodations 171 rooms and suites in 3-story wings and executive casitas with red-tile roofs and Spanish colonial accents. Rooms have king-size beds, full bath, dressing area, TV, and private balcony. Casitas have wood-burning fireplaces, full kitchen, expansive views.

Rates $170–$280 per day; 4-night spa package $980–$1,120 single, $790–$860 double. Summer rates lower. Golf packages. Tax and service charges additional. Credit cards: AE, DC, MC, V.

Meal Plans 3 meals daily in the spa package. 1,200-calorie (per day) diet low in sodium and cholesterol. Vegetarian lasagna or pizza for lunch, broiled swordfish, pasta primavera, and steamed vegetables for dinner.

Services and Facilities	**Exercise Equipment:** 10-station Universal weight training gym, Lifecycles, stationary bikes, rowing machines, treadmill, free weights. **Services:** Massage, herbal wrap, aromatherapy, loofah salt-glow body scrub; manicure, pedicure, hairstyling. Nutritional counseling, private exercise training. **Swimming Facilities:** 75-foot outdoor pool. **Recreation Facilities:** 4 tennis courts, 27-hole golf course, horseback riding, ballooning.
In the Area	Sabino Canyon tourmobile, Indian arts and crafts at Mission San Xavier del Bac in Santa Cruz Valley, Mexican crafts in Nogales, Mt. Lemmon observatory.
Getting Here	*From Tucson.* By car, I–10 north to Cortaro Farms Rd., Shannon Rd. to club entrance (25 min). Airport shuttle service, taxi, rental car available.
Special Notes	Elevators provide access for the disabled. No smoking in the spa and in designated areas of the dining room.

The Aspen Club

Sports conditioning
Weight management
Life enhancement
Stress control

Colorado
Aspen

The program of the Aspen Club is designed to help you improve your general health and fitness level by integrating exercise, healthy eating, and modern medicine. The schedule on a typical Monday in February includes cross-country skiing, tennis, cycling, and volleyball, but it's the personal training at the Aspen Fitness and Sports Medicine Institute, the club's high-tech health facility, that sets it apart from other sports programs.

The advanced center for therapy and training employs a comprehensive approach to well-being that considers the individual's personal needs and goals in prescribing small, short-term lifestyle modifications aimed at making significant health improvements.

The fitness program, which is open to nonmembers, is concerned chiefly with weight loss, stress reduction, and the rehabilitation of sports-related injuries. Visitors stay a few days or a few weeks, scheduling exercise classes and diagnostic appointments among the activities of a world-class resort.

A complete physical evaluation by a team of physicians, physical therapists, and trainers is the first order of business; you undergo a stress test with EKG readings, pulmonary-function tests, and body-fat, strength, and flexibility measurements. A nutritionist evaluates your eating habits and body chemistry (and schedules blood tests when appropriate) prior to recommending a diet that meets your nutritional needs.

Each program is personalized: You work out with a personal trainer, you may be coached on how to order a nutritional meal from a restaurant menu, you could take a cooking class. The custom-made character of the program emphasizes the benefits of continuing your new regimen at home. The more immediate benefits tend to be increased energy and improved self-esteem.

Athletes make up a large percentage of the institute's active members, as the special equipment attracts pro football players and amateur skiers. Celebrities, too, come here, and the program director, Julie Anthony, knows how to handle them all; she was formerly team psychologist for the Philadelphia Flyers.

The Aspen Club
Fitness and Sports Medicine Institute
1450 Crystal Lake Rd., Aspen, CO 81611
Tel. 303/925–8900 or 800/882–2582 (800/443–2582 in CO)

Administration Program director, Julie Anthony; medical director, Barry Mink, M.D.

Season Year-round.

Accommodations Studios, 4- and 5-bedroom condominiums, private homes—all with Jacuzzi, fireplace, sun deck—by arrangement with the Aspen Club Management Company. 2-bedroom apartments at the Aspen Club have oak furnishings, queen-size and twin beds, bath, and full kitchen. Linens, daily maid service, newspaper delivery. Health-club facilities included.

Rates Studio apartments $98–$172. (Prices higher during ski season.) 2-bedroom Aspen Club condominium $232–$742 per day in winter. The Fitness and Sports Institute services and tests à la carte or as part of the $650–$800 program. Some costs may be covered by medical insurance. Services and programs billed separately. 50% advance payment within 10 days of booking. Credit cards: AE, MC, V.

Meal Plans Club dining facility; recommended restaurants include Gordon's, Syzygy, Piñon.

Services and Facilities **Exercise Equipment:** David and Keiser Cam III pneumatic weight training units, Nautilus, Polaris, Lifecycles, StairMasters, VersaClimbers, treadmills, stationary bikes, rowing machines, cross-country ski machines, free weights. **Services:** Swedish massage, nutritional and food-allergy evaluation, strength and flexibility tests, blood-profile analysis, private exercise training; post-injury therapy. **Swimming Facilities:** Indoor lap pool. **Recreation Facilities:** Skiing, 2 indoor and 7 outdoor tennis courts, 6 racquetball courts, 3 squash courts, basketball, volleyball, wallyball, fencing, cycling, aikido. Golf and horseback riding nearby. **Evening Programs:** Athletics, tournaments, fitness and nutrition seminar.

In the Area Mountain hiking and dogsledding offered by local tour operators. Aspen Music Festival and Ballet/Dance Festival (July–Aug.), ballooning, rafting. Crafts shows and classes at the Anderson Ranch at (Snowmass). Nature walks at Hallam Lake Wildlife Sanctuary. Mineral-water baths at Glenwood Springs.

Getting Here *From Denver.* By train, Amtrak to Glenwood Springs (2 hr). By bus, Greyhound to Glenwood Springs (3 hr). By car, I–70 to Dillon, Rte. 91 to Hwy. 24, Rte. 82 via Independence Pass (closed in winter) is scenic route (3½ hr). By plane, commuter flights on United or Continental Express (40 min). Free pickup to and from Aspen airport. Rental car, taxi, limousine available.

Special Notes Full facilities for the disabled. Children's athletic programs in swimming, tennis, squash, racquetball, and dance; nursery and toddler swim class by reservation. No smoking in public areas. Some nonsmoking apartments.

The Cascade Club at The Westin Hotel

Non-program resort facilities

Colorado
Vail

Skiers and hikers get a bonus here: free use of the newest, largest, and most complete sports and fitness facility this side of the Rockies. Adjacent to the luxurious Westin Hotel, the Cascade Club has a full range of aerobics and sports-training programs plus sports-medicine clinics. In addition to an indoor track and tennis, squash, and racquetball courts, there is a year-round outdoor swimming pool and thermal whirlpool. Sports instruction is also available.

After a day on the slopes or the trails, you can have an alfresco soak or enjoy the steam room in the men's and women's pavilions. Tired muscles can be soothed in individual massage rooms, and an aerobics studio allows you to work out any kinks.

The hotel is set in the exclusive Cascade Village, a few steps from the new Ford Amphitheatre, where summer shows range from symphonic pops to rock. To skiers' delight, a new four-passenger chairlift whisks you from the hotel to the upper slopes in eight minutes.

The Cascade Club at The Westin Hotel
Cascade Village, Vail, CO 81657
Tel. 303/476–7111

Administration Westin Hotel general manager, Michael Sansbury; Cascade Club general manager, Herb Lipsman

Season Year-round.

Accommodations 344 luxury rooms and suites with king- and queen-size beds, sofas, color TV.

Rates $195–$285 per day, depending on the season; premier guest rooms and suites higher; value seasons mid-Sept.–mid-Nov., mid-Apr.–June 1. Confirmation by credit card. Credit cards: AE, CB, DC, MC, V.

Meal Plans Robust soups, salads, sandwiches; a skier's breakfast; a "fanny lunch" for mountainside picnics in The Cafe. Alfredo's features rotisserie-grilled meats, chicken, and fish for dinner. No special diet menu.

Services and Facilities **Exercise Equipment:** Complete line of Nautilus, free weights, stationary bikes, rowing machine, cross-country ski machine, treadmills. **Swimming Facilities:** Heated outdoor pool. **Recreation Facilities:** 3 outdoor and 4 indoor tennis courts, 4 squash courts, 2 racquetball courts, golf.

In the Area Vail Nordic and Nature Center and Snowmobile Tours offer various programs. Colorado Ski Museum, Dobson Ice Arena (indoor skating), white-water rafting on the Eagle River.

Getting Here *From Denver:* By car, I–70 to Vail (2 hr). By plane, commuter flights to Avon Airport. Free airport transfers.

Special Notes No smoking in the Cascade Club.

Eden Valley Lifestyle Center

Preventive medicine
Weight management
Spiritual awareness

Colorado This homelike retreat set amid woods, lakes, and streams on
Loveland 550 acres in the foothills of the Rocky Mountains teaches physical conditioning and nutrition in comprehensive programs
lasting seven to 24 days. The Eden Valley Lifestyle Center's approach emphasizes the pursuit of traditional Seventh-day
Adventist philosophies of diet and mental and spiritual health
under medical supervision.

Following thorough individual physical evaluations by the medical director, small groups of guests are counseled on health
and disease prevention. Cooking demonstrations show how the
vegetarian diet can be adapted to one's own kitchen routines.

The doctor monitors each guest's progress and may suggest additional activities. Drinking lots of pure water, walking in the
clean mountain air and sunshine, and taking hydrotherapy and
whirlpool baths are all part of the program.

Personalized strategies for attaining a healthy lifestyle are prepared for those with heart disease, diabetes, degenerative
disease, and digestive problems. Chronic fatigue, obesity, arthritis, and high blood pressure are also treated, and there is
therapy for quitting smoking.

The Lifestyle program began in 1987 as an extension of services at a nearby home for senior citizens. People of all ages
come here to gain new vitality and stamina and to relax in the
company of a small supportive group. There is lots of camaraderie here—and a very attentive staff.

Eden Valley Lifestyle Center
6263 N. County Rd. 29, Loveland, CO 80537
Tel. 303/669–7730 or 800/637–9355

Administration Program director, Mark LaVantura

Season Year-round.

Accommodations 5 guest rooms with twin beds in a new ranch-style facility, 3
with private bath. Draperies and flowered bedspreads. Private
sun deck.

Rates 7-day program $550, 17 days $1,495, 24 days $1,995, all per per-
son, double occupancy. An accompanying spouse participating
in the program but not receiving treatment pays $20 per day
less. $10–$20 per day additional for a private room when available. Medical costs may be covered by health insurance. $300 in
advance for the 17-day and 24-day programs, $100 for the 7-day
program, nonrefundable. Credit cards: MC, V.

Meal Plans 3 vegetarian meals daily, buffet style. Adventist diet of fruit,
raw vegetables, legumes, and grains. No butter, oils, or dairy
products. Some olives, nuts, and avocado. Vegetarian lasagna
with mock-cheese topping of pimiento. Bean haystack with rice
on corn chips, topped with cashew-nut mixture. Green salads,

steamed vegetables, and baked tofu for dinner. No coffee, tea, or condiments. Whole-grain bread baked daily.

Services and Facilities **Exercise Equipment:** Stationary bike and trampoline. **Services:** Complete physical examination, blood-chemistry analysis, computerized lifestyle inventory, daily hydrotherapy treatments with hot and cold showers, Jacuzzi, sauna. **Swimming Facilities:** Community pool and lakes. **Recreation Facilities:** Mountain trail hiking, fishing, boating; downhill and cross-country skiing. Golf course, tennis courts, horseshoe and picnic facilities nearby.

In the Area Estes Park (mountain resort), greyhound racetrack, county fair and rodeo, trail rides, ghost towns, antiques shops. Performing-arts and museum exhibitions.

Getting Here *From Denver.* By car, I–80 to Idaho Springs (45 min).

Special Notes All facilities on ground floor. No smoking indoors.

Glenwood Hot Springs Lodge

Taking the waters

Colorado
Glenwood Springs

The biggest natural mineral-water pool this side of the Rockies attracts guests to the Glenwood Hot Springs Lodge. Even in subfreezing temperatures the water's lingering warmth should keep you warm long enough to get to the locker room.

Summer and winter, the 130-degree water is cooled for comfort in the Olympic-size outdoor swimming pool. In a smaller therapy pool equipped with underwater jets for a free massage, the water temperature is 104 degrees. Together the pools contain 1.5 million gallons of mineral water, changed three times daily. The entire complex is two blocks long.

Located on I–70, the principal east-west route across the state, the Victorian-looking town has motel lodging in every price category as well as camping and RV hookups. The new facility was opened in 1986 for the resort's centennial.

In the nearby vapor caves (coed), the hot springs create temperatures that reach 115 degrees and make for a great sweat. Cold-water hoses are available here, but there is no soaking pool. Day visitors are welcome in the vapor caves and at the pools. Lodge guests have the use of the athletic club, which has an indoor hydrojet pool, sauna, and steam bath.

Glenwood Hot Springs Lodge
Box 308, Glenwood Springs, CO 81601
Tel. 303/945–6571

Administration Manager, Kjell Mitchell

Season Year-round.

Accommodations 105 modern rooms furnished with two queen-size beds (some are king-size), private bath and double vanity. Deluxe rooms with balcony or patio overlooking the pools, coffee maker, safe, air conditioning, geothermal heating.

Rates $42–$50 per day single, $46–$55 double; deluxe rooms $59–$65 single, $59–$70 double. Discount on admission to baths and health club for lodge guests. 1 night payable in advance. Credit cards: AE, DC, MC, V.

Meal Plans Meals served at the lodge cafe and nearby motels. Broiled chicken and mountain trout are local specialties.

Services and Facilities **Exercise Equipment:** 10-station Nautilus units. **Services:** Massage, facials, chiropractic adjustment. **Swimming Facilities:** 4 outdoor pools. **Recreation Facilities:** Hiking, water slide, trout fishing, 4 indoor racquetball courts.

In the Area Ski resorts, Aspen Music Festival, Wheeler Opera House, Anderson Ranch arts center at Snowmass, galleries and shops in Aspen.

Getting Here *From Denver.* By train, Amtrak twice daily (3 hr). By bus, Greyhound (4 hr). By car, I–70 (3 hr). Rental car available.

Special Notes No smoking in the health club or caves.

Indian Springs Resort

Taking the waters

Colorado
Idaho Springs
At the historic Indian Springs Resort you can swim in mineral water surrounded by tropical foliage beneath a translucent arched roof. Built in 1869, the lodge is a Victorian relic down to its ornate dining room.

The soaking pools cater to guests' naturalist tendencies. Separate caves for men and women have walk-in pools hewn into rock. Water flows from three springs at temperatures ranging from 104 to 112 degrees. No bathing suits are allowed in the caves, and couples and families may soak together. Private tubs are booked by the hour.

Sacred to Native Americans, the hot springs were first developed during the local gold rush, and devotees have traveled from around the world to bathe in them ever since.

Chemical analysis of the water has found that it contains trace minerals essential to good health. While no scientific claims are made for the waters, experts cite the benefits of bathing to those who suffer from arthritis and rheumatism. Unlike most hot springs, the waters here do not smell of sulfur.

Both day visitors and overnight guests are welcome. Located on Soda Creek, with a national forest to the west, this bargain getaway is easily reached from Denver.

Indian Springs Resort
Box 1990, Idaho Springs, CO 80452
Tel. 303/567–2191

Administration Manager, Jim Maxwell

Season Year-round.

Accommodations 32 lodge rooms, single and double, furnished with Victorian antiques and brass beds; few modern conveniences. Deluxe new rooms in the inn with king-size or double beds, color TV, coffee maker, full modern bath.

Rates Lodge rooms $47.93 per day, single or double; deluxe inn rooms $53.33. Weekend package with room, dinner for 2, baths, $39.95. 1 night payable in advance by credit card. Credit cards: MC, V.

Meal Plans Rocky Mountain brook trout and fresh vegetables are frequently on the menu; the dining room serves 3 meals daily.

Services and Facilities Services: Massage, chiropractic treatment. **Swimming Facilities:** Indoor pool. **Recreation Facilities:** Hiking, walking, horseback riding, fishing.

In the Area St. Mary's Glacier.

Getting Here *From Denver.* By car, I–70 east to Idaho Springs exit, Hwy. 385.

Special Notes No smoking in pool area or baths.

Mountain Biking at Winter Park

Sports conditioning

Colorado
Winter Park
Pedaling along backcountry trails and roads in the Rockies is a great way to burn calories while enjoying some of the country's most spectacular scenery. The gentle, rolling hills and valleys around Winter Park have long been popular with hikers and bikers, and in 1988 a new system of biking trails was mapped and marked, heralding the first full-service mountain-bike resort program, run by volunteers in cooperation with the National Forest Service. It's a unique way to vacation on a budget.

Winter Park occupies a high, wide mountain valley surrounded by steep mountain ranges and forests. The area was originally pioneered by ranchers and loggers who left behind hundreds of miles of trails. In 1987 members of the Winter Park Fat Tire Society began marking and mapping these trails to include the new mountain-bike trail system.

Fitness buffs quickly began arriving with their bikes aboard the two daily Amtrak trains from Denver. Following routes rated according to steepness, the bikers discovered a world of alpine meadows, timberline wilderness, and mountain valleys that few riders had had access to before.

From the center of the resort, 500 miles of trails now wind through the valley and up into the mountains. Tour operators in town have organized overnight biking trips, even a downhill ride for those who don't want to expend all their energy pedaling uphill. Outfitted with gourmet lunch, map, and fat-wheel bike, riders can set their own pace.

For those not inclined to venture out on their own, there are guided group outings. The YMCA of the Rockies features a nature tour of the trails, with riders identifying flowers and wildlife along the route. A group of race enthusiasts is organizing a summer series of invitational competitions for locals and visitors alike.

The mountain bike is a durable bicycle frame equipped with 18 speeds that can be shifted from the handlebar grip with the thumb. Six speeds on one hand are controlled by three ranges on the other to make the going easier on steep grades.

Bikes can be rented from eight well-equipped outfitters in town, several more in outlying areas. The Winter Park Fat Tire Society provides a complete map of the trail system free of charge. The map uses international biking symbols and shows points of origin, trails, degrees of difficulty, and scenic attractions along the route.

Dozens of hotels, motels, lodges, and condominiums line the valley. A toll-free central reservation service can find you a bed at the YMCA dormitory in Snowmountain Ranch or a studio suite at the Snowblaze Athletic Club. Bikes rent for $10–$14 a day.

Once you master them, the fat, knobby-tired bicycles are your passport to rugged terrain and flower-filled meadows.

Mountain Biking at Winter Park
Winter Park Resort
Box 3236, Winter Park, CO 80482
Tel. 303/726–4118 or 800/453–2525

Season June–Oct.

Accommodations 11,000 beds in hotels, motels, lodges. The Snowblaze Athletic Club on the south edge of town has studio suites with queen-size and sofa beds, private bath, indoor swimming pool, weights room, racquetball court, Jacuzzi.

Rates $55 per person per day for a 4-person studio at Snowblaze. Reservation by credit card. Credit cards: MC, V.

Meal Plans 40 restaurants in Winter Park.

Services and Facilities **Exercise Equipment:** Nautilus units. **Swimming Facilities:** Indoor and outdoor pools, lake at Snowmountain Ranch. **Recreation Facilities:** Pole Creek Golf Club, trout fishing, horseback riding, rafting, boating, tennis.

In the Area Jeep tours, ultralight aircraft flights; Tippary Creek Classic (30K mountain-bike race in August), Alpine Slide, High Country Stampede Rodeo (Saturday evening), chair-lift rides, Central City Opera House.

Getting Here *From Denver.* By car, I–70, Rte. 40 (90 min). By train, Amtrak twice daily (60 min). Bike, taxi, rental car available.

Rocky Mountain Health Ranch

Life enhancement
Holistic health
Stress control

Colorado
Meredith
The Rocky Mountain Health Ranch began as a dream for Dr. Rob Krakovitz and his sister Maxine Rose. Inspired by the majesty and splendor of the Rockies, they designed a life-energizing program filled with fun and activities for guests of all ages.

Welcomed at the main lodge, you are assigned to a room or private cabin. After a consultation, Dr. Krakovitz tailors a program to meet your needs and fitness level. A variety of natural healing techniques and bodywork are offered by the professional health services staff for an additional charge.

Outdoor recreation is the focus here. Hiking and touring the backcountry fill most days. Horseback riding continues to be a major attraction at this former dude ranch. A variety of recreational excursions, from white-water rafting to kayaking and glider rides, is available for an additional fee.

One unique activity is a program in Native American folklore and rituals. Guests are invited to a traditional sweat lodge and listen to members of local tribes.

By adhering to a course of exercise and attending classes on topics ranging from improving communication skills and personal relations to the enhancement of mental, emotional, and physical energies, the sense of well-being you acquire in this magical place will put you on the road to peak vitality.

Rocky Mountain Health Ranch
32042 Frying Pan River Rd., Meredith, CO 81642
Tel. 303/927-3570 or 303/927-4793

Administration	Manager, Maxine Rose; program director, Rob Krakovitz, M.D.
Season	Year-round.
Accommodations	18 rooms in main lodge and guest cabins. Rustic charm, ranch-style furnishings, private modern baths. Lodge with high beam ceiling and open fireplace. Jacuzzi on sun deck.
Rates	$110–$140 per person, double occupancy. $40 more for singles, less with shared bath. $100 per person per week payable in advance. Credit cards: MC, V.
Meal Plans	3 meals daily, family style, plus snacks. Mainly vegetarian menu with fresh fish and free-range chicken dishes. Meals low in fat, sodium, and sugar, high in fiber. Breakfast pancakes with whole-grain buckwheat; lemon soup, Greek salad, vegetable shish kebabs for lunch; a vegetable stir fry for dinner.
Services and Facilities	**Services:** Massage, natural healing bodywork, yoga and meditation training, dance kinetics instruction. Personal consultation on medical and health problems, with holistic therapies. Horseback-riding instruction (fee). **Swimming Facilities:** Nearby lake. **Recreation Facilities:** Horseback riding, trout fishing, rowing, canoeing, mountain biking. **Evening Programs:** Informal workshops on health and nutrition.
In the Area	Cross-country and downhill skiing, trail rides; skiing, shopping, summer arts festival in Aspen; mineral baths at Glenwood Springs; Olympic training center at Colorado Springs.
Getting Here	*From Denver.* By car, I–70 to Glenwood Springs, Rte. 82 to Basalt (3 hr). By air, commuter flights to Aspen (40 min). Free pickup in Aspen on Sun. and Wed.
Special Notes	Riding instruction programs for children. No smoking indoors, smoking discouraged elsewhere.

Rocky Mountain Wellness Spa

Nutrition and diet
Weight management
Stress control
Taking the waters

Colorado
Steamboat
Springs

The fresh, pine-scented air is enough to give you a Rocky Mountain high at these altitudes. The Rocky Mountain Wellness Spa, a short walk from the ski area, is surrounded by 150,000 acres of national forest where you can hike, ski, and bathe at the hot mineral springs for which the town is named. Yet this is not the resort for those who want to spend most of their time on the slopes or indulging in massages and facials.

The "wellness" experience is based on a scientific approach to nutrition, stress reduction, and exercise. The program directors begin by analyzing your metabolism in an effort to ascertain links between stress and weight control. Their prescription of a stress-release technique is intended to be the key to your attaining peak performance.

The highly structured program eliminates decision making; you simply relax and follow the schedule. It can begin with early morning stretching and de-stressing exercises, breakfast, and a brisk walk. Walks of 20–30 minutes after each meal are considered essential here for guests who complain that they can't lose weight regardless of diet.

Dieters begin to lose one or two pounds a week as their metabolism is affected by the post-meal exercise, and hiking the scenic trails around the resort makes exercise seem like fun.

Mornings are often devoted to learning about the causes and symptoms of stress and how to control them. After your low-calorie lunch and a stroll, you spend the afternoon relaxing in the exercise room, on the tennis courts, or in the swimming pool. During the winter, a special cross-country ski program is planned for all levels under the supervision of instructors and guides.

Weight loss is an important aspect of the program, but it does not require a drastic reduction in calories. You are tested for food allergies over a five-day period during which all suspected items are eliminated from your diet, then reintroduced one at a time.

The program is designed to modify your lifestyle. The limited size of the group—never more than 15 participants at a time—and the staff's concern for each person's progress create a personal atmosphere for improvement.

The vitamin and mineral needs of each guest are analyzed, and supplements are prescribed as necessary. The staff evaluates each guest's cardiovascular system, metabolism, allergies, body-fat percentage, and toxic levels at the beginning and end of the program for comparison. These provide clues to body-system trends, and they also provide the basis for the diet, exercise regimen, and stress-release techniques recommended to the participants.

A special program to quit smoking is offered with other activities. Detoxification and behavior modification are part of the 10-day schedule. One-on-one counseling and the pleasant, controlled environment help reduce anxiety. Meals are designed to help rid the body of toxins, and massage and loofah scrubs enhance body cleansing. Other special treatments, similar to the Seventh-day Adventist program, include hot and cold showers and drinking large amounts of water and fresh fruit and vegetable juices.

A new division, the Rocky Mountain Wellness Institute, helps business executives develop and strengthen their decision-making capabilities. The "brain training" process focuses on controlling fears, anxieties, jealousy, guilt, and other negative reactions.

The view from the mountain and the invigorating air make all things seem possible.

Rocky Mountain Wellness Spa
Box 777, Steamboat Springs, CO 80477
Tel. 303/879–7772 or 800/345–7770 (800/345–7771 in CO)

Administration	Program directors, Larry and Dorothy Allingham
Season	Year-round.
Accommodations	7 bedrooms in a modern 4-story ski chalet, singles or doubles, with queen-size beds, private bath. Rooms on each floor grouped around a lounge with fireplace. Contemporary furnishings, maid service.
Rates	1-week Wellness experience $1,125 per person double occupancy, $1,285 single; 10-day program $1,690 per person double, $1,930 single. $150 additional for smoking program. Tax and gratuities additional. Longer or shorter stays by arrangement. $500 deposit on booking, nonrefundable. Credit cards: AE, MC, V.
Meal Plans	3 mainly vegetarian meals daily, family style. Some fish. No wheat, egg yolk, corn, soy, salt, sugar, chocolate, coffee, tea, or dairy products. Breakfast includes freshly baked bran muffins and fruit; lunch can be lentil soup and salad; baked salmon is a typical dinner entree.
Services and Facilities	**Exercise Equipment:** Stationary bike, hand weights, stretch bands, slant board. **Services:** Nutritional testing, personal wellness consultation, aerobics instruction; massage, facials, skin and hair care, afternoon outings. **Swimming Facilities:** Outdoor and indoor pools. **Spa Facilities:** Outdoor hot tub; the nearby hot springs is a modern facility. **Recreation Facilities:** Tennis courts, sailing, biking, hiking, river rafting. **Evening Programs:** Workshops on health, nutrition, stress control.
In the Area	Bathing at the hot springs, hiking, bike tours; Continental Divide; Denver; summer music festival, shops, entertainment in Aspen.
Getting Here	*From Denver.* By car, I–70 to Hwy. 40, exit at Steamboat Springs (3½ hr). By plane, commuter service to Steamboat Springs (40 min). Free transport to and from Steamboat Springs Airport.
Special Notes	No smoking. Remember to bring medical records, outdoor clothing, backpack, and rain gear.

Waunita Hot Springs Ranch

Taking the waters

Colorado
Gunnison
National Forest

A family-oriented dude ranch with a thermal water swimming pool, Waunita Hot Springs Ranch offers a taste of the Old West and modern comforts. The 200-acre ranch, family owned and operated, was among the first settlements in western Colorado. Today horseback riding and outdoor recreation are the main attractions.

A log barn houses the riding instruction program, with classes for children and adults. There are corral games and an all-day ride to snow-capped peaks near the Continental Divide. Other activities, scheduled daily, include hayrides and an overnight mountain camp out.

The pool, fed by hot mineral springs at a temperature of 95 degrees, soothes and relaxes after riding or hiking. There are heated dressing rooms, and the area is lit at night.

Meals at the ranch house consist of hearty buffets. A bowl of fresh fruit is always on hand, and you can help yourself to coffee, tea, hot chocolate, or punch. Alcoholic beverages are not permitted.

Nature lovers and families with children make up most of the 45 guests. You can bird-watch, collect rocks, or hike in the national forest. Bring casual clothes, jeans, and boots and discover real Western hospitality.

Waunita Hot Springs Ranch
8007 County Rd. 887, Gunnison, CO 81230
Tel. 303/641–1266

Administration Manager, Junelle Pringle

Season June–Sept.

Accommodations 22 rooms in the ranch house, all with private bath, wood paneling, leather chair. TV in the library.

Rates $525 a week per person, double occupancy; children's rates on request. $80 deposit per person. No credit cards.

Meal Plans 3 meals daily, buffet style. Cookouts and steak-fry dinners. Home-cooked food to suit any diet. Barbecued chicken and grilled trout specialties.

Services and Facilities **Swimming Facilities:** 90-foot outdoor pool. **Recreation Facilities:** Hiking, horseshoes, Ping-Pong, corral games, fishing, softball, volleyball. **Evening Programs:** Country-Western Music Hall, movies.

In the Area Cookout rides, overnight camp out; river float trip, mountain rides, Jeep trips offered by local outfitters; Continental Divide, ghost towns, mining relics.

Getting Here *From Denver.* By car, Hwy. 285 to Salida, Hwy. 50 to Doyleville, County Rd. 887 (3 hr).

Special Notes No smoking indoors.

Weight Watchers Camp Rocky Mountain

Youth camps for weight loss

Colorado
Aspen

The Colorado Rocky Mountain School, about 30 minutes from the center of Aspen, is the location of Weight Watchers Camp Rocky Mountain, a coed summer camp for young people age 10–21. The program focuses on a diet, exercise, and education. Campers have exclusive use of sports fields, indoor swimming pool, gymnasium, and fitness center complex with weights and aerobics rooms. The surrounding streams and forests offer opportunities for hiking, mountain climbing, and country walks.

Meals are prepared from the recipes of Weight Watchers International, Inc., and in classes on food preparation and lectures on nutrition, campers learn how to eat properly. The dining room is the social center.

Counselors supervise full weeks of workouts with Nautilus equipment, slimnastics and aerobics classes, and sports. Those who complete the course are guaranteed weight loss—or they get a refund.

Weight Watchers Camp Rocky Mountain
1493 Country Rd. 106, Carbondale, CO 81623
Tel. 303/963–3984
Weight Watchers Camps
183 Madison Ave., New York, NY 10016
Tel. 212/889–9500 or 800/223–5600 (800/251–4141 in Canada)

Administration Program director, Anthony Sparber

Season July–Aug.

Accommodations Spacious rooms in rustic residence halls accommodate 2 campers each; modern lavatory and shower facilities; 1 counselor to every 5 campers.

Rates Sessions of 2–7 weeks from $1,450. $100 in advance. Credit cards: AE, DC, MC, V.

Meal Plans 3 meals a day in the cafeteria; 2 snacks a day in the residence halls.

Services and Facilities **Exercise Equipment:** Weights room with Nautilus equipment, gymnasium equipment, aerobics room. **Swimming Facilities:** Indoor pool. **Recreation Facilities:** Soccer, basketball, tennis, softball, volleyball; horseback riding (additional fee); tubing. **Evening Programs:** Dramatics, game nights, talent shows.

In the Area Hiking, mountain climbing, country walks.

Getting Here Pickup at Aspen airport. Taxi, rental car available.

Special Notes No smoking indoors.

Wiesbaden Hot Springs Lodge

Taking the waters

Colorado
Uncompahgre
National Forest

Begun as a mountainside motel with mineral water baths, the family owned and operated Wiesbaden Hot Springs Lodge has become a full-fledged health resort in recent years. Its facilities include an exercise room with daily aerobics classes, a weights room, a sauna, and an indoor soaking pool. Mud baths and a steam room are planned.

The geothermal water that heats the building as well as the swimming pool flows from two springs at temperatures of 111 and 117 degrees.

Scenic canyons in the national forest are a major attraction for hikers. The makings for a picnic can be found at the cafe and store in town, a few blocks away (the lodge has no dining room).

At an altitude of 7,700 feet, the picturesque old mountain town is sheltered from winds by the surrounding forest. Few roads traverse these mountains that are the source of the Rio Grande and several hot springs. A public swimming pool and a visitor information complex are nearby.

Wiesbaden Hot Springs Lodge
625 5th St., Box 349, Ouray, CO 81427
Tel. 303/325-4347

Administration Manager, Linda Wright-Minter

Season Year-round.

Accommodations 18 modern rooms, each with private bath. Glass-walled lounge overlooks the pool and sun deck. Rustic, mountain furnishings.

Rates $59–$78 per day, double occupancy. 1 night payable in advance. Credit cards: MC, V.

Services and Facilities **Exercise Equipment:** Universal weight training gym, stationary bike. **Services:** Swedish massage, acupressure, aromatherapy, facials. **Swimming Facilities:** Outdoor pool. **Recreation Facilities:** Hiking; bike rental nearby.

In the Area Antiques shops, Box Canyon falls, Telluride (historical mining town) film festival, Ute Indian reservation.

Getting Here *From Denver.* By car, I–70 to Grand Junction, Hwy. 550 (4 hr).

Special Notes No smoking in the spa.

Desert Inn Hotel & Casino

Luxury pampering

Nevada
Las Vegas The combination of a complete health and fitness club within a country club and casino resort has made the Desert Inn popular. Devoted to exercise and pampering, this well-equipped health emporium can be enjoyed without entering the casino. Guests pay a daily facilities charge ($10–$15) or sign up for a package plan that includes 10 exercise classes to choose from.

Sunlight streams through floor-to-ceiling glass walls in the central rotundas of the men's and women's pavilions. Dual facilities, including private therapy pools, hot or cold plunges, and a big central Jacuzzi, are separate and private. The steam rooms, saunas, and hydrotherapy room are a few steps away.

The water-focused treatments include loofah body scrub with sea salts and herbal wraps. Thermotherapy consists of varied applications of heat and cold to soothe and cleanse the body: Moving from Turkish steam room to Finnish sauna, you are wrapped like a mummy in warm sheets soaked with herbal fragrances.

A private swimming pool for lap swimming, exercise classes, and water volleyball is also part of the spa complex. Indoor coed facilities include two gyms: one for weight training and cardiovascular fitness and the other for aerobics.

Set on 200 parklike acres, the Desert Inn offers everything from golf to shuffleboard, plus a 1/16th-mile parcourse with 10 exercise stations. You can't lose on health even if your luck at the tables isn't up to snuff.

Desert Inn Hotel & Casino
3145 Las Vegas Blvd. S, Las Vegas, NV 89109
Tel. 702/733–4444 or 800/634–6909
Telex 684481

Administration Manager, Kevin Malley; spa director, Peter Stein

Season Year-round.

Accommodations 821 rooms with a desert theme in a high-rise hotel. Recently refurbished suites and rooms have balconies, full baths, many small amenities.

Rates $85–$175 a day, single or double; suites from $180. Spa packages $139 a day additional, $389 for a deluxe 4-day plan. 1 night payable in advance. Credit cards: AE, CB, DC, MC, V.

Services and Facilities **Exercise Equipment:** Lifecycles, 12 Keiser Cam II pneumatic pressure units, free-weight dumbbells (2–60 lbs.), rowing machine, ergometer, Quinton treadmill, NordicTrack, rebounders. **Services:** Massage, loofah body scrub, facials, herbal wrap; hair, nail, and skin care. **Swimming Facilities:** Lap pool, Olympic-size recreational pool. **Recreation Facilities:** 10 tennis courts, water volleyball, golf. **Evening Programs:** Celebrity shows in casino.

In the Area Waterworld theme park, Lake Mead recreational area and Hoover Dam, the Grand Canyon.

Getting Here *From Los Angeles.* By bus, Greyhound-Trailways (5 hr). By car, I–15 (4½ hr). By plane, scheduled flights (1½ hr). Limousine on request; rental car, taxi.

Special Notes Ramps and elevators provide access for the disabled; all facilities are on one level.

Walley's Hot Springs Resort

Taking the waters

Nevada A health club and hot mineral baths are the attractions at the
Genoa charming cluster of Victorian cottages called Walley's Hot Springs Resort. Located in the foothills of the Sierra Nevadas, 12 miles from Lake Tahoe's south shore and 50 miles from Reno, the secluded resort offers a pay-as-you-go treatment plan and free exercise classes.

The main building, a two-story health club, has separate men's and women's sections that contain sauna, steam bath, and massage rooms. A coed weight training room is modestly equipped, but there are plans for expansion.

Mineral water is piped from a pond into the bathhouse, where it continuously flows through the bathing tubs. For an outdoor soak, the 104-degree water is collected in six cement pools, where it is cooled for the swimming pool.

Exercise classes in the pool are scheduled Monday, Wednesday, and Friday mornings and Tuesday and Thursday evenings. Guests can hike the scenic Carson Valley and make day-trips to nearby resorts and casinos. Of special interest are the mud baths and mineral-water treatments at nearby Steamboat Springs, a historic resort that dates from 1904.

Walley's Hot Springs Resort
2001 Foothill La., Box 26, Genoa, NV 89411
Tel. 702/782–8155

Administration Program director, Deborah Pope

Season Year-round.

Accommodations 5 private cottages, 1 with queen-size bed, others with twins. Private baths, country antiques, turn-of-the century ambience. Full hotel service; breakfast delivered.

Rates $75–$115 per day for 2 with breakfasts; 1 night payable in advance. Credit cards: AE, MC, V.

Services and Facilities **Exercise Equipment:** 7-station Universal weight training gym, free weights, stationary bikes. **Services:** Massage, herbal wraps. **Swimming Facilities:** Outdoor pool. **Spa Facilities:** Indoor and outdoor mineral-water pools. **Recreation Facilities:** 2 tennis courts, downhill and cross-country skiing nearby. **Evening Programs:** 2 exercise classes weekly.

In the Area Lake Tahoe resorts and casinos, Reno casinos, historic Carson City.

Getting Here *From Reno.* By car, Hwy. 395 south to Genoa, Genoa Lane to Foothill Lane (60 min). By bus, Greyhound to Gardnerville (45 min). Rental car, taxi available.

Special Notes Limited access for the disabled. Children under 12 not permitted in the health club. No smoking in the health club.

SunRise Springs Resort

Life enhancement
Holistic health
Stress control

New Mexico
Santa Fe Hidden behind the adobe walls of an old *paraje* stagecoach stop on the King's Highway between Mexico City and Santa Fe, an adventure in human potential awaits today's traveler. The surprisingly modern SunRise Springs Resort hugs a hillside where spring-fed ponds and century-old cottonwood trees add to a sense of seclusion. The desert air is crystal clear, and sunlight streams into a peaceful atrium where guests practice yoga. Outside, an organic garden of flowers and herbs is used

for teaching and meditation, and eight Alpha Chambers are used to enhance brain activity and relax the body and mind.

Attuned to nature, this is a place where the body, mind, emotions, and spirit are addressed, and at the Living Center you can participate in a multidimensional program that embraces all four. Packages for four to 10 nights allow guests to choose from a smorgasbord of bodywork, nutritional and wellness consultations, seminars, and personal services that range from astrology to image enhancement with makeup, hair, and color analysis. Meals, juice bar, and aerobics classes are included.

The Wellness Program focuses on personal health. Stretched, exercised, massaged, and put through a battery of physical, medical, and nutritional tests, participants learn the meaning of peak performance. The program is mandatory, tightly scheduled, and progresses to more demanding levels.

The Excellerated Learning Forum encourages a different outlook. Cocooned in an oversize "learning" pod, you are surrounded by sounds and visual stimuli, part of a system intended to increase relaxation and enhance your ability to act on intuition.

Another component of the retreat is a computer center and library with tutoring and research resources. A workshop on organic gardening takes place in the botanical garden, where participants tune in to nature in the process of digging and pruning.

The resort, built on 69 acres, is surrounded by mountain and desert views; in the distance are the Sangre de Cristo and Jemez ranges, and the rosy sunsets seem to last for hours. Here the spiritual and healing atmosphere is consonant with jogging trails, bike tracks, and cultural celebrations. The sauna has the traditional log-and-stone design of an Indian sweat lodge, and there are tepees and hot tubs in the woods. Flagstone paths connect the adobe house and lodges. And a museum recreates the everyday life of 19th-century New Mexico.

SunRise Springs Resort
R.R. 14, Box 203, La Cienega, Santa Fe, NM 87505
Tel. 505/471–3600 or 800/772–0500

Administration Owner and manager, Megan Hill

Season Year-round.

Accommodations 4 guest rooms in the old adobe house share baths in the garret. 32 rooms with garden and pond views in 2 lodges. 1 studio with clerestory windows, fireplace, a raised adobe hearth. Most garden rooms with private balconies, floor-to-ceiling glass doors, white adobe walls, with king-size or 2 twin beds. All garden rooms with private bath (tub or shower), telephone. No TV.

Rates Garden room $120 double occupancy, $100 single, June 1–Oct. 15; $63–$90 Oct. 15–June 1. Breakfast included. Garret rooms $50, single or double. 7-night package (3 meals) from $950 per person double occupancy, $1,100 single, to $1,070 and $1,310 in high season. 1 night payable in advance, $200 deposit for package. Credit cards: AE, MC, V.

Meal Plans Spa menu at the gourmet Blue Heron restaurant in the main lodge. 1,000-calorie diet includes yogurt and fresh fruit for breakfast, broiled breast of chicken on wild rice with steamed vegetables or broiled eggplant for lunch. Typical dinner entrees are venison medallion with steamed sunchokes and baked onions filled with couscous.

Services and Facilities   **Exercise Equipment:** 6-station Universal weight training gym, 2 stationary bikes, rowing machine, rebounder. **Services:** Acupuncture, chiropractic, massage therapy (Swedish, shiatsu, Trager, Reiki), crystal work, facials, manicure, pedicure. Consultation on nutrition, wellness, vocational transition, conflict resolution. Seminars on stress reduction, gardening, meditation, communications, astrology, astronomy, and tarot readings. **Swimming Facilities:** Outdoor pool. **Recreation Facilities:** 2 tennis courts, mountain-bike rental, roller skates. Nearby downhill and cross-country skiing, golf, horseback riding. **Evening Programs:** Lectures and workshops on health and well-being.

In the Area   Rancho de las Golondrinas (living history museum), Santa Fe Downs Race Track, the Museum of Fine Arts (Mexican and American Indian art), Palace of the Governors, Museum of International Folk Art; Santa Fe Opera (July–Aug.), chamber music, theater, and concert seasons.

Getting Here   *From Albuquerque.* By bus, shuttle service from the airport and downtown hotels (80 min). By car, I–25 north to La Cienega, Rte. 22 to Frontage Rd., turn left near racetrack (60 min). Courtesy van for pickups in Santa Fe. Rental car, taxi available.

Special Notes   Limited access for the disabled. No smoking in program facilities or in designated areas of the restaurant.

Truth or Consequences

Taking the waters

New Mexico
Truth or Consequences   Named after a radio show popular in the 1950s, the town of Truth or Consequences may be the bargain basement of health spas. Springwater is channeled to bathhouses and guest lodges along Broadway and the adjoining streets. Some offer little more than a tub, most do not accept credit cards. A 20-minute soak in unchlorinated 110-degree mineral water typically costs $3.

Naturopathic treatments are offered at some of the older establishments, but a massage is the principal therapy after bathing. Water sports in mile-long Elephant Butte Lake just outside town, hiking, and tubing on the Rio Grande are mentioned in Chamber of Commerce publications.

What is not mentioned is the run-down appearance of the town and its once famous baths. Yet local operators say the area is picking up, and there are newer motels on the main road.

At the Sierra Natural Healing Center, a former hotel on Broadway, the baths are open daily, 8 AM–8 PM. Brice Callahan, a massage specialist, uses an imported vibrator along with his hands and muscles, and sunken tubs in three private massage rooms are filled with fresh, hot mineral water after being sanitized following each use. The older bathhouses rely on nature for constant water circulation; they have a potential for algae buildup.

Bathers at the Yucca Lodge can exercise in two big pools equipped with metal support bars. Massages are also offered. The Charles Motel in town has separate facilities for men and women. Each has sauna, steam bath, and four individual tubs. Massages cost $20 an hour.

Ralph Edwards, former host of *Truth or Consequences*, bathes here as guest of honor during the town fiesta the first weekend in May. Before his time it was a favorite of Geronimo.

Truth or Consequences
Chamber of Commerce
500 McAdoo St., Drawer 31, Truth or Consequences, NM 87901
Tel. 505/894–3536

Season Year-round.

Accommodations Standard motels on the highway, without mineral baths, include Super 8 and the Western Motel.

Rates $28 a night at the Charles Motel. Confirmation by credit card. Credit cards: MC, V.

Services and Facilities **Swimming Facilities:** Nearby lake. **Recreation Facilities:** Hiking, tubing.

Getting Here *From Albuquerque.* By car, I–25 north (2½ hr).

Cliff Lodge at Snowbird

Sports conditioning
Stress control
Luxury pampering

Utah
Snowbird
Alpine views from a penthouse spa, mountaineering courses, and 1,900 acres of groomed ski slopes are the attractions of the sports-oriented Cliff Lodge. Set in Utah's scenic Wasatch Mountains near Salt Lake City, Cliff Lodge is more like a Swiss spa than any other ski resort in America.

The Mountaineering Center complements the spa-and-ski program with rock-climbing classes, overnight backpacking trips, bike tours, and guided treks to the peaks of the national forest. Open from July through mid-October, the center attracts outdoors people and climbers of all achievement levels. Hiking can be an aerobic workout at an altitude of 8,000 feet.

For golfers, there is helicopter service to the courses in nearby Wasatch National Park and at Jeremy Ranch. Skiers can also be whisked up to powder snow conditions on upper slopes.

The active, youthful vacationers here get into shape with stress-management classes and relaxation exercises led by a certified neurolinguistic programmer. Body-movement techniques, stress control for shoulders and stomach, and the attainment of a relaxed frame of mind are seen as leading to improved results on the slopes.

The two-story fitness center on the top floors of the 11-story luxury hotel provides a tranquil environment for morning stretch classes, hydrotherapy, or an herbal wrap. Mountains are everywhere you look. After skiing, a hike through Little Cottonwood Canyon, or tennis in the crisp mountain air, you can swim laps in an outdoor pool on the roof. The scenery adds a special dimension to workouts in the glass-walled weights room or relaxation in a whirlpool. Inside, the hotel atrium provides architectural drama.

The spa atop the Cliff Lodge, opened in 1987, was the crowning touch in a master plan for year-round recreation developed by Dick Bass, a Texas-born oilman, rancher, and amateur rock climber. There are saunas and steam rooms for men and women and private treatment rooms for sophisticated therapies such as the French Phytomer process of cleansing and toning the bust with marine products. A skin treatment for the back, popular with men, uses steam, a prep scrub, a Phytomer marine peel, and massage cream to deep-cleanse the pores and moisturize the skin. All treatments are available à la carte or as part of summer and winter packages.

There's plenty for children to do while their parents exercise or pamper themselves. Special skiing and tennis training are offered for children five and older, and kids stay free in their parents' room. Children's lift tickets are free when children accompany adults on outings.

Cliff Lodge at Snowbird
Little Cottonwood Canyon Rd., Snowbird, UT 84092
Tel. 801/742–2222 or 800/453–3000
Telex 9102400389 Snowbird UT USA

Administration	Manager, Edward Pilkerton; spa operations manager, Jane Brennan
Season	Year-round.
Accommodations	532 rooms and suites with mountain views and balconies that open onto the 11-story atrium. Luxury furnishings and baths, king-size beds, cable TV, full service.
Rates	Rooms from $88 a day, suites to $380; $10 additional for use of the spa. Spa program and treatments $330 single, $265 double, per day, high season. Packages for 4–7 nights, with room, 3 meals, and spa services from $1,275 single, $1,025 double. Mountaineering Center activities charged separately. $100 per person advance payment for packages. Credit cards: AE, DC, MC, V.
Meal Plans	Packages include dining in 3 lodge restaurants. The Aerie's low-fat, low-cholesterol offerings may include vegetarian lasagna or pizza, grilled salmon, broiled chicken, luncheon salads, chicken teriyaki, meatless chili. The Spa Cafe serves fruit smoothies, high-fiber breakfast, and lunch.
Services and Facilities	**Exercise Equipment:** 12 Keiser Cam III pneumatic weight-resistance units, Lifecycles, Bodyguard 900 bikes. Aerobics studio with suspended wood floor. **Services:** Massage, hydrotherapy, herbal wrap, parafango wrap, Phytomer deep-cleansing treatments, manicure, pedicure, facial, hairstyling. Daily classes in aerobics and stretching. Stress-management course (additional fee). **Swimming Facilities:** Outdoor lap pool. **Recreation Facilities:** 7 tennis courts; hiking, skiing, rock climbing. Golf and horseback riding nearby. **Evening Programs:** Outdoor adventure films and talks.

In the Area   Helicopter rides, Western barbecues, backpacking, mountain bike tours, tram rides; Salt Lake City sports and entertainment centers, Mormon Tabernacle, mineral springs at Heber City, historic Alta (19th-century silver mine).

Getting Here   *From Salt Lake City.* By bus, Utah Transit Authority scheduled service from city terminal and airport during winter season (45 min). By car, I–75, I–80, Rte. 210 to Little Cottonwood Canyon (40 min). Free pickup on arrival and departure at Salt Lake City airport with package plans. Limousine, taxi, rental car available. Resort parking; valet service and indoor parking at the lodge only.

Special Notes   Ski-training course for the disabled. Ski and tennis instruction, day-care center for children. No smoking in the spa, the 9th-floor guest rooms, and designated areas of the dining room.

Green Valley Health Resort

Nutrition and Diet
Weight management
Luxury pampering

Utah
St. George   If you've read *How to Lower Your Fat Thermostat* or seen Sybervision's audio and video series on the neuropsychology of weight control, you'll find the Green Valley Health Resort the place to put those theories into practice. The live-in program, based on lowering weight by making changes in the control centers of your body, was designed by the same team that wrote the book, and the authors are here about two days a month for personal consultation.

The desert resort provides a pleasant environment for fun and fitness; the tensions and pressures of daily life can melt away with the pounds. As you begin to regain energy, you'll appreciate the opportunities to explore the wonderland that surrounds the valley. Settled by Mormon pioneers, the area is rich in history, and there are heritage buildings to be visited.

Beginning with an introduction to how the body's weight-regulating mechanism works, your learning experiences include trips to restaurants and supermarkets, cooking workshops, and discussion groups. The nutritious high-energy meals are a revelation about the variety and quantity of food that one can enjoy while losing weight. The effect on brain chemistry is to decrease depression, increase alertness, and foster a sense of well-being.

The program's educational approach to obesity confronts food allergies and addictions. Instructors teach you how to control cravings with techniques developed by Dr. Dennis W. Remington at Brigham Young University's Eating Disorder Clinic.

Once the mind and body are in sync, the exercise and the hiking become more challenging. The training emphasizes correct posture and body movements, shaping and contouring as weight is lost. The program is limited to 15 to 20 participants per week to maintain personal interaction with staff physiologists and nutritionists.

Subconscious stresses are also addressed. Dr. Edward A. Parent, the psychological consultant and director, and Garth

Fisher, the exercise director, have developed specific processes and treatments for relaxing. Certainly one of the best tonics is the peace and quiet, the crisp air, and the bright sunlight of this green oasis.

Green Valley Health Resort

1515 W. Canyon View Dr., St. George, UT 84770
Tel. 801/628–8060 or 800/237–1068 (800/654–7760 in UT)

Administration Manager, Coleen Breeze; program director, Roy Fitzell

Season Year-round.

Accommodations Furnished condominium apartments have spacious contemporary interiors with living room, dining counter, kitchen, private bath, balcony. Some have a Jacuzzi on the deck.

Rates 1-week program $995 per person, double occupancy. $100 deposit. Credit cards: MC, V.

Meal Plans 3 meals daily. Low-fat diet, no sugar or salt. Sunday breakfast is scrambled eggs, buttermilk biscuits, turkey sausage, assorted fresh fruit. Lunches include soup, salad, steamed vegetables, a tuna-salad sandwich on whole-grain bread or turkey salad on pita. Typical dinner entrees are swiss steak with mashed potatoes and steamed broccoli, beef stew, baked chicken with tarragon, poached red snapper in tomato sauce. Desserts include Key lime pie, banana pudding, apple strudel.

Services and Facilities **Exercise Equipment:** Lifecycles, rowing machines, treadmills, stationary bikes, Politas Reformers (stretching). **Services:** Swedish massage, hand and foot reflexology, herbal wraps, facials, powdered-pearl body rub; hair, nail, and skin care. Personal counseling on tension control, wardrobe, coloring and makeup, skin care, shopping. **Swimming Facilities:** Outdoor and enclosed pools, diving pool. **Spa Facilities:** Steam rooms, saunas, whirlpool. **Recreation Facilities:** 15 outdoor and 4 indoor tennis courts, volleyball, shuffleboard, basketball, lawn chess, 9-hole executive golf course, putting green, bowling alley, roller skating, squash and racquetball courts. Use of bicycles. Horseback riding, downhill skiing, water sports nearby. **Evening Programs:** Talks on health and nutrition.

In the Area Zion National Park excursion with picnic lunch, hiking in Snow Canyon, Vic Braden Tennis College (on site), North Rim of Grand Canyon, Snow Canyon sandstone cliffs, Bryce National Park, Nevada casinos, country and western entertainment, river rafting.

Getting Here *From Las Vegas.* By car, I–15 to St. George (2 hr). By plane, commuter flights on Skywest (40 min). Free pickup to and from St. George airport. Van service from Las Vegas (fee). Car rental available.

Special Notes Elevators, oversize bathroom facilities for the disabled. Summer fitness/health camp for children, tennis camp at Vic Braden College. No smoking. Remember to bring a medical release from your doctor, casual workout clothing, walking shoes.

The Last Resort

Spiritual awareness

Utah
Sunset Cliffs

Yoga studies, meditation, and nature walks are the cornerstone programs for rejuvenating the body and the mind at the Last Resort, an informal mountain retreat. Operated as a bed-and-breakfast inn, the 2-story log building 8,700 feet above sea level boasts spectacular mountain views and accommodates up to 12 guests.

Marked trails attract hikers and backpackers in summer and autumn. In winter the light powder snow makes ideal conditions for cross-country skiing.

Iyengar yoga adapts to the seasons and to nature. During year-end retreats, total silence is observed for 10 days. A seven-day program that explores human and physical relationships is scheduled for July and August, limited to eight persons. Spring is celebrated with a 10-day detoxification and spring cleaning of the body.

The hosts, who have been associated with the Yoga Institute in San Diego for more than a decade, make guests feel at home and encourage them to seek inspiration from nature.

Beginners and advanced students are all welcome.

The Last Resort
Box 6226, Cedar City, UT 84720
Tel. 801/682–2289 or 619/283–8663

Administration Program directors, Pujari and Abhilasha (Ed and Barbara Keays)

Season Year-round, with retreats scheduled in June, July, Dec., and Jan.

Accommodations Dormitory beds and private rooms for couples. Simple furnishings, communal bath.

Rates $25 a day for 1 person, $35 for 2, including breakfast. 5-day retreat in Jan. $220; 10-day "spring cleaning" $650; 7-day yoga intensive $550. 50% payable in advance for a program. No credit cards.

Meal Plans Vegetarian meals prepared by a nutritionist, tea, and juice come with retreats. Menus include steamed fresh vegetables, whole grains, rice, dahl.

Services and Facilities **Swimming Facilities:** Nearby lakes. **Spa Facilities:** Mineral baths at Pah Tempe Hot Springs. **Recreation Facilities:** Hiking, cross-country skiing. **Programs:** Meditation instruction, rebirthing, Iyengar yoga classes, lectures on lifestyle.

In the Area Bryce Canyon National Park. North Rim of the Grand Canyon, Zion National Park, Cedar Peaks. Shakespeare Festival in Cedar City (mid-July–Aug.).

Getting Here *From Las Vegas.* By car, I–15 to Cedar City, Rte. 14 (3 hr).

Special Notes No smoking.

National Institute of Fitness

Weight management
Nutrition and diet

Utah Designed by an exercise physiologist, the National Institute of
Ivins Fitness no-frills fitness and weight-loss program is based on
nutrition, movement, and recreation in some of the most glori-
ous canyon country in the West.

Vigorous exercise, rather than pampering or bodywork, is central here. On arrival participants are given a fitness evaluation
that includes a cardiovascular endurance test. Based on that
assessment, individuals are assigned to a fitness group and instructor. Participation in the scheduled classes and exercise
sessions is encouraged but not required; many guests stay for a
month or more.

Group support plays an important role in this regimen. The
program moves along at a fast pace, and instructors concentrate on teaching techniques that guests can practice on their
own at home. The indoor facilities include an aerobics studio,
weights room, racquetball court, and the largest covered swimming pool in southern Utah for laps and aquaerobics. A
whirlpool and massage are also available.

Set in a geological paradise of red sandstone canyons near Zion
National Park, the resort complex features dome-shaped housing units that blend in with the rugged terrain.

National Institute of Fitness
202 N. Snow Canyon Rd., Box 938, Ivins, UT 84738
Tel. 801/673–4905

Administration Manager, Jay Cooper; program director, Vicki Sorenson

Season Year-round; program begins Mon.

Accommodations 39 rooms with 1–4 beds each. Modern furnishings, private
bath. Semiprivate rooms have partitions, single beds. Daily
maid service weekdays.

Rates 1-week program from $419 per person (4 in a room) to $799 (single occupancy). $100 (nonrefundable) payable in advance.
Credit cards (3% surcharge): MC, V.

Meal Plans Low-calorie weight-loss diet, nutritionally balanced, controlled portions. Low in salt, fat, sugar; high in complex
carbohydrates. Pritikin-style entrees for lunch are turkey loaf,
tuna sandwich on wheat bread; dinner includes vegetarian lasagna, pizza with turkey.

Services and **Exercise Equipment:** 11-station Magnum II weight training
Facilities gym, free weights, StairMaster, Exercycles, treadmills,
rebounders. **Services:** Massage; hair, nail, and skin care; fitness
evaluation; yoga and exercise instruction. **Swimming Facilities:**
Heated indoor pool. **Recreation Facilities:** Tennis court, indoor
racquetball court; horseback riding nearby. **Evening Pro-**
grams: Workshops on nutrition and health.

In the Area Snow Canyon State Park, Las Vegas, Salt Lake City, Zion National Park.

Getting Here *From Las Vegas.* By car, I–15 to St. George, Bluff St. north to Santa Clara, Sunset Blvd. to Ivins (2 hr). By plane, commuter flights on Skywest Airlines to St. George (45 min). Free pickup to and from St. George Airport. Taxi, rental car available.

Special Notes No smoking. Remember to bring medical records, exercise clothing, aerobic and hiking shoes.

The Northwest

Native Americans believed long ago that the Great Spirit lived at the earth's center and that steaming hot springs produced "big medicine" waters. Rediscovered by a new generation, the hot springs of the Northwest can be enjoyed in settings of great natural beauty or at large new resort developments. One such sacred spot in Oregon is now the popular resort Kah-Nee-Ta, owned and operated by the Confederated Tribes of the Warm Springs. Wyoming has developed Hot Springs State Park on land purchased from the Shoshone and Arapahoe Indians near Yellowstone National Park. The Sol Duc Hot Springs Resort in Olympic National Park, Washington, is another warm watering spot.

Montana's "big sky" country offers the family-oriented Fairmont Hot Springs Resort and the rustic Chico Hot Springs Lodge, along with 39 ski runs and posh dude ranches. In a verdant valley rich with gold rush lore outside Fairbanks, Alaska, the sulfur sprites of Chena Hot Springs have welcomed homesteaders and "cheechako" travelers since 1905.

Chena Hot Springs Resort

Taking the waters

Alaska
Fairbanks

A soak at the historic Chena Hot Springs Resort near Fairbanks comes accompanied by reminders of pioneer days. There are cabins and pools here that were built in the early 1900s, when the main visitors were gold miners who had traveled by dogsled and on horseback in search of relief from rheumatism and arthritis in the hot springs. Images of the miners still smile from the photographs of the Victorian era that decorate the dining room and lounge.

Despite some recent development, the old-time character of the resort has not changed. The bathhouse is a ramshackle affair of wood and plastic that provides just enough protection from the chill as you prepare to swim or bathe. The hot mineral water that bubbles to the surface at 156 degrees is cooled to a tolerable 110 degrees in the soaking pools, 90 degrees for swimming.

The cluster of cabins around the main lodge has the general appearance of a mining camp. In the gardens between the steaming ponds, where the spring waters run into a creek, the machinery, carts, and tools that the miners once used have taken on the role of memorabilia. Moose have been spotted wandering on the grounds, and antlers adorn some of the buildings.

Set in a quiet valley that is part of the state park and recreation system, the hot springs now attract winter and summer vacationers. A lively crowd from the university in Fairbanks, 60 miles down the road, comes to ski the nearby slopes and well-marked trails, and the springs are popular with Japanese tourists. Yet most guests are Alaskans, and they set the informal

The Northwest

0 ——— 300 miles
0 ——— 300 km

N

ALASKA

CANADA

ALBERTA

Yukon River
Fairbanks ○ ⓐ 14
ⓐ 15

Anchorage ○

Gulf of Alaska

Juneau ★

C

A

PACIFIC OCEAN

① ②
○ Everett
ⓐ 97
Spokane River
Coeur d'Alene ○
③
○ Seattle
WASHINGTON
Spokane ○
ⓐ 90
★ Tacoma
Olympia ○
ⓐ 5
④
ⓐ 97 ⓐ 82
Snake River
Walla Walla ○
Missoula ○
Vancouver ○
⑤ ⓐ 84
Columbia River
Portland ○
ⓐ 84
★ Salem
⑦ ⑥
IDAHO
Corvallis ○
○ Eugene
ⓐ 5
ⓐ 20
Boise ★
OREGON
ⓐ 26
Snake River
⑧
Medford ○

CALIFORNIA

NEVADA

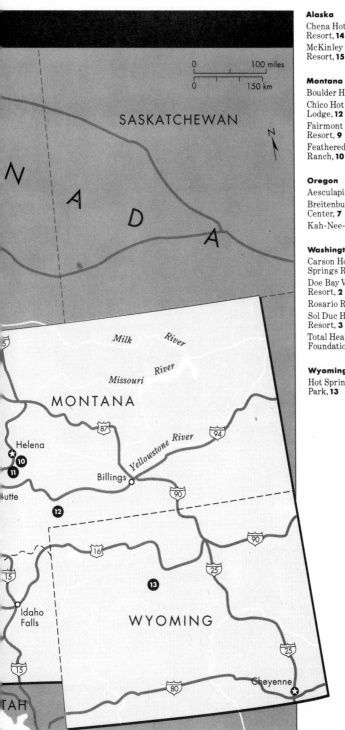

Alaska
Chena Hot Springs
Resort, **14**
McKinley Chalet
Resort, **15**

Montana
Boulder Hot Springs, **11**
Chico Hot Springs
Lodge, **12**
Fairmont Hot Springs
Resort, **9**
Feathered Pipe
Ranch, **10**

Oregon
Aesculapia, **8**
Breitenbush Retreat
Center, **7**
Kah-Nee-Ta Resort, **6**

Washington
Carson Hot Mineral
Springs Resort, **5**
Doe Bay Village
Resort, **2**
Rosario Resort, **1**
Sol Duc Hot Springs
Resort, **3**
Total Health
Foundation, **4**

Wyoming
Hot Springs State
Park, **13**

tone of the resort. Don't expect calorie-counted food or anything fancy. Wild blueberry daiquiris are the specialty at the bar.

Chena Hot Springs Resort
Chena Hot Springs Rd., Fairbanks, AL 99071
(Reservations) Drawer 25, 1919 Lathrop St., Fairbanks, AL 99071
Tel. 907/452-7867

Administration	Manager, Bird Curtiss
Season	Year-round.
Accommodations	Lodges and cabins, plainly furnished, for 160 guests. Baths private or shared, geothermal hot water, maid service. Cabins with double and single beds, wood-burning fireplace for heat, propane lights, washbasin, chemical toilet; no linens. RV hookup, campsites. Single rooms on request.
Rates	$35–$45 per day for 2 persons; 1-week package $250–$300 for 2. 1 night's lodging in advance. Credit cards: AE, MC, V.
Meal Plans	Pancakes with berries, hot cereal for breakfast; generous servings of roast beef, ham, roast turkey for lunch and dinner. Fresh produce in season.
Services and Facilities	**Spa Facilities:** 2 indoor whirlpools, swimming pool. **Recreation Facilities:** Volleyball court, croquet, horseshoe pitch; fishing, hiking, mountain climbing; downhill and cross-country skiing, ice skating, snowmobiling, sledding.
In the Area	Chena River cruise, boating, canoeing.
Getting Here	*From Fairbanks.* By car, Rte. 2 (Steese Hwy.) to Chena Springs Rd. (80 min). Rental car available.
Special Notes	Limited access for the disabled.

McKinley Chalet Resort

Non-program resort facilities

Alaska
Denali National Park

Overlooking majestic mountains at a scenic turn in the Nenana River, the McKinley Chalet Resort consists of a cluster of rustic cabins and a modern mountain lodge in an accessible area of the wilderness of Denali National Park. Guests enjoy free use of the only indoor health club and swimming pool this side of Mt. McKinley. Fitness facilities at the resort's Chalet Club include an exercise room with weights, whirlpool, and sauna, and an aerobics studio is used for classes.

Dominated by Mt. McKinley, the Denali experience is a mixture of rugged outdoor treks and guided bus tours.

Naturalists and park rangers accompany trips along park roads that are closed to private cars in the summer. River rafting and a scenic float are other possibilities here.

McKinley Chalet Resort
George Parks Hwy., Denali National Park, AK
(Reservations) 825 W. 8th Ave. (240), Anchorage, AK 99501
Tel. 907/276-7234

Administration Manager, Carson Flaherty; fitness director, Beth L. Handley

Season May–Sept.

Accommodations 216 deluxe 2-room suites in an alpine chalet, with hotel service. Units include simply furnished sitting rooms with sofa and reading chair, 2 single beds, modern bath, wooden balconies and walkways. Dining in the main building (adjoining the Chalet Club).

Rates 1-night visit with 6-hour Tundra Wildlife bus tour $94.50 per person double occupancy. 3-day/2-night package with tours, river rafting, and evening entertainment $201 per person double occupancy. 1-night's lodging in advance. Credit cards: MC, V.

Meal Plans A la carte menu offers fresh salmon baked and grilled, salads with Alaskan crab, pasta, shrimp fettucini, steaks, chicken, roast pork. For breakfast, home-baked muffins and breads.

Services and Equipment **Exercise Equipment:** 10-station Universal weight training gym, stationary bikes, rowing machine, free weights. **Services:** Swedish massage. **Swimming Facilities:** Indoor pool. **Recreation Facilities:** River rafting, backcountry hiking. **Evening Programs:** Cabin sourdough banquet.

In the Area Tundra Wildlife bus tour (6 hr), air sightseeing, sled-dog demonstration; Vistadome rail excursion to Fairbanks or Anchorage.

Getting Here *From Anchorage.* By bus, Gray Line of Alaska (5 hr). By train, McKinley Explorer private car, Alaska Railroad scheduled service daily (5 hr). By car, Rte. 3 (George Parks Hwy.) to National Park gateway (5 hr). Free pickup to and from train station.

Special Notes Ramps at health club and some lodging allow access for the disabled. Swimming lessons and nature trail hikes for children. No smoking in the Chalet Club, Chalet Center, and designated areas of the dining rooms.

Boulder Hot Springs

Taking the waters
Holistic health

Montana
Boulder

Mineral-spring baths and mountain hikes at the Boulder Hot Springs resort in the foothills of the Elkhorn range of the Rocky Mountains have been an attraction since the early 1800s. Then, in the early 1950s, controversy arose as stories of a radioactive "miracle mine" appeared in the national media.

Operators of the Free Enterprise Radon Mine make no claims for medical benefits. Instead, they point to the documentation of treatments at similar mines near Bad Gastein, Austria, where more than 7,000 patients a year breathe radon under medical supervision.

Those who come to the Free Enterprise mine seeking relief from asthma, arthritis, bursitis, and other forms of chronic, crippling pain bundle up in sweaters and coats and stretch out in deck chairs to breathe the radon gas and drink the radioactive water. Some visitors have claimed to experience improved freedom of movement and relief from pain after a week.

As for the degree of radioactivity involved, the Montana Health Department says that guests are exposed to less than 10% of the maximum legal allowance of radiation to which miners may be exposed. No authoritative medical evaluation of the theraputic value of the mines has been established.

Located three miles from the hotel and 85 feet below ground, the mine is surprisingly dry and comfortable. A large elevator, capable of handling wheelchairs, descends to well-lighted, timbered tunnels equipped with warming lamps. Visits last a maximum of 80 minutes, and a series of up to 32 treatments is suggested.

Guests at the big old inn enjoy a variety of therapies from massage to hot and cold plunges, and one may consult with a natural-health specialist. Around the indoor pools is a lounge area with a bar that serves vitamins, mineral supplements, and herbal tea as well as beer. Meals must be ordered in advance; the restaurant is open only on weekends. For those who want to cook for themselves, a central kitchen may be used free of charge. The temperature of the mineral water is 175 degrees when it reaches ground level. Pure enough to drink, it has the effect of a laxative and diuretic. Chemical analysis shows the water to be full of the same medicinal salts used at European spas to treat rheumatism, gout, and some kidney and bladder disorders.

As renovations progress, the resort's owners hope to rejuvenate the health programs. The inn's mission architecture is being preserved.

Boulder Hot Springs
Box 1020, Boulder, MT 59632
Tel. 406/225–4273

Administration	Manager, Robert Johnson
Season	Year-round.
Accommodations	25 rooms remain open while the original 125-room hotel undergoes renovation. Furnishings have a turn-of-the-century look: heavy wooden pieces, oversize beds, old-fashioned baths. Hostel beds, camp sites, RV connections available.
Rates	$28–$40 a night. Mine health treatment packages $140 a week for 2, $105 single. Dormitory beds $8 a night. 1 night's lodging payable in advance. No credit cards.
Meal Plans	The Hot Spot Restaurant (hotel) features grilled mountain trout, vegetable lasagna, broiled chicken. Fruit, yogurt, vitamins, distilled water available.
Services and Facilities	**Services:** Massage (acupressure, deep-muscle), biofeedback therapy, consultation on nutrition and health. **Swimming Facilities:** Naturally heated outdoor mineral-water pool. **Spa Facilities:** Separate men's and women's bathhouses have hot and cold plunge pools. **Recreation Facilities:** Hiking, walking, fishing; cross-country skiing.
In the Area	Glacier National Park, Lewis & Clark Caverns, Montana State Capitol in Helena, Yellowstone National Park.

Getting Here *From Helena.* By car, I–15 to Boulder, Hwy. 69 to Boulder Springs (40 min). Free pickup to and from Helena or Butte. Service to the radon mine. Rental car available.

Special Notes Limited access for the disabled. No smoking in dining room.

Chico Hot Springs Lodge

Taking the waters

Montana After a day in the saddle, the prospect of a hot soak makes sore
Pray muscles bearable. There's nothing glamorous about the Chico Hot Springs Lodge, but the two hot-springs pools on its 157-acre grounds encourage many visitors to Yellowstone Park to detour. Located about 30 miles from the park's northern gateway, the resort offers horseback riding and pack trips into the Gallatin National Forest and the Absaroka range of the Rockies.

Surrounded by spectacular mountain scenery, the open-air pools are fed by 110-degree untreated mineral water from several springs. Four private areas in the bathhouse have redwood hot tubs large enough for a family of four.

The pools are open to the public as well as to registered guests, and as you soak you might even spot deer on the slopes.

Chico Hot Springs Lodge
Pray, MT 59065
Tel. 406/333–4933

Administration Managers, Michael and Eve Art

Season Year-round.

Accommodations 52 rooms in the main lodge, 12 motel units, several family-size A-frame cabins. Lodge rooms have Western furnishings, twin beds, private bath.

Rates About $50 a day for 2. Confirmation by credit card. Credit cards: MC, V.

Meal Plans Continental fare. A la carte lunch menu includes grilled fish, salad, fruit plate; dinner entrees can be roast venison, saddle of lamb, grilled or sautéed trout.

Services and **Swimming Facilities:** Mineral-water outdoor pool. **Spa Facili-**
Facilities **ties:** 4 private tubs, 2 outdoor pools. **Recreation Facilities:** Boating, trout fishing (private lake), horseback riding; cross-country skiing, snowmobiling.

In the Area Trail rides; Yellowstone National Park; Crow Indian Reservation.

Getting Here *From Bozeman.* By car, I–90 to Hwy. 89 (2 hr).

Fairmont Hot Springs Resort

Taking the waters

Montana Big Sky country and big springs come together here. Nestled
Anaconda near the Pintlar Wilderness in an area of boundless views and numerous springs, the Fairmont Hot Springs Resort combines

striking modern architecture and Western hospitality. The range of amenities and activities makes it ideal for a family vacation in summer or a skiing holiday in winter.

Native Americans worshiped the "medicine water" of the natural hot springs. The mineral water, 160 degrees when it surfaces, is treated and cooled for the two Olympic-size swimming pools and the indoor and outdoor soaking pools. Resort facilities include men's and women's saunas but no bodywork.

The family-oriented activities include hayrides and visits to the petting zoo; among the sports options are horseback riding, golf, tennis, and, for children, a huge water slide.

Guests have the choice of a fully equipped condominium apartment or rooms and suites in the main lodge. The indoor pool ensures swimming and soaking in comfort year-round.

Fairmont Hot Springs Resort
1500 Fairmont Rd., Anaconda, MT 59711
Tel. 406/797–3241 or 800/443–2381 (800/332–3272 in MT)

Administration	Manager, Edward Hemrich
Season	Year-round.
Accommodations	135 guest rooms in the lodge; time-share condominium apartment rentals. Double beds, quality furnishings, private bath. RV hookup, campsites.
Rates	Rooms $50–$60, depending on season; suites $80–$120; condominiums $150. 1 night payable in advance. Credit cards: AE, MC, V.
Meal Plans	Standard American breakfast and dinner in the restaurant.
Services and Facilities	**Swimming Facilities:** Outdoor and indoor Olympic-size pools. **Spa Facilities:** Large soaking pools, indoor and outdoor. **Recreation Facilities:** 4 tennis courts, 18-hole golf course, horseback riding, hayrides; trout fishing, cross-country skiing, sleigh rides.
In the Area	Yellowstone National Park, Glacier National Park.
Getting Here	*From Missoula.* By car, I–90 (60 min).
Special Notes	Limited access for the disabled. Hayrides, sleigh rides for children.

Feathered Pipe Ranch

Holistic health
Spiritual awareness

Montana
Helena

Feathered Pipe Ranch is a magical place that sets spirits soaring, since 1975 a center for workshops in yoga and holistic health that attracts world-renowned teachers and practitioners. Almost every week from spring to autumn sees an intensive program here on subjects as diverse as astrology, Rubenfeld Synergy, massage training, and Iyengar yoga. People from many backgrounds, professionals in the healing arts, and novice students come here to gain new ideas and experience.

A catalyst for change, the Feathered Pipe Foundation offers vacations that help visitors recognize their wholeness and the interconnectedness of all life. Some even maintain that the ranch wilderness has a healing power.

Located in the Montana Rockies close to the Continental Divide, the retreat sits on land that was once inhabited by a Native American tribe. Climbing to "sacred rocks" for meditation, you gain a panoramic view of the 110-acre ranch. Miles of hiking trails, a sparkling lake and stream, and the dry, clear air make a heady combination that can generate a tremendous feeling of release.

Workshops address many areas of the human-potential movement. There is an annual course in miracles, and another is devoted to the shamanistic rituals of the Huichol Mexicans. Iyengar yoga is a popular topic in this intimate environment; a one-week course teaches yoga as the means to personal transformation.

Log and stone buildings give the impression of a frontier outpost. Beyond the main lodge are Native American tepees, Mongolian yurts, and basic tents. A cedar bathhouse holds huge hot tubs, a sauna, and a massage room staffed by professional therapists.

The search for insight is the ranch's principal attraction. Serious concentration is the norm here, with little of the fun-and-fitness holiday atmosphere.

Feathered Pipe Ranch
2409 Colorado Gulch, Helena, MT 59601
Tel. 406/443-9611
(Foundation programs) Box 1682, Helena MT 59624
Tel. 406/442-5138

Administration	Executive Director, India Supera; seminars director, Heidi Goldman
Season	Late Apr.–Sept.
Accommodations	10 dormitory rooms with bunk beds for 4–6 people in the main lodge. Linens, blankets, towels provided. Tents, yurts, campsites, RV space available; tepees sleep 2–4 persons.
Rates	4-day workshop $275–$495, 1-week program $750. Lodging, meals, instruction included. $250 payable in advance. Credit cards (4% surcharge): MC, V.
Meal Plans	3 gourmet vegetarian meals daily, cafeteria style. Organically grown produce. Breakfast includes yogurt, home-baked bread or muffins, fresh fruit; lunch may be tuna-fish salad with pita bread, green salad, or pasta with vegetables; typical dinner selections are baked trout, eggplant and cheese casserole, zucchini baked with tomatoes, baked chicken. Special diets accommodated.
Services and Facilities	**Services:** Massage, bodywork. **Swimming Facilities:** Mountain lake. **Recreation Facilities:** Volleyball, hiking. **Evening Programs:** Talks related to study programs; entertainment.
In the Area	Helena historical area and shopping; Gates of the Mountains boat tour, hot springs.
Getting Here	*From Helena.* By car Hwy. 12 (15 min). Rental car and limo available.

Special Notes No smoking indoors. Remember to bring flashlight, sun protection.

Aesculapia

Spiritual awareness
Holistic health

Oregon Created as a community of healers and named after the Greek
Grants Pass god of healing and ancient dream temples, Aesculapia is a retreat that teaches self-healing. Visitors take part in shamanistic ritual, hike in the woods, or meditate; help is available from body healers and hypnotherapists, nutritionists and psychotherapists.

Spontaneous creative energy is applied to healing in six related programs, or "communities." Matters of the body, the mind, and the spirit; healing through the arts; and transpersonal psychologies create a certain synergy.

Aesculapia strives to provide those in search of healing with supportive relationships and natural-health specialists in a low-key environment. Individual and group therapy are offered, along with scheduled workshops, seminars, and rituals that include a Rune circle to consult ancient Viking oracles and ceremonies from a wide range of Eastern, Western, and New Age traditions.

Unstructured and informal, the activities are different from one day to the next. You can work with healers, practice natural healing techniques, and attend as many workshops as you like; you set your own pace. Each summer sees a week-long gathering of healers at the nearby Breitenbush Retreat Center, which is open to all.

Aesculapia
1480 Dutcher Creek Rd., Grants Pass, OR 97527
Tel. 503/476–0492 or 503/342–5472

Administration Managers, Jeannie Eagle and Graywolf Swinney

Season May–Oct.

Accommodations Rustic, comfortable rooms in small mountain houses are shared by community members. Guests bring their own linens, towels, blankets.

Rates $20–$30 a day per person, including meals. 1 night payable in advance. No credit cards.

Meal Plans Vegetarian meals, fresh fruit and produce in season. Buffets offer salads of sprouts, greens, and grains, vegetarian lasagna, tofu casserole, and home-baked whole-wheat breads.

Services and Facilities **Services:** Massage; counseling on nutrition and health. **Swimming Facilities:** Lake. **Recreation Facilities:** Walking, hiking. **Evening Programs:** Informal workshops, rituals.

In the Area Ocean beaches, vineyard tours, hot springs; Shakespeare Festival (July–Aug.).

Getting Here *From Eugene.* By bus, Greyhound to Medford (2 hr). By car, I–5 south to Grants Pass (90 min). Rental car available.

Special Notes Programs for children include Emergent Design group sharing of thoughts, feelings, conflicts; outings and adventures.

Breitenbush Retreat Center

Taking the waters
Spiritual awareness
Holistic health

Oregon The Esalen of the Northwest, the Breitenbush Retreat Center
Detroit is a holistic community retreat for groups and individuals; its rustic cabins cluster on the banks of the Breitenbush River, surrounded by the Willamette National Forest.

The hot mineral waters are a major attraction: Natural springs and artesian wells supply 180-degree water for the steam bath and outdoor pools. At an idyllic spot in the woods, four hydrojet pools are filled with chlorinated water for alfresco baths with adjustable temperatures. In the meadow you can dip into footbaths where the hot mineral water flows naturally.

Beyond sybaritic pleasures, the community is dedicated to fostering personal health and spiritual growth. Visitors can join workshops and ceremonies, even experience a meditation pyramid and a Native American sweat lodge. A sanctuary building provides space for a private retreat.

Breitenbush Retreat Center
Box 578, Detroit, OR 97342
Tel. 503/854–3314

Administration Manager, Peter Moore; program director, Alex Brenner

Season Year-round.

Accommodations 40 cabins, each with 2–4 beds (sheet only), bath with toilet. 20 tents, some campsites.

Rates $30–$40 a day per person includes meals. 1 night payable in advance. No credit cards.

Meal Plans Ovo-lacto vegetarian diet. Breakfast is granola, hot cereal of mixed grains, yogurt, fruit, and home-baked wheat breads. Lunch can be a salad with sprouts or tuna fish, vegetarian pizza. Dinner entrees may include pasta, char-broiled salmon, casserole of tofu and rice.

Services and Facilities **Services:** Massage, counseling on health and healing. **Swimming Facilities:** Outdoor pool to be renovated; glacial river. **Spa Facilities:** 4 outdoor tiled pools, indoor hot tubs. **Recreation Facilities:** Fishing, hiking; downhill and cross-country skiing. **Evening Programs:** Workshops on health and nutrition.

In the Area Native American cultural center at Warm Springs Indian Reservation; Mt. Hood National Forest.

Getting Here *From Portland.* By car, I–5 south to Salem, Hwy. 22 to Detroit (2 hr).

Special Notes Smoking only in designated outdoor areas. Remember to bring bedding, towels, flashlight.

Kah-Nee-Ta Resort

Taking the waters

Oregon
Warm Springs

The Kah-Nee-Ta Resort, owned and managed by a confedera-
tion of tribes whose ancestors once worshiped at the springs on
their reservation, strikes a delicate balance between tradition
and modernity. Guests are invited to tribal ceremonies and festivals and to share a guinea hen baked in clay. Huge swimming
pools and bathhouses offer private soaks and a massage. And
the tranquillity of the brown hills, the distant snow-covered
mountains, and the vast expanse of blue sky where hawks hang
like kites on invisible currents of air may seem to have curative
powers.

The guest lodge and conference center sit atop a rocky ridge
overlooking the Warm Springs River and a recreation complex.
Open to the public, this Indian village of tepees and vacation
villas offers mineral baths and pools, a golf course, tennis
courts, and stables. Trails for biking, hiking, and riding fan out
toward the distant Cascade Mountains.

All activities are priced à la carte, and the fees are modest: $10
for an hour on horseback, $3 for a 25-minute mineral bath. Ar-
rangements can be made on short notice on any day of the week.
In the separate men's and women's bathhouses, the five tiled
sunken tubs are refilled after each use. The odorless mineral
water is piped in at 140 degrees and cooled to suit the bathers.

Named after the Native American spirit of the hot springs, this
cheery, family-oriented resort protected by mountains enjoys
a dry and sunny climate most of the year. Native Americans say
it is a place to make peace with yourself.

Kah-Nee-Ta Resort
Box K, Warm Springs, OR 97761
Tel. 503/553–1112 (800/831–0100 in the Northwest)

Administration Manager, Deborah Berman

Season Year-round.

Accommodations Luxury rooms in the cedar lodge, cottages in the village, and
furnished tepees accommodate 325. Lodge rooms have balco-
nies with views, oversize beds, full bath. Campsites, RV and
trailer hookup available.

Rates Lodge rooms $49–$59 a day single, $59–$69 double. Cottages
$39–$49 for 2, $59–$99 for up to 4 persons. 1 night payable in
advance. Credit cards: AE, CB, DC, MC, V.

Meal Plans Breakfast includes eggs, ham, bacon or sausage, Indian fry
bread, huckleberry muffins or croissants. For lunch, salads,
pizza, grilled salmon. Dinner selections may be seafood fettu-
cine, Swiss steak, baked salmon, venison steaks, game bird
baked in clay. Native salmon bake on Sat., Memorial Day–
Labor Day.

Services and
Facilities

Services: Massage. **Swimming Facilities:** Olympic-size outdoor
pool (village), outdoor pool (lodge). **Spa Facilities:** 5 tiled Roman tubs in men's and women's bathhouses. **Recreation
Facilities:** 4 tennis courts, golf course, horseback riding, trout

fishing, mountain-bike rental. **Evening Programs:** Drumming, ceremonies, rituals; salmon bake.

In the Area Nature trail walks with resident naturalist; Mt. Hood National Forest, The Dalles recreation area, white-water rafting on the Deschutes River.

Getting Here *From Portland.* By car, Hwy. 26 to Warm Springs (2½ hr). By air, scheduled commercial service to Redmond (30 min); private and charter flights land at Madras Airport 25 miles away. Van shuttle service from airport. Rental car available.

Special Notes Limited access for the disabled. Guided tours of cultural center, films for children. No smoking in pool area and designated dining areas.

Carson Hot Mineral Springs Resort

Taking the waters

Washington
Carson
The claw-footed enamel tubs are characteristic of the old-fashioned friendliness bathers enjoy at the Carson Hot Mineral Springs Resort. Proud of using "the same bath methods for over 100 years," the management strives to remain unpretentious and comfortable. The rustic cabins, a landmark hotel, and bathhouses located on the banks of the Wind River near its junction with the mighty Columbia date from 1876. The oldest remaining structure, a two-story wood hotel, was built in 1897 to accommodate bathers who traveled by steamboat from Portland, Oregon. The cabins were built in the early 1920s.

Taking the waters is a simple, two-step procedure: a tub soak followed by the traditional sweat wrap, in which an attendant wraps bathers in sheets and heavy blankets to induce a good sweat. Separate bathhouses for men and women offer some privacy.

The 126-degree mineral water is piped directly into the tubs (eight for men, six for women), which are drained and refilled after each use. The water is not treated with chemicals; analysis shows it to be high in sodium and calcium, like springs at principal European spas. The crowning touch is the half-hour ($10) or hour ($18) massage.

The mountains behind the hotel are laced with hiking trails, and there is good fishing nearby. Guests can dine at the hotel or do their own cooking in the cabins.

Carson Hot Mineral Springs Resort
Box 370, Carson, WA 98610
Tel. 509/427–8292

Administration Manager, Gloria Collins

Season Year-round.

Accommodations 9 large hotel rooms, 23 cabins, all simply furnished with double beds. No private bath, TV, or telephone. Cabin rooms have toilet and sink.

Rates Rooms and cabins $20 a day for 2 persons. Housekeeping cabins $22.50. Baths $5. 1 night payable in advance. Credit cards: MC, V.

Meal Plans 3 hearty meals daily, à la carte. Lunch menu includes pasta salad, beef lasagna, vegetarian sandwiches. Dinner entrees are a vegetarian "gardenburger," fruit platter, grilled salmon, steak, ham.

Services and Facilities **Services:** Massage. **Spa Facilities:** Individual tubs in men's and women's bathhouses. **Recreation Facilities:** Hiking, fishing.

In the Area River trips, The Dalles recreation area, Bonneville Dam, Shakespeare Festival (summer), Portland museums and cultural centers.

Getting Here *From Portland.* By car, I–84 to Bridge of the Gods, Rte. 14 to Carson (70 min).

Special Notes Limited access for the disabled. No smoking in the bathhouses.

Doe Bay Village Resort

Taking the waters

Washington
Orcas Island
The hot tubs at the rustic Doe Bay Village Resort afford spectacular views of the San Juan Islands, and the constant 106-degree temperature of the mineral water from nearby springs protects bathers from the chilly mist. Waterfalls, the ocean, hidden beaches, and a sauna with stained-glass windows help to create a special feeling of seclusion and communion.

Native Americans were the first to make a sanctuary here. Loggers and trappers came to enjoy the springs and a tavern in the town, where a general store and post office have operated since the early 1900s. In time the area became an artists' colony and a human-potential center; today the resort is a laid-back haven for lovers of hot springs, hiking, kayaking, and other outdoor life.

The village may strike you as having been caught in a time warp. The old-time general store, listed in the National Register of Historic Buildings, is now a communal kitchen—where you can cook your own meals—and the resort's main dining room. Cabins linked by covered walkways line a grassy slope above the bay.

The paint may be peeling and the plumbing may not always work, but the prices are reasonable. There are campsites (with communal baths and showers) for those who go for seclusion in the woods. Some sites have a dome of plastic sheeting for protection from the rain. Hostel-style dormitory beds at $9.50 per night are the least expensive accommodation.

Canoe, rowboat, and kayak rentals are available during the tourist season, and Moran State Park, a large, isolated part of the island, has hiking trails throughout. Its picnic areas and warm-water lakes for fishing and swimming are a few miles from the resort. A large number of day visitors come here by ferry from the mainland for a soak at the springs.

The open-air hot tubs at the resort are equipped with Jacuzzi jets; two have hot water, one is naturally cold. A wood deck surrounds the bathing complex, which is attached to a big sauna hut in which 20 people can enjoy the wood-fired heat comfortably. The price for eight hours is $5 (plus parking if you drove over from the ferry). Bring your own towels.

The tranquilizing effect of the sea air, warm water, and perhaps a massage makes up for the lack of programs or amenities. A modest series of meditation sessions has been scheduled, and this may grow into a permanent program under the resort's current owner, a former psychiatric counselor.

Doe Bay Village Resort
Star Rte. 86, Olga, WA 98279
Tel. 206/376–2291 or 206/376–4755

Administration Owner and manager, Michael Pierson

Season Year-round; meals in summer only.

Accommodations Rustic cabins for up to 100 guests range from duplexes to large cottages with private shower, heat, and bedding. No maid service, TV, telephone. Campsites, tents, RV hookups available.

Rates Cottages $29.50–$59.50 a day (2 persons). 1 night payable in advance. Credit cards: AE, MC, V.

Meal Plans Vegetarian cuisine in the resort cafe (summer season only).

Services and Facilities **Exercise Equipment:** 5-station Paramount weight training gym. **Services:** Massage, kayaking instruction. **Swimming Facilities:** Ocean beach, mountain lake. **Spa Facilities:** 3 outdoor tubs. **Recreation Facilities:** Kayaking, fishing, hiking. **Evening Programs:** Meditation.

In the Area Ferry trips to nearby islands; kayak excursions (for 4 or more); whale-watching boat trips; Seattle museums and cultural life; Olympic National Park.

Getting Here *From Seattle.* By car, I–99 to Mt. Vernon, ferry from Anacortes. Drive through Olga to east end of the island (3 hr).

Rosario Resort

Luxury pampering
Weight management

Washington
Orcas Island

Sea-inspired treatments for the body and the seaside setting are the lure of the Rosario Resort, built around the former mansion of the shipbuilder Robert Moran. Many of the guest lodges and public rooms have a nautical look; portholes and other parts salvaged from old ships pop up in the indoor swimming pool and other unexpected places. An organ room with a spectacular cathedral ceiling and stained-glass windows is the setting for concerts and lectures.

The carved figurehead of a woman, saved from a sailing ship, looks out to sea from the front lawn of the mansion. Yachters dock here on their trips through the San Juan Archipelago, and the next best way to get here is by seaplane.

Simple pleasures such as hunting for driftwood on the two-mile-long beach, wandering in the pine woods, and relaxing in the sauna attract most visitors. Families with children, senior citizens, and fitness buffs come for a few days or weeks. Canada, the Rockies, and sophisticated Vancouver are a few hours' drive north; charming Victoria is just seven miles away by water.

Orcas Island is protected by hills on one side, warmed by the Japanese current of the Pacific Ocean on the other. The winters are mild and see no snow accumulation.

The resort offers weekend retreats and five-day packages, with all services available to resort guests on an à la carte basis. The daily schedule includes low-impact and aquatic aerobics, dance exercise, stretching and toning (flexercise) calisthenics, and yoga. This is one of the few places on the West Coast to offer thalassotherapy; a body wrap with seawater or a loofah scrub with algae and oils leaves the skin tingling and refreshed.

Guests stay in villas overlooking the water that offer country-home atmosphere and great views. Fresh fish is an important part of the low-calorie spa cuisine.

Rosario Resort
Eastsound, Orcas Island, WA 98245
Tel. 206/376–2222 (800/562–8820 in WA)

Administration Manager, Sarah Geiser; spa program director, Jaylin McGuire Peacock

Season Year-round.

Accommodations 215 rooms, condominium apartments, villas, all with country antique furnishings, modern beds, private bath, color TV, air conditioning, patio. No room service.

Rates Double rooms $83 a night, studios with fireplace $89–$99. 5-day/4-night package with meals and spa treatments $399 per person double occupancy, $525 single. Weekend retreats $225 per person double, $290 single. Midweek revitalizers, 2 nights from $214.50 per person double occupancy. $100 per person deposit on spa packages or 1 night payable in advance. Credit cards: AE, MC, V.

Meal Plans 3 meals daily in the Orcas Room. Lunch can be a green salad dressed with fresh fruit juice and cayenne pepper or chicken baked in romaine lettuce. Dinner entrees may include grilled salmon with peppercorn, basil, and red-pepper sauce; veal topped with crab and asparagus. Special diets on request.

Services and Facilities Exercise Equipment: 4-station Marcy weights unit, 4-station Apollo II gym, 2 Precor rowers, 2 Monark bikes, treadmill, rebounders, dumbbells (3–50 lbs.). **Services:** Massage (Swedish, Trager, shiatsu, reflexology), body wrap, facials, salt-glow loofah body scrub, lymphatic cleansing, pedicure, manicure; full-service beauty salon. **Swimming Facilities:** 2 outdoor pools, indoor pool, ocean beach, mountain lake. **Spa Facilities:** Hot springs at Doe Bay Village Resort. **Recreation Facilities:** 6 tennis courts, horseback riding, hiking; 9-hole golf course nearby; marina; kayaking center. **Evening Programs:** Talks on health-related topics; movies.

In the Area Whale-watching boat trips, kayaking excursions, ferry trips; island crafts and antiques in Eastsound; Orcas Island Historical Museum. Seattle; Vancouver; Olympic National Park.

Getting Here *From Seattle.* By car, I–99 to Mt. Vernon, ferry from Anacortes to Eastsound (3 hr). By plane, scheduled flights to Eastsound by San Juan Airlines; seaplane and air taxi (20 min). Van service provided to and from Eastsound.

Special Notes   Limited access for the disabled; some ground-floor rooms wheelchair accessible. No smoking in the spa or in designated dining areas.

Sol Duc Hot Springs Resort

Taking the waters

Washington   Here's the place to bring the family for a soak and a swim after
Olympic National   a drive or a hike in Olympic National Park. Located within the
Park   park, the Sol Duc Hot Springs Resort maintains public and private pools, including four indoor whirlpools, filled with mineral water that flows from springs on federal land.

Piped into a heat exchanger at a temperature of 128 degrees, the mineral water is cooled for use in the three large outdoor soaking pools. The water's continuous flow into the pools makes chlorination unnecessary. Creek water is heated and treated for the large outdoor swimming pool.

Operating as a concession of the Department of the Interior, the resort has been updated and expanded in recent years. In addition to private cabins, a new six-unit motel has a country-kitchen restaurant.

The park's rugged Pacific coastline, forests, and alpine meadows draw more than 2.8 million visitors a year. A short drive from Seattle, it can be visited for a day or an extended stay during the resort season.

Sol Duc Hot Springs Resort
Soleduc River Rd., Olympic National Park, WA
(Reservations) Box 2169, Port Angeles, WA 98362
Tel. 206/327–3583

Administration   Manager, Connie Langley

Season   May–Oct.

Accommodations   36 cabins with double bed (or twin beds and sofa bed), kitchen, bath. 6 motel rooms with 2 beds, toilet, sink. No TV, telephone, dresser, or air-conditioning.

Rates   Cabin with kitchen $53 day, without kitchen $49. Motel room $38 day. 1 night payable in advance. Credit cards: MC, V.

Meal Plans   Vegetarian, fish, and chicken dishes. Granola, yogurt, smoked salmon omelet, buckwheat pancakes with fresh berries for breakfast; burgers and deli selections for lunch; char-broiled chicken, baked cod with mushrooms, steaks, or zucchini-cheese casserole for dinner.

Services and   **Swimming Facilities:** Large public pool. **Spa Facilities:** 4 indoor
Facilities   whirlpools, outdoor soaking pools. **Recreation Facilities:** Fishing, hiking. **Evening Programs:** Talks by park rangers.

In the Area   Nature hikes with park rangers. Seattle museums, cultural centers, Pioneer Square (Klondike Gold Rush museum).

Getting Here   *From Seattle.* By car, Hwy. 101 to Fairholm, Soleduc Rd. 11 miles to resort (4 hr). By car ferry, scheduled service to Winslow, Hwy. 101 to Soleduc Rd. (2 hr).

Special Notes Ramps at geothermal pools allow access for the disabled; rooms are wheelchair accessible. Nature walks for children with park ranger. No smoking in the bathhouse.

Total Health Foundation

Life enhancement
Weight management
Spiritual awareness

Washington
Yakima Valley

Coming to the Total Health Foundation is like visiting elderly cousins in the country. The rambling 50-year-old house has a wide veranda and a green lawn big enough for croquet and badminton, and it is surrounded by apple and pear orchards. The family rooms have a lived-in look. Only the presence of doctors' offices detract from the homelike ambience.

The medically supervised programs of this Seventh-day Adventist natural-healing center are designed to educate guests and restore health; they combine treatments that promote spiritual, mental, and physical well-being. The foundation-sponsored facilities are nondenominational and nonsectarian, open to everyone, and intended for those suffering from obesity and degenerative disease. Participants, limited to 10 per week, are mostly over 50 and include couples.

Camaraderie develops easily here. Everyone participates in the food and cooking demonstrations, baking bread and learning to prepare vegetarian meals. The Adventists are known for their interest in nutrition, and their "Vegan" diet of fruits, vegetables, legumes, and naturally fat foods like nuts and avocados is observed in the dining room.

The doctors treat angina, high blood pressure, atherosclerosis, diabetes, chronic fatigue, and gastrointestinal disorders. Therapy is structured for each individual.

Hiking orchard trails and country roads is part of the daily program. The closely monitored participants are expected to maintain an exercise chart and keep a personal record of physical improvement. A steam bath, whirlpool, and Swiss 12-point shower are in the house. Walking is the preferred exercise here, so there's little in the way of exercise equipment.

The personal attention from the doctors and nine staff members (including a registered dietician) helps motivate guests to help themselves. Lecture notes, reference materials, and recipes are prepared to take home.

Total Health Foundation
Old Naches Rd., Rte. 1, Box 176, Naches, WA 98937
(Office) Box 5, Yakima, WA 98907
Tel. 509/965–2555 or 800/348–0120

Administration Medical director, David Trott, M.D.

Season Year-round.

Accommodations 8 upstairs bedrooms with private bath, built-in dressers and closets, old-fashioned furniture, two beds.

Rates 7-day all-inclusive program $1,365, 14-day program $2,415. 15% discount for spouse as patient, 50% discount for nonparticipating companion. (Medical insurance may cover some costs.) 10% deposit required. Credit cards: MC, V.

Meal Plans 3 vegetarian meals daily, family style. Lunch may include green salad, cashew chow mein, steamed vegetables. Typical dinner entrees are vegetarian lasagna with mock mozzarella topping, baked tofu, or eggplant Parmesan with cheeseless topping. Lots of complex carbohydrates; no dairy products, eggs, or oils. No coffee, tea, condiments.

Services and Facilities **Exercise Equipment:** Treadmill. **Services:** Guided walks and hikes; medical tests and fitness evaluations; behavior modification program for addictions. **Swimming Facilities:** Outdoor pool. **Recreation Facilities:** Community tennis courts and golf course; fishing. **Evening Programs:** Worship hour.

In the Area Ginkgo Petrified Forest, Mt. Rainier National Park, Mt. St. Helens Volcanic Monument, Moses Lake, winery tours, Ellensburg Rodeo (Labor Day weekend), Grand Coulee Dam.

Getting Here *From Seattle.* By bus, Greyhound to Yakima (2½ hr). By car, I-90 south to Ellensburg, I-82 to Yakima, Hwy. 12 toward Naches, Eschbach Rd. to Old Naches Rd. (3 hr). Taxi or prearranged pickup at bus station.

Special Notes No smoking indoors.

Hot Springs State Park

Taking the waters

Wyoming
Thermopolis
Long before explorers discovered the Big Spring, it was a bathing place for the Shoshone and Arapahoe tribes. When the land was purchased by the federal government in 1896, the deed stipulated that the springs remain open and free to all. Thus there is no charge to bathe in the indoor and outdoor pools maintained by the State of Wyoming. A Holiday Inn, resort apartments, and a rehabilitation center are located within the one-square-mile Hot Springs State Park.

The water wells from the earth at a temperature of 135 degrees and spills down a series of mineral-glazed terraces on its way to the Big Horn River. Some of the flow is diverted to privately operated bathhouses and swimming pools and into the state-run baths. The sparkling clean and airy facilities are patronized by families en route to Yellowstone and by senior citizens from a nearby retirement home. Park and pools are open daily, 9 AM–10 PM.

The Holiday Inn on the bank of the Horn River offers the most complete facilities. There are separate men's and women's bathhouses for private soaks (coed on request), and an outdoor hydrojet pool is filled with warm mineral water. The outdoor swimming pool contains chlorinated tap water. The Athletic Club facilities are free to inn guests.

Located in central Wyoming, the town of Thermopolis is surrounded by high buttes and range land where a herd of bison still roam free; it's a pleasant stop on the way to Yellowstone from Denver and Cheyenne.

Hot Springs State Park
Thermopolis Chamber of Commerce
220 Park St., Thermopolis, WY 82443
Tel. 307/864–2636
Holiday Inn of the Waters
100 Park St., Box 1323, Thermopolis, WY 82443
Tel. 307/864–3131 or 800/465–4329

Administration Manager, James Mills; program director, Terry Johnson

Season Year-round.

Accommodations 80 rooms with modern furniture, bath, queen-size or twin beds or waterbed. Separate exercise rooms for men and women in the Athletic Club.

Rates $49 a day, double room, $45 single; $69 with two beds. Weekend Hot Water package (Jan.–May) $99.95 for 2 nights with steak dinner for 2. 1 night payable in advance. Credit cards: AE, CB, MC, V.

Meal Plans 3 meals daily in hotel restaurant. Special diets accommodated. Western steaks, grilled fish, baked mountain trout, salads in season.

Services and Facilities **Exercise Equipment:** 9-station Paramount weight training gym in men's and women's areas; punching bag, stationary bikes, 2 racquetball courts. **Services:** Massage, beauty shop. **Swimming Facilities:** Outdoor heated pool. **Spa Facilities:** 4 private mineral water tubs, outdoor Jacuzzi; sauna, steam bath, men's and women's bathhouses. **Recreation Facilities:** Bicycle rental (tandem, single); golf, fishing, skiing, snowmobiling nearby.

In the Area Outfitters offer hunting and fishing trips, scenic tours, river floats. Yellowstone National Park, Wind River Canyon, County Historical Museum (Hole in the Wall Bar), Jackson winter-sports area, Wind River Indian Reservation.

Getting Here *From Cheyenne.* By car, I–25 to Casper, Hwy. 20 via Moneta (3 hr).

Special Notes No smoking in the Athletic Club and designated areas of the dining room.

The Central States

Dallas has been in the forefront of recent fitness developments in the Central States. Dr. Kenneth Cooper, who did pioneering research in exercise and nutrition in the U.S. Air Force and at the Cooper Clinic, is the guiding spirit for the Aerobics Center's residential program. In the suburbs, the Greenhouse now offers luxury pampering and body conditioning during mother-and-daughter weeks, and the Four Seasons's preventive medicine center allows a busy executive to get a checkup between rounds of golf.

A new trend involving the crossover of European hydrotherapy and American fitness has been introduced at the recently renamed Chrysalis resort in Argyle, Texas, near Dallas. This is the first American center to feature the Kniepp herbal treatments and water exercises from Austria. Meanwhile, those who want to work out on President George Bush's home turf can head for the Phoenix Fitness Resort in the Houstonian Hotel complex.

Akia

Weight management   *Women only*
Stress control

Oklahoma Camping out with a dozen women, following a rigid weight-loss
Chickasaw diet, and getting lots of exercise are the main ingredients of the
National no-frills program at Akia. Guests are required to participate in
Recreation Area full days of hiking, stretching, and body toning in a rigorous
dawn-to-dusk schedule that takes advantage of the scenic
Arbuckle Mountains and nearby lakes and forests.

The day begins at 6 AM with exercise on the redwood deck that surrounds the main building. The two-mile hike before breakfast is followed by more stretching and toning in a lakeside pavilion.

Aerobics classes, contouring, and relaxation exercises begin the afternoon. Then participants have the option of soaking in the hot tub, getting a massage, walking, bicycling, or swimming in a nearby lake.

Akia is run like a boot camp, and its guests find the regimented program effective in reducing stress and improving fitness. Participants bring their own linens and towels and help with housekeeping. Lectures on developing healthy habits are given at the campfire around which guests cluster after dinner.

Akia
Sulphur, OK
(Office) 2316 N. W. 45th Place, Oklahoma City, OK 73112
Tel. 405/842-6269

Administration Program director, Wilhelmina Maguire

Season 6-week spring and fall seasons.

Accommodations Stone cottages and wood duplex for 11 guests. Cottages have 3 single beds, private bath.

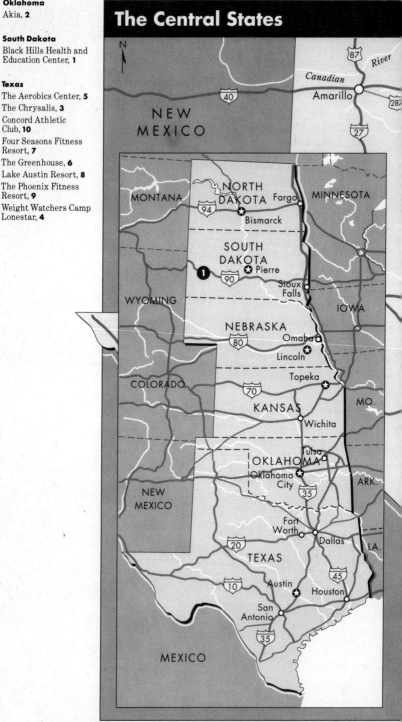

The Central States

N

NEW MEXICO

MONTANA

NORTH DAKOTA
Fargo
Bismarck

MINNESOTA

SOUTH DAKOTA
Pierre
1
Sioux Falls

WYOMING

IOWA

NEBRASKA
Omaha
Lincoln

COLORADO

Topeka

KANSAS
Wichita

MO.

NEW MEXICO

OKLAHOMA
Tulsa
Oklahoma City

ARK.

Fort Worth
Dallas

LA.

TEXAS
Austin
Houston
San Antonio

MEXICO

Amarillo
Canadian River

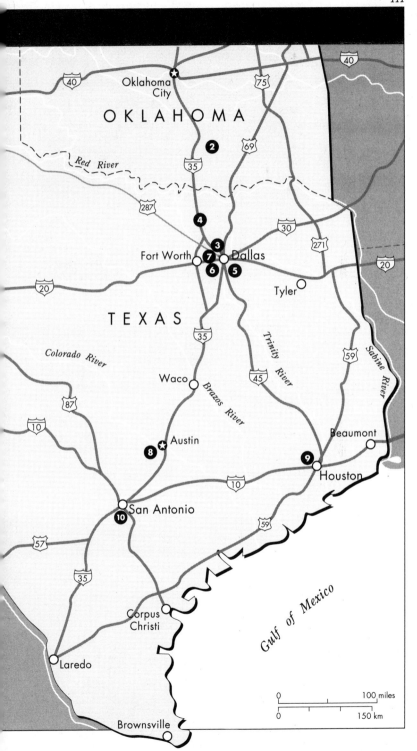

Rates $500 for 1-week session; $350 for 5-day session Sun.–Fri.; $300 for 4-night weekend. $150 advance payment. No credit cards.

Meal Plans 3 simple meals daily total 800–1,000 calories. Breakfast is cereal with fruit and juice, lunch a high-fiber protein shake. Typical dinner entrees are spinach lasagna, baked fish, eggplant Parmesan, peppers stuffed with lentils and brown rice; ricotta cheesecake is a favorite dessert.

Services and Facilities **Services:** Massage, facial, personal color analysis, body-composition test, nutritional counseling. **Swimming Facilities:** Nearby lake. **Recreation Facilities:** Bicycling. **Evening Programs:** Lectures on nutrition, shopping for health food.

In the Area Oklahoma City's Kirkpatrick Center (Native American and African art), National Cowboy Hall of Fame, Guthrie (Victorian prairie capital), Cherokee Heritage Center in Tahlequah.

Getting Here *From Oklahoma City.* By car, I–35 south to Davis, Rte. 12 to Sulphur (2 hr).

Special Notes No smoking.

Black Hills Health and Education Center

Life enhancement
Stress control
Spiritual awareness

South Dakota
Hermosa

Across three creeks and up a woodland trail, in a lodge that looks like a mountain resort, you'll find the Black Hills Health and Education Center, a Seventh-day Adventist healing center that offers programs of 12 to 25 days and a five-day vacation package.

Black Hills's medically supervised programs are designed to teach guests to develop healthy habits and to help those who suffer from diabetes, arthritis, hypertension, heart problems, and obesity. Each person's lifestyle is analyzed and a suitable regimen of exercise and diet prescribed. Rehabilitation therapy is provided for persons who have had cardiac surgery.

The program begins with a complete physical examination, blood tests, and medical counseling. Hydrotherapy (included in the program fee) and massage may be recommended; the lodge is equipped with a whirlpool, a Russian steam cabinet, and a shower that alternates hot and cold water from six sprays. Once or twice a week an excursion takes participants to a fitness center and a swimming pool fed by warm springs.

While the lectures cover stress control and nutrition, the central philosophy is one of learning by doing. Everyone joins in bread-making and cooking classes, and outings to a supermarket and restaurant are led by staff members who demonstrate how to shop for and order nutritious foods.

The health center is located in the scenic Banana Belt of the Black Hills, so named for the temperate climate and sunny days that prevail even in winter. Guests explore the canyons, cliffs, and farmlands on daily hikes.

The combined focus on spiritual, mental, and physical health attracts persons of all ages to this informal resort, though most of the participants are over 50. They arrive in motor homes that can be hooked up outside, or they stay in the lodge; some bring children and a baby-sitter.

An affiliate of the Black Hills Missionary College, the health center draws on the campus for services. Friday evening is a time when students and guests traditionally gather around the big stone fireplace in the lounge and join in a music program.

Black Hills Health and Education Center
Box 1, Hermosa, SD 57744
Tel. 605/255–4101

Administration	Program director, Klaus Irrgang; medical director, Glen Wiltse, M.D.
Season	Year-round.
Accommodations	12 rooms in a 2-story lodge, modern furnishings, mostly double beds, private and shared baths. Motor-home services.
Rates	12-day program $1,250 single, $1,899 couple; 25-day program $1,980 single, $2,990 couple. $84–$160 reduction for motor-home occupants. Wellness vacation packages, 5–12 days, $645–$1,999. $100 per person advance payment. No credit cards.
Meal Plans	3 vegetarian meals daily, buffet style. Fruits, vegetables, legumes, and natural fat sources such as nuts and avocados. Lunch and dinner include salad bar, water-steamed vegetables, entrees such as vegetarian lasagna with mock-cheese topping, baked tofu, cashew chow mein. Whole-grain bread baked daily. No dairy products, eggs, coffee, tea, condiments.
Services and Facilities	**Exercise Equipment:** Schwinn Air-Dyne bikes, rowing machines, trampoline. **Services:** Massage, hydrotherapy, medical consultation. **Swimming Facilities:** At nearby fitness center. **Spa Facilities:** Mineral hot springs nearby. **Recreation Facilities:** Gold panning, rock collecting; downhill skiing nearby. **Evening Programs:** Informal talks and films on health-related topics. Music program Fri.
In the Area	Evans Plunge hot springs, a naturally heated indoor mineral-water pool; Custer State Park wildlife preserve; Rapid City; Mt. Rushmore; the Black Hills Passion Play (summer); The Homestead, a working gold mine at Lead; antique train ride from Hill City; Badlands National Park; Wind Cave National Park (caverns); prehistoric excavations.
Getting Here	*From Rapid City.* By car, Hwy. 79 south to Hermosa, Hwy. 40 west to entrance road (40 min). Free pickup to and from Rapid City airport and bus station.
Special Notes	Specially equipped rooms, ramps for the disabled. No smoking indoors.

The Aerobics Center

Weight management
Nutrition and diet
Preventive medicine

Texas Developed by the Cooper Clinic, a recognized leader in the
Dallas study of the medical value of exercise, the Aerobics Program
for Total Well-Being at the Aerobics Center is a residential program designed to help participants achieve permanent changes
in lifestyle. Programs of 7–13 days and a 3-day wellness weekend teach the adoption and cultivation of healthy habits.

At first look, the Aerobics Center Guest Lodge seems more like
a country club than a medical clinic; the stately redbrick mansion is for the exclusive use of guests, members, and visiting
professionals.

Four exercise sessions are part of each day's program. You can
work out on a treadmill or walk and jog on paved and lighted
trails that wind through the 30-acre wooded estate. A gymnasium has basketball and racquetball courts and a three-lane
running track. Two heated outdoor lap pools are six lanes wide
and 75 feet long. The four outdoor Laykold lighted tennis
courts are equipped with automatic ball machines.

Your stay begins with a full physical examination. The first
day's schedule sees a chest X-ray, a test for pulmonary function, and vision, hearing, and dental exams. A standard skin-
fold test and weigh-in on an underwater scale determines your
ideal body weight. Blood pressure is measured during and after
exercise, and an ECG treadmill test measures stress. Before
and after the program, 24 blood tests, including HDL and LDL
for cholesterol, are administered. (Your health insurance may
cover this part of the program cost.) The comprehensive medical report determines the exercise program that will be
recommended for you.

Classes begin on your second day. Specialists lecture on nutrition and health, and you participate in cooking and bread-
making demonstrations. Volleyball, aerobics in the swimming
pool, and other forms of group exercise are scheduled. Evenings are reserved for massages or a walk. The whirlpool,
sauna, and steam room are open every night; participants are
entitled to two 30-minute massages a week, one on the weekend.

The combination of a supportive environment, state-of-the-art
equipment and facilities, and the professional staff creates a
disciplined program, and significant results have been seen in
lowering cholesterol and triglyceride levels in only two weeks.
Follow-up calls and return visits have confirmed participants
success in lowering blood pressure and increasing vitality and
alertness.

Limited to groups of no more than 20, the program appeals to
high-powered executives who have lost control of their health.
Here they work with a team of nine full-time physicians, a den-
tist, nutritionists, and exercise technologists. Guided by Dr.
Kenneth H. Cooper, whose pioneering research on aerobics inspired the founding of the center, these professionals make

wellness meaningful to everyday life. The center encourages friends and couples to work together on behavior modification.

The Aerobics Center

12230 Preston Rd., Dallas, TX 75230
Tel. 214/386–0306 or 800/527–0362
Telex 791578/AEROBICCTR DAL, Fax 214/386–5415

Administration Program director, Roy E. Vartabedian; medical director, Kenneth H. Cooper, M.D.

Season Sessions scheduled year-round.

Accommodations 32 rooms, 8 suites, with heavy mahogany king- or queen-size beds, wing chairs, private bath. A grand staircase dominates the marble lobby.

Rates 13-day program $3,795 all-inclusive, 7-day program $2,595, 3-day weekend $925. With a spouse or companion, 13 days $3,301 per person, 7 days $2,329 per person, weekend $877 per person. Suites: 13 days $3,587 per person; 7 days $2,483 per person; weekend $877–$1,087 per person. $500 advance payment, 7-day and 13-day programs; $250 in advance for the weekend. Credit cards: AE, MC, V.

Meal Plans 3 calorie-controlled meals daily. Low in fat and cholesterol, lunch choices include spinach lasagna or Cajun chicken fillet sandwich on whole-grain bread. Typical dinner entrees are a skewer of sea scallops and fresh vegetables on rice pilaf; medallions of veal with fresh steamed vegetables. Tossed salad and dessert (poached pears, raspberry sorbet) served with lunch and dinner. Decaffeinated coffee and tea.

Services and Facilities **Exercise Equipment:** 15-station Nautilus units, 5-station Universal weights gym, free weights, 5 Lifecycles, 5 Aerobocycles, 13 Schwinn Air-Dyne bikes, 2 recumbent bikes, 4 Pacer treadmills, Bally Liferower, Concept II rowing machine, StairMaster, Versaclimber. **Services:** Personal counseling on fitness, diet, and exercise; medical testing and evaluation. Swedish massage; hair, nail, and skin care in beauty salon. **Swimming Facilities:** 2 heated outdoor pools. **Recreation Facilities:** 4 25-yard racquetball courts, 4 tennis courts, volleyball, basketball, handball. Golf course nearby. **Evening Programs:** Talks on nutrition and health; walks and massage.

In the Area Dinner at an Italian restaurant; White Rock Lake; the Omnimax film theater in Fort Worth; Dallas Museum of Art, Kennedy Memorial, Fort Worth Science Center, Dallas Arboretum and Botanical Garden.

Getting Here *From Dallas.* By car, Hwy. 635 (LBJ Freeway), Preston Rd. (20 min). Free limousine service to and from Dallas–Fort Worth International Airport for 7-day and 13-day program guests.

Special Notes Ramps and elevator provide access to all areas. No smoking indoors. Remember to bring recent medical records, a watch with second hand, calculator, exercise clothing.

The Chrysalis

Life enhancement
Luxury pampering

Texas
Argyle

European hydrotherapy and American fitness concepts meet at the attractive hillside hacienda of the Chrysalis in Denton County, where Spanish colonial buildings open onto a gracious courtyard. Water treatments stimulate circulation and soothe your nerves while physiologists, therapists, and a nutritionist devise programs to revitalize your entire body.

The therapy, based on the teachings of Father Sebastian Kniepp, an early health advocate in Bavaria, relies on the curative properties of water. It involves bathing in herbal essences, contrasting hot and cold footbaths, and a hay pack heat treatment for liver ailments. Specially designed hydrotherapy tubs have whirlpools and underwater massage. The refrigerator in each guest room is stocked with mineral water.

The holistic approach to health attempts to release stress and detoxify the body. Following a fitness-level assessment, your personalized program is prepared and exercise classes scheduled; participants do the latest in low-impact aerobics and work out with stretch bands.

A heated indoor pool provides space for hydroaerobics, and the panoramic views from the exercise rooms are a special treat.

The Chrysalis
294 Country Club Rd., Argyle, TX 76226
Tel. 817/464–7220 or 800/458–7727

Administration Executive director, Laura Lewis

Season Year-round except Christmas Day–New Year's Day.

Accommodations 19 rooms decorated in desert tones, with wicker chairs, queen-size beds with fluffy comforters, dressing room, bath, and TV.

Rates 2-night/3-day weekend $369 single, $295 per person double, $195 per person with 4 in a room; 5-day Vitalizer package $859 single, $649 per person double; 1-day visit with Kniepp treatment and lunch $195. $200 in advance for packages, $100 for weekend. Credit cards: AE, MC, V.

Meal Plans 3 gourmet meals. 850-calorie diet includes buckwheat pancakes with fresh blueberries for breakfast; a luncheon salad of watercress with coconut-lemon dressing, couscous, or tabouli; and perhaps grilled swordfish or braised scallops for dinner. Coffee and tea.

Services and Facilities **Exercise Equipment:** Treadmill, Monark bike, Lifecycle, rowing machine, free weights, ankle and hand weights, stretch bands. **Services:** Hair, skin, and nail care, including facials, clay packs, and hay pack; loofah body scrub, herbal whirlpool bath, alternate foot or arm baths, sitz bath; health consultations. **Swimming Facilities:** Indoor pool with sun deck. **Recreation Facilities:** Croquet, volleyball, badminton, nature trail walks. Golf and tennis nearby. **Evening Programs:** Lectures on health and fitness, concerts, cooking classes; videocassette library.

In the Area Fort Worth museums, shopping.

Getting Here *From Dallas.* By car, I–35 to Denton, left on Fort Worth Dr. to Argyle, left of Country Club Rd. (40 min). Free pickup to and from Dallas–Fort Worth International Airport. Taxi, car rental available.

Special Notes Limited access for the disabled. No smoking indoors.

Concord Athletic Club

Luxury pampering
Sports conditioning

Texas The four floors and 60,000 square feet of the Concord Athletic
San Antonio Club contain an extraordinary health facility that offers a seven-day physical fitness training program whose participants range in age from two to 80. The wide expanses of glass in the spectacular contemporary structure provide dramatic vistas of San Antonio and add to a general sense of spaciousness.

Body toning through water sports in the Olympic-size pool is a primary goal. Racquetball and squash are popular. A physician supervises workouts with weight training equipment, treadmills, and bicycling. Out-of-town guests of the club stay at nearby hotels.

Concord Athletic Club
7700 Jones Maltsberger, San Antonio, TX 78216
Tel. 512/828–8880

Administration Program director, Steve Jensen

Season Daily except Thanksgiving, Christmas Day, New Year's Day.

Accommodations Nearby hotels are the Marriott and Embassy Suites.

Rates $10 per day for hotel guests. Hotel concierge makes arrangements.

Meal Plans 3 meals daily in the Concord Cafe. Fruit plate, cereals, yogurt for breakfast; salad bar, pasta, chicken Sicilian style for lunch; broiled fish, steak, spinach lasagna for dinner. Salt only on request.

Services and **Exercise Equipment:** 15-station Nautilus weight training units,
Facilities Liferowers, NordicTrack cross-country ski machine, stationary bikes, treadmills, StairMaster, free weights. **Services:** Massage; hair, skin, and nail care; aerobics classes, fitness evaluation. **Swimming Facilities:** 25-meter indoor lap pool. **Recreation Facilities:** 6 racquetball courts, 4 squash courts, indoor running track, full-court gym; golf and tennis courts nearby. **Evening Programs:** Seminars on health and fitness.

In the Area The Alamo, historic Old Town, theaters, shopping.

Getting Here *From San Antonio.* The club, located 3 miles from the airport, can be reached from I–37 (McAllister Freeway) at the Jones Maltsberger exit. Free airport pickup by hotel.

Special Notes Elevator provides access for the disabled. No smoking indoors.

Four Seasons Fitness Resort

Life enhancement
Preventive medicine
Luxury pampering

Texas
Irving

Teamwork between health professionals, a luxury hotel, and an urban developer has produced the stunning new Four Seasons Fitness Resort near the center of the Dallas–Fort Worth business belt. For corporate executives this is a one-stop health club where productivity and fitness are partners; for vacationers with a taste for elegance and romance, this may be the ultimate urban escape.

Space-age design and Old World architecture meet in the 12,000-acre Las Colinas Urban Center, where the Four Seasons Hotel and Spa is the centerpiece of a golf course surrounded by canals and a monorail system. Lining the waterway are shops, cafes, and the Mandalay Hotel—reminiscent of a Mediterranean village. The spa, connected by an underground tunnel, offers 23 daily exercise classes, weight training, total fitness regimens, stretch groups, water works, and a range of indoor sport and workout facilities.

The bonus is the Preventive Medicine Center, where cardiologists, internists, and orthopedists evaluate your health in order to prescribe a fitness regimen. Using computers and high-tech stress tests, the team assembles a comprehensive physical profile that includes diagnostic exercise testing, evaluations of blood chemistry and body mass, and an overall assessment of your fitness level. This option, available to hotel guests staying seven nights or more, is $550 in conjunction with the spa package.

Programs can be tailored to suit your needs: You can work out on the advanced Nautilus equipment, do aerobics and bodybuilding exercises, and play a round of golf or team up for tennis. Packages for two to seven nights include accommodations, meals, and unlimited participation in resort activity; golf and medical services are extra.

Spa treatments and beauty salon services are included in all packages and can be booked on an à la carte basis. Services range from massage to aromatherapy, herbal wraps, and baths. There are two sets of Jacuzzis, saunas, steam rooms and hot/cold pools. The spa program, limited to 50 people, assures personal attention from the staff. You can arrive here any day of the week. Because the hotel hosts corporate meetings, and members of the Sports Club have access to the spa, there is no group camaraderie. Spa activities include excursions to museums, a health-food shop, and shows in town. Lectures on health and nutrition are scheduled during lunch and dinner.

Two Tournament Players golf courses, indoor and outdoor tennis courts, and jogging tracks leave little to be desired in the way of sports facilities. Squash and racquetball courts, indoor and outdoor swimming pools, clinics, and private instruction are also available.

The "alternatives" menu served in the garden cafe and the main dining room keeps dieters on course. Regular selections are available as well.

Four Seasons Fitness Resort
4150 N. MacArthur Blvd., Irving, TX 75062
Tel. 214/717–0700 or 800/332–3442
Telex 735319

Administration Manager, Jim FitzGibbon; program director, Mary Beth Harrison

Season Year-round.

Accommodations 315 rooms in the Four Seasons Hotel; spa guests get superior and deluxe rooms with private balconies when available, comfortable living area, 3 telephones, cable TV, marble bath with separate tub and shower.

Rates $100 per day on average; can be combined with $150 pampering package. Weekends $580 single, $444 per person double. 7-day/6-night program $1,745 single, $1,339 per person double. $100 advance payment or credit card confirmation. Credit cards: AE, DC, MC, V.

Meal Plans 3 meals daily in package, with caloric, cholesterol, sodium monitoring. Menu selections are broiled chicken, Mexican chicken enchilada, grilled salmon, roast quail with fresh berry sauce. Preselected menu totals 1,000 calories per day.

Services and Facilities **Exercise Equipment:** 12-station Nautilus units, free weights, 6 Lifecycles, 4 treadmills, 2 rowing machines, 10 Schwinn Air-Dyne bikes, 4 ergometers, cross-country ski unit. **Services:** Massage, aromatherapy, herbal wraps, herbal baths, loofah body scrub, shiatsu. Beauty salon for facials, hair, skin, and nail care. Physical examination and counseling at Las Colinas Preventive Medical Center. Personal health and lifestyle profile, body-composition and nutritional analysis. Daily change of workout clothing. Guided morning walks; exercise classes. **Swimming Facilities:** 25-meter and Olympic-size outdoor pools, 75-foot indoor lap pool. **Recreation Facilities:** 8 outdoor, 4 indoor tennis courts, 7 racquetball courts, 2 squash courts, basketball court, 2 golf courses. **Evening Programs:** Talks during dinner on health, lifestyle, work, parenthood.

In the Area Scheduled trips to museums, health-food store, shopping malls; Texas Stadium, Market Center, State Fair Music Hall, Arts District.

Getting Here *From Dallas.* By car, Hwy. 183 (Airport Freeway), Hwy. 35 (MacArthur Blvd.) (20 min). Free limousine service to and from Dallas–Fort Worth International Airport; taxi, rental car available.

Special Notes Limited access for the disabled. Programs for children include supervised activity on weekends, golf and tennis clinics, and hotel plan allows free or shared accommodations. No smoking in the spa or designated dining areas. Nonsmoking rooms available.

The Greenhouse

Life enhancement   *Women only*
Luxury pampering

Texas
Arlington

Privacy and freedom from stress are precious commodities to the harried young career women and the celebrities who check into the Greenhouse for a week of physical and emotional rejuvenation. Completely self-contained, with a staff of more than 125 serving just 39 guests, the retreat focuses on well-being and beauty.

You hardly notice the tacky neighborhood as you are whisked from the airport in a chauffered limousine. Arlington, better known for its Six Flags Over Texas theme park, has been a special destination for the knowledgeable spa set since 1965, when the Greenhouse was built by the fashion trendsetters Neiman Marcus and Charles of the Ritz. While the resort has maintained its high standard of service and elegant accommodations, it has expanded its program to appeal to the special needs of its guests. Repeaters make up 75% of the clientele.

Thoughtful attention to detail distinguishes a stay here. Each guest is assigned a personal facialist, hairdresser, manicurist, and masseuse for the week. A resident physiologist and nurse help plan a schedule to the individual's needs.

Breakfast in bed begins the day at 7 AM. Your daily schedule comes on the tray, and a fresh leotard and robe await you. A brisk guided walk through the garden is followed by exercise classes to flex and tone the body. Choices include low-impact aerobics, weight training techniques, cardiovascular workouts, and water workouts in the pool. Your personal trainer studies your fitness profile (prepared on your arrival) and works with you at your pace. Interval training and relaxation techniques are among the new concepts introduced under the direction of Toni Beck.

Lunch is served poolside, perhaps to be followed by a massage and serious pampering. Daily schedules are adhered to unless guests request otherwise. Evenings tend to be dressy or informal, depending on the guests, yet the setting reflects everything you've ever seen on TV about Texan elegance and style.

Airy, bright, and expensively furnished, the Greenhouse has the look of a semitropical sybaritic hideaway. The skylighted marble-floored atrium for swimming and the luxuriously feminine bedrooms are very much a part of the therapy.

The Greenhouse
107th St., Box 1144, Arlington, TX 76010
Tel. 817/640–4000 or 800/637–5882
Fax 817/649–0422

Administration
Executive director, Judy Stell; spa operations director, Toni Beck

Season
Year-round except early July and Dec. Programs begin and end on Sun.; 3-day miniweeks sometimes available.

Accommodations
39 single rooms, 2 suites with queen-size half-canopied beds, matching drapes. Hand-embroidered linens, large dressing area, sunken tubs.

Rates $2,975–$3,025 per week; suite shared by 2, $2,950 per person; 3 days $1,200. $500 in advance, nonrefundable. Credit cards: AE, MC, V.

Meal Plans 850–1,200 or 2,000 calories a day. 3 meals plus midmorning snack and afternoon fruit frappe. Homemade bran muffin, fresh melon and raspberries, coffee or tea for breakfast; vegetable pizza with green salad, lobster-and-crab salad, cheese soufflé with fruit at lunch; Cornish hens stuffed with shallots and breast meat, broiled lamb chops, grilled salmon at dinner. Gooey chocolate cake or hot apricot soufflé for those not dieting.

Services and Facilities **Exercise Equipment:** 6-station Universal weight training gym, Nautilus units, 2 Trotter treadmills, 8 stationary bikes, cross-country NordicTrack, StairMaster, body-ball weights, hand weights, poles, elastic Thoro-bands. **Services:** Massage, facials; hair, skin, and nail care; one-on-one workouts. Personal fitness, nutrition, health, beauty, and relaxation programs. Cooking classes. **Swimming Facilities:** Indoor and outdoor pools. **Recreation Facilities:** 2 tennis courts, parcourse, jogging track. **Evening Programs:** Discussion topics are stress, wellness, makeup, cosmetic surgery; entertainment, feature films, fashion shows.

In the Area Neiman Marcus, Dallas Arts District, State Fair Music Hall, Texas Stadium, shopping malls.

Getting Here *From Dallas.* By car, I–30 to Arlington, Hwy. 360 to Avenue H, left to 107th St. (20 min). Free transportation to and from airport; taxi, rental car available.

Special Notes No smoking in public areas.

Lake Austin Resort

Life enhancement
Luxury pampering

Texas
Austin
Hill-country walks, water aerobics, and a range of body-toning exercise classes make up the week-long program at the Lake Austin Resort. The family-oriented retreat provides a great escape in a part of Texas noted for scenic rolling hills and placid lakes.

European facials with Clarins skin-care products and a full-service salon for hair and skin care are available à la carte. Package rates are limited to 16 physical-fitness classes offered daily, meals, and programs on lifestyle enhancement.

One of the nice touches here is a roommate-matching service. If you want to share accommodations for extra savings, ask about a compatible person who is registered for the program. Stays of less than a week are available, and you can arrive on any day of the week. First-time visitors get an added bonus: $100 toward pampering services during a week's stay.

The facilities include a set of saunas and steam rooms for men and women, coed Jacuzzi, and indoor and outdoor swimming pools. The glass-walled gym and parcourse overlook Lake Austin. Hiking and jogging trails extend into the woods. Guests have free use of classes and exercise equipment, or they can simply relax outdoors.

"Renewal" is the buzzword of the new management that took over the resort in 1983. Formerly a fishing village (and at one time a nudist colony), the spa now specializes in casual and sophisticated spa treatments.

Lake Austin Resort
1705 Quinlan Rd., Austin, TX 78732
Tel. 512/266–2444 or 800/847–5637

Administration	Manager, Deborah Evans
Season	Year-round.
Accommodations	40 small cabins provide rustic comfort with twin beds, TV, air conditioning, private bath. Larger deluxe units have vaulted ceilings and lake views.
Rates	$105–$160 a day. Sun.–Sun. package $623–$693 double, $875–$945 single, plus $165 service charge and 6% tax. $200 per person deposit for 1-week program. Credit cards: AE, MC, V.
Meal Plans	3 meals daily, 900 calories suggested for women, 1,200 for men. Fruit or juice, scrambled eggs, tortilla, or muffin for breakfast. Lunch and dinner feature seasonal salads, artichoke-mushroom quiche, fish and asparagus roll-ups, honey-crunch chicken, enchilada casserole, vegetarian lasagna. Yogurt ambrosia with fruit and ricotta cheese for dessert.
Services and Facilities	**Exercise Equipment:** 6-station Universal weight training gym, Lifecycle, Schwinn Air-Dyne bikes, treadmill, rowing machine, hand weights. **Services:** Massage therapy; skin, hair, nail care; facials. Personal consultation on fitness, nutrition, skin analysis, special dietary needs. **Swimming Facilities:** Indoor and outdoor pools. **Recreation Facilities:** Volleyball, badminton, tennis; golf and horseback riding nearby. **Evening Programs:** Talks on health and fitness.
In the Area	University of Texas, state capitol, L. B. Johnson Library and museum.
Getting Here	*From Austin.* By car, Ranch Rd. 2222, FM 620 to Quinlan Park Rd. (45 min). Free transfers to and from Austin Airport. Taxi, rental car available.
Special Notes	All facilities on one level. No smoking in public areas.

The Phoenix Fitness Resort

Life enhancement
Nutrition and diet
Luxury pampering

Texas
Houston
Providing the motivation for lasting change rather than a quick fix has been the goal at the Phoenix Fitness Resort since 1980. Practical habits that you can take home are emphasized here, and diet is not considered synonymous with self-denial.

Until you've had a brisk two-mile morning walk through the pine trees of this complex, it's hard to imagine that the 22-acre retreat is just minutes from the city's smoggy freeways. The combination of the Houstonian Medical Center and the deluxe Houstonian Hotel makes it possible to enjoy a healthy getaway for a few days or a full week.

The fitness program, held in a former mansion that sits in the center of the complex, has changed with the times. Pampering and weight loss are deemphasized now; the majority of the stressed-out professionals who come here are women, but more men and couples are showing up for special weeks designed around their needs. Options include health and fitness, stress control, and total-image weeks.

The goal is to improve one's self-image while learning healthy eating habits and exercising properly within one's limits. Tests to measure basal metabolism, cardiovascular capacity, body composition, and muscular flexibility and strength are administered at the medical center upon your arrival. A fitness specialist uses the data to help you formulate a take-home program during a midweek consultation.

The tightly scheduled program is challenging, but the staff and exercise instructors give lots of support. And camaraderie develops quickly among the 20 or so participants. The high-tech exercise system called Powercize, with computerized machines that greet you by name and keep tabs on calories burned, brightens workouts. Facilities at the health club include an indoor banked running track, Olympic-size swimming pool, whirlpools, saunas, steam rooms, and tennis and racquetball courts.

Each week's program has a different emphasis: a fitness plan concentrates on exercise, with guest specialists for lectures and classes; stress management programs feature pampering. All include low-impact aerobic workouts in a specially designed studio that has a cushioned floor, exercise sessions in the pool, bodywork, and beauty-salon services. Additional professional and personal services, available à la carte, can be booked and billed through the hotel.

The Phoenix Fitness Resort
111 N. Post Oak La., Houston, TX 77024
Tel. 713/680–1601 or 800/548–4700 (800/548–4701 in TX)

Administration Manager, Kathleen Hargiss; program director, Kathy Driscoll

Season Year-round.

Accommodations Fitness plan guests stay in a wing of the 300-room Houstonian Hotel; luxury single rooms have cable TV, private bath.

Rates $475 a day includes room; 2-night weekend $550, single or double. Week-long package plans $2,500–$2,800 per person. $750 in advance for one-week program, nonrefundable; credit card confirmation for hotel. Credit cards: AE, MC, V.

Meal Plans Simple meals at a buffet breakfast, table service at lunch and dinner, and juice breaks. 1,000 calories daily, mainly fresh vegetables, fruits, lean meats, whole grains. No caffeine, sugar, or salt. Low-fat, high-carbohydrate meals include asparagus spears in whole-wheat crepes, baked chicken breast in lemon-saffron sauce, and poached chicken with carrots. Desserts are baked apple in parchment, pumpkin mousse.

Services and Facilities **Exercise Equipment:** 6-unit Powercise system, David pneumatic weight training units, stationary bikes, Universal weight training gym, free weights, wrist and ankle weights. **Services:** Massage, manicure, pedicure, facials, aromatherapy, herbal wrap, body scrub, makeup, hairstyling. Medical examination, fitness evaluation, nutritional counseling. Daily spa wardrobe provided. **Swimming Facilities:** 1 indoor, 2 outdoor pools. **Recreation Facilities:** 8 racquetball courts, 5 outdoor tennis courts, parcourse, jogging trail. **Evening Programs:** Talks on health and nutrition.

In the Area Shopping, museums, concerts, opera season, Alley Theater.

Getting Here *From Houston.* By car, Hwy. 610 N, Woodway Memorial Exit (20 min). Free limousine service on arrival and departure; taxi, rental car available.

Special Notes Elevators, ramps provide access for the disabled. No smoking.

Weight Watchers Camp Lonestar

Youth camps for weight loss

Texas Weight Watchers Camp Lonestar, a coed summer camp for
Denton young people 10 to 21 years old, provides a balanced regimen of fitness, diet, and education on an active vacation. Located on the Selwyn School campus in the Dallas–Fort Worth area, the camp features outdoor sports facilities, outdoor swimming pool, private lake, and weights room.

Meals are prepared from the recipes of Weight Watchers International. Campers learn to eat properly in classes on food preparation and lectures on nutrition.

Accredited counselors supervise full weeks of workouts, slimnastics and aerobics classes, and sports. Those who complete the course are guaranteed to lose weight—or they get a refund.

Weight Watchers Camp Lonestar
3333 University Dr. W, Denton, TX 76201
Tel. 817/387–4201
Weight Watchers Camps
183 Madison Ave., New York, NY 10016
Tel. 212/889–9500 or 800/223–5600 (800/251–4141 in Canada)

Administration Program director, Anthony Sparber

Season June–Aug.

Accommodations Dormitories with modern bath; lounge facilities. Bedrooms shared by 2.

Rates Sessions of 2–7 weeks from $1,450. $100 in advance. Credit cards: AE, DC, MC, V.

Meal Plans 3 balanced meals a day in the cafeteria, 2 snacks in residence halls.

Services and Facilities **Exercise Equipment:** Weights room with Universal equipment; gymnasium equipment. **Swimming Facilities:** Outdoor pool, private lake. **Recreation Facilities:** Basketball, soccer, softball, tennis; jogging; rowing, canoeing, sailing. **Evening Programs:**

Campfires, fashion shows, dramatics, talent shows, movies, lighted outdoor amphitheater for stage productions.

In the Area Nature walks.

Getting Here Campers picked up at Dallas–Fort Worth airport. Taxi, rental car available.

Special Notes No smoking indoors.

The Middle West

Fitness resorts are a relatively recent phenomenon in the Middle West; their programs are informal and outdoors oriented, they capitalize on scenic locations, and their focus tends to be on weight loss and general well-being.

Wisconsin offers the widest variety of choices, from the no-frills Wooden Door to the sophisticated pampering of the Olympia Village Resort. In Ohio you can work out in a registered historic landmark at the Kerr House, and Americana and Victorian antiques enhance the ambience of the newly expanded Aurora House Spa. French Lick Springs in Indiana and the Elms in Missouri are older, traditional resorts that offer thermal waters.

Heartland Health and Fitness Retreat

Life enhancement
Stress control
Nutrition and diet

Illinois
Gilman

Guests are made to feel at home in the Heartland Health and Fitness Retreat's lakefront mansion, which is rather like being at an adult camp in the country. The guest list is limited to 28, and your day can be as structured or unstructured as you please. You don't need to sign up for scheduled exercise classes, but appointments for massage and facials should be made in advance. Since bodywork and beauty treatments are included in the package price, most guests take advantage of them—and add further pampering services at their own expense.

The weekend is the busiest time; van loads of Chicagoans arrive on Friday evening via complimentary transportation from the Loop. Yet the best deal is a five-day stay, from Sunday to Friday noon, that includes four massages and a facial for $1,100 double occupancy.

High-tech workouts with weight machines are held in the barn, an impressive three-level fitness center reached through an underground passage from the house. This barn is unlike anything on the neighboring farms; it has a full complement of cardiovascular workout equipment, pneumatic resistance muscle movers, an indoor swimming pool, whirlpool, sauna, steam room, and private massage rooms. The 30-acre estate is ideal for winter and summer sports, including ice skating when the lake freezes.

Personal consultation with staff members is encouraged, the quick-fix approach discouraged. They advise you to concentrate on activities you enjoy and to keep them up when you return home. (Try yoga and race walking!)

Group support is important here. Workout clothing—T-shirts, shorts, sweat suits, socks, and outdoor gear for cold weather—serves as a uniform. At 6:30 AM, ready for the brisk morning walk, everyone lines up to massage the shoulders of the person in front. The general-issue sweat suit is acceptable attire for lounging fireside or watching a movie on the VCR in the evening.

Heartland Health and Fitness Retreat

Gilman, IL 60938
(Office) 18 E. Chestnut St., Chicago, IL 60611
Tel. 312/266–2050 (office) or 815/683–2182 (spa)

Administration   Executive director, Michael Livesay; nutrition and education director, Susan Witz

Season   Year-round.

Accommodations   28 pine-furnished rooms with country antiques, down-filled comforters, twin beds, private bath with hair dryer, toiletries, large fluffy towels.

Rates   2-day weekend package $440 per person double occupancy, $660 single; 7 days $1,450 double, $2,175 single. Roommate matching on request. Taxes and gratuities included. 50% deposit. Credit cards: AE, MC, V.

Meal Plans   3 meals daily (table service). Snacks and fruit all day. Breakfast includes freshly baked muffins, hot and cold cereal, coffee on request. Vegetarian menu; dairy products, fish served occasionally. No salt, sugar, or added fats. 1,200 calories a day for women, 1,500 for men. Lunch can include hearty soup, vegetable pâté, or Japanese mushroom salad; typical dinner entrees are grilled swordfish with rosemary, Peruvian fish stew, corn crepes with spinach soufflé, fish and vegetable brochettes.

Services and Facilities   **Exercise Equipment:** Keiser Cam II pneumatic resistance equipment, Cybex and Tunturi exercycles, Amerec rowing machines, free weights, hand weights, StairMaster, soft joggers, NordicTrack cross-country ski machine, trampolines. **Services:** Massage therapy (sports, relaxation, foot), facial, manicure, pedicure, hair and skin care; personal fitness assessment, nutrition evaluation, color analysis, image enhancement. **Swimming Facilities:** Indoor pool, 3-acre lake. **Recreation Facilities:** Outdoor tennis court, parcourse, hiking, cross-country skiing (equipment provided), running track. **Evening Programs:** Informal discussions on health-related topics. Guest speakers on stress management, life enhancement.

In the Area   Architecture of Frank Lloyd Wright in Oak Park, Abraham Lincoln's home and tomb in Springfield.

Getting Here   *From Chicago.* By car, the Dan Ryan Expwy. south, I–57 to Kanakee Exit 308, Hwy. 52/45 (becomes Hwy. 49) to Rte. 24, R.R. 122 (90 min). Free van service to and from downtown Chicago.

Special Notes   No smoking indoors.

French Lick Springs Resort

Taking the waters
Non-program resort facilities

Indiana
French Lick   Modeled on the great spas of Europe, the French Lick Springs Resort was built in the early 1800s and attracted a wealthy elite who came from all over the country to "take the waters" in as many ways as they could. The sulfurous spring water was

Illinois
Heartland Health and
Fitness Retreat, **7**

Indiana
French Lick Springs
Resort, **9**
Weight Watchers Camp
Hoosier, **8**

Minnesota
Birdwing Spa, **1**

Missouri
The Elms Resort, **5**
Marriott's Tan-Tar-A
Resort, **6**

Ohio
Aurora House Spa, **11**
The Kerr House, **10**
Sans Souci Health
Resort, **12**

Wisconsin
The American Club, **2**
Olympia Village
Resort, **3**
The Wooden Door, **4**

The Middle West

NORTH DAKOTA

SOUTH DAKOTA

MINNESOTA

Duluth

St. Cloud

St. Paul

Minneapolis

NEBRASKA

IOWA

Sioux City

Des Moines

Cedar Rapids

MISSOURI

Kansas City

Jefferson City

KANSAS

Springfield

Missouri River

Des Moines River

0 100 miles

0 150 km

Lake Superior

ONTARIO

N

Sault Ste. Marie

WISCONSIN

Lake Huron

75

Green Bay

41 43

27

Lake Michigan

2

90
94

3

MICHIGAN

Madison

Milwaukee

Grand Rapids

75

Beloit

4 94

96

Lansing

Detroit

196

94

Ann
Arbor

Lake Erie

90

venport

90

Toledo

80
90

11

80

Chicago

8

South
Bend

10

Cleveland

55

Gary

71

77

ILLINOIS

7

Fort
Wayne

OHIO

57

65

69

70

74

74

41

ingfield

55

70

Indianapolis

Dayton

12

Columbus

St. Louis

INDIANA

Cincinnati

55

65

52

57

9

Ohio River

64

Wabash River

KENTUCKY

bottled and marketed as Pluto Water, and today it is still used in the Pluto Bath in the hotel health club.

Recently restored to its original Victorian elegance in a costly renovation, the 450-room resort hotel has high-ceilinged rooms with ceiling fans, French doors, carved woodwork, and verandas that overlook formal gardens. Its 2,600 acres of lawns and rolling woodland add to the charm and attract families and conventions.

The spa can be enjoyed on a daily-rate basis or with baths and beauty services included in two-night and five-night packages. No formal program of activities is offered; you set your own schedule. The spa director will consult with you on a meal plan, exercise classes, and bodywork.

French Lick Springs today is a place to have fun and enjoy a bit of pampering. With a championship golf course, tennis courts, and other recreation facilities at hand, the springs are no longer the sole attraction. Yet you can still have a sip from a well beneath a gazebo or take a bath in spring water piped into a claw-footed tub. Eighty years ago the water was widely advertised as a laxative: "When nature won't, Pluto will!" Today the therapeutic pitch is "medicine for the ego."

French Lick Springs Resort
French Lick, IN 47432
Tel. 812/935-9381 or 800/457-4042

Administration	Spa director, Gail Spencer
Season	Year-round.
Accommodations	Deluxe suites and large double rooms with king- or queen-size bed, antique furniture, modern private bath, color TV.
Rates	$159 a day for 2, including breakfast, dinner, spa facilities. Deluxe 5-night spa program, Sun.–Fri. noon, $1,088 per person double occupancy, $1,250 single; 2-night midweek package $300 per person double, $379 single. Winter rates about 50% lower. Credit card confirmation or $100 per person deposit for spa packages. Credit cards: AE, DC, MC, V.
Meal Plans	3 meals daily with spa packages. Low-calorie selections from dining-room menu include poached salmon for dinner, shrimp shish kebab and teriyaki chicken for lunch. Vegetarian meals on request.
Services and Facilities	**Exercise Equipment:** 7-station Universal weight training gym, stationary bikes, rowing machines, treadmill. **Services:** Swedish massage, aromatherapy, reflexology, body toning, facials, pedicure, manicure, loofah body scrub; makeup lessons, beauty salon for hair and skin care; personal consultation on nutrition and exercise. **Swimming Facilities:** Indoor and outdoor pools. **Recreation Facilities:** Golf, tennis, horseback riding, bicycling, bowling, skeet- and trapshooting, miniature golf, billiards; fishing, sailing, skiing. **Evening Programs:** Resort entertainment.
In the Area	Surrey rides. Evansville historic district (19th-century homes), Old Vanderburgh County Courthouse, New Harmony colony near Vincennes, Amish farms.

Getting Here *From Louisville, KY.* By bus, Greyhound (2 hr). By car, I–64 west, Hwy. 150 to Paoli, Rte. 56 west (60 min). Hotel limousine, rental car available.

Special Notes Elevators and ramps connect hotel rooms and spa facilities. Supervised day camp for children during summer months; playground, miniature train ride, wading pool. No smoking in the spa.

Weight Watchers Camp Hoosier

Youth camps for weight loss

Indiana
La Porte Weight Watchers Camp Hoosier is a coed summer camp for young adults and teenagers that offers a balanced program of fitness, diet, and education in the course of an active vacation. Located on the campus of La Lumiere School in La Porte, the camp sessions are organized by age group for youngsters 10 to 21 years old. Campers may use a nine-hole golf course, an indoor swimming pool, and a weights room. Living quarters are in a residence hall with modern facilities.

Meals feature trademarked Weight Watchers recipes, and campers learn how to eat properly through classes on food preparation and lectures on nutrition.

Supervised by accredited counselors, campers enjoy full weeks of workouts with Nautilus equipment, slimnastics and aerobics classes, and sports. Those who complete the course are guaranteed weight loss or they get a refund.

Weight Watchers Camp Hoosier
Box 5005, La Porte, IN 46350
Tel. 219/326–7450
Weight Watchers Camps
183 Madison Ave., New York, NY 10016
Tel. 212/889–9500 or 800/223–5600 (800/251–4141 in Canada)

Administration Program director, Anthony Sparber

Season June–Aug.

Accommodations Residence hall with separate rooms for men and women; modern bath, laundry facilities, central lounge, private dining room overlooking the campus.

Rates Sessions of 2–7 weeks from $1,450. $100 payable in advance. Credit cards: AE, DC, MC, V.

Meal Plans 3 balanced meals daily in the cafeteria, 2 snacks in the residence halls.

Services and Facilities **Exercise Equipment:** Fully equipped gymnasium. **Swimming Facilities:** Private lake. **Recreation Facilities:** Ping-Pong, basketball, volleyball, tennis, soccer, football, slimnastics. **Evening Programs:** Dramatics, musical presentations, talent shows.

In the Area Nature walks.

Getting Here Pickup at South Bend airport. Taxi, rental car available.

Special Notes Smoking discouraged.

Birdwing Spa

Nutrition and diet
Life enhancement
Luxury pampering

Minnesota The only full-service spa in the upper Midwest, Birdwing Spa
Litchfield blends European therapy and Minnesota traditions. The
Tudor-style mansion set on a lakeside estate accommodates 18
guests; an exercise studio occupies the former barn/garage,
and an outdoor swimming pool and miles of shoreline trails
for walks and cross-country skiing are on the grounds. The
manor house has a sauna, Jacuzzi, and beauty-treatment facilities.

Oriented to outdoor activity, the spa provides equipment for
skiing, canoeing, and biking rather than weight training. In
two daily "image sessions," guests have a choice of facial, massage, or manicure. Aerobic exercise or an hour of yoga
completes the daily schedule.

Birdwing ranks high as a relaxing experience on a country estate. The owner, Elizabeth Carlson, was born and raised in
Salzburg, Austria, and knows the meaning of quality and service; her staff includes registered dieticians, European-trained
chefs, and a fitness director. Working with this dedicated team
makes sense for those who are just beginning a diet and fitness
program. Others will simply enjoy the breakfast in bed, low-
calorie gourmet dining, and unabashed pampering. Lake Wo-
begon this is not.

Birdwing Spa
R.R. 2, Box 104, Litchfield, MN 55355
Tel. 612/693–6064

Administration Director, Elizabeth Carlson; fitness director, Diane Gilmer

Season Year-round.

Accommodations 9 bedrooms (singles and doubles) with Ethan Allen furnishings, draperies, down-filled comforters, shared baths. The
master suite has fireplace, private bath, Jacuzzi, and steam
bath.

Rates Full-week spa program, Sun. evening–Sun. noon, $980 per per-
son for two in the master suite, $1,190 single, $880–$990 other
rooms. 5-day program from Sun. evening, $795 per person in
the master suite, $995 single, $695–$795 other rooms. Weekend
retreat, Fri.–Sun., $285 per person in the master suite, $345
single, $235–$295 other rooms. $100 in advance for weekends,
$250 for other programs. Credit cards: MC, V.

Meal Plans 900–1,100 calories per day. 3 weight-loss meals daily: cinnamon
raisin French toast with 3-berry sauce for breakfast, fruit ke-
babs followed by chicken tacos with salsa or turkey pizza for
lunch, chicken asparagus rolls and butterscotch brownies for
dinner. Skim milk and dairy products.

Services and **Services:** Swedish and Esalen massage, facials, hair and nail
Facilities care, reflexology, tanning booth. Nutritional counseling, fit-

ness evaluation, exercise instruction. **Swimming Facilities:** Outdoor pool. **Recreation Facilities:** Bicycling, canoeing, cross-country skiing, bird-watching. Tennis and golf nearby. Special weeks for art and nature studies. **Evening Programs:** Guest speakers on stress control, nutrition, cardiac health, and problems of career women. Cooking classes and feature films.

In the Area Minneapolis–St. Paul museums, shopping malls.

Getting Here *From Minneapolis.* By bus, shuttle service morning and afternoon from the Twin Cities airport (80 min). By car, I–394, Hwy. 12 west to Litchfield, Rte. 1 and 23 (90 min). Birdwing makes arrangements for local transportation on request.

Special Notes No smoking in public areas indoors.

The Elms Resort

Taking the waters
Non-program resort facilities

Missouri
Excelsior Springs In the 1800s high-living health seekers descended on this sleepy little Missouri town each season to take the mineral waters. The Elms, built to accommodate them in the grand manner, became a tradition that survived two devastating fires; the present limestone and concrete structure was built in 1912 and incorporates the New Leaf Spa.

Ten "environmental rooms" are programed for jungle rain, wet steam, or dry sauna and equipped with a hot tub for two. The European swim track, swimming in which can be a mildly claustrophobic experience, is a one-lane lap pool filled with tap water.

Downtown you'll find the Hall of Waters, an Art Deco treasure that boasts of having the world's longest mineral water bar; other facilities include a large indoor swimming pool and private baths. Built in 1937, the Hall of Waters is run by the city and is open to the public. There's a fee for bathing or swimming, and an appointment is required for a private mineral bath (tel. 816/637–0752). Pool hours are 8–5 Monday–Friday, noon–5 on summer weekends.

Lovingly restored, the Elms is Missouri's most unusual resort. When you walk through corridors lit by reproductions of antique gas lamps, it's easy to imagine Al Capone arriving with his bodyguards for an all-night poker game. Harry Truman also slept here.

Today there's a lot of nostalgic charm about the Elms. Croquet and badminton are played on the lawn, and the tennis court is free to guests. A quaint village of boutiques, crafts, books, and art opened recently. Popular for conventions and sales meetings, the 23-acre wooded resort is less than an hour from Kansas City.

The Elms Resort
Regent and Elms Blvd., Excelsior Springs, MO 64204
Tel. 816/637-2141 or 800/843-3567
Fax 816/637-1222

Administration	Manager, Robin Steinkritz; spa manager, David Hayes
Season	Year-round.
Accommodations	106 rooms newly furnished with traditional wood dresser and table, writing desk, ceiling fan, cable TV, old-fashioned tiled bath.
Rates	$49 per night for 2 persons Sun.-Thurs., $79 Fri. and Sat., midsummer. Suites $110-$160. Credit cards: AE, DC, MC, V.
Meal Plans	American and European cuisine. Salads, fresh fish, meat, or chicken for lunch and dinner.
Services and Facilities	**Exercise Equipment:** Nautilus circuit gym, Liferower, Lifecycle, treadmill, stationary bike. Indoor running track circles the lap pool (23 circuits = 1 mi). **Services:** Swedish massage, facial, cosmetology, beauty salon. **Spa Facilities:** Private mineral baths by appointment ($7.50). Hot and cold whirlpools. 3-level spa complex with separate saunas and steam rooms for men and women. **Swimming Facilities:** Outdoor pool; municipal indoor pool. **Recreation Facilities:** Golf course, tennis, croquet, badminton, volleyball, horseshoes, shuffleboard; racquetball court nearby; bicycle rental. **Evening Programs:** Resort entertainment.
In the Area	Watkins Woolen Mill (19th-century textile factory) in state park; fishing, swimming, hiking, picnicking, camping. Kansas City Zoo, Country Club Plaza (shopping), Crown Center (Hallmark museum), Nelson Atkins Museum of Art.
Getting Here	*From Kansas City.* By car, I-35 north to Excelsior Springs, Hwy. 69 to Rte. 10 (30 min). Limousine, rental car, taxi available.
Special Notes	No smoking in the spa.

Marriott's Tan-Tar-A Resort

Non-program resort facilities

Missouri *Osage Beach*	Outdoor recreation is the principal attraction of Marriott's Tan-Tar-A Resort, surrounded by 400 acres in the Lake of the Ozarks region. The lake, created by a dam in 1931, has countless coves for water sports, boating, and fishing. The hotel caters to conventioneers as well as family vacationers.
	Resort guests enjoy full use of an indoor/outdoor fitness center. Aerobics classes are offered three mornings a week, aquatics two mornings. The weights room, staffed by fitness specialists, is open daily. Massage and beauty services are available à la carte.

Marriott's Tan-Tar-A Resort
State Road KK, Osage Beach, MO 65065
Tel. 314/348-3131 or 800/228-9290 (800/268-8181 in Canada)

Administration	Manager, Bill Bennett; fitness director, Gary DeAngelis
Season	Year-round.

Accommodations	1,000 rooms in the hotel and cottages have fireplace, kitchenette, bar (in some rooms and suites), coffee maker, TV, private bath.
Rates	Double rooms $79–$129, 1-bedroom suites $130–$210, 2-bedroom suites $190–$275. Package plans include condo, breakfast and dinner, unlimited golf. Deposit of 1 night's lodging applied to last night reserved (and forfeited on early departure). Credit cards: AE, CB, DC, MC, V.
Meal Plans	The Cliff Room has Continental cuisine and light fare as well as fried catfish. Windrose on the Water serves fish cooked to order (broiled, baked, sautéed, blackened).
Services and Facilities	**Exercise Equipment:** 3 Trotter treadmills, 2 Liferowers, 3 Nautilus stationary bikes, 9-station Universal weight training gym, abdominal-muscle exerciser. **Services:** Swedish massage, reflexology, acupressure, facials; hair, nail, and skin care for men and women. **Swimming Facilities:** 4 outdoor pools, private beach on lake. **Recreation Facilities:** 6 outdoor and 2 indoor tennis courts, 4 indoor racquetball courts, 2 golf courses, 8 bowling lanes, billiards, moped rental, boat rental with fishing guide, trapshooting range, miniature golf, ice skating. **Evening Programs:** Resort entertainment.
In the Area	Trail rides, fishing; Bridal Cave, HaHa Tonka Castle monument and state park, antiques shops; Abraham Lincoln home and tomb in Springfield, IL; Harry Truman home and library in Independence, MO.
Getting Here	*From St. Louis.* By car, I–44 to Rte. 65 (70 min). Limousine service to and from the airport; rental car available.
Special Notes	Supervised morning play camp for youngsters, teenage games and indoor activity in summer. No smoking in the weights room.

Aurora House Spa

Luxury pampering

Ohio *Aurora*	Clevelanders enjoy formal dinners by candlelight, business executives shift from meetings to massage appointments, and a dozen or so spa guests in terry-cloth robes take tea in a Victorian parlor, all at the Aurora House Spa. Located a few miles from the Ohio Turnpike, the spa gives you a sense of having journeyed back to another century; one of the buildings was a stagecoach inn more than 130 years ago.

In addition to the spa building and a new conference center, the complex is headquarters for Mario's International, owned and operated by Mario and Joanne Liuzzo, who have combined their experience in the beauty salon business with a love of Victoriana. Their salon outgrew two Victorian houses in eight years. The recent expansion includes an Olympic-size pool in the manner of ancient Roman baths, an enclosed jogging track, 10 new guest rooms, and the Cabin Lounge, which celebrates Aurora's landmark coach stop.

Fitness is now the focus of the programs for corporate members and health-conscious men and women who come here. Aquaerobics, a Dynastic stretch-and-tone class, weight-loss diets, and thalassotherapy are new features. Recreation includes hiking and biking along country trails and other outdoor sports. The spa has widened its selection of exercise equipment.

Pampering is what the spa does best: eight facial and throat treatments for men and women, massages, pedicures, manicures, makeup application, and a top-quality salon for hairstyling and dressing. Repechage, the house specialty facial, involves a layered thermal mask with applications of concentrated aloe vera juice, powdered seaweed, and clay. When the hardened clay mask is removed, your complexion feels softer and firmer. The price is $65.

Therapy, diet, and exercise are intended to work together here. Your day can begin with breakfast in bed, a walk, hike, or jog, and continue in the gym with cardiovascular training. Exercise sessions are tailored to the individual and designed to relax muscles while burning surplus calories. The dining room, known for its low-calorie cooking, looks onto a waterfall.

Aurora House Spa
35 E. Garfield Rd., Aurora, OH 44202
Tel. 216/562–9171

Administration	Director, Joanne Liuzzo
Season	Year-round.
Accommodations	15 rooms in the new wing and the original mansion, furnished with period pieces and modern comforts: Jacuzzi, large modern bath, hair dryer, terry-cloth robe. Executive suite has fireplace.
Rates	$135 a day for 2 persons, $100 single; executive suite $150 for 2 persons. 2-day pampering package with spa meals and aerobics $284.50 per person double occupancy, $299 single; 3-day/2-night program $799.50 per person double, $839 single. Spa package with suite from $349 single (1 night) to $1,699.50 per person double occupancy (5-night/6-day program). One-third of total payable on booking. Credit cards: AE, MC, V.
Meal Plans	3 meals daily with packages. Oatmeal buttermilk pancake topped with fruit sauce (breakfast), shrimp and vegetable kebab (lunch), ricotta-stuffed zucchini rounds with tomato puree, grilled veal medallions with *shiitake* mushrooms, and grape mousse made with skim milk (dinner). Controlled use of fats, salt, sugar: yogurt substituted for sour cream, fruit juices and honey for sugar, garlic and citrus for salt.
Services and Facilities	**Exercise Equipment:** Nautilus and Universal weight machines, stationary bikes. **Services:** Massage, facials, body scrub with dulce (a nutrient-packed seaweed) and almond oil, manicure, pedicure, parafango muscle treatment with mud/paraffin mix, aromatherapy, hairstyling, makeup consultation, personalized exercise instruction, Habitat environmental sauna; health and diet analysis. **Recreation Facilities:** Bicycling; golf, tennis, horseback riding nearby; downhill and cross-country skiing. **Evening Programs:** Lectures on health topics.
In the Area	Antiques shops, flea markets, shopping areas, Sea World.
Getting Here	*From Cleveland.* By bus, Greyhound (50 min). By car, I–480 to Rte. 91, Rte. 82 and 306; or the Ohio Turnpike (I–80) to exit 13

(40 min). Limousine service from Cleveland Hopkins Airport; rental car available.

Special Notes   Limited access for the disabled. Nonsmoking areas designated.

The Kerr House

Life enhancement
Luxury pampering

Ohio
Grand Rapids   The Kerr House is an antiques-filled Victorian mansion that functions as a hideaway for men and women who seek privacy and a complete overhaul. With just eight guests in residence at a time, the facility takes on the atmosphere of a private club. Your fellow guests might include a Toledo schoolteacher, a doctor from Pittsburgh, and an Australian business executive. Some may be physically and emotionally burned out; others may just want to enjoy a bit of pampering. Some weeks are reserved for men only or women only.

The chatelaine, Laurie Hostetler, sets the program. Breakfast arrives at 7 AM on a wicker tray, and with it comes your personal schedule—massage, facial, nature walk, exercise.

Yoga, the specialty of the house, is taught in a carpeted exercise room on the top floor. Hostetler encourages guests by providing her own book of *asanas*, the exercise positions of Hatha yoga. "Listen to your body," she says, "it will tell you how much you can do." You can't work out on weight machines or swim laps here, unless you use the community swimming pool. Exercise is limited to low-impact aerobics, walking, and three hours of yoga daily.

Personal counseling and accessible health specialists make this spa experience attractive for those who want to learn healthy habits. A good deal of time is spent discussing ways to build self-esteem and to deal with everyday stress. Guests begin to feel a balance between mind and body and to appreciate the excitement of functioning at capacity on natural rather than nervous energy.

Addictions to smoking, caffeine, and sugar can be addressed. Avoiding temptation, changing one's daily routine, and being in a supportive group often inspire success. During the initial chemical withdrawal, positive support and breathing exercises to cleanse the lungs and flush impurities from the body are prescribed. Drinking lots of water from local wells, eating natural foods, and cleansing the colon are also advised.

Whirlpool, sauna, and massage sessions are part of the pampering. Guests appear radiant and relaxed by dinnertime in the formal family dining room, where places are set with period china and silver. A harpist plays in the background.

The Kerr House
17777 Beaver St., Grand Rapids, OH 43522
Tel. 419/832–1733 or 419/255–8634

Administration   Director, Laurie Hostetler

Season   Year-round.

Accommodations 5 guest rooms with high ceilings, antiques, lace curtains. The house has massive wood doors, stained-glass windows, a hand-carved staircase.

Rates $1,950 a week per person double occupancy; $2,350 single (1 room available). Tax, gratuities, all services included. Weekends $575. 50% payable in advance. Credit cards: AE, MC, V.

Meal Plans Diet of 750–1,000 calories per day, mainly vegetarian, with fish and chicken. Low in fat and cholesterol; no salt, sugar, refined flour, additives. Lunch can include a Senegalese carrot soup, lettuce salad, pita bread with couscous stuffing, and herbal tea. Typical dinner entrees are eggplant Parmesan with tomato sauce; baked chicken breast on wild rice; shrimp and baked potato. Fresh fruit desserts and sorbets are specialties.

Services and Facilities **Exercise Equipment:** Rebounders. **Services:** Massage, pedicure, facial, hair and skin care, reflexology, polarity, herbal body wraps, mineral baths. **Swimming Facilities:** Community pool nearby. **Recreation Facilities:** Walks along the Maumee River and the Miami & Erie Canal towpath; paddleboat rides. **Evening Programs:** Occasional guest speakers.

In the Area Visit to a glass craftsman's studio, the Ludwig Mill (water-powered saw and grist mill), the restored Fort Meigs, farms and country fairs, hydroplane races (Sept.).

Getting Here *From Toledo.* By car, I–475 to Rte. 65 (20 min). Complimentary pickup and return at Toledo Express Airport.

Special Notes No smoking indoors.

Sans Souci Health Resort

Weight management
Nutrition and diet
Stress control

Ohio
Bellbrook

On a beautiful, secluded 80-acre estate, a small band of health seekers follows the owner and director of the Sans Souci Health Resort, Susanne Kircher, on a parcourse fitness trail across the immaculate lawn of the country retreat. Birdsong and gentle breezes enhance the outdoor sessions of stretching, breathing, and wakeup exercises. Miles of hiking trails crisscross the woods and meadows of the estate, which borders a 600-acre wildlife preserve.

Kircher, a registered nurse and a former consultant to Olympic athletes, mixes European spa philosophy with no-frills fitness training. The men and women who come here to shed a few pounds learn how to kick the habits that caused them to gain weight. The daily agenda is full of aerobics, from dance steps to slimnastics, and water workouts in the swimming pool during warm months.

The programs in the spacious country home where the Romanian-born Kircher began her fitness resort in 1978 are devoted to pampering, stress management, and stopping smoking. The guest list is limited to seven for the week so that programs can be tailored to meet individual needs. An hour a day is set aside for rest and relaxation; meditation walks or yoga classes add another quiet period to the day's schedule.

Sans Souci He[...]

3745 Rte. 725, Bel[...]
Tel. 513/848-4851

Administration	Director, Susanne K[...]
Season	May–Oct.
Accommodations	Spacious, airy rooms [...] private bath, dressing [...]
Rates	5-night program Sun.–F[...] $1,190 single; weekend r[...] single. Daily rate $92 (no r[...] it cards: MC, V.
Meal Plans	800-calorie daily diet includ[...] [...], snacks, mineral water, luncheon omelet of egg [...]tes and vegetables, dinner selections such as seafood divan, fruit-garnished chicken. Dinner served by candlelight. Juice fast recommended on day of arrival.
Services and Facilities	**Exercise Equipment:** 18-station parcourse. **Services:** Massage, facials, herbal wraps, manicures, pedicures, hair and skin care; cooking demonstrations, personal consultation on nutrition and diet. **Swimming Facilities:** Outdoor pool. **Recreation Facilities:** Horseback riding, badminton, volleyball, croquet; golf and fishing nearby. **Evening Programs:** Workshops on behavior modification, stress management, nutrition; assertiveness training; therapeutic massage and Jacuzzi relaxation. Guest lecturers and films on alternate evenings.
In the Area	Picnic lunches, tour of Bellbrook, 600-acre Sugarcreek Reserve.
Getting Here	*From Dayton.* By car, I–75 to Rte. 725 East (30 min). Free service to Dayton International Airport; $20 for pickup on arrival.
Special Notes	No smoking indoors.

The American Club

Non-program resort facilities

Wisconsin
Kohler

In a town dominated by the nation's leading manufacturer of plumbing fixtures and bathtubs, it can be no surprise that luxury and bathing are synonymous at the American Club's 160-room hotel owned and operated by the Kohler Company. With the recent additions of a 28-hole golf course designed by Pete Dye, a Sports Core with indoor and outdoor tennis courts and a spa salon, and a 600-acre nature preserve where heart-healthy meals are served in a secluded log lodge, the American Club has become an oasis of fitness in the Midwest.

Built in 1918 to house and educate immigrant workers, the American Club gained a new lease on life in 1981 when members of the Kohler family decided to create a showcase for their products while providing the best of dining and recreation in Wisconsin. Bed and bath are discussed in detail when you make your reservation; there are five levels of luxury to choose from, and the plumbing fixtures become more lavish and imaginative as the price increases.

s for two are set on glass-covered terraces and in
ed baths. For the ultimate in hedonism, ask for a
te equipped with Habitat, a master bath with an hour's
serenity programmed into it: The sounds of a rain forest, soft
breezes, a gentle mist, a steam bath, even desert tanning are
simulated.

The club's facilities extend around the village of Kohler and
past the factory. Registered guests are issued passes that allow
them to charge meals and services and ride a trolley to activities. Part of the club's charm lies in being in a place that looks
like a Hollywood vision of middle America yet functions with
the precision of a posh resort. The original Tudor-style dormitory, reminiscent of a country inn, has been duplicated across a
garden courtyard where a Victorian greenhouse serves as an
ice cream parlor.

Checking in at the Sports Core, you get a locker and towel and
the opportunity to schedule herbal wraps, massage, and court
times. In addition to three racquetball courts (used for handball and wallyball, too), six indoor tennis courts are available
for an hourly fee, while the outdoor courts are free. The Peter
Burwash International staff offers professional instruction.
Exercise rooms, aerobics studio, and health services are down-
stairs. A glass-walled 60-foot swimming pool and the Lean
Bean restaurant (a happy discovery for dieters) are off the
lobby.

Outdoor and indoor whirlpools and a man-made lake
surrounded by a 2.2-mile exercise parcourse get heavy use
from members and guests. Men's and women's locker rooms
have Habitats in case your room isn't equipped with one. The
Core is open from 6 AM–11 PM daily. Bodywork, indoor courts,
fitness and aquacize classes, and the use of Nautilus and computerized equipment in the weights rooms require additional fees.
Racquets and cross-country skis can be rented.

River Wildlife is a place apart, one where the outdoors and good
food are celebrated. Marksmen practice, hikers explore more
than 30 miles of woodland trails, and canoers and fishermen enjoy
the winding Sheboygan River. A rustic lodge with log beams and
fieldstone is the centerpiece. Lunch is served daily, dinner on
weekends in front of the huge fireplace. In winter the trails are
groomed for cross-country skiing, and hot cider is served before
a crackling fire. American Club guests need only a $5 pass to
use the facilities; the trails are open to all. Hunting parties can
be arranged. Fishing licenses and archery lessons are available.

As a playground, the American Club and the nearby state parks
are tops. Sheboygan, minutes away, offers cultural attractions.
The combination of small-scale pleasures, an eager staff, and
woodland creatures make this a cozy retreat.

The American Club
Highland Dr., Kohler, WI 53044
Tel. 414/457–8000

Administration Manager, Susan P. Green; fitness director, Alice Hubbard

Season Year-round.

Accommodations 160 rooms with a range of whirlpool baths, four-poster brass beds with feather comforters and pillows, wood paneling, carved oak doors, sitting areas, glassed-in terrace with hot tub, wet bar, and mirrored bath in some rooms. Suites in the renovated Carriage House are reached by crossing the parking lot or using an underground walkway. Free transportation between facilities.

Rates $98–$237 double room, $81–$207 single. 2-night getaway packages for 2 persons, including a bubble massage at the Sports Core and some meals, $134–$239 per person. For golfers, 2 rounds at Blackwolf Run, plus amenities, $245–$340 per person double occupancy. 2-night retreat in sybaritic suite $304 per person double occupancy. 1 night payable in advance. Credit cards: AE, CB, DC, MC, V.

Meal Plans Breakfast buffet in the Wisconsin Room, expanded menu at Sunday brunch. Dinner at The Immigrant is a dress-up affair in small rooms dedicated to the club's original European occupants; specialties are Wisconsin whitefish caviar roe, scallops, shrimp, seafood sausage on spinach pasta, mesquite-roasted loin of Iowa pork, Kohler Farms beef. The River Wildlife menu, changed every weekend, can feature pheasant pâté, grilled rabbit, broiled fresh brook trout stuffed with vegetables, veal scallops with pesto and 5-cheese sauce. Salad of sprouts and seasonal greens or hamburgers at the Lean Bean or the Horse & Plow pub restaurant for lunch.

Services and Facilities **Exercise Equipment:** 16-station Nautilus circuit, 5 Lifecycles, StairMaster, Liferower; 16-station Universal gym, 2 aerobic bikes, rowing machine, free weights; indoor and outdoor jogging tracks, 2.2-mile parcourse. **Services:** Massage, herbal wrap, body wrap; facial skin care, manicure, pedicure; fitness consultation; hydrotherapy. Aerobics classes throughout the day ($4.80 each). Clay marksmanship course, crazy-quail shooting, archery instruction. **Swimming Facilities:** Indoor lap pool, lake with sandy beach. **Recreation Facilities:** Indoor and outdoor tennis courts, 3 handball/racquetball courts, fishing, canoeing and boating, bicycle rentals, hiking, cross-country skiing. **Evening Programs:** Dancing, concerts by visiting ensembles.

In the Area Half-day canoe trip, nature walks, charter-boat fishing on Lake Michigan; Kettle Moraine State Forest (Ice Age formations), dunes on Lake Michigan beaches, nature trail at Sheboygan Indian Mound Park, Kohler Arts Center, Kohler Design Center, cheese plant tour, Kohler Company tour, Manitowac Maritime Museum.

Getting Here *From Milwaukee.* By car, I–43 to Exit 53B, Rte. 23 west to Kohler (about 80 min). By bus, Greyhound to Sheboygan (90 min). Sheboygan Limousine Service to Milwaukee's Mitchell Airport, Amtrak, and bus stations. The American Club arranges pickup in Sheboygan. Limo service from hotels in Milwaukee and Chicago.

Special Notes Elevators link all floors. The Sports Core has supervised activities for children 1½–6. Older children can join week-long summer-camp programs or sign up for tennis and swimming lessons. No smoking in the Sports Core athletic and therapy areas.

Olympia Village Resort

Luxury pampering

Wisconsin
Oconomowoc

Olympia Village, a first-class vacation resort for relaxation and rejuvenation, is a good place to escape for a few days or a week. The spa's aerobics studio offers a full schedule of classes that includes yoga and a workout in the pool, and a full-service Lancôme beauty salon is located here.

An invigorating walk begins the day at 7 AM; then you're free to exercise in the weights room or work on your appearance. A personalized fitness program and daily diet will be tailored to your needs and physical abilities by the staff director. A follow-up regimen to take home comes with the package for two to seven days.

Coed whirlpools and sunken Roman baths allow socializing or a private soak. Separate saunas and steam rooms for men and women and private massage rooms are among the extensive facilities for guests and residents of nearby condominiums. Luxuriously tiled and carpeted, the spa combines glamorous atmosphere and gentle discipline.

Olympia Village Resort
1350 Royale Mile Rd., Oconomowoc, WI 53066
Tel. 414/567–0311 or 800/558–9573

Administration General manager, Frank J. Kumberg; program director, Wanda Shields

Season Year-round.

Accommodations 380 modern rooms facing a lake and ski lifts. Fully carpeted and air conditioned, all rooms have private bath and color TV.

Rates 2-night spa sampler $387.22 per person double occupancy, $305.22 single; 4-day retreat $581 per person double, $721 single; 7-night/8-day renewal plan $1,088 per person double, $1,375.07 single. Daily rate $131.50 per person, double occupancy, with spa admission, meals, services. $50 per person payable in advance. Credit cards: AE, CB, MC, V.

Meal Plans Diet menu dining room for spa guests serves 30. Low in fat and cholesterol, dinner choices include broiled herbed chicken, broiled pike in lemon dill sauce, steamed lobster. Luncheon menu changes daily, features spinach quiche, chef's salad. 3 meals, 2 snacks included in spa plans.

Services and Facilities **Exercise Equipment:** Biocycles, 12-station Universal weight training gym, rowing machine, dumbbells, 30 free weights, wrist weights. **Services:** Exercise classes, yoga instruction, massage, herbal wrap, facial, pedicure, manicure, loofah body scrub, hair and skin care; makeup instruction; workout suit, robe, and scuffs provided. **Swimming Facilities:** Indoor and outdoor pools, private beach on lake. **Recreation Facilities:** Indoor and outdoor tennis, racquetball courts, golf, horseback riding, bicycle rental (1 hr free with spa plans), water sports; downhill and cross-country skiing. **Evening Programs:** Resort entertainment, movie theaters.

In the Area Old World Wisconsin (living history village), Octagon House (historic home), fishing, Milwaukee Brewers baseball.

Getting Here *From Milwaukee.* By car, I–94 to Rte. 67 (40 min).

Special Notes Elevators and ramps connecting all floors provide access for the disabled. No smoking in the spa and spa dining room.

The Wooden Door

Weight management *Women only*
Life enhancement

Wisconsin For the frugal fitness buff, the 54-acre lakeside retreat of The
Lake Geneva Wooden Door offers a weight-loss week about twice a month. Run like a summer camp, with an early-bird schedule that keeps you on the go all day, the program is a rewarding getaway for women who enjoy total programming and can't afford The Golden Door. Up to 95 guests can be accommodated.

The no-frills concept even permits guests to bring their own linens and towels (or to rent them for $20 per session). Guests scrape their own dishes, keep their own cottages tidy.

A typical day begins with sunrise yoga at 6 AM, followed by walking and jogging before breakfast. Strenuous exercise sessions alternate with aerobics, stretching, and dance routines. Weather permitting, fitness classes are held in a charming gazebo overlooking the lake. Afternoon and evening programs focus on personality enhancement, perhaps some pampering. Bodywork and beauty treatments are not included in the program cost, but their prices are reasonable.

Don't expect high-tech exercise equipment or a steam room; activity here is oriented toward enjoying the great outdoors in water sports, hiking, and tennis. The main lodge has a gym for indoor workouts. Discussions of the place of women in today's society take place around a big stone fireplace in the evening.

The Wooden Door
Rte. 50, Covenant Harbor, Lake Geneva, WI 53147
(Mailing address) Box 830, Barrington, IL 60010
Tel. 312/382–2888

Administration Program director, Jill Adzia

Season Apr.–Oct., Jan. ski weeks.

Accommodations Roomy cabins sleeping 2–4 have wall-to-wall carpeting, steel-frame bunk beds, large bath, electric heat. Larger cottages have a lounge area with fireplace.

Rates Sessions of 5 or 6 nights $475 per person in summer, $425 other times. Weekend getaways in the spring $190. $100 deposit upon booking. Credit cards: MC, V.

Meal Plans 3 meals and snacks total 900 calories a day. 8 glasses of water per day mandated. Dinner dishes include chicken breast with mushroom sauce, herbed rice; lunch could be zucchini pizza or peaches with yogurt.

Services and **Services:** Massage, facials, pedicure, manicure. **Swimming Fa-**
Facilities **cilities:** Lake with private beach. **Recreation Facilities:** Hiking, bicycling, sailing, canoeing, waterskiing, volleyball, cross-country skiing; tennis and golf nearby. **Evening Programs:** Workshops and lectures on health, beauty, fashion, social issues.

In the Area   Resort town (4-mi hike).

Getting Here   *From Chicago.* By bus, scheduled departures from O'Hare International Airport on Wisconsin Lines (tel. 312/427–3102), $15 one way (90 min). By car, I–94, Rte. 50 (90 min).

Special Notes   No smoking indoors.

The South

From hot-springs spas to New Age retreats, the range of health facilities in the South includes some of the oldest and some of the newest resorts in the nation. Virginia's Warm Springs baths, Hot Springs National Park in Arkansas, and the ultramodern therapies of the Doral Saturnia International Spa Resort in Florida make dramatic contrasts that show how far the pursuit of fitness has come over the last century.

Advancing to a new generation of preventive medicine programs, Duke University in North Carolina sponsors a Diet and Fitness Center, and the Palm-Aire Spa Resort & Country Club in Florida has a University Health Program run by medical authorities from several institutions. The emphasis on modifying one's lifestyle for healthier living is reflected at the Wildwood Lifestyle Center, a Seventh-day Adventist medical center in Georgia, and at the private Hilton Head Health Institute set amid sea pines in South Carolina.

For the combination of fitness facilities and sports opportunities, few resorts can match the programs of the PGA Sheraton Resort, the Saddlebrook Golf and Tennis Resort, and the Safety Harbor Spa and Fitness center, all in Florida.

Uchee Pines Institute Health Center

Preventive medicine
Weight management
Spiritual awareness

Alabama
Seale

This homelike retreat offers health conditioning and special diets in comprehensive three-week sessions that appeal mostly to persons over 50. Medically directed, the Uchee Pines Institute program treats most degenerative diseases.

The Health Conditioning Center expounds traditional Seventh-day Adventist philosophies on nutrition and mental and spiritual health. Led by three physicians, the staff combines medical and natural healing. A nutritional analysis, aided by computers, gives each patient specific diet recommendations and takes into account each individual's physical condition, nutritional needs, and weight loss goals. Following each guest's complete physical examination (some of which may be covered by medical insurance), a physician prescribes a personal schedule and continues to monitor the patient's progress throughout the program.

Treatments to stop smoking, drinking, or other lifestyle problems are also offered.

Diet plays a key role in the cleansing and healing process. The food here is fresh from the farm, and vegetarian meals are totally oil-, salt-, and gluten-free. There are special diets for cancer and menopausal patients.

Secluded in a 200-acre woodland preserve near the Chattahoochee River, the center's live-in accommodations for 14 guests

The South

Alabama

Uchee Pines Institute Health Center, **5**

Arkansas

The Arlington Resort Hotel & Spa, **1**

Evergreen Manor, **2**

Hot Springs National Park, **3**

Florida

Bonaventure Resort & Spa, **27**

Doral Saturnia International Spa Resort, **31**

Fontainebleau Hilton Resort and Spa, **29**

Hippocrates Health Institute, **25**

Palm-Aire Spa Resort & Country Club, **26**

PGA Sheraton Resort, **24**

Pritikin Longevity Center, **30**

Russell House, **23**

Saddlebrook Golf and Tennis Resort, **21**

Safety Harbor Spa and Fitness Center, **20**

Turnberry Isle Yacht and Country Club, **28**

Weight Watchers Camp Vanguard, **22**

Georgia

Southwind Health Resort, **6**

Wildwood Lifestyle Center, **7**

Kentucky

Bluegrass Spa, **8**

Louisiana

EuroVita Spa at the Avenue Plaza Hotel, **4**

North Carolina

Camp Camelot, **16**

Duke University Diet and Fitness Center, **14**

Structure House, **15**

Weight Watchers Camp Asheville, **17**

South Carolina

Hilton Head Health Institute, **18**

OHIO

WEST VIRGINIA

nkfort

Lexington

KENTUCKY

Knoxville

hattanooga

Washington, D.C.

Richmond

Norfolk

Roanoke

VIRGINIA

Greensboro

Winston-Salem

Rocky Mount

Raleigh

NORTH CAROLINA

Charlotte

Greenville

Columbia

SOUTH CAROLINA

Atlanta

Augusta

Macon

Charleston

Savannah R.

GEORGIA

Savannah

Chattahoochee River

Flint River

Valdosta

Jacksonville

Tallahassee

FLORIDA

Orlando

Daytona Beach

ATLANTIC OCEAN

200 miles

300 miles

The Westin Resort, **19**

Virginia

Hartland Health Center, **10**

The Homestead, **9**

The Kingsmill Resort, **11**

The Lotus Center, **13**

The Tazewell Club, **12**

Tampa

Fort Myers

Miami

Fort Lauderdale

Key West

provide privacy and comfort. Walks, gardening, exercise, and hydrotherapy balance out daily lectures on preventive medicine, nutrition, and lifestyle change.

The health center is equipped with a heated, full-body whirlpool, steam bath, massage tables, and ultrasound therapy units. Special treatments include fomentation—application of moist heat to the body for relief from congestion or pain—and the use of ice packs to slow down circulation or arrest a physical reaction. Only a few pieces of exercise equipment are available to those who want an active program.

The warm, caring atmosphere and small size of the facilities make this an ideal place for older persons who need constant attention and who are searching for a life-restoring experience. It is nondenominational and nonsectarian.

Uchee Pines Institute Health Center
Rte. 1, Box 273, Seale, AL 36875
Tel. 205/855–4764

Administration	Manager, Greg Griffith; medical director, David Miller, M.D.
Season	Year-round.
Accommodations	7 twin-bedded rooms with modern furniture, flowered bedspreads, ceiling fans, reading lamps. Private bath.
Rates	$2,520 for a 3-week live-in session, all-inclusive; $2,320 for a spouse as a patient, $1,475 as a nonpatient (includes physical exam and medical consultation). Daily rate $120. $500 per person advance payment; 5% discount for full payment. Credit cards (4% surcharge): MC, V
Meal Plans	3 vegetarian meals daily, family style. Adventist diet of fruits, vegetables, legumes, and grains. No fats, butter, or oils. Olives, nuts, and avocado in moderate amounts. Entrees include vegetarian lasagna, whole-wheat pizza, baked tofu.
Services and Facilities	**Exercise Equipment:** Stationary bike, jogger trampoline. **Services:** Massage, showers. **Spa Facilities:** Whirlpool, steam bath. **Recreation Facilities:** Nature hiking, bicycling, gardening, orchard work. **Evening Programs:** Informal discussions of health-related topics.
In the Area	Group outings to Callaway Gardens; Providence Canyon, Tuskegee Institute Museum (history and agriculture).
Getting Here	*From Atlanta.* By bus, Trailways to Columbus, GA (5 hr). By plane, Delta Airlines to Columbus, GA (30 min). By car, I–185 via Columbus, Rte. 80 to Rte. 431, south to Rtes. 24 and 39 (about 5 hr). Free pickup to and from airport and bus station.
Special Notes	No smoking indoors.

The Arlington Resort Hotel & Spa

Taking the waters
Non-program resort facilities

Arkansas *Hot Springs*	Quiet elegance, spacious accommodations, and old-world charm distinguish the landmark Arlington Resort Hotel & Spa, which overlooks Bathhouse Row in the heart of Hot Springs National Park. There are no special programs, but the hotel

has private facilities for bathing, including 50 rooms with springwater-filled tubs. There are weekend packages for couples and for families.

Book a room on the Club Level for the most privacy and luxury. Hostesses make your reservations, a complimentary Continental breakfast is served daily, and a cotton robe is provided for your trip to the spa.

With the Bath House on the third floor, there's no need to fight the crowds at the public baths outside. The complete treatment takes about 1½ hours, with sauna, whirlpool, and massage. The naturally heated mineral water leaves your skin feeling silky smooth and relaxes tense muscles.

Twin cascading mountain pools, where you can swim in the mineral water, and hot tubs are outside. Walking and jogging paths wind through the woods behind the hotel.

Catering to families and convention groups, the hotel has grand lobbies and open loggias, as well as bars and other temptations. For arthritis and neuritis sufferers the Libbey Memorial Physical Medicine Center (within walking distance) offers underwater massage and special hot springs mineral-water hydrotherapy. Also nearby is the Levi Arthritis Hospital, which offers outpatient care.

The Arlington Resort Hotel & Spa
Central Ave. and Fountain St.;
Box 5652, Hot Springs, AR 71901
Tel. 501/623–7771 or 800/643–1502

Administration Manager, Horst Fischer

Season Year-round.

Accommodations 490 guest rooms with 2 queen-size beds or 1 king-size, wicker chairs, flowered chintz curtains. Preferred rooms are in the towers and the Arlington Club level, or those equipped with mineral water baths.

Rates High-season (summer and fall) $48–$72 double occupancy, $40–$70 single; with mineral-water bath $75 single, $85 double. Weekend package for two (including thermal bath, massage, and deluxe room) $169. Family Plan $54 per night for up to four persons. One night advance payment. Credit cards: AE, DC, MC, V.

Meal Plans Breakfast and dinner à la carte in the Venetian Room. Dinner entrees include broiled red snapper with red peppercorns, broiled lamb chops, seafood fettucini, veal marsala, and salads. No diet or low-cal menu, but special diets accommodated.

Services and Facilities **Exercise Equipment:** Weights room with MGI fitness system with curl/high-pull combo unit, knee machine, leg abduction/adduction, overhead press, lats, triceps, and chest units; treadmill, recumbent bike, sit-up bench. **Services:** Massage, pool, beauty salon for hair and skin care, including facials. **Swimming Facilities:** Outdoor mineral-water pools. **Spa Facilities:** Whirlpool in separate pavilions for men and women, mineral-water bath. Bath House open to public; treatments in individual alcoves. **Recreation Facilities:** Country club golf, tennis, and dining privileges for hotel guests. Three nearby lakes for fishing, boating, and swimming. **Evening Programs:** Resort entertainment.

In the Area Local sightseeing tours, Thoroughbred horse racing at Oaklawn Park (Feb.–April), Magic Springs Family Theme Park, Mid-America Museum (science and history) and outdoor amphitheater, Observation Tower.

Getting Here *From Little Rock.* By bus, Trailways (60 min) or scheduled van from the airport. By car, I–30 south, Rte. 70 (45 min). Airport shuttle bus directly to and from hotel ($12 each way). Rental car, taxi available. Parking available on site.

Special Notes Elevator connects all floors to bath house. Game room for children on pool deck. No smoking in bath house.

Evergreen Manor

Holistic health
Weight management
Taking the waters

Arkansas Evergreen Manor is a secluded retreat on a parklike estate,
Hot Springs where fasting and hot springs bathing are supervised by fitness specialists. The coed program teaches how to recover from stress, condition your body, and gain vitality.

A week of resting and cleansing begins with a consultation to determine the best way to lose weight. For those who can adjust to a restricted diet, fasting is recommended to rid the body of waste. Optional treatments include colonics and therapeutic massage.

Visits to the facilities in nearby Hot Springs National Park provide the main exercise. Thermal baths, massage, and yoga classes are included in the program fee. Bicycles are available at no charge for outings on miles of trails through the park.

This is a closely monitored and restful way to try new healthy options.

Evergreen Manor
214 Daffodil La.;
Box 1154, Hot Springs, AR 71902
Tel. 501/625–0600

Administration Program director, Kitt Smith

Season Year-round; closed Dec. 15–Jan. 15.

Accommodations 7 bedrooms for 12 guests in manor house. Mixture of old and new furnishings. Well-maintained bath.

Rates $595 for a 1-week all-inclusive program, double occupancy; otherwise, $100 per person per day. $100 advance payment for 1-week program. Credit cards: MC, V.

Meal Plans Three vegetarian meals served daily, family style. Diet of raw food, fruits, and vegetables, plus generous amounts of spring water.

Services and **Exercise Equipment:** Trampoline, stationary bikes. **Services:**
Facilities Massage, colonics, iridology, deficiency testing, program to stop smoking. **Swimming Facilities:** Indoor pool and nearby

lake. **Spa Facilities:** Hot Springs National Park. **Recreation Facilities:** Biking.

In the Area Hot Springs National Park.

Getting Here *From Little Rock.* By bus, Continental Trailways (60 min). By car, I–30 to Hot Springs Exit, Rte. 70 west (60 min). Pickup at Little Rock airport $40. Car rental, taxi available.

Special Notes No smoking indoors.

Hot Springs National Park

Taking the waters

Arkansas Hot Springs National Park was once called the Valley of the Va-
Hot Springs pors. Indians and conquistadores were attracted by billowing clouds of steam from the 47 springs that bring hot mineral water to the surface in what is now a national park within a resort city.

Local lore has it that Hernando de Soto and his explorers relaxed here in 1541, but park rangers are skeptical. They tell visitors about the springwater's 4,000-year journey from deep within the earth, where it is heated to 143 degrees, and its mineral content from which its therapeutic properties derive.

The federal government got into the spa business in 1832 and set aside four sections of the springs as a health reservation, the first in the country's history. A partnership system evolved with private bathhouse and hotel operators, so the National Park Service now regulates operations and maintains the reservoirs, where the springwater cools down to a comfortable 100 degrees for bathing.

Six bathing facilities are open to the public, and plans are underway for renovation and adaptive reuse of several Art Deco buildings on Bathhouse Row. The most splendid of the eight buildings surviving here, The Fordyce, was built in 1915 by a Colonel Fordyce, who credited the springwaters with saving his life. The interior has stained-glass windows and a skylight with scenes of water nymphs, appropriate for the museum of bathing soon to open here. Perhaps the gymnasium where Jack Dempsey and Billy Sunday reportedly hoisted wooden dumbbells will again be used for demonstrations. Other bathhouses will display art and musical instruments; one will be an exclusive health spa.

For the time being, a bath at the Buckstaff gives a taste of the glory days. Plan on about 1½ hours for a soak in the thermal waters, the whirlpools, and a massage. The entire treatment at Buckstaff Baths, including hot packs on sore muscles and a multineedled shower, costs about $20.

Vacationing here is like taking a step back in time. Grand old hotels as well as mansions offer bed and breakfast. Hot Springs is also a modern medical center for advanced therapy of degenerative diseases and rehabilitation treatments for postcardiac or surgery patients. The town has the flavor of a 19th-century European spa—all the charm without the exaggerated claims.

Hot Springs National Park
Box 1860, Hot Springs, AR 71902
Tel. 501/624–3383
Hot Springs Chamber of Commerce
Box 1500, Hot Springs, AR 71901
Tel. 501/321–1700 or 800/643–1570 (800/272–2081 in AR)

Administration	Superintendent, Roger Giddings
Season	Year-round.
Accommodations	Bathing facilities in the Arlington, Hilton, and Majestic hotels. Guest houses and camping facilities.
Services and Facilities	**Swimming Facilities:** Indoor and outdoor pools at hotels; lakes nearby. **Spa Facilities:** 6 bathhouses operate under the auspices of U.S. Department of the Interior. All open Mon.–Sat. 7 AM–11:30 AM, 1:30 PM–3:30 PM. Majestic closed Sat. afternoons. Arlington closed Sun. morning. **Recreation Facilities:** Hiking trails in Ouachita Mountains, boating, fishing, biking, horseback riding; cross-country skiing. Hotels offer tennis, golf. **Evening Programs:** 12-minute slide program scheduled in park headquarters auditorium. Campfire talks at Gulpha Gorge Campground.
In the Area	Conducted hikes, nature walks, bathhouse tours; Ouachita Lake recreational area, Oaklawn Park (Thoroughbred racing, late Jan.–mid-April), Hot Springs Mountain Tower in Ouachita National Forest, Alligator Farm.
Getting Here	*From Little Rock.* By bus, Continental Trailways (60 min). By car, I–30 to Hot Springs Exit, Rte. 70 west (60 min).
Special Notes	Ramps and specially equipped rooms in most hotels and Buckstaff Baths. Nature walks for children with National Park Service naturalists. No smoking in bathhouses.

Bonaventure Resort & Spa

Luxury pampering
Weight management
Non-program resort facilities

Florida
Fort Lauderdale

When you want to go first class on a tight budget, a holiday at the Bonaventure Resort & Spa offers first-rate services à la carte or on a package basis. The difference between the two is in quantity of services, not quality. You can stay a weekend, four days, or a full week; take unlimited exercise classes and enjoy expert bodywork and beauty treatments; or orient your visit around sports—tennis, golf, and horseback riding. But beware adding too many extras to your spa schedule, as your bill will quickly run up.

The hotel also offers a one-day spa sampler—a fixed-price package of pampering and nutritious meals that is popular with people attending conventions. These bookings are limited when spa facilities are crowded. (There is a large local membership, as the residential community around the resort has grown enormously since the spa opened in 1982.)

Separate facilities for men and women, plus a coed gym and pool, are among the features of the free-standing fitness center. Once past the registration desk, you're handed workout clothing and a cotton robe, assigned to a locker where your personal schedule is posted, and then left to your own pursuits.

Sybaritic pleasures aside, management takes a serious approach to fitness here. A resident physician and two nurses are on staff to provide complete medical examinations and laboratory tests to determine individual exercise programs. Special diets are determined from this data by a nutritionist. After your body composition has been measured, and after intensive training on the Keiser weight training machines, you'll receive a computerized nutrition profile.

A typical day begins with a walk or jog around the golf course before breakfast, then an hour-long aerobics class. Three levels of conditioning are offered in a dozen different classes that range from easy stretches and energizing routines to deep toning calisthenics. Workouts in the water are popular, especially for people with orthopedic problems. There's no risk to joints and the back while doing aquatics.

There are cardiovascular exercises for men only, general conditioning and contouring for women only, and separate salons for facials, hair, and skin treatments. One of the specialties, available only here and in California, is Kerstin Florian's complexion revitalizer with fresh cell extracts.

What sets this spa apart from others is the wide range of body and skin-care treatments. Always on the cutting edge, Bonaventure recently introduced a sea kelp bath to its repertoire of hydrotherapy. There is an imported line of essential oils and a patented European process called Nutriol, which enhances hair growth and helps cases of psoriasis and acute dandruff.

The latest in spa cuisine is served at the hotel in a separate dining room decorated in soft colors, bamboo screens, and mirrors. Dinner dress is casual, but meals can be served in your room if you prefer.

Bonaventure Resort & Spa
250 Racquet Club Rd., Fort Lauderdale, FL 33326
Tel. 305/389–3300 or 800/327–8090 (800/432–3063 in FL)
Telex 568–632 (Bonaventure VD), Fax 305/389–3300, ext. 7810

Administration Spa director, Josefine Feria; medical director, Robert Dollinger, M.D.

Season Year-round.

Accommodations 493 luxury guest rooms and suites in nine 4-story buildings; Spacious rooms with balconies overlook lake or golf course with 2 beds (queen-size or twin) or 1 extra-large king-size. Rattan seating and tropical colors. Oversize bath with dressing area.

Rates $105–$195 single, $125–$225 double occupancy. The Perfect Day package $129 per person, plus tax and gratuity. Fitness weekend with meals, 2 half-hour massages, treatments, and classes: $380–$505 single, $315–$405 double (per person). Additional bodywork and beauty treatments included in 4-day plan: $1,113–$1,413 single, $936–$1,200 double. 7-day fitness plan $1,844–$2,369 single, $1,562–$1,960 double. Golf and tennis packages available. 1 night's advance payment 7 days after booking or AE confirmation.

Meal Plans 3 meals with calorie-counted selections served daily in private Spa Dining Room. 1,200 calories suggested for those not on weight-loss diet. Lunch specialties include pasta primavera, curried chicken soup, baked vegetables marinara with tofu, and fresh fruit. Dinner entrees include Maine lobster with asparagus spears, stir-fried chicken and vegetables on cellophane noodles, dessert crepe with blueberry and cheese filling. Decaffeinated and regular coffee and herbal tea; also acidophilus milk. Food is low in fat, cholesterol, refined sugar, and sodium, high in natural fiber, nutrients, and flavor. Dietitian on hand for special requests. Evian bottled mineral water.

Services and Facilities **Exercise Equipment:** 10-station Keiser gym, 3 Lifecycles, 4 Precor treadmills, 3 stationary bikes, Bodyguard ergometer, rowing machine, 3 minitrampolines. **Services:** Massage (Swedish, shiatsu, aromatherapy), loofah body scrub, herbal wrap, facials, skin and nail care, hairstyling. Private exercise, golf, tennis, and horseback-riding instruction. Individualized fitness profile, nutrition profile, and body composition analysis. Medical screening. **Swimming Facilities:** Outdoor and indoor pools, ocean beach nearby. **Spa Facilities:** 3½-foot exercise pool, outdoor Jacuzzi, Finnish sauna, Turkish steambath, hot and cold plunge baths, refreshment bar with Evian water, herbal tea. **Recreation Facilities:** 23 tennis courts, 2 golf courses, racquetball, squash, horseback riding, bicycle rental. **Evening Programs:** Lectures on health and stress, psychic readings.

In the Area Shopping trip to Galleria Mall; local sightseeing on request. Everglades tour by airboat, jai-alai fronton, Bahamas cruises, dog and horse racing tracks, Seminole Indian village, Fort Lauderdale museums and performing arts center.

Getting Here *From Miami.* By car, I–75 to Fort Lauderdale, Arvida Parkway Exit, State Rd. 84 (40 min). By plane, scheduled service (15 min). Free limousine service from Miami International or Fort Lauderdale airports included in 4-day and 7-day packages; scheduled van service. Taxi, rental car available.

Special Notes Ramps, elevators, and specially equipped rooms for the disabled. Supervised activity Fri.–Sun. mornings for children 5–13: guided trail rides at Saddle Club, paddleboats, bowling, roller-skating. No smoking in spa building or in designated areas of the dining room.

Doral Saturnia International Spa Resort

Luxury pampering
Life enhancement

Florida
Miami Like a vision of Tuscany, the villa's red-tile roof rises above formal gardens, statuary, and cascading fountains at the Doral Country Club. The mood inside is modern, without a trace of sweaty workouts to disturb the calm. Yet the spa is self-contained, with a wing of suites and dining pergola just for those participating in one of the deluxe packages.

Around the upper levels of the central atrium are the men's and women's locker rooms, equipped with whirlpool, saunas (dry and steam), sun deck, and lounge; 15 private massage rooms with a selection of treatments; a coed beauty salon and skin-care treatment rooms that feature an exclusive line of Italian cosmetics; and a running track. Gymnasium and weights room are located below the lobby level.

A grand staircase from a Paris department store provides a grand entrance for lunch in the rotunda. You come as you are; fresh outfits and robes are issued throughout the day in the locker room. Country club and one-day spa guests also dine here. The menu features traditional Italian favorites (pizza and pasta) adapted to meet the standards of the Doral Saturnia Fat Point Nutrition System.

Inspired by the ancient baths at Terme di Saturnia, north of Rome, the Doral Saturnia spa blends European and American health concepts. There are one-on-one workouts with pneumatic resistance equipment imported from Finland, aerobics in two cushion-floored studios, and an indoor pool. Treatments for muscular and skin problems are a specialty; warm mud packs from the same Saturnia volcanic springs used by Italian dermatologists are part of the massage therapy.

Daily regimens are flexible. The classes tend to be jazzy, low-impact workouts that appeal to men as well as women. Refreshing trays of fruits, veggies, and tall frosted fruit drinks are set out on a marble-topped buffet during breaks. For those who prefer tennis, 16 courts are nearby.

Appointments for personal services begin in the locker room lounge, where fresh workout clothing is issued. A therapist then escorts you by elevator to private rooms around the lofty rotunda. Serious regimens are planned after consultation with staff specialists who compare your health profile with a computerized model. All this personalized attention—a three-to-one ratio of staff to guests—comes at a price: about $300 per day, including three meals. Treatments are priced individually; various packages focus on fitness and beauty, or on golf, tennis, and horseback riding.

The dressy informality of a country house prevails in the spa villa. The mood of prosperity carries into the suites, where you'll find wall-to-wall marble, twin baths (one with Jacuzzi), dressing rooms furnished with robes and cosmetics, and an alcove where fresh fruit and Italian mineral water are supplied daily. Videocassettes are available for those who want to watch a feature film in their living room.

For a fully sybaritic retreat, guests may book one of five suites decorated by Piero Pinto of Milan to evoke regions of Italy. Furnished with original artwork and custom-made seating and beds, the suites are Italian fantasies.

Evenings in the glass-walled Villa Montepaldi Ristorante are elegant yet informal. Predinner nonalcoholic drinks are served in the library, where a fast game of billiards might whet one's appetite. The menu combines Tuscan specialties with fresh Florida produce and seafood. You may choose the size of your portion; fat points are listed, and a calorie counter is attached to the menu.

Talks by health specialists are scheduled after dinner, but many guests succumb to the temptation to enjoy the luxurious accommodations and prepare for an early morning walk around the golf course. The Spa Villa is air-conditioned, which is essential during the high-humidity summer months. Weather permitting, breakfast is served alfresco, with your choice of newspapers.

Miami's museums, shopping, and nightlife are less than 30 minutes away; Coral Gables and Coconut Grove are even closer. You can take off for the beach in the Doral private bus and use a cabana and exercise room at a sister hotel. Another alternative is a natural massage under cascades of water designed in the spirit of the original Italian spa.

Doral Saturnia International Spa Resort

8755 N.W. 36th St., Miami, FL 33178
Tel. 305/593-6030 or 800/331-7768 (800/247-8901 in FL)
Telex 990471/Doral Saturnia UD, Fax 305/593-6030, ext. 5101

Administration Resident manager, Offer Nissenbaum

Season Year-round.

Accommodations 48 suites, all with twin baths, Jacuzzi, wet bar and refrigerator, VCR. 5 grand suites ($150 additional per night), 1 supreme suite ($300 additional per night). Suites with private terrace or balcony overlook golf courses.

Rates Spa plan, 4 nights, $1,250 per person double occupancy, $1,675 single; 7 nights with choice of health, sports, or total-image emphasis, $1,975 per person double occupancy, $2,625 single; Grande Get-A-Way, 3 days/2 nights, $555 per person double occupancy, $770 single; Spa Day $185 with lunch, classes, massage (1 treatment, no room). Summer rates lower. $500 advance payment within 7 days after booking 7-night plan, balance 14 days before arrival. Full payment within 7 days after booking short stays. Refundable (less $50) up to 14 days prior to arrival date. Credit cards: AE, DC, MC, V.

Meal Plans Specialties include buckwheat waffles with fruit topping (breakfast), small pizza topped with turkey sausage (lunch), grilled honey basil chicken with rice and fresh vegetables (dinner). All meals, snacks, and dinner wine included in spa villa suite rate. Italian-accented, low-fat menu; special diets accommodated.

Services and Facilities **Exercise Equipment:** 11-station David system, free weights, Lifecycles, Liferovers. **Services:** Fango mud facial and body treatments; facials, herbal wraps, underwater massage, Swedish massage. Beauty salon. Cooking classes. **Swimming Facilities:** Large outdoor pool with cascades, separate lap pool, indoor pool for aquatics. **Recreation Facilities:** Golf, tennis, horseback riding, hiking trail. **Evening Programs:** Lecture and discussion group daily.

In the Area Complimentary use of beach club at Doral Hotel On-the-Ocean; shopping at Bal Harbour, Coral Gables; performing arts seasons and festivals in Miami and Miami Beach; museums and Vizcaya mansion; Orange Bowl games and concerts; jai alai and racetracks; sailing and deep-sea fishing.

Getting Here *From Miami International Airport.* 15 min away, served by major airlines. Amtrak station in Miami. Free limousine service in the spa villa plan. Taxi, rental car, limo arranged by concierge. Free scheduled shuttle bus to Miami Beach. Free parking, restricted to spa guests.

Special Notes Barrier-free facilities and dining rooms for the disabled; elevators throughout the spa center and villa. No smoking indoors.

Fontainebleau Hilton Resort and Spa

Sports conditioning
Luxury pampering
Preventive medicine

Florida
Miami Beach

Behind the monumental lobby, the half-acre lagoon with rock grotto and cascades, and the deli bar is The Spa. Located in the Fontainebleau's Old South building, where convention guests stay, it is developing into a self-contained fitness and health retreat. The ambience is more that of a city club than a fitness resort. The clientele includes local members and visiting businessmen. Access to a sports medicine institute and special salons for skin care expand the range of this glamorous beach resort.

The medical services, including pre-exercise physical examinations, rehabilitation, and treatment of sport related injuries, are provided by the Mount Sinai Medical Center. Computer software makes health-risk appraisals and nutritional assessments. The results from these tests help the staff plan comprehensive exercise and lifestyle programs on an individual basis.

Exercise physiologists in the spa team up with the medical specialists to work on a one-to-one basis. They outline a plan and monitor your progress.

Athletes are given an assessment of their oxygen consumption. The center's state-of-the-art equipment is helpful in developing sports training regimens. Factors evaluated include climatic conditions, age, and body composition.

Another computer program measures cardiovascular strength and evaluates diet. It might help beforehand for you to compare notes with your personal physician at home and start working under the supervision of experts on the link between diet, exercise, and health. The spa also organizes workshops for convention groups and half-day seminars in lifestyle management. Special charges apply for all medical services.

Another attraction is the natural-foods restaurant and its dining area beside an outdoor swimming pool. Lunch here is not included in the hotel's spa package. Dinner is served in the main dining room.

The Christine Valmy salon and treatments with herbal products developed by plastic surgeon Paula Moynihan are skincare options. After a dose of Florida sunshine, a fresh herbal and fruit mask has a soothing effect. The Moynihan Skin Care Center and the beauty salon serve both men and women in the penthouse.

Fitness and fun go together on the beach and in the freshwater pool, from a prebreakfast walk to an afternoon aquaerobics class. You can get a serious workout in the weights room or get caught up in the many activities offered all guests at the Fontainebleau. Be massaged alfresco or slip into the sauna, steam bath, and Jacuzzi.

Fontainebleau Hilton Resort and Spa
4441 Collins Ave., Miami Beach, FL 33140
Tel. 305/538–7600, 800/445–8667, or 800/548–8886
Telex 51–9362

Administration Spa director, Marc H. Siegel

Season Year-round.

Accommodations 1,224 rooms, all with private bath, and 61 suites. Deluxe bedrooms with king-size or large double beds, color TV, and balcony.

Rates Rooms $125–$600 per day. Spa refresher package 4 days/3 nights: $667 single, $427 double, with treatments and classes, no meals. 1 night's lodging advance payment. Credit cards: AE, CB, DC, MC, V.

Meal Plans Self-service at the Spa Veranda for lunch includes salads, low-cal drinks, fresh juice and fruit. Heart-healthy items on the dinner menu at the hotel's 6 restaurants are the broiled snapper, pasta primavera, and broiled chicken. All meals à la carte.

Services and Facilities **Exercise Equipment:** Nautilus circuit, Lifecycles, rowing machines, StairMasters, treadmills, free weights. **Services:** Massage, aromatherapy, loofah body scrub, herbal wrap; personal instruction on exercise, fitness profile, private whirlpool mineral baths, skin-care treatments, manicure, pedicure, hairstyling. Medical consultation, skin consultation. **Swimming Facilities:** Exercise pool, free-form recreational pool, and ocean beach. **Recreation Facilities:** 7 lighted tennis courts, Hobie and Catyak catamaran sailboats, windsurfing, beach volleyball. Nearby golf course and horseback riding. **Evening Programs:** Resort entertainment, cabaret.

In the Area Local sightseeing tours and cruises, Caribbean cruises, 1 day Bahamas flights and cruises, Thoroughbred horse races, harness track, dog races, jai alai fronton, Miami Dolphins stadium. Metropolitan Museum (major art shows), Gusman Performing Arts Center (concerts), opera season (winter), chamber music series, theater.

Getting Here *From Miami International Airport.* Limousine van service operates at all times (20 min). Taxi, rental car, limousine, public bus available. Free indoor parking included in spa package.

Special Notes Elevator to all floors and some specially equipped rooms for the disabled. Free children's accommodation with parents. No smoking in spa or designated dining areas.

Hippocrates Health Institute

Holistic health
Weight management

Florida
West Palm Beach A raw vegetarian diet, bodywork, and beach outings are central to the health renewal program that brings people to the Hippocrates Health Institute from all over the world. Sessions three weeks or longer are planned on an individual basis for 15 to 20 participants. Highly structured, the program includes nutritional education, regular exercise, massage, detoxification, and relaxation.

Guests stay in a spacious hacienda or private cottages on the 10-acre wooded estate. A peaceful, healing serenity pervades the grounds, where walkways wind through tropical surroundings.

The Hippocrates lifestyle involves learning to be self-sufficient in matters of food and medicine. A typical day begins at 8 AM with light exercise before breakfast, then a blood-pressure check, and discussion session on health and diet. Guests learn and practice how to sprout and grow greens for home use.

Personal counseling comes with the program. A psychologist works closely with the medical director to monitor your progress and advise you on personal problems. Deep-relaxation techniques are taught to enhance healing, creativity, and inspiration.

The program is run by health promoters (who moved the institute from Boston) with 30 years' experience teaching vegetarianism.

Hippocrates Health Institute
1443 Palmdale Ct., West Palm Beach, FL 33411
Tel. 407/471–8876

Administration Director, Brian R. Clement; program director, Alix Weill

Season Year-round; scheduled 3-week programs.

Accommodations 12 guest rooms, from luxury suite in Spanish-style hacienda to garden apartments and cottages, some with marble-walled bath and whirlpools. Colonial New England furnishings, views of lush tropical greenery, privacy.

Rates 3-week Health Encounter $2,400–$4,500 single, $3,000–$5,500 double occupancy. Shorter and longer stays on space-available basis; weekend programs. 50% of room rate nonrefundable deposit by certified check or major credit card. Credit cards: AE, MC, V.

Meal Plans 3 meals daily, buffet style, with days designated for juice fasting. Live Food diet of unprocessed raw vegetables, fruits, nuts, seeds, sprouts, sea plants and algae, and herbs. Raw juices and legumes in enzyme-rich menu, including combination of red pepper stuffed with cheeselike mix of nuts and seeds or sauerkraut and seed loaf. No dairy products, eggs, fish, meat, coffee, tea, or condiments.

Services and Facilities **Exercise Equipment:** 3 stationary bikes. **Services:** Health consultations, chiropractic treatment, full body massage, facials, supervised exercise program, wheatgrass detoxification schedule. **Swimming Facilities:** Outdoor pool, ocean beach nearby. **Recreation Facilities:** 2 tennis courts, golf and boating nearby. **Evening Programs:** Informal discussions nightly.

In the Area Organized trips to the beach, local museums, shopping excursion at a health-food store. Evening concerts and dinner at a local restaurant included. Disney World, Sea World, Miami museums, deep-sea fishing charters.

Getting Here *From Miami.* By bus, Greyhound to West Palm Beach (90 min). By car, Florida Turnpike (I–75) to Palm Beach Exit 40, Okeechobee Blvd. to Skees Rd. (60 min). Free service to and from

West Palm Beach airport and bus station. Taxi, rental car available.

Special Notes Ramps provided for the disabled; one specially equipped guest room. No smoking.

Palm-Aire Spa Resort & Country Club

Life enhancement
Weight management
Luxury pampering

Florida
Pompano Beach Three worlds coexist among the palm-lined streets of this 1,500-acre country club community: the University Health Center, devoted to comprehensive fitness and weight control programs; a spa complex for exercise and pampering; and a luxurious resort hotel. Surrounded by five 18-hole championship golf courses, 37 clay and hard-surface tennis courts, and condominium apartment buildings, the Palm-Aire is constantly expanding its services and facilities.

A former playground for the rich and famous, Palm-Aire now promotes physical fitness and stress reduction programs for executives. Although the glamorous clientele and 19th-hole parties still keep the hotel busy, a quiet revolution has been taking place across the street at the spa.

In 1987 a wellness program was developed by nutritionists and psychologists from several major universities to help participants overcome weight, nutrition, stress, fitness, and self-esteem problems. Limited to 12 men and women, and supervised by a staff of nutrition, health education, and psychology experts, the University Health Center program is the nucleus for a totally integrated medical and health complex that capitalizes on all of Palm-Aire's resources.

Whereas the two-week university program requires a total commitment, the spa is more flexible. Separate men's and women's pavilions have private sunken Roman baths, Swiss showers (17 nozzles that alternate warm and cool water), and some of the most experienced hands in the massage business. Each has sauna, cold plunge, steam room, and outdoor exercise pool (try aquaerobics in the buff). There's a well-equipped coed gym, racquetball courts, and an Olympic-size outdoor swimming pool.

A typical day begins with 10 minutes of warm-up stretches after breakfast, then a brisk walk on a half-mile parcourse. An instructor monitors your pulse rate on every lap. Fresh workout clothing is handed out in the locker room, and you can relax in the lounge while waiting for your next appointment or class. There's a clublike atmosphere as resident members and regular guests swap gossip and watch the stock market reports. Staff members are attentive and accustomed to gratuities.

Aerobics classes, scheduled throughout the day, range from mild to tough. A fitness exam may be required by an instructor before you may take an advanced class. Many guests mix pampering with their workout, then nap in the afternoon by the pool.

Calories count in the private spa dining room; the food is portion controlled, high in carbohydrates and low in fat. The 800-

calorie-per-day plan is sufficient, but second helpings are available. A regular, "fattening" menu is served in the adjoining dining room. Avoid the bar scene and head for the spa guests' lounge, where snacks of raw vegetables and fruit and a video-cassette library are available.

Salon services for men and women, in a newly decorated facility adjoining the spa, are charged à la carte. If you plan to stay two nights or longer, ask about package plans.

Palm-Aire Spa Resort & Country Club
2501 Palm-Aire Dr., Pompano Beach, FL 33069
Tel. 305/972–3300 or 800/327–4960
Telex 510–956–9606

Administration	Executive director, Michael C. McCaffrey; University Health Center administrator, Michael Stanton
Season	Year-round.
Accommodations	194 newly redecorated (1988) guest rooms larger than most hotel suites. All with separate dressing rooms and some with two baths. Private terraces, about half overlooking golf course. King-size beds and sofas, remote-control TV, built-in wet bar.
Rates	"Instant Tone-Up" package, 3 days/2 nights, spa treatments, 10 exercise classes, unlimited tennis, 1 round of golf: $425–$432 per person, double occupancy; 4-night package (winter season only): $678; "Complete Shape Up," 7 days/6 nights: $1,275–$1,296 (in winter, 8 days/7 nights: $1,582 per person). 13 day/14 night University Health Center program, with deluxe room: $3,640–$4,130 per person, double occupancy; single accommodations $4,340–$5,120 depending on season, more for golf view or deluxe room. Golf and tennis packages available. 50% advance payment for University Health Center; other packages, 2 nights advance payment by credit card. Credit cards: AE, DC, MC, V.
Meal Plans	3 meals daily in Spa Dining Room. Breakfast can include poached egg on wheat bread or cottage cheese and a bran muffin. Lunch choices include spinach-mushroom salad followed by baked potato stuffed with cottage and Jarlsberg cheeses or Spanish omelet made with egg whites. Broiled or poached snapper, chicken cacciatore, and vegetable lasagna for dinner. Whipped-mousse dessert or fresh fruit, decaffeinated or regular coffee, herbal tea. The Peninsula Room serves gourmet fare à la carte.
Services and Facilities	**Exercise Equipment:** 2 Trotter treadmills, 4 Precor treadmills, 2 rowing machines, 2 Liferowers, 4 Lifecycles, 2 Biocycles, 2 Schwinn Air-Dyne bikes, 2 recumbent bikes; 13-station Bodymaster strength conditioning system; complete Olympic free-weight gym, barbells (1–100 lbs.). **Services:** Body massage (Swedish, Trager, deep muscle), thalassotherapy, seaweed treatments, full-body fango mudpack, facial treatments, loofah body scrub, herbal wrap, body composition analysis. Separate men's and women's salons for hair, nail, and skin care. Golf and tennis clinics, personal conditioning. **Swimming Facilities:** 2 outdoor pools; beach club nearby. **Recreation Facilities:** 37 tennis courts, 5 18-hole golf courses, 2 racquetball courts, trails and beaches, indoor squash court. **Evening Programs:** Lectures on behavior modification, stress management, nutrition, other health-related topics.

In the Area   Fishing in the Everglades, scuba course; Fort Lauderdale Museum of the Arts, performing arts center, Parker Playhouse; one-day Bahamas cruise; Pompano Harness Track, Dania Fronton (jai alai), dog and Thoroughbred racing; deep-sea fishing charters, canal cruises.

Getting Here   *From Miami.* By bus, vans depart from Miami International Airport (60–80 min). By car, I–95 north to Exit 34, Atlantic Blvd., 27th Ave. to second entrance road (45 min). Limousine service (fixed fee) available to and from Fort Lauderdale International Airport and Miami. Rental car, taxi available. Valet service at hotel.

Special Notes   Spa facilities on ground level, elevators. No smoking in the spa, the spa dining room, and the lounge.

PGA Sheraton Resort

Sports conditioning

Florida
Palm Beach
Gardens

The golf and tennis champions exercise here during tournaments, but that's the extent of the glamour. This is a no-frills, down-to-earth fitness center. The PGA Sheraton overlooks four golf courses, five croquet courts, a 26-acre sailing lake, biking and jogging trails, and the Health and Racquet Club. All are available to registered guests.

The fitness instructors recommend a varied workout program to develop specific muscle groups and cardiovascular strength. Skiers might train on a cross-country exercise machine, a stair-climbing machine, and alternate 20-minute sessions on Nautilus equipment. For the tennis player, there's the treadmill, selected Nautilus units, and tennis aerobics, taught by a tennis pro.

Variety makes the exercise fun, and the staff helps keep you on the right track. Tennis, swimming, or golf alternates with walking, weightlifting, and croquet.

Even the golf pros are taking to croquet. Since the United States Croquet Association made this their national headquarters in 1987, the game has moved from the backyard to the mainstream. In addition to five tournament-size courts, there is an instruction area where beginners learn the basics of golf croquet. This recreational hybrid can be played by a couple or singles who want a mental workout with mallet and wicket. It looks easy but requires coordination and strategy. Don't forget to bring your whites; all-white dress is required.

Golf, however, is the principal recreation here. The home of the Professional Golfers' Association of America, the four courses challenge any style player, professional or Sunday duffer. Getting in shape for the ultimate golfing experience, a round on the General (a course designed by Arnold Palmer), could be the goal of a fitness regime devised by a team of golf pros and fitness instructors.

There is a specific circuit of Nautilus equipment to help golfers loosen up muscles and gain strength and flexibility. Twenty minutes to an hour on the treadmill will increase cardiovascular endurance. If you're really out of shape, there are daily clinics, private lessons, and three-day golf schools. Or you can go into the advanced "killer golf" school as part of a four-day resort package.

At the beginning and end of the day, a whirlpool massage will relax sore muscles. Aerobics classes are scheduled daily, from 8:00 AM to 7:45 PM, and six training combinations are offered. Afro–Caribbean aerobics are based on island rhythms. A combination of tennis strokes and aerobic steps is set to music—one way to increase endurance while improving your tennis game.

All of these activities are priced separately, with packages offered for golf, tennis, and croquet. There's a $10 daily charge for using the Nautilus equipment, swimming laps at the health club, or taking tennis aerobics classes. Make arrangements well in advance to get what you want.

The hotel operates more like a private club than a Sheraton, and food and drink are expensive. Transportation to local attractions is provided by obliging attendants at fixed prices. And when the PGA Seniors' Championship is in full swing, nongolfers are the minority.

With a new building for hydrotherapy and a fitness restaurant scheduled to open in late 1989, PGA Sheraton will be one of Florida's most complete sports and spa resorts.

PGA Sheraton Resort
400 Ave. of the Champions, Palm Beach Gardens, FL 33418
Tel. 407/627–2000 or 627–4444 (800/325–3535 for reservations)

Administration Managing director, Stephen P. Stearns; fitness director, Ruth Barnett

Season Year-round.

Accommodations 336 spacious guest rooms, redecorated (1987–1988) with conventional amenities. Tropical bamboo and palms decor. Large suites and 85 cottage units along golf course, each with 2 bedrooms, 2 baths, and kitchen. All rooms with balcony or terrace, private bath, and walk-in closet.

Rates Winter: double occupancy $170–$225 per person, singles $150–$200; suites $380–$655; cottages $250 for 2 persons, $65 for additional persons. Spring and fall tariffs about $40 less; summer, at least 50% less. 1 night advance payment. Credit cards: AE, CB, DC, MC, V.

Meal Plans 3 hotel restaurants, snack bar at Health & Racquet Club. No fitness menu. Colonel Bogey's à la carte selections include Florida red snapper grilled over mesquite wood, Cajun blackened beef, grilled chicken, plus extensive salad bar. Exotic dining at The Explorers includes marinated braised lion loin and black buck antelope, plus sushi, Dover sole, Maine lobster. At health club, salads and "smoothie" fruit drinks available all day.

Services and Facilities **Exercise Equipment:** 18-station Nautilus circuit, 2 Trotter treadmills, 2 Lifecycles, 2 StairMasters, 2 Monark stationary bikes, Nordic Track cross-country ski machine, free weights (5–50 lbs.) **Services:** Tennis, golf, and croquet instruction; massage, facials, skin care; beauty salon; fitness evaluation; sports equipment rental. **Swimming Facilities:** Family pool at hotel, health club 5-lane lap pool; ocean beaches nearby (15 min). **Recreation Facilities:** 4 golf courses, 29 outdoor tennis courts (10 lighted), 6 indoor racquetball courts, 6 croquet courts, sailboats, aquacycles, bicycles; walking and jogging trails, horseback riding nearby; fishing in private lake; kite flying festival in July. **Evening Programs:** Disco, resort entertainment; lectures during scheduled golf and tennis programs.

In the Area Palm Beach shops and museums, Golf Hall of Fame, The Gardens (5 min away), Burt Reynolds Dinner Theater, Palm Beach Symphony Orchestra, opera and pops concerts, Polo Club.

Getting Here *From West Palm Beach.* By car, I–95 to Exit 57, PGA Blvd. west to resort entrance; Florida Turnpike to Exit 44, PGA Blvd. (20 min). Limousine and van service (fixed fee) to and from airport. Taxi, car rental available.

Special Notes Ramps, elevators, and specially equipped rooms provide access for the disabled. Daily baby sitting, summer day-camp; golf and tennis clinics or private instruction for children. No smoking in Health and Racquet Club.

Pritikin Longevity Center

Nutrition and diet
Weight management

Florida
Miami Beach
Dieting at the Pritikin Longevity Center may be the healthiest holiday in Florida. Everyone, from the doctors on staff to the exercise instructors, eats Pritikin-style.

The revolutionary diet introduced by the late Nathan Pritikin in 1974 is the foundation of 13- and 26-day programs designed to treat and control medical problems. The medically supervised live-in program here, like the original in California and another in Pennsylvania, provides the support many people need in changing their lifestyles.

The regimen demands discipline, so don't expect a fun-in-the-sun holiday. Along with 50 other participants, you work out in the gym or pool and walk on the beach. If you enjoy ocean swimming, it can be part of your exercise plan. The staff doctor decides what's best.

Exercise, nutrition, stress management, health education, and medical services are the core curriculum. The 13-day program is recommended for sufferers of heart disease, insulin-dependent diabetes, obesity, or uncontrolled high blood pressure. The full course offers individual attention, counseling, and close supervision.

Healthy people come to learn how to safeguard their health. The daily schedule includes cooking demonstrations, lectures, and three exercise sessions. A full physical examination is a major feature of the program and includes a treadmill stress test and complete blood chemistry analysis. Depending on your personal history and fitness level, you are assigned to a specialist in cardiology or internal medicine who monitors your progress on the prescribed diet and exercise program.

Eating the Pritikin meals encourages a taste for food without added fats, salt, or sugar. Caffeine is not permitted. Meals are mostly vegetarian, with lots of fresh fruit and whole grains, and fish is served several times a week. Some nutritionists and doctors consider the diet unnecessarily austere, but the results are proof that the concept works.

The beachfront resort is a bonus. There are plenty of diversions for a nonparticipating spouse or companion.

Pritikin Longevity Center
5875 Collins Ave., Miami Beach, FL 33140
Tel. 305/756–5353 or 800/327–4914
Fax 305/866–1872

Administration Executive director, Joy Aronson; medical director, Robert E. Bauer, M.D.

Season Year-round, scheduled dates.

Accommodations 100 rooms in beachfront hotel, some facing traffic on Collins Ave., others with an ocean view on penthouse floor, and suites. Smaller rooms included in program with single or double beds, private baths, and comfortable furniture. All with air conditioning, color TV, telephone, maid service.

Rates 13-day program $4,902 single, $2,322 spouse or companion; 26-day program $8,195 single, $3,965 spouse or companion. More for larger rooms. $500 advance payment for 13-day program, $1,000 for 26-day. Credit cards: MC, V.

Meal Plans 3 meals plus 3 snacks daily. Buffet-style breakfast and lunch, table service and menu choices at dinner. Lunch and dinner salad bar. Lunch includes Pritikin vegetarian pizza, eggplant patties with marinara sauce, and rice-tofu *moo goo gai pan;* chicken teriyaki or poached salmon in dill sauce for dinner.

Services and Facilities **Exercise Equipment:** 23 Trotter treadmills, 6 Schwinn Air-Dyne bikes, 2 rowing machines. **Services:** Private counseling on nutrition and health, complete medical and physical examination, including blood tests. Massage, beauty salon appointments by request. **Swimming Facilities:** Olympic-size outdoor pool for aerobics; direct access to beach. **Recreation Facilities:** Nearby tennis courts and golf course, boardwalk. **Evening Programs:** Nightly entertainment by local talent; yoga.

In the Area Group trips to shows and jai alai games; Miami museums and sightseeing, deep-sea fishing.

Getting Here *From Miami.* By car, I–95 to Rte. 195, Julia Tuttle Causeway to Collins Avenue (15 min). Public bus, airport shuttle service, taxi, rental car available. Private parking on site.

Special Notes Ramps and elevators provide access for the disabled. No smoking in public areas.

Russell House

Holistic health
Weight management

Florida The juice fasts and 550-calorie diet here have been known to
Key West knock off 10 pounds in a week, but most of the guests come for casual relaxation and the laid-back, colorful scene. Located in the historic area where Ernest Hemingway once lived and Har-

ry Truman vacationed, the Russell House is a hideaway at prices well below luxury resorts. The program, like the town, is refreshingly informal.

Consult with staff members on fitness, nutrition, and dieting to set your goals. Activities are divided between active exercise like aerobics in the swimming pool, yoga, and bodywork, including reflexology, acupressure, and herbal wraps. Personal services are à la carte. The basic program costs as little as $525 for a week, but minimum-rate rooms are cell-like.

Guests dine in wet bathing suits, or whatever they like. The low-key atmosphere helps put you in the mood for stress-management workshops and lectures on healthier living. Lifestyle changes are discussed in group sessions on behavior modification, disease prevention, and negative habits. Private counseling and fasting supervised by a registered nurse help guests lose weight or stop smoking.

Russell House

611 Truman Ave., Key West, FL 33040
Tel. 305/294-8787

Administration	Manager, Enid Badler; fitness director, Len Guidone
Season	Year-round.
Accommodations	24 guest rooms for 1–4 persons, with bath, air conditioning, TV, telephone. Simple, small motel rooms and charming old Conch cottages vary in price.
Rates	1-week program with meals and accommodations $525–$1,600. Tipping not permitted. $200 advance payment. Credit cards: AE, MC, V.
Meal Plans	3 low-cal vegetarian meals daily. Organic fruit, nuts, seeds, and whole grains. Special diets for hypoglycemia, diabetes, arthritis, and high blood pressure. No salt, sugar, or cholesterol. 550 calories advised for dieters. Dinner includes a vegetable stir-fry or brown noodle spaghetti; lunch features green salad.
Services and Facilities	**Services:** 5 daily exercise classes, body wraps, massage, facials, program to stop smoking, acupuncture, astrology, chiropractic. **Swimming Facilities:** Outdoor pool, beach nearby. **Spa Facilities:** Garden-level sauna and sunken Roman whirlpool. **Recreation Facilities:** Beach, tennis, and golf nearby. Bicycles, snorkeling, and fishing gear can be rented. Exercise deck. **Evening Programs:** Informal discussion groups.
In the Area	Local sightseeing by open-air trolley; fishing trips available; Mallory Sq. sunset ceremony in Old Town, Duvall St. boutiques and art galleries, house tours during "Old Island Days" (Feb.-Mar.), Hemingway and Audubon house tours, the Wreckers Museum (maritime history) and Mel Fisher's Sea Salvors exhibit (Spanish treasure), Cuban cultural center and restaurants.
Getting Here	*From Miami.* By bus, Greyhound has scheduled daily service (5 hr). By plane, Piedmont Airlines scheduled service, Eastern Airlines commuter aircraft (40 min). By car, Florida Turnpike to Hwy. 1, 7-mile ocean causeway to southern terminus (3½ hr). Taxi, rental car available. On-street parking.
Special Notes	No smoking.

Saddlebrook Golf and Tennis Resort

Sports conditioning

Florida
Wesley Chapel
(Tampa Bay)

An active, sports-oriented vacation comes in a variety of packages at Saddlebrook. The United States Professional Tennis Association calls this home, as do the Harry Hopman tennis clinics.

The newly emerging field of sports biomechanics underlies Saddlebrook's programs. Directed by sports trainer Dr. Jack Groppel, they are designed for business executives interested in improving productivity and athletes seeking peak performance. Both groups learn to handle stress more efficiently while maintaining high levels of energy.

Program flexibility allows you to spend part of the day on the courts or golf course and part of it in consultation with fitness and nutrition specialists. Six services are available, including a psychological profile of how you handle stress in the office or in competitive sports. Based on these assessments, along with your interests and goals, a personal exercise program is designed for you.

Weight loss isn't a top priority here, but the restaurants do have low-calorie items on the menu. A computerized evaluation of your daily food consumption compares your nutritional intake to your recommended dietary allowance. The appraisal takes into account age, sex, weight, and amount of exercise.

Rolling greens and tree-lined fairways surround a traffic-free "walking village" where everything is conveniently located. The centerpiece is a 270-foot Superpool, big enough for racing, water aerobics, or volleyball. There's also a diving area and children's wading pool. The Jockey Club Spa nearby has ultramodern saunas, whirlpools, steam rooms in separate facilities for men and women, massage rooms, and a fully equipped exercise room.

Weight training sessions and aerobics classes are available separately or as part of a Sports and Health Getaway. The four- to seven-day packages include a hotel room or suite.

Families feel comfortable in this country club community, where there are sports activities for young people as well as competitive-minded parents. Even the convention groups that meet here take time off for sports workshops and a mini-Olympics.

Saddlebrook Golf and Tennis Resort
100 Saddlebrook Way, Box 7046, Wesley Chapel, FL 34249
Tel. 813/973–1111 or 800/237–7519 (800/282–4654 in FL).
Telex 52261

Administration Sports and health development director, Jack Groppel

Season Year-round.

Accommodations 790 guest rooms in 3 resort clusters, from spacious rooms with large baths to 1- and 2-bedroom suites with fully equipped kitchens. All units have color cable TV, modern furniture, queen- and king-size beds, balcony or patio.

Rates Deluxe room, single or double, $135 Jan. 15–Apr. 30, $60 in summer. Suites $130–$220, $70–$90 in summer. 4-day/3-night Sports and Health Getaway package $471–$525 single, $285–$399 double, in peak season. 4-day golf and tennis packages available. 1-night's advance payment for short visits, 25% for longer. Credit cards: AE, DC, MC, V.

Meal Plans Meals not included in packages. The Cypress Room open for gourmet dining and Friday night seafood buffet. The Little Club has special ovens for smoked meats and poultry, entrees such as mesquite-grilled snapper and pompano, steaks. Low-calorie options by special request.

Services and Facilities **Exercise Equipment:** 12-station Nautilus circuit, computerized Biocycle, Monark stationary bike, StairMaster, free weights (2–50 lbs.) and curl bar. **Services:** Swedish massage, facial, manicure. Computerized fitness analysis, health-risk appraisal, nutrition profile, stress management index, competitive sports profile. Tennis and golf clinics, including videotaped swing analysis. **Swimming Facilities:** 3 outdoor pools. **Recreation Facilities:** 41 tennis courts (hard and clay, some with lights), 2 18-hole golf courses designed by Arnold Palmer. Also fishing (equipment provided), 2-mi jogging trail.

In the Area Busch Gardens (family-oriented theme park and wildlife preserve), Sea World (performing whales and dolphins), Disney World, Cypress Gardens, Ybor City (Tampa's Cuban quarter).

Getting Here *From Tampa.* By car, Rte. 275 to I–75, Hwy. 54 (40 min). Limousine, rental car, taxi available.

Special Notes Ground-floor accommodations for the disabled, ramps to spa facilities. Programs for children 5–13: tennis and golf instruction, special camps, supervised activities during holidays. No smoking in spa and designated dining areas.

Safety Harbor Spa and Fitness Center

Life enhancement
Weight management
Luxury pampering
Taking the waters

Florida
Safety Harbor
(Tampa Bay)

Walking along Bayshore Drive in the morning, swimming laps under swaying palms, and soaking in mineral spring water are among the pleasures of a vacation at Safety Harbor. For centuries the springs attracted "cure" seekers from around the country; today the emphasis is on fitness and beauty, but you can still take the waters.

A fountain of youth this is not. Hernando de Soto, the Spanish explorer, supposedly bathed here in 1539 and named the five springs *Espiritu Santu* for their curative powers. Modern chemical analysis shows that each spring has a different proportion of calcium, magnesium, sodium, potassium, and other minerals. One water is recommended as a mild laxative, and the housekeeper will bring a free supply to your room on request. Otherwise, the best way to enjoy the waters is to bathe briefly in one of the Jacuzzi whirlpools next to the exercise pools. Unfortunately, they're loaded with chlorine.

Aquatics is a strong feature of the health-oriented program introduced in 1986, when the facilities got a $15-million face-lift. Exercising in the specially designed shallow indoor and outdoor pools burns calories efficiently without straining the body. The instructors here specialize in a variety of routines, from gentle to active, to keep you from getting bored. Coed classes attract people of all ages and are specially suited to exercise beginners.

An emphasis on total wellness has come with the new health and fitness orientation. Guests are encouraged to learn health habits and follow a low-cal diet that can be incorporated into their routines at home. The Safety Harbor experience is a good turning point for people who are not fit and need to make changes.

Staff doctors treat cardiovascular and other special problems. A member of the fitness staff will check your overall physical condition, monitor your aerobic heart rate, and analyze your body-fat to muscle ratio. Based on a computer analysis, a specific combination of exercise and diet will be recommended.

The various package plans allow you to pick and choose from the daily schedule of classes without advance registration. Nothing is required. More than two dozen activities, from cardiovascular circuit training at 6 **AM** to evening classes, are available.

The exercise studios, locker rooms, beauty salon, and massage rooms are on the garden level, an easy sprint from guest and dining rooms. Convenience is a plus in inclement weather, but it doesn't promote outdoor activity. Despite a few wall murals, the exercise area is spare. The locker rooms are downright dowdy, but the friendly staff helps guests look beyond appearances.

Bodywork appointments are made in the locker room and charged on an à la carte basis. Private tubs for thermal springwater baths are also available, along with the sauna and the steam room. Both men's and women's locker rooms have direct access to the exercise pool, but it's a good idea to bring footwear, even aquatic socks for water aerobics.

There's a view of Tampa Bay from the two well-equipped weight rooms and three aerobics gyms. Exercise instructors promote low-impact routines, and the shock-absorbing floors are specially constructed to help avoid tendinitis and shin splints. However, the workouts are peppy, and the sports training routine is for advanced fitness buffs only.

Both regular and calorie-controlled menus are served in the dining room. Don't be surprised to see a celebrity or two. Performers at nearby Ruth Eckerd Hall often stay here for the workouts and diet meals, and the exercise room is used by professional athletes.

Safety Harbor Spa and Fitness Center
105 N. Bayshore Dr., Safety Harbor, FL 34695
Tel. 813/726–1161 or 800/237–0155

Administration Manager, Alan Helfman; executive director of the spa, Fred Banke

Season Year-round.

Accommodations 215 bedrooms and suites; 30 full-service apartments in annex across the street. Tropical ambience, 1950s modern. Newer large deluxe units in the towers with balcony or terrace, 2 queen-size beds, dressing room, oversize bath. Air conditioned buildings connect to the spa.

Rates Fitness program and meals $246 per day single, deluxe room; $170 per person, double-occupancy, standard room, high season. "Perfect Day" package without room $139. "Total Fitness Plan" 8 days/7 nights $1,925 single, deluxe room; $1,470 per person, double occupancy, standard room. Tax and 16% service charge additional. 1 night advance payment. Credit cards: AE, MC, V.

Meal Plans 3 meals daily in formal dining room. Fitness plan breakfast includes fresh-baked pumpkin muffins, whole-wheat pancakes with raspberry puree, and egg-white omelete with farmer cheese. Lunch includes vegetable chili with white or brown rice, vegetable lasagna, pizza with whole-wheat crust, and breast of chicken with herbed ricotta cheese. Special dinner salads, such as romaine lettuce with Parmesan dressing, then broiled lobster, crab Mornay, shrimp with linguini. Coffee and herbal tea. Suggested daily 900-calorie special diet is high in complex carbohydrates, low in fat and sodium.

Services and Facilities **Exercise Equipment:** Paramount sports trainer system with adductor, abductor, abdominal pullover, pull-down, butterfly back press, lateral raise, leg-kick pulley, bicep/tricep machine. Nautilus hip/back, leg curl, lower back, and abdominal machines. 12 Precor treadmills, 4 stationary bikes, 2 rowing machines. 2 Heartmate TV bikes, 2 Schwinn Air-Dyne bikes, Versaclimber, 2 Concept II rowing machines, upper body ergometer, 4 trampolines, Hydra Fitness Total Power machine, Roman Chair abdominal unit. Free weights (1¼–45 lbs.) and dumbbells (3–40 lbs.) with bench press, incline bench. 2 speed bags for boxers. **Services:** Medical consultation, fitness evaluation, massage, herbal wraps, salt-glow loofah body scrub. Lancôme Skin Care Institute offers facials, haircuts and styling, makeup consultation, manicure, pedicure. Tennis instruction. **Swimming Facilities:** 2 outdoor and indoor pools. Mineral spring water in all swimming pools and Jacuzzis. **Recreation Facilities:** 7 Har Tru tennis courts, 3-hole golf course and driving range, free use of bikes, basketball, water volleyball. Golf and horseback riding nearby for a fee. **Evening Programs:** Lectures on stress management and health-related topics, cooking demonstrations, cultural programs, lounge dancing on weekends.

In the Area Organized outings for canoeing, biking, fishing (fee). Evening trips to performing arts centers in Tampa and Clearwater, shopping centers, movies; Ybor City (Tampa's colorful Cuban quarter), one-day Bahamas cruise, ocean beaches, Busch Gardens (family theme park and wildlife preserve), history museums, Tarpon Springs sponge harvest and sales center.

Getting Here *From Tampa.* By bus, scheduled van service from Tampa International Airport. By car, I–275 south to Exit 20, Rte. 60 toward Clearwater, exit on Bayshore Blvd. (20 min). Hotel van to the airport. Taxi, rental car available.

Special Notes Elevators but no specially equipped rooms for the disabled. No smoking in the spa and in designated dining areas.

Turnberry Isle Yacht and Country Club

Life enhancement
Luxury pampering

Florida
Turnberry Isle
(North Miami)

Here's a luxury hideaway for the executive who wants to shape up in privacy. Boasting spacious accommodations on the Intracoastal Waterway, with a medical director, nutritionist, and full staff of therapists, Turnberry Isle accepts no more than 10 outside guests at a time to share the members' privileges.

A well-kept secret, the spa here must be sought out. You proceed through the security gate past the imposing condominium apartment towers, tennis courts, and lush gardens to the marina hotel.

Health and nutrition programs are an integral part of this posh preserve. The professionals who run the spa talk privately with you about losing weight and arranging appointments for bodywork at your convenience. With a minimum amount of stress and bother, you begin a rejuvenating regimen.

A menu planner comes with the daily schedule of exercise classes. One muscle builder, one fruit or fruit juice, one bread and cereal add up to just 200 calories for breakfast. Men take in more protein than women—seven ounces per day versus six. An egg-white mushroom omelet is 65 calories, a poached egg, 75.

The morning walk around the five miles of waterway and golf course gives you a chance to get acquainted with club members and guests. Then you have a choice of four to six classes daily, from water works to a power workout with hand weights, all rated for fitness level.

Clothing for exercise and swimming is supplied daily at the spa reception desk and locker rooms. Bring just leotards and tights. Staff members greet guests by name and quickly make newcomers feel at home.

For a break in the routine, try the beach. There are cabanas, a swimming pool, and light fare for lunch at the private Ocean Club. Relax in a Turkish steam bath and Swedish sauna.

Small and exclusive, Turnberry Isle is a special place to escape from pressure and routine. Rarely crowded, it has first-class facilities and equipment, complete with hydrotherapy, indoor and outdoor whirlpools, and medical consultation.

Turnberry Isle Yacht and Country Club
19735 Turnberry Way;
Box 630578, Turnberry Isle, FL 33163
Tel. 305/932–2504 or 800/327–7028
(305/932–6200 for hotel reservations)
Telex 80–8013 AVTURN

Administration   Spa director, Hugh Jones

Season   Year-round.

Accommodations   118 rooms and suites in Marina Hotel (adjoining spa building) and country club, with curving terraces and views. Wicker and wooden furnishings, dining and reading areas. Suites with double Jacuzzi tub, private solarium, redwood hot tub. For golfers, Country Club Hotel can be part of spa package.

Rates Rooms $125–$140 a day in summer, $275 in winter. Spa facilities admission $12.50 daily for registered guests. Spa nutrition and fitness plan 8 days/7 nights $1,982 single, $1,584 double, including tax and gratuity, May–Oct. 5- day/4-night package with meals $1,230 single, $1,004 double, May–Oct. One night's advance payment with credit card. Credit cards: AE, CB, DC, MC, V.

Meal Plans 3 low-cal meals daily in nutrition and fitness plan (900 calories per day). High-carbohydrate luncheon includes grilled swordfish, pasta primavera, and cold shrimp plate. Typical dinner entrees are steamed lobster tail, tenderloin brochette, eggplant Parmesan, mesquite-grilled redfish with scallions. Meals in your room or in the main dining room.

Services and Facilities **Exercise Equipment:** Nautilus circuit, free weights, Liferower, StairMaster, Lifecycles, treadmills, hand weights. 34-station Vitacourse. **Services:** Therapeutic massage, Swedish massage, herbal wrap, loofah body scrub, Swiss shower, Vitabath, skin care. Computerized body composition analysis, nutrition consultation, blood cholesterol test, medical consultation. **Swimming Facilities:** 2 pools at spa, Ocean Club, Country Club. **Recreation Facilities:** 2 championship golf courses, 24 tennis courts with 5 different surfaces (18 lighted), 3 indoor racquetball courts, bicycle rentals.

In the Area Yacht and deep-sea fishing charters; shopping at Aventura Mall, Thoroughbred races at Gulfstream Park, Disney World, Miami and Fort Lauderdale museums.

Getting Here *From Miami.* By car, I–95 to Exit 20, Ives Dairy Rd., U.S. Rte. 1, Biscayne Blvd. (25 min). By boat, Intracoastal Waterway to Turnberry Isle Marina. Airport shuttle service to Fort Lauderdale and Miami. Taxi, limousine, rental car available.

Special Notes No smoking in the spa and in designated dining areas.

Weight Watchers Camp Vanguard

Youth camps for weight loss

Florida
Lake Wales This summer coed camp for teenagers and young adults—10 through 21 years old—offers diet, exercise, and education on an active vacation. Campers have exclusive use of a weights room, gymnasium, outdoor swimming pool and other facilities. Water sports, boating, and fishing opportunities are also available at Camp Vanguard, on the Vanguard School campus in the Tampa/Orlando area. Men and women campers are housed separately in modern dormitories.

Meals feature Weight Watchers recipes. Campers learn how to eat properly through cooking classes and lectures on nutrition.

Accredited counselors supervise workouts with Nautilus equipment, slimnastics and aerobics classes, and sports. Those who complete the course without losing weight get a refund.

Weight Watchers Camp Vanguard
2249 Hwy. 27 North, Lake Wales, FL 33853
Tel. 813/676–7083
Weight Watchers Camps
183 Madison Ave., New York, NY 10016
Tel. 212/889–9500 or 800/223–5600 (800/251–4141 in Canada)

Administration Program director, Anthony Sparber

Season June–Aug.

Accommodations Dormitories with TV lounges, modern lavatories and baths. Campers grouped by age, overseen by counselors.

Rates Sessions of 2–7 weeks from $1,450. $100 advance payment. Credit cards: AE, DC, MC, V.

Meal Plans 3 balanced meals daily in the cafeteria, 2 snacks daily in residence halls.

Services and Facilities **Exercise Equipment:** Weights room with Nautilus, gymnasium equipment. **Swimming Facilities:** Outdoor swimming pool, beach nearby. **Recreation Facilities:** Softball, soccer, tennis, football, volleyball, jogging, track; water sports, boating, fishing. **Evening Programs:** Outdoor barbecues, picnics, talent shows, disco.

In the Area Nature walks; Disney World.

Getting Here Campers picked up at Orlando airport. Taxi, rental car available.

Special Notes No smoking indoors.

Southwind Health Resort

Luxury pampering   *Women only*
Weight management

Georgia
Cartersville Southern hospitality comes with the room in this turn-of-the-century Victorian mansion. The spa program is designed for women who are serious about losing weight. Atlanta matrons and working women come here for a week, weekend, or one-day sampler. Set on 16 wooded acres overlooking Lake Allatoona, Southwind is an upscale retreat with a down-home atmosphere. Programs are limited to 16 participants. The totally structured program includes four hours each day for individual counseling. Personalized beauty consultations emphasize the benefits of exercise and diet. A swimming pool, Jacuzzi, exercise machines, and Nautilus gym are nearby.

Health professionals conduct seminars daily, and two medical doctors, a nurse, a cardiovascular fitness specialist, and a nutritionist are on hand. Personal attention begins during prebreakfast fitness walks and continues through discussions after dinner.

The formal mansion dining room gives a sense of occasion to calorie-controlled gourmet meals. A complimentary beverage bar serves herbal teas, decaffeinated coffee, and water. By the end of the day many guests are content to settle into a rocking chair on the veranda and just enjoy the fresh country air.

Scheduled programs run from Sunday afternoon to Saturday morning and Thursday afternoon to Sunday brunch. Fitness classes, bodywork and beauty treatments, and shopping and sightseeing can be added to the basic program for about $300 to $400 extra—still below costs at many luxury spas.

Southwind Health Resort

Rte. 2, Sandtown Rd., Cartersville, GA 30120
Tel. 404/975–0342 or 800/832–2622

Administration	Director, Doreen MacAdams
Season	Year-round sessions and day visits.
Accommodations	8 double rooms with Old South charm. Queen-size beds, some shared baths.
Rates	6-night program $795 per person, weekends $395. Optional fitness and beauty packages with unlimited exercise classes (some massage and salon services) $100–$150 weekends, $300–$400 weekly. 1-day sampler $150. $500 advance payment weeks, $200 weekends. Credit cards: AE, CB, DC, MC, V.
Meal Plans	3 balanced meals (800–1,000 cal) daily. Specialties include organically grown vegetables and home-made dietetic ice cream. Medallions of lobster in sherry and cream sauce, Cajun-style blackened chicken, *moo goo gai pan* with chicken and bok choy specialties, and spaghetti squash Parmesan are among choices.
Services and Facilities	**Exercise Equipment:** Hand weights, 2 stationary bikes, 2 rowing machines; Nautilus gym nearby. **Services:** Massage, facials, manicures, hair and skin care, beauty consultations; cooking class. **Swimming Facilities:** 40-foot pool, lake beach nearby. **Recreation Facilities:** Nature hiking, fishing in private pond, golf nearby. **Evening Programs:** Talks on practical and humorous sides of health; library of videocassettes and publications on health and self-help.
In the Area	Atlanta museums.
Getting Here	*From Atlanta.* By car, I–75 north to Exit 122, Cartersville, Allatoona Rd. (45 min). Service to and from Hartsfield International Airport ($20). Taxi, rental car available.
Special Notes	No smoking indoors.

Wildwood Lifestyle Center

Life enhancement
Preventive medicine
Weight management

Georgia
Wildwood
Converts to fitness come here to learn a healthier way of life. Up to 26 middle-aged professionals and housewives participate in each session of the Wildwood Lifestyle Program. Medically oriented and devoted to education and exercise, the 24-day program provides a basis for self-help.

Wildwood, a hospital as well as a lifestyle center, has been devoted to preventive medicine for more than 40 years. The doctors, nurses, and staff, all Seventh-day Adventists, see medicine as a means of disease prevention. Their nutritional computer analysis makes specific recommendations for diet and takes into account present physical condition, nutritional requirements, and weight-loss goals. After a complete medical examination a physician—who monitors your progress throughout the three-week program—prescribes a program for you. One-week programs to stop smoking are scheduled at various times during the year. Personal counseling tailored to the health needs of the individual and 10- to 17-day programs are available.

The hospital's live-in accommodations provide privacy and comfort in a secluded valley among the mountains of North Georgia. Each program participant gets a blood chemistry profile, EKG-exercise stress test, lung function evaluation, and chest X-ray. (Health insurance may cover some expenses.) The philosophy is to treat the causes of disease rather than the symptoms. High blood pressure, coronary heart disease, angina, arteriosclerosis, diabetes, stress, constipation, arthritis, and obesity are addressed.

Hydrotherapy and massage may be recommended at extra cost. Hiking twice a day along 35 miles of wooded trails helps guests get in shape. Every afternoon during the week there is a nutrition lecture, followed by cooking classes.

The Adventists, known for their interest in health and nutrition, admit anyone who is committed to a strictly vegetarian diet and the need for continuing exercise at home. Wildwood is nondenominational and nonsectarian.

Wildwood Lifestyle Center
Wildwood, GA 30757
Tel. 404/820–1474 or 800/634–9355

Administration Director, Charles H. Cleveland; Lifestyle Program director, Larry Scott; medical director, Marjorie Baldwin, M.D.

Season Year-round.

Accommodations 26 mountain lodge bedrooms with twin beds, private patio; some share large bath. Woodland views. Lounge for informal lectures around fireplace, laundry facility.

Rates 24-day program $2,950 semi-private. Private rooms when available. $20 less daily for spouses participating in nonmedical parts of program. Transportation included certain times of year. 7-day stop-smoking program $1,150. $100 per person advance payment, refundable up to 2 weeks before program begins. Credit cards (4% surcharge): MC, V.

Meal Plans Fruits, vegetables, legumes, and grains. No butter or oil, but nuts, olives and avocados available. 3 daily buffets without dairy products, fish, or meat. Specialties include vegetarian lasagna with melty "cheese" topping of tahini, pimiento, and tomato; oat-burger roll; steamed vegetables with rice; seven-grain bread.

Services and Facilities **Exercise Equipment:** 2 Lifecycles, 2 trampolines, rowing machines. **Services:** Swedish massage, hydrotherapy showers, medical treatment. **Swimming Facilities:** Lake on property. **Spa Facilities:** Sauna and steam room. **Recreation Facilities:** Hiking, boating. **Evening Programs:** Lectures on health-related and spiritual topics.

In the Area Picnics, outings to historical sites and Civil War memorials; Atlanta museums, shopping; Chattanooga museums.

Getting Here *From Atlanta.* By bus, Trailways to Chattanooga (2 hr). By plane, scheduled flights to Chattanooga metropolitan airport.

By car, I–24 past Chattanooga, Exit 169 (about 2 hr). Free service to and from Chattanooga airport and bus station. Rental car available.

Special Notes All rooms on ground level; wheelchair patients accepted when accompanied by companion. No smoking indoors. Remember to bring an alarm clock, laundry detergent, umbrella, rain gear.

Bluegrass Spa

Stress control
Holistic health
Life enhancement

Kentucky
Stamping Ground Time seems suspended at Bluegrass Spa. It comes as a surprise that, behind the antebellum mansion set amid great old trees and green pastures, is a modern holistic health center with bodywork and spiritual-awareness programs.

The holistic approach to health is intended to nurture the mind and spirit as well as the body. Daily classes, workshops, and mini-lectures address physical and metaphysical aspects of health. There are outings with a channeler and a visit to an equestrian center.

Many career women come here to relax and learn about holistic health while indulging in some spa pampering. Guests typically range in age from 30 to 60, with a few men who enjoy the exercise classes along with golf at a nearby course. Individuals choose their activities, but their progress is monitored by the fitness director.

Limited to 20 guests, the program capitalizes on resources in the Lexington area. There is a carriage house and pool for fitness classes, but no exercise equipment other than bicycles, hand weights, and a rebounder. Choices on a typical day include a workshop in tai chi chuan, bicycling on country roads, relaxing in the sauna and Jacuzzi, and sunbathing. Beauty and bodywork are à la carte or included in packages.

Misty views of horse farms and old tobacco barns reward early risers. The ranch bell at 7 AM heralds a prebreakfast stretch followed by a walk or jog along lanes lined with stone and log fences.

Blueberry bran muffins fresh from the oven are morning compensation. The 900-calorie daily diet—all-natural, low in fat and high in fiber, without salt, sugar, or chemicals—leaves room for treats like cheesecake and stir-fried vegetables. There is an organic garden on the property.

Bluegrass Spa
901 Galloway Rd., Stamping Ground, KY 40379
Tel. 502/535–6261

Administration Program director, Nancy Rutherford

Season Apr.–Oct.

Accommodations 2 guest rooms, high ceilings, fireplaces, antiques, large, modern beds, private baths, in 1819 Greek Revival mansion. 2 cabana rooms by pool, 4 bedrooms in lodge for groups of 3 or more with shared bath. White wicker chairs, down comforters add to old-fashioned comfort.

Rates $165–$225 daily includes all spa activities and meals. Beauty
and bodywork extra. A la carte plan $297–$405 weekends,
$743–$1,051 for 5 nights, $1,042–$1,418 for 7 nights. Package
plans with some massages and beauty treatments $125 daily
(not overnight), $322–$430 weekends, $843–$1,115 5 nights,
$1,190–$1,568 for 7 nights. $400 deposit 7- and 5-day plans,
$150 weekends. Credit cards: MC, V.

Meal Plans Mainly vegetarian, meals include fish and chicken. Fruit and
muffins for breakfast, tortilla with garden vegetables, salsa
sauce and cheese topping for lunch. Dinner entrees include
spinach-mushroom lasagna, snapper baked with lime and
served with papaya chutney. Frozen bananas and grapes available twice daily for snacks.

Services and **Exercise Equipment:** Stationary bikes, hand weights, trampo-
Facilities line. Bicycles for outings and personal use. Additional
facilities, with exercise machines, planned for 1989. **Services:**
Massage (Swedish, Esalen, shiatsu, Trager, polarity, and
reflexology), salt glow, facials, herbal wrap, aromatherapy.
Swimming Facilities: Outdoor pool, nearby lake. **Recreation
Facilities:** Bicycling, basketball, volleyball, croquet; horseback
riding, tennis, golf nearby for a fee. **Evening Programs:** Workshops on stress control, energy enhancement, astrology, and
consciousness expanding.

In the Area 2 or more outings weekly organized to suit guests. Options include Kentucky Horse Park, a restored Shaker village,
antiques shops along Railroad St. in historic Midway, and a
session of trance channel work at Phoenix Inst. in Lexington;
summer theater, concerts, Kentucky Derby complex,
Keenland Race Track, Churchill Downs, Red River Gorge.

Getting Here *From Cincinnati.* By car, I–75 to Georgetown, KY, Rte. 460 to
Galloway Pike (about 80 min). By plane, scheduled flights to
Lexington, KY (20 min). Free service to and from Lexington
airport; pickup at Louisville or Cincinnati, $40 each way.

Special Notes No smoking.

EuroVita Spa at the Avenue Plaza Hotel

Luxury pampering

Louisiana Amid Cajun capers and blackened redfish restaurants is an oa-
New Orleans sis of fitness in New Orleans. The EuroVita Spa is located in a
pleasant hotel in the Garden District and is heavily patronized
by knowledgeable local fitness buffs and visitors on business.
The best deal is a spa plan package for two, four, or six nights.

The fitness facilities spread from a garden patio pool to a mirrored rooftop aerobics studio. An outdoor whirlpool on the sun
deck has a view of the city.

Yoga or aerobics begin the day, Monday through Friday, and
two or three classes are scheduled daily. Massage, herbal
wrap, or loofah body scrub, complete with Swiss shower, are
by appointment. Sauna and steam room are available, and
robes are provided daily.

The extensive array of exercise equipment is unusual for city
spas in this part of the country. The Avenue Plaza is a real discovery.

EuroVita Spa at the Avenue Plaza Hotel
2111 St. Charles Ave., New Orleans, LA 70130
Tel. 504/566–1212 or 800/535–9575

Administration	Manager, Joan B. Tarver; fitness director, Anthony Chetta
Season	Year-round.
Accommodations	240 1- to 3-bedroom suites in elegant, 12-story stone building. Traditional or Art Deco furnishings, modern baths, air conditioning, TV. King-size or double beds, foldouts.
Rates	$69–$165 single, $79–$206 double, includes spa facilities without program. Spa plan with treatments and meals from 2-night package, $315 single, $256.50 per person double occupancy, to 6-night program, $882 single, $711 per person double occupancy. With companion sharing room, but not plan, $167.50 for 2 nights, $471 for 6 nights. 25% payable in advance. Credit cards: AE, DC, MC, V.
Meal Plans	Breakfast and lunch diet cuisine for spa plan guests (dinner not included). Special menu selections arranged on request. Entrees at lunch include breast of chicken with cognac and raisins, oysters en brochette with chilled seafood salad, shrimp à la Nantua.
Services and Facilities	**Exercise Equipment:** Paramount circuit and Universal multistation unit in weights room open Mon.–Fri. 7 AM–9 PM, weekends 9–5. Free weights (2–50 lbs.), and barbells (2–50 lbs.), 3 Lifecycles, 3 Schwinn Air-Dyne bikes, Monark ergometer, 2 rowing machines, 2 Precor treadmills, StairMaster and Versaclimber. **Services:** Massage, herbal wrap, loofah scrub, facial, pedicure, manicure, hairstyling. A health-risk appraisal included in spa plan. **Swimming Facilities:** Heated outdoor pool in garden patio. **Recreation Facilities:** Concierge can make arrangements for tennis, golf, horseback riding.
In the Area	Local sightseeing and scheduled tours; bayou tours, antiques shops, Mississippi River cruises.
Getting Here	*From New Orleans International Airport.* By bus: Rhodes Public service $8. Taxi or limo: $18 per person (30 min). Rental car available. Private parking for hotel guests.
Special Notes	Elevator connects all floors. No smoking in the spa. Remember to bring exercise clothes and tennis shoes.

Camp Camelot

Youth camps for weight loss   *Women only*

North Carolina *Boone*	Located in the heart of the Appalachian Mountains, on the Appalachian State University campus, the all-girl Camp Camelot focuses on diet, exercise, nutritional education, and personal grooming. The camp offers recreational, educational, and cultural opportunities for young women in age groups 8–12, 13–17, 18–21, and 21–29.
	Sports facilities include an 8,000-seat gymnasium, gymnastics room, exercise room with Universal gym, health-fitness room, and dance studio. Basketball, volleyball, racquetball, tennis courts, indoor and outdoor tracks, and a baseball field are also available.

In addition to an Olympic-size swimming pool, there are nearby lakes for waterskiing and canoeing. Personal grooming workshops cover poise and grace, posture, wardrobe, etiquette, skin and body care, and makeup and hairstyling.

The exercise regimen and calorie-controlled meal complement each other. The 1,200-calorie diet is served in colorful dining halls with modern cooking facilities. A nutrition consultant oversees daily preparation of three meals and two snacks of assorted vegetables and fresh fruits.

Camp Camelot

Appalachian State University, Boone, NC;
(Office) 949 Northfield Rd., Woodmere, NY 11598
Tel. 516/374-0785 or 800/421-4321

Administration Program director, Thelma Hurwitz

Season July–Aug.

Accommodations Campers have exclusive use of fully equipped dorms with mountain views; lounges and game room for socialization and evening activities. Modern baths and post office.

Rates 7 weeks $3,650, 4 weeks $2,450, 3 weeks $1,925. $375 deposit. Credit cards: MC, V.

Meal Plans Balanced meals 3 times daily. Diet determined by each camper's growth and nutritional needs. Specialties: Polynesian chicken, veal scaloppine, broiled steak, barbecued chicken, beef Stroganoff, turkey divan.

Services and Facilities **Exercise Equipment:** Exercise room with Universal gym, gymnastics and health fitness rooms, dance studio. **Swimming Facilities:** Indoor pool; lakes and beaches nearby. **Recreation Facilities:** Softball, basketball, soccer, volleyball, tennis, racquetball, track, bicycling, aerobics. **Evening Programs:** Dramatics, skating, bowling, movies, dancing.

In the Area Linville Caverns, Tweetsie Railroad, Grandfather Mountain, Mystery Hill, Blowing Rock; concerts and theaters; indoor ice-skating rink, golf courses.

Getting Here Pickup by prior arrangement. Rental car, taxi available.

Special Notes No smoking indoors.

Duke University Diet and Fitness Center

Life enhancement
Weight management

North Carolina This weight-control program resembles a college course in
Durham healthier living. The combination of classes and nutritional and psychological counseling, with focus on sports and exercise, emphasizes strategies for long-term success and lifestyle change rather than immediate results. For more than 15 years the Duke University Diet and Fitness Center has achieved an enviable success rate.

Obesity 101 could be the course title of the educational program designed to fit into a two-week vacation period. Many people come for four weeks or longer, hoping to lose from 20 to 200 pounds after unsuccessfully trying various other weight-loss plans without mastering long-term weight management. The average weight loss is two to five pounds per week.

Supervised by a team of doctors, behavioral psychologists, nutritionists, and fitness specialists, the program draws on the resources of Duke University and its distinguished faculty. Housing arrangements, however, are left to the individual, and there are no rooms on campus.

New participants arrive on Monday. After an initial assessment and evaluation, including laboratory tests and a treadmill stress test, a schedule of classes and lectures is prescribed (about four per day on the two-week program), with free time on weekends to explore the area. Daily check-ins with staff members monitor progress.

The medically supervised part of the program can include psychotherapy on an individual basis and additional laboratory tests. The fitness component—the gym and the swimming pool—enables sedentary types to get some exercise into their lives. Once group camaraderie develops, there are volleyball, basketball, and badminton games.

Education continues outside the classroom in local supermarkets and restaurants. Duke staffers demonstrate how to shop for and order the right foods. Cooking classes are a popular feature, and meals made at the center's demonstration kitchen can be eaten.

The improved self-esteem and confidence that comes with weight loss accounts largely for the program's long-term success rate. Instructors illustrate how age, sex, and level of physical activity affect weight and show ways to lower cholesterol, decrease blood pressure, and avoid problems of diabetes.

The center attracts people from all walks of life, of all ages and both sexes. Programs are structured for seriously overweight persons and are without the social strains found in some resorts. A platoon of obese joggers "walking the wall," a 1.6-mile route around the university, is a common morning sight. Later there are water aerobics in the heated indoor swimming pool. It's a full day, from the walk at 7:30 to the after-dinner lecture.

The center encourages family members or close friends to accompany program participants. Arrangements can be made to eat together, attend lectures, and use the exercise facility. Support program costs range from $75 a day to $345 a week.

Durham has been known as a diet and fitness center for more than 40 years. Continuing education at Duke's program is a commitment for those who need to change their lifestyle. Dieters return periodically for reinforcement, and some even move here.

Duke University Diet and Fitness Center
804 W. Trinity Ave., Durham, NC 27701
Tel. 919/684–6331

Administration Program director, Michael A. Hamilton, M.D.; manager, Jonathan Carmel

Season Year-round.

Accommodations Local inns cater to dieters. Duke Tower, across from center, has suites with bedroom, living room, kitchen $1,200 per month. Rooms in private home 2 miles from center $400 per month.

Rates 2-week program $2,400, 4-week program $2,950. $500 advance payment. $200 deposit Duke Tower suites, refundable. Credit cards: AE, MC, V.

Meal Plans 3 low-calorie, portion-controlled meals daily at Center. 800-calorie daily diet low in sodium, fat, and cholesterol. Vegetarian and kosher diets accommodated. Seafood gumbo with rice, lamb stew, and eggplant Parmesan for lunch. Italian baked fish, roast barbecued pork, sirloin steak, and black bean tortillas for dinner. Menu published weekly, with calorie counts.

Services and Facilities **Exercise Equipment:** Schwinn Air-Dyne bicycles, all equipment in university gymnasium. **Services:** Massage, supervised exercise on bikes, swimming instruction; individual psychotherapy; on-site medical clinic; clinic to stop smoking. **Swimming Facilities:** 25-meter indoor pool. **Recreation Facilities:** University campus and city parks provide full range of sports, including tennis, golf, fishing. **Evening Programs:** Lectures on health-related topics scheduled nightly Mon.–Fri.: Image consultant, dance instructor, Overeaters Anonymous speakers. Duke University performing arts and cultural programs open to participants.

In the Area Low-cost day-trips on weekends include mountains, beach resorts, numerous historic sites. Brevard Music Center concerts late June–mid-Aug., Asheville folk arts. Biltmore Estate near Asheville.

Getting Here *From Raleigh-Durham Airport.* By car, Rte. 70 to I–85, Gregson St. to Trinity Ave. (20 min to center). Duke Towers provides free service to and from airport. Taxi, rental car available.

Special Notes Ramps in most buildings provide access for the disabled. Theater, arts, recreational outings for children through community organizations. No smoking indoors and in patio area. Remember to bring appropriate seasonal clothing, exercise and swimming outfits, jogging or walking shoes; notebooks and pens, wristwatch, alarm clock, padlock for gym lockers.

Structure House

Weight management
Life enhancement

North Carolina **Durham** Settling into your apartment in "the village" is like getting a new lease on life. The cluster of residential units around the new Life Extension Center Building and the big, redbrick Structure House, where one goes for meals, classes, and professional services, gives off a college campus atmosphere. Healthy habits, in fact, are what you learn here.

Most people come here to lose weight quickly and safely, but the program is designed to teach long-term weight control. The new environment helps, particularly if you have failed to lose weight at home or in other programs. Over 40 qualified professionals help you to understand the reasons behind unhealthy lifestyles and to practice problem solving.

The medically managed program involves mental and physical conditioning. A full physical examination and diagnosis precedes the planning of an individual diet and exercise regimen. For the elderly, the handicapped, and those with health problems, the medical staff consults with patients' private physicians in order to monitor and continue health services.

Therapy does more than reduce stress. Structure House tries to help people understand why they gain weight. Divorce, serious illness, financial setbacks and other major changes often lead to overeating. Everyday stresses, too little activity, depression, and boredom are treated, along with serious cases of obesity, in group sessions with a stress therapist and in private counseling.

The body-image workshop shows how people view themselves. This therapy helps you to accept your body and integrate it into a new self-image as you lose weight.

A two-week session at the Executive Lifestyle Institute and at least four weeks of intensive treatment are recommended for serious weight problems. Alumni can return for a week or more of reinforcement; many bring their spouse or a companion.

The integration of medical and psychological aspects of weight loss, alongside dietary and exercise programs, makes this program work for people who need a structured environment. The exercise facilities and classes at the Life Extension Center are the equal of many leading spa resorts.

Success stories—losses of 100 pounds and more—are celebrated regularly. The actor James Coco wrote about his experience in a 1984 best-seller; he called it "restructuring."

Structure House
3017 Pickett Rd., Durham, NC 27705
Tel. 919/688–7379

Administration	Program director, Gerard J. Musante; medical consultants, Sigrid Nelius, M.D.; Robert Berger, M.D.; David Hawkins, M.D.
Season	Year-round; sessions begin 8 AM Mon.
Accommodations	1- and 2-bedroom apartments in 6 two-story houses on campus and nearby lodging. New modern units, sliding glass door opens onto porch. Washer/dryer, linens, telephone, color TV with HBO, weekly maid service. 60 rooms on campus, 40 off.
Rates	2-week Executive Lifestyle Institute $2,500, including housing, double occupancy. 4-week Intensive Treatment Program $2,425, plus $1,075 for campus housing or $675 for in-town apartments, double occupancy. (Health insurance may cover medical and psychological services.) $500 per person advance payment. Credit cards: MC, V.
Meal Plans	Selections based on weekly diary system in which each person plans own meals. Suggested 700-calorie menu includes meat loaf, turkey sandwich, French toast, and oatmeal. Fri. lunch is a potato bar with toppings. Dinner entrees include stuffed zucchini Florentine, baked chicken, and filet mignon. Vegetarian and special diets accommodated.
Services and Facilities	**Exercise Equipment:** Nautilus machines, stationary bikes, rowing machine, bench press and free weights, trampoline. **Services:** Massage (Swedish, Trager, deep-muscle, polarity), medical consultation and testing, consultation with clinical

psychologist, dietary reeducation workshops, consultation. **Swimming Facilities:** Indoor pool, lakes nearby. **Recreation Facilities:** Nature trails, hiking, basketball, badminton, Ping-Pong, tennis, golf; horseback riding nearby. **Evening Programs:** Occasional parties.

In the Area   Eastern Piedmont mountains and shoreline, plus numerous historic sites. Brevard Music Center concerts late June–mid-Aug., Asheville area folk arts and Biltmore estate. Minor-league baseball at *Bull Durham* park.

Getting Here   *From Raleigh-Durham Airport.* By car, Rte. 70 to I–85 (20 min to Structure House). Shuttle service from airport prearranged by Structure House $15. Taxi, rental car available.

Special Notes   Ramps for wheelchairs; some apartments specially equipped for the disabled. No smoking indoors and in designated dining areas. Remember to bring recent medical records, exercise clothing, wristwatch with second hand, walking or jogging shoes.

Weight Watchers Camp Asheville

Youth camps for weight loss

North Carolina   Located on the campus of Warren Wilson College, this recent-
Swannanoa   ly relocated coed summer camp offers a program of diet, exercise, and education. The 10- to 21-year-old campers at Camp Asheville are housed in residence halls where they share spacious double rooms.

Meals feature Weight Watchers recipes, and campers learn to eat properly through cooking classes and lectures on nutrition.

Accredited counselors supervise workouts with Nautilus equipment, slimnastics and aerobics classes, and sports. Those who complete the course are guaranteed to lose weight or get a refund.

Weight Watchers Camp Asheville
701 Warren Wilson Rd., Swannanoa, NC 28778
Tel. 704/298–3325
Weight Watchers Camps
183 Madison Ave., New York, NY 10016
Tel. 212/889–9500 or 800/223–5600 (800/251–4141 in Canada)

Administration   Program director, Anthony Sparber

Season   June–Aug.

Accommodations   Double rooms for 225 campers. A counselor for every 4 campers.

Rates   Sessions of 2–7-weeks, from $1,450. $100 advance payment. Credit cards: AE, DC, MC, V.

Meal Plans   3 balanced meals daily in cafeteria, 2 snacks daily in residence halls.

Services and Facilities   **Exercise Equipment:** Weights room with Nautilus equipment, gymnasium equipment, dance studio. **Swimming Facilities:** Indoor pool. **Recreation Facilities:** Soccer, basketball, tennis, football, softball, volleyball. **Evening Programs:** Campfires, cookouts, disco, fashion shows, talent shows.

In the Area   Hikes, nature walks, Biltmore Estate.

Getting Here Campers picked up at Asheville Airport. Taxi, rental car available.

Special Notes Smoking discouraged.

Hilton Head Health Institute

Life enhancement
Stress control
Weight management
Nutrition and diet

South Carolina Compact courses on healthy living are aimed at modifying be-
Hilton Head havior in order to achieve practical results: changes in your
Island home life and work habits, nutritional education for weight
maintenance, and the enhancement of executive stamina.

A few weeks here will not change your life immediately, but it
can be a step toward taking control. The effect of food on the
body's metabolism and the effect of stress on productivity and
health are taught by a team of psychologists, nutritionists, and
physical fitness specialists.

The island environment encourages change. Part of the exercise regime is walking on the beach—called a "thermal walk"
here because of the effects of sun and air on mood and appetite.

Activities center in a campuslike cluster of villas. Participants
share well-decorated apartments, fully equipped for laundry or
cooking. The island's laid-back atmosphere will certainly ease
stress, and the self-management course will help you resist
food temptations in high-rise hotels down the beach. The medically supervised programs are suited for individuals and
couples who have reached a point in their lives where change is
necessary and they need a boost to get started.

Hilton Head Health Institute
Box 7138, Hilton Head Island, SC 29938
Tel. 803/785–7292

Administration Executive director, Peter M. Miller; medical consultant, Jack
M. Catlett, M.D.

Season Scheduled programs monthly, year-round.

Accommodations Villas accommodate 44. Twin beds, private baths. Traditional
furniture, fine fabrics, color TV. Living area shared by 2 bedrooms. Private porch, parking space, pedestrian walkways.

Rates 12-day executive health course $2,600 per person double occu-
pancy, in a condominium-style apartment. 26-day weight-
control program $4,200 per person. 2-week "Healthy Lifestyle"
program (early Dec. only) $2,600 per person. $600 advance
payment for 12-day program, $1,000 for 26-day program. No
credit cards.

Meal Plans 3 meals and "Metabo" fruit snack daily. Mon.–Fri. diet totals
approx. 800 calories daily, more on weekends, when outdoor
activity increases. Food high in complex carbohydrates, moderate protein, low fat, no sugar or salt. Lunch can feature pasta
primavera with raw vegetables, dinner entrees include chicken
enchilada with salsa and brown rice.

Services and **Exercise Equipment:** 8-station Paramount weight system, 5
Facilities stationary bikes, 2 rowing machines, 2 treadmills. **Services:**

Massage, beauty salon nearby. **Swimming Facilities:** Outdoor pool, ocean beach. **Recreation Facilities:** 24 tennis courts and 3 golf courses within walking distance, for a fee. Nature preserve of subtropical marshes for hiking. Horseback riding, bicycling, windsurfing, sailing, deep-sea fishing available through resort services.

In the Area Community theater, cinema, shopping mall. Nature tours by boat; Historic Savannah, GA (1 hr), Beaufort, Charleston (antebellum homes and gardens, 2 hr north).

Getting Here *From Savannah.* By car, I-95 to Rte. 278 (50 min). By plane, Hilton Head Island airport has scheduled service on Piedmont-Henson (via Charlotte), Eastern (via Atlanta). Limousine service hourly from Savannah airport. Taxi, rental car available.

Special Notes Programs for children at community centers. No smoking indoors. Remember to bring an alarm clock, flashlight, medical records.

The Westin Resort

Non-program resort facilities

South Carolina
Hilton Head
Island

On an island noted for golf, tennis, and fishing, the newly opened health facilities at the posh Westin Resort are a happy addition. The price is also good news. Equipment, classes, and outdoor recreation on 24 acres of landscaped, subtropical dunes is free to hotel guests.

The sprawling, five-story hotel has big-city airs and a breezy, Southern Low Country ambience. Enjoy the view of the grand courtyard and three swimming pools from the mirrored weights room. One of the pools is glass-enclosed for year-round swimming and water aerobics classes.

Mornings begin with a beach walk, the so-called "thermal walk" recommended by doctors at the Hilton Head Institute. Invigorated by sun, sea, and air, you can join an exercise class or have a personal program planned for you. The club's full-time fitness pro is available for consultation and cardiovascular testing.

Other facilities include a steam room with Swiss shower, a sauna misted with eucalyptus oils, three outdoor whirlpools, and private rooms for massage appointments.

The marriage of low-calorie cooking with Low Country cuisine is a special attraction of the hotel's flagship restaurant, the Barony. The American Heart Association has honored the menu for low-cholesterol selectons of seafood and salads. For informal dining, there's Hudson's Seafood House, on the dock at Skull Creek where the fishing boats unload their daily catch, a few miles from the hotel.

The Westin Resort
135 South Port Royal Dr., Hilton Head Island, SC 29928
Tel. 803/681-4000 or 800/228-3000
Telex 805030, Fax 803/681-1087

Administration Manager, Patrick Burton; health club manager, Spencer Kurtz

Season Year-round.

Accommodations 416 luxury rooms (including 48 suites), with separate dressing areas, hair dryers, large baths. Furnishings and architecture are reminiscent of grand southern homes.

Rates Room with balcony $165–$225 for 2 people in summer. Full oceanfront view $225; suites $250 and up. 3-night family package $510 for parents' room, $247 for children's. "To Your Health" fitness package includes fruit basket with granola bars and Gatorade, massage, bicycle rental 1 hr daily: 3 days $192, 7 days $530, Mar. 15–Oct. 31, per person, double occupancy. Golf and tennis packages available. Reservations and deposit by credit card. Credit cards: AE, CB, DC, MC, V.

Meal Plans Brasserie buffet serves breakfast, lunch, dinner. Barony Restaurant 600-calorie meal includes chilled coconut and pineapple soup, asparagus salad with quail eggs, sorbet, poached fillet of Dover sole with seafood mousse, fresh fruit. Poached snapper, grouper, salmon, and tilefish specialties. All meals à la carte; dinner in the Barony about $50, including tip, tax, and wine.

Services and Facilities **Exercise Equipment:** Weights room with Universal, free-weight dumbbells (3–50 lbs.), Lifecycle, rowing machine, stationary bike, bilateral board equipment, Nautilus abdominal machine. **Services:** Fitness testing, personal instruction on exercise equipment, classes and beach activity; massage by appointment (fee); golf and tennis clinics. **Swimming Facilities:** Indoor pool, outdoor pool with lap lanes; ocean beach. **Recreation Facilities:** Beach runs and walks, volleyball, water polo; 3 golf courses, 16 tennis courts (clay, hard, and grass, 6 lighted), croquet lawn; horseback riding, windsurfing, sailing, and fishing nearby. **Evening Programs:** Resort entertainment.

In the Area Historic Savannah (1 hr), Beaufort, and Charleston (antebellum homes and gardens, 2 hr north).

Getting Here *From Savannah.* By car, I–95 to Hardeeville, Rte. 278 (50 min). By plane, Hilton Head Island airport has scheduled service on Piedmont-Henson (via Charlotte), Eastern (via Atlanta). Also, private aircraft facilities. Hourly limousine service from Savannah airport. Taxi, rental car available.

Special Notes Ramps, specially equipped rooms, elevators to all floors provide access for the disabled. The Kids Korner for children, free to hotel guests, has arts and crafts, games, pool and water activities morning and evening May–Sept., Nov.–Apr. Scheduled daily excursions for teenagers Apr.–Sept. No smoking in the health club.

Hartland Health Center

Life enhancement
Weight management
Preventive medicine

Virginia The 25-day program of health, education, and exercise at
Rapidan Hartland Health Center teaches you how to help yourself. The core program consists of cooking school experience, private and group counseling, and physical therapy guided by a team of physicians, dietitians, educators, chaplains, and therapists.

The doctors and staff, all Seventh-day Adventists, focus on disease prevention. Their computer-aided nutritional analysis makes specific recommendations for diet and takes into account physical condition, nutritional requirements, and weight-loss goals. Hydrotherapy treatments and calisthenics also help you get in shape.

The serious, medically-oriented approach and the relaxed, gracious atmosphere in the plantation mansion suit this program to older persons who need personal attention. Spouses are welcome and encouraged to participate at a reduced fee. Heart disease, arthritis, cancer, diabetes, and obesity seem manageable on this 575-acre estate in the foothills of the Blue Ridge Mountains.

Activities begin with breakfast at 6:45 on weekdays. A personal schedule is designed after your medical consultation, and you are taught what kind of exercise works best for you. Hydrotherapy, including contrasting hot and cold showers, hot packs, or sitz baths may be recommended.

The program is associated with Hartland College, a small, four-year training program for health professionals. The intensive, outpatient-style program has motellike facilities adjacent to physicians' offices and treatment areas in the mansion. During a 25-day stay, each participant receives a complete physical examination, with EKG test, treadmill fitness test, blood chemistry analysis, urinalysis, and body-composition evaluation. (Health insurance may cover some costs.)

Shorter stays can be arranged, especially if you've been here before and want a follow-up visit or refresher. There's also a 10-day program and shorter visits for $150 a day.

The dedicated physicians and educators believe medical technology often overshadows simple ailments that can be prevented with good living habits.

The Adventists, well-known for their interest in health and nutrition, make their service—nondenominational and nonsectarian—available to anyone willing to commit themselves to healthy living.

Hartland Health Center
Box 1, Rapidan, VA 22733
Tel. 703/672-3100

Administration Director, Warren Peters, M.D.

Season Sessions monthly except Dec.

Accommodations 30 bedrooms in mansion, and 2-story annex completed in 1988. Large new rooms with contemporary furnishings and private baths in the annex. Residential atmosphere in the redbrick mansion, built at the turn of the century. Two-story porch with limestone pillars, expansive views of fields and lakes, semiprivate baths.

Rates 25-day program $3,750, $2,750 for accompanying spouse, $1,250 for a nonparticipating companion sharing room. Shorter visits $150 per day, including treatments, programs, and meals. $300 per person advance payment. No credit cards.

Meal Plans 3 vegetarian meals daily. Lunch may include baked tofu loaf, water-steamed vegetables, green salad, baked potato, and homemade bread. Fruit served only at breakfast and dinner, along with grains, cereals, and legumes. No butter or oils. The "Vegan" diet is high in complex carbohydrates. No dairy products, cheese, eggs, meat, fish.

Services and Facilities **Exercise Equipment:** 2 stationary bikes, 2 treadmills, rowing machine, NordicTrack cross-country ski simulator, free weights. **Services:** Hydrotherapy, massage, stress-management classes, exercise counseling, smoking cessation program, cardiac and cancer rehabilitation; medical tests, body-composition evaluation, physician's visits; cooking school, weight control counseling; spiritual guidance. **Swimming Facilities:** Indoor pool. **Recreation Facilities:** Hiking, jogging trails; cross-country skiing (no equipment provided). **Evening Programs:** Medical lectures.

In the Area Scheduled weekend tours to Monticello (estate of Thomas Jefferson), Montpelier (home of James Madison), museums in Washington, DC; Shenandoah National Park and the Skyline Drive, Colonial Williamsburg, historic Fredericksburg, factory outlets.

Getting Here *From Washington, DC.* By train, Amtrak to Culpepper (80 min). By bus, Trailways and Greyhound to Culpepper (90 min). By car, I–66 to Lee Highway (Rte. 29) into Culpepper, Rte. 15 toward Orange, to Rte. 614 (about 2 hr). By plane, Dulles International and National Airports, commuter service to Charlottesville. Pickup arranged at airports, bus and train stations for fixed fee. Rental car available.

Special Notes No smoking indoors.

The Homestead

Non-program resort facilities
Taking the waters

Virginia
Hot Springs Style accounts for the enduring popularity of this historic spa. Although there's a newly outfitted exercise room with Universal's dynamic variable resistance equipment, antique machines for exercising arms and legs, designed at the turn of the century, are still in use at the Homestead. People pay to have the attendant crank them up, and the Smithsonian Institution has expressed an interest in acquiring them.

The mineral springs that made the Homestead famous as long ago as 1766 still gush in front of the Bath House, furnished with 1920s-style wicker furniture and flowered chintz draperies, and there are huge marble tubs for mineral-water soaks. The "spout bath," prescribed here by an advocate of European hydrotherapy in 1937, is faithfully followed today. A doctor's prescription is still required to "take the cure," though not all spa services come under that category.

Bath, sauna, massage, and an herbal wrap for deep-heat penetration that relaxes muscles and removes toxins are spa services outside "the cure." The Olympic-size indoor swimming pool, built in 1903, is great for laps and crowded only on weekends. Beginner and intermediate aerobic classes are scheduled. Services are free of charge except baths and body work.

The naturally heated mineral water, high in sulfur and magnesium, reaches your tub at 104 degrees and overflows to keep the temperature constant. After a few minutes in the sauna or steam room (the men's side has a Turkish bath), you're led to a marble slab for a rubdown with coarse salt, then hosed off in the Scotch Douche. After cooling down, you're treated to a massage by an old-timer. The cost is $34.50.

Another combination of mineral wrap and tub features a water massage, the original Homestead spout bath, that simulates European fountain treatments. The rate is $18. A "5-star" package with massage, sunlamp, facial, manicure, and pedicure costs $145.

Most people come here today to bathe for pleasure rather than therapy. Weekenders are typically family groups from the South and a few Washingtonians who relish the old-fashioned ambience and service. Tea is served afternoons to the accompaniment of a string quartet in the Edwardian hall. Dinner is a dressy affair, with a live band for dancing.

The spa will put a spring in your step, but beware the dining room menu. The Modified American Plan for all guests includes breakfast and dinner. People have been known to sample all 75 items. Lighter dishes are available in a deli-cafe, located among the resort boutiques, or you can make a salad at the luncheon buffet near the tennis courts in summer.

Three golf courses and 19 tennis courts, playable most of the year, are big outdoor attractions. There's horseback riding, mountain trout fishing, archery, and trap shooting. Surrounded by a 15,000-acre mountain preserve, the Homestead has miles of hiking trails. Snowmaking equipment on the slopes and groomed trails for cross-country skiing are winter attractions.

Despite its rambling size and dated grandeur, the Homestead makes you feel at home, even as it caters to conventions. Each season, from blossoming spring dogwood to blazing fall foliage, has special appeal. The southern hospitality is seasonless.

The Homestead
Hot Springs, VA 24445
Tel. 703/839–5500 or 800/336–5771 (800/542–5734 in VA)

Administration Acting manager, Clifford Nelson

Season Year-round.

Accommodations 600 guest rooms in main section and tower, built 1902–1929, and South Wing, added with conference center in 1973. Choice rooms and best views in the tower. Mahogany bedsteads, writing tables, lounge chairs, lacy white curtains, damask draperies. Some rooms with French doors that open on to private balconies or screened porches. Private baths.

Rates Modified American plan includes breakfast, dinner, and tea. $225–$275 single, $135–$175 per person, double occupancy; $85–$120 more for parlors. Children with adults $50 each through age 15, $75 over 16. Packages for golf and tennis. $100 advance payment. Credit cards: AE, MC, V.

Meal Plans Country breakfasts include grits, omelets, steak, mountain trout. Dinner features Virginia ham stuffed with greens, roast beef, broiled chicken, farm produce, sautéed whole trout or smoked fish appetizer.

Services and Facilities **Exercise Equipment:** Universal weights gym, with leg extension, chest press, shoulder press, hip and arm units; stationary bikes, abdominal board, rowing machine, free weights. Exercise room open daily 8 AM–7:30 PM. **Swimming Facilities:** Large indoor pool with mix of mineral and well water, two outdoor pools. Indoor pool open daily 10 AM–7:30 PM. **Recreation Facilities:** 3 golf courses, 19 tennis courts (Har-Tru and Gras-Tex), horseback riding, hiking, skeet and trap shooting, archery, fishing, lawn bowling, carriage rides, bowling alley; skiing, ice-skating, cross-country skiing (equipment rental). **Evening Programs:** Movies, dancing.

In the Area Carriage rides. Country boutiques, the baths at Warm Springs (Jeffersonian structure), chamber music concerts at Garth Newel, historic Lexington (Washington and Lee University), Virginia Military Institute (George Marshall Library).

Getting Here *From Washington, DC.* By train, Amtrak from Union Station or Alexandria, VA, to Clifton Forge (4 hr). By car, I–66 west to I–81, at Mt. Crawford Exit, Rtes. 257 and 42 to Goshen, Rte. 39 to Warm Springs, Rte. 220 south to Hot Springs (about 6 hr). By plane, commuter flights on United Express from Dulles International to Ingalls Field at the Homestead, Piedmont Airlines or USAir from National Airport to Roanoke, VA (1 hr). Private aircraft also land here. Limousine meets train or plane by arrangement (fixed fee). Rental car available. Daily parking charge $2.50. Valet service.

Special Notes Ramps and elevators in all buildings and some specially equipped rooms provide access for the disabled. Swimming, tennis, and skiing lessons for children; supervised playroom (summer only) and outdoor activity at the spa building (fee). No smoking in the spa building and in designated areas of the dining room.

The Kingsmill Resort

Non-program resort facilities

Virginia
Williamsburg For a family vacation combining sports and entertainment, the Kingsmill Resort villas provide an ideal base from which to explore Busch Gardens, Colonial Williamsburg, the scenic Tidewater area, and Atlantic beaches.

Built and managed by Anheuser-Busch, the 2,900-acre resort borders the historic James River, where there's a private marina. Golfers play the River Course, designed by Pete Dye, and the Plantation Course, designed by Arnold Palmer. The big news for fitness buffs was the 1988 opening of the Sports Club, a 23,000-square-foot structure with indoor and outdoor exercise facilities, restaurant, and adjacent conference center.

There is no charge to registered guests for using the Sports Club facilities. The well-equipped weights room is staffed by instructors. There's an indoor lap pool and an outdoor pool for family play. Five-day golf and tennis school programs will improve your game.

Busch Gardens, a 360-acre park, has rides, animal acts, Broadway revues, and many activities for families. Evening entertainment for teenagers has broadened the park's appeal without changing its low-key sense of fun. Located a few minutes from the resort, Busch Gardens is popular with the kids and senior citizens.

In Colonial Williamsburg, a few miles up the road, there's plenty of culture to complement your fitness regime. Take a walk through the 18th century in Virginia's original capital. Local museums exhibit everything from Art Deco glass to Fabergé eggs, and a treasure trove of English and American decorative arts dating from 1600 can be seen at the new DeWitt Wallace Gallery.

In southeastern Virginia's rolling hills and forests, Kingsmill Resort possesses both cosmopolitan sophistication and Colonial gentility. It's big enough so corporate conferences and vacationers needn't mix. The atmosphere is more residential than resort, and if you enjoy planning your own program, the elements are all here.

The Kingsmill Resort
1010 Kingsmill Rd., Williamsburg, VA 23185
Tel. 804/253–8201 or 800/832–5665

Administration General manager, Harry D. Knight; Sports Club manager, Beverly Cutchins

Season Year-round.

Accommodations Private villas overlooking river or golf course. 1–3 bedrooms, some complete kitchens, living rooms with fireplace. Residential furnishings, daily maid service. Air conditioning, king- or queen-size beds, color cable TV.

Rates Seasonal pricing. $75–$125 for guest room, $365 for 3-bedroom suite in new Riverview Rooms. 5-day golf package from $860 for double guest room to $1,150 for 1-bedroom suite. 5-day tennis school from $710 for double guest room to $1,000 for 1-bedroom suite. 1 night's advance payment with AE. Credit cards: AE, MC, V.

Meal Plans Sports Club bistro-style restaurant serves light fare, including grilled chicken breast on brioche, pasta salad, and individual pizzas 11 AM–10 PM. Fruit dishes, nut breads, and whipped drinks of yogurt, honey, and fruit prepared daily.

Services and Facilities **Exercise Equipment:** 15-station Nautilus exercise machines, 2 treadmills, 2 stationary bikes, 2 Schwinn Air-Dyne bikes, Liferower, StairMaster, NordicTrack, power rack, incline bench, bench press, free weights. **Services:** Aerobic classes and water aerobics ($5 per class), instruction on exercise equipment. **Swimming Facilities:** Indoor 56-foot lap pool, outdoor recreational pool. **Recreation Facilities:** 2 golf courses, 12 tennis courts, 2 racquetball courts, game lounge with billiards, darts, table-top shuffleboard; coed whirlpool, separate saunas and steam rooms for men and women. **Evening Programs:** Summer season of pop and rock concerts.

In the Area Colonial Williamsburg (88 restored 18th-century buildings, shops, and residences), James River plantation tour, Jamestown Festival Park (replicas of 3 historic ships), Yorktown (Revolutionary War battlefield), Williamsburg Pottery (outlet shops and boutiques), Virginia Beach, Mariner's Museum, Nature Museum and park.

Getting Here *From Washington, DC*. By train, Amtrak from Union Station or Alexandria, VA, to Williamsburg (all seats reserved, 3 hr). By bus, Greyhound (3 hr). By car, I–95 south to I–64 east, Exit 57A to Rte. 199W.

Special Notes Interpretive tours for children at historic sites. No smoking in sports club.

The Lotus Center

Holistic health
Spiritual awareness
Stress control

Virginia Healthy living is taught at the Lotus Center in a residential set-
Buckingham ting where small groups focus on programs to achieve and sustain maximum health. Formerly a private home, the center was remodeled to resemble a bed-and-breakfast inn.

Week-long programs concentrate on coping with specific physical conditions, especially cancer or heart disease. Through yoga, gentle stretches and relaxation techniques help rejuvenate and balance the body.

Meditation helps guests find quiet and understanding, and breathing techniques build energy. The scenic location, overlooking a historic river valley, contributes to a sense of peace and fulfillment.

Spiritual teacher Sri Swami Satchidananda teaches that our whole being can be healed even when it's not possible to entirely heal the body. When a young public relations executive came here after undergoing chemotherapy, she mastered visualization, a method of directing energy in a conscious manner, to speed her recovery. Others come for weight-loss and nutrition weeks or extended stays supervised by the medical staff.

Staff members are certified in holistic health sciences. Guest speakers and program leaders add expertise. Yogaville, a residential community for yoga students and monastics on the adjoining Satchidananda Ashram enhances the spiritual atmosphere.

The Lotus Center
Rte. 1, Box 172A, Buckingham, VA 23921
Tel. 804/969–3300

Administration Director, Vivekan Flint; medical director, Sandra McLanahan, M.D.

Season Year-round.

Accommodations 7 modern bedrooms, private or shared baths. Sauna. 12 guests maximum.

Rates Weekly programs $600 couples, $400 single. Basic daily program, including meals and yoga instruction, $60 single, $100 double. Service charges and tips included. $30 advance payment single accommodations, $50 couples. Credit cards: MC, V.

Meal Plans 3 vegetarian meals served family style in dining room. Rice, dahl, steamed vegetables with brown rice, green salad, Indian bread.

Services and Facilities **Services:** Guided relaxation, medically supervised fasting, instruction in meditation, cooking, visualization; Swedish massage, shiatsu, herbal wraps. **Swimming Facilities:** Private beach on nearby lake. **Recreation Facilities:** Country roads, hiking trails. **Evening Programs:** Meditation.

In the Area Yogaville and the Light of Truth Universal Shrine; Charlottesville (University of Virginia), Monticello (Palladian villa designed by Thomas Jefferson), Civil War sites (Appomattox Courthouse).

Getting Here *From Washington, DC*. By train, Amtrak to Charlottesville (3 hr). By bus, Trailways to Charlottesville (4 hr). By car, I–66 south to Rte. 29, at Lovingston Rte. 56 to Rte. 604 (3½ hr). By plane, commuter flights on USAir or Piedmont to Charlottesville. Service to and from Charlottesville train and bus stations or airport by prior arrangement (fixed fee). Rental car available.

Special Notes Ashram classes in yoga, meditation, and cooking for children. No smoking. Remember to bring slippers and walking shoes.

The Tazewell Club

Non-program resort facilities

Virginia
Colonial
Williamsburg

The first health club in the old Colonial capital opened in 1988. A part of the Williamsburg Lodge and Conference Center complex, facing a golf course, the Tazewell Club is minutes from the 173-acre historic area. It's an escape to the latest in pampering and exercise after immersing in 18th-century life.

Designed for newcomers to fitness, the club also challenges fitness buffs. The well-equipped weight training room is open from 8 AM to 8 PM, Monday through Friday, till 6 PM on Saturday, and from 11 to 4 on Sunday. Low-impact aerobics classes are taught morning and evening on weekdays. The swimming pool is popular with families, but certain hours are reserved for lap swimmers.

Safety is stressed by the club management, which offers individual instruction on the use of exercise equipment. Aerobics instructors increase or decrease exercise routines to suit your fitness level. It's a shipshape operation with polite, enthusiastic staff.

The workout area has views of the surrounding valley, once part of the Tazewell estate. The swimming pool opens onto a sun deck. The spa, with separate saunas, steam rooms, whirlpools for men and women, and private massage areas, is on the same floor. Try a loofah body scrub or a combination massage with avocado oil and salt.

The club is open to guests staying in any of the five hotels operated by the Colonial Williamsburg Foundation. There is a $7 daily admission fee. Two Robert Trent Jones golf courses, eight tennis courts, croquet court, bowling green, and two outdoor swimming pools are nearby. Personal services, court time, and greens fees are extra.

The nation's largest and oldest living history museum is within hiking distance. Williamsburg re-creates the 18th century as it was during the British Colonial era. In the musick master's house, a string quartet may be rehearsing for a concert. At the Raleigh bake shop, you can sample gingerbread and cookies straight from the wood-fired oven.

The Tazewell Club
Williamsburg Lodge
Box C, Williamsburg, VA 23187
Tel. 804/220-7690 or 800/447-7869

Administration   Club manager, William A. Doig

Season   Year-round.

Accommodations   25 Tazewell Club guest rooms in the Williamsburg Lodge, color TV, spacious baths. Also 5 hotels and group of Colonial houses, plus 2 deluxe suites with Jacuzzi, fireplace, wet bar, and private balcony on penthouse level of club. 235 guest rooms in the Williamsburg Inn, a short walk from the health club and 85 rooms in restored homes with Colonial atmosphere.

Rates   Double or single occupancy in Tazewell wing $125 high season; regular lodge rooms $89–$93; suites $320 for 1–4 persons. Williamsburg Inn $150–$190, suites and bed-sitting rooms available. House rooms $120–$200. Variable deposits, about $90–$100 per room. Credit cards: AE, MC, V.

Meal Plans   No meals at the Tazewell Club, but guests can charge meals at historic area restaurants. In Regency Dining Room (jacket and tie required) at the Williamsburg Inn, specialties include Chesapeake crabmeat sautéed in wine, picatta of shrimp and veal, and scaloppine of lamb with garlic. Traditional Virginia recipes in the town's taverns—King's Arms, Christiana Campbell's, Josiah Chowning's. Peanut soup to stuffed trout. Chesapeake Bay specialties on Friday seafood buffet at the Williamsburg Lodge.

Services and Facilities   **Exercise Equipment:** 11 Keiser Cam II stations, Nautilus gym, 2 Lifecycles, 2 Liferowers. **Services:** Massage, loofah scrub, facials, manicures, pedicures, nonsurgical face-lift, hair/skin care; individual instruction on exercise equipment. **Swimming Facilities:** 60-ft 4-lane lap pool, large outdoor pool. **Recreation Facilities:** 18- and 9-hole golf courses, 8 tennis courts, lawn bowling and croquet, jogging trail, bicycle rentals; badminton, volleyball, and water aerobics on request. Miniature golf. **Evening Programs:** 18th-century concerts, seasonal ceremonies, tavern entertainment. Shakespeare productions.

In the Area   Busch Gardens (family-oriented theme park), James River plantation tour, Jamestown Festival Park (replicas of 3 historic ships), Yorktown (Revolutionary War battlefield), Virginia Beach, Mariner's Museum, Nature Museum and park.

Getting Here   *From Washington, DC.* By train, Amtrak from Union Station or Alexandria, VA, to Williamsburg (all seats reserved, 3 hr). By bus, Gold Line or Trailways (3 hr). By car, I–95 south to I–64 east (3 hr). By plane, scheduled flights to Norfolk or Richmond, VA (30 min). Taxi, car rental available; limousine on request. Scheduled van service to airports from Williamsburg hotels.

Special Notes Elevator to all floors, some specially equipped rooms provide access for the disabled. Tours of historic sites and golf lessons for children. No smoking in club. Remember to bring fitness shoes (white-soled aerobics), workout clothing, leotards (robes provided).

The Middle Atlantic States

George Washington made taking the waters in West Virginia fashionable at about the same time that Europeans discovered a place called Spa in Belgium. Health resorts flourished over the years in the Poconos, the Alleghenies, and the southern Appalachians. These resorts tend to be small-scale and conservative, emphasizing service and personal attention, and oriented to golf and tennis rather than to high-energy workouts. While the renowned Greenbrier Resort in White Sulphur Springs, West Virginia, recently made the great leap from traditional to contemporary in its health spa, Berkeley Springs—where George Washington bathed—remains a sleepy country town with modest accommodations for spa-goers in a state park. The introduction of snow-making equipment has added a new dimension to resorts throughout the area, with downhill and cross-country skiing now complementing indoor exercise.

In building the nation's first boardwalk, Atlantic City touched off a development boom along the New Jersey shore. The introduction of casino gambling in 1978 brought the town out of a long decline, and when the manufacturer of Lifecycles and other exercise equipment became a Bally company, the shore gained its first full-scale fitness center at Bally's Park Place. Like most spas in the area, it is an amenity rather than a comprehensive health vacation program.

Abunda Life Health Hotel

Holistic health
Nutrition and diet
Weight management

New Jersey
Asbury Park

Naturopathic treatments and Christian inspiration are provided in equal measure at the Abunda Life Health Hotel in a holiday intended to enrich body, mind, and spirit. Abunda Life's fundamental principles call for fasting, detoxification, colon cleansing, chiropractic care, cardiovascular conditioning, and a diet of natural foods. Combining herbal remedies with the beneficial effect of ocean air, this seaside retreat on a quiet tree-lined street a block from the beach has special programs for losing weight, stopping smoking, and subliminal motivation.

The scheduled exercise classes, walks, and meals are required of all guests. Supervised fasting, detoxification, beach recreation, and fishing are optional. Additional therapy, nutritional testing, and psychological care are available and recommended.

Hour-long sessions of meditation and listening to tapes are intended to teach guests to relax and lead healthier lives. Programs emphasize nutrition and natural remedies; staff members urge new arrivals to be tested for metabolic type, food sensitivity, and energy levels (cost of testing $195), and the test results determine the program of activities recommended for the individual.

The Bach Flower Emotional Health Remedies and a line of homeopathic food supplements and power drinks are sold in the dispensary. The shop stocks more than 400 items, including health food and remedies formulated by Professor Robert Sorge, the hotel's guiding spirit. Participants are expected to abide by the house rules. Outside eating is prohibited, and personal luggage is subject to search for junk food or cigarettes. Prayer is encouraged; Bible-related literature and tapes are discussed daily.

The practical approach to "becoming a better you" involves workshops in food preparation, drinking raw juices, massage, and foot reflexology. Snacks are provided for those who go out during the day. But don't be late in returning; the doors are locked at 11 PM week nights, 1 AM weekends. Most guests seem to find sitting in rocking chairs on the windswept front porch entertainment enough.

Abunda Life Health Hotel
208 Third Ave., Asbury Park, NJ 07712
Tel. 201/775–7575

Administration Director, Robert H. Sorge

Season Year-round.

Accommodations 55 clean and simple rooms with 2 single beds, TV, air conditioning, private bath with shower. Dormitory beds (4–6 guests per room) available.

Rates $95 a day per person double occupancy (all-inclusive); programs $250 for 3 nights, $595 for a week. Programs of 2 weeks to a month $1,095–$1,995. Add 20% for single occupancy. Non-program guests $40 single, $50 double. $95 deposit per person. Credit cards: MC, V.

Meal Plans 3 meals daily plus snacks and juices. Ovo-lacto-vegetarian diet features fresh, natural foods with some fish or chicken. No coffee, salt, pepper, white sugar, chocolate. Only certified raw milk (cow and goat). Breakfast includes eggs, fresh fruit, grain cereal. Lunch may be a cheese-vegetable casserole, salad, or fish. Juice fasts and purified water.

Services and Facilities **Exercise Equipment:** Rebounders, stationary bikes, free weights. **Services:** Massage, iridology, colonics, acupuncture, medical care. **Swimming Facilities:** Beach. **Recreation Facilities:** Boardwalk, bicycling, fishing. Lake and riverboat rides and canoeing. **Evening Programs:** Free concerts at a band shell. VCR or cable TV, bingo, Ping-Pong, table games. Concerts and shows year-round in the nearby Convention Hall.

In the Area Garden State Arts Center (popular shows and symphony concerts), Ocean Grove Tabernacle (Christian entertainment and spiritual programs), Atlantic City casinos.

Getting Here *From New York City or Philadelphia.* By car, Garden State Pkwy. to Asbury Park exit, Rte. 195 East to end (90 min). By bus, Jersey Shore Lines from Port Authority and other stations; stops 1 block from hotel. Taxi, rental car available.

Special Notes No smoking indoors.

New Jersey
Abunda Life Health Hotel, **8**
The Shoreham Hotel & Spa, **9**
The Spa at Bally's, **10**
Vivanté at the Centrium, **7**

Pennsylvania
Deerfield Manor, **3**
The Himalayan Institute, **2**
Kripalu Yoga Ashram, **4**
Pritikin Longevity Center, **6**
Weight Watchers Camp Colang, **1**
Weight Watchers Camp Perkiomen, **5**

West Virginia
Berkeley Springs State Park, **13**
Coolfont Resort, **15**
The Greenbrier, **16**
The Spa at the Country Inn, **14**
Sheraton Lakeview Resort, **11**
The Woods Fitness Institute, **12**

The Middle Atlantic States

Lake Erie

Allegheny River

OHIO

Pittsburgh

West

Ohio River

Wheeling

Morgantown

Parkersburg

Clarksburg

Potomac River

WEST VIRGINIA

Charleston

50

75 kr

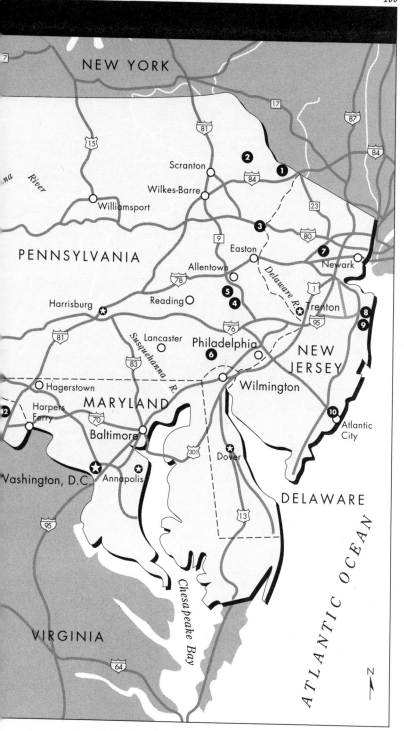

The Shoreham Hotel & Spa

Luxury pampering

New Jersey
Spring Lake

The Shoreham Hotel & Spa's midweek package consists of an easygoing, traditional seashore holiday combined with exercise and beauty treatments. The personalized approach emphasizes healthy living rather than strenuous exercise; classes offer stretch, toning, low-impact aerobics, and exercise in the heated swimming pool.

The hotel, built in 1890, has a Victorian charm enhanced by the addition of facilities for spa treatments. Herbal wraps, massage, and facials are available à la carte or as part of a package. Most guests are over 40, and they enjoy long walks on the beach and avail themselves of the resort's motorized carriages to shop at nearby boutiques.

The Shoreham Hotel & Spa
Box 225, 115 Monmouth Ave., Spring Lake, NJ 07762
Tel. 201/449–7100 or 800/648–4175

Administration	Program director, Adiline Schofel
Season	May 1–Oct. 31
Accommodations	108 spacious rooms with ocean and lake views, private bath, some with porch.
Rates	$70–$170 a day per person double occupancy, Modified American Plan (breakfast and dinner). 5-night package (Sun.–Fri.) $750 single or double, with 3 meals daily. $250 per person in advance for spa package. Credit cards: AE, MC, V.
Meal Plans	Light cuisine and a resort menu. Fresh seafood and locally grown vegetables.
Services and Facilities	**Exercise Equipment:** Toning tables, bicycles. **Swimming Facilities:** Heated outdoor pool, ocean beach. **Recreation Facilities:** Boardwalk; golf, tennis, sailing nearby.
In the Area	Atlantic City, Monmouth Park Race Track, Garden State Arts Center.
Getting Here	*From New York City.* By car, south on New Jersey Turnpike and Garden State Parkway to Rte. 34 (1 hr). By plane, Newark International Airport is served by major airlines; Allaire Airport accommodates private planes. By train, New Jersey Coastline from Penn Station. By bus, New Jersey Transit. Guests are met at the train station (short walk from hotel) on request; motorized surreys and rental car available.

The Spa at Bally's

Luxury pampering

New Jersey
Atlantic City

Amid the glitz and glamour of the beachfront casinos, The Spa at Bally's is a health and fitness oasis. The spacious facilities and top-of-the-line equipment would be the pride of any fitness resort; here they serve as a complement to gambling and entertainment. It's possible not to set foot in the casino, but the majority of the people working out in the weights room also exercise the one-armed bandits.

Four racquetball and squash courts and a complete health-food restaurant flank the reception desk. Anyone may watch the action and enjoy a diet snack. The pool, saunas, whirlpools, and treatment rooms are open to hotel guests and members; others must pay a daily fee. The fee is waived for those who book a minimum of services such as massage and herbal body wrap. There's also a beauty salon.

The spa's exotic gardens and waterfalls and its dramatic view of the Atlantic heighten the sense of luxury that guests get in some of the most luxurious pampering on the East Coast. Spa hours are Monday–Saturday 7:30 AM–9 PM, Sunday 8 AM–7 PM.

The Spa at Bally's
Bally's Casino Hotel
Boardwalk and Park Place, Atlantic City, NJ 08401
Tel. 609/340–2000 or 800/772–7777 (800/225–5977) for room reservations)

Administration	Spa manager, Deborah Smith
Season	Year-round.
Accommodations	468 rooms with private bath; 42 suites with balcony; 9 restaurants. Art Deco touches in the original building, casino luxury in the new tower.
Rates	Rooms $105–$155 per day. Spa admission $10 for hotel guests, $17.55 others. Treatments priced individually. Packages of 1, 2, and 5 nights available midweek. Payment in advance for packages and weekends. Credit cards: AE, CB, DC, MC, V.
Meal Plans	Fresh salads and low-calorie lunches in the Spa Cafe; nonalcoholic drinks. Spa cuisine in the main dining room.
Services and Facilities	**Exercise Equipment:** Computerized Lifecycle bikes, rowing and weight-lifting machines. **Swimming Facilities:** Indoor pool, ocean beach. **Recreation Facilities:** Bike rental on the Boardwalk; golf and tennis nearby. **Evening Programs:** Cabaret and celebrity shows.
In the Area	Brigantine National Wildlife Refuge, Farley State Marina, The Noyes Museum (contemporary art), Historic Town of Smithville, Atlantic City Race Track.
Getting Here	Atlantic City is served by daily casino bus from points throughout the region. By plane, USAir's Allegheny commuter flights use close-in Bader Field. By train, a new express line from Philadelphia offers daily service. By car, the Garden State Parkway from points north and south, the Atlantic City Expressway from Philadelphia (60 min). Taxi, rental car, minibus available locally.
Special Notes	Facilities for treatments and hotel accommodations available for the disabled. No smoking.

Vivanté at the Centrium

Luxury pampering *Women only*

New Jersey
Morristown

Add the charm of a historic town to all-out pampering, state-of-the-art exercise equipment, and an upscale hotel, and you have a new breed of health resort. Located one hour from New York City, Vivanté at the Centrium makes an ideal getaway for weekends or longer. The Headquarters Plaza Hotel in which it is located adjoins a mall with 50 shops.

The program, limited to 20 women a week, is tailored to each person's goals, as determined with reference to a personal health history questionnaire sent to all guests in advance of their stays. Consultations can be arranged with nutritionists, a chiropractor, and specialists at the local hospital. Participants are coached on the proper use of the exercise equipment—more than 110 pieces in a spacious gym that adjoins the hotel. Herbal wraps and a facial come with the package.

The Centrium Club complex includes a large indoor swimming pool, jogging track, and health-food restaurant. There are coed aerobics classes and a Jacuzzi, saunas, plunge pools, and steam rooms for men and women, and a beauty salon. Many corporate executives have memberships here.

Vivanté at the Centrium
65 Headquarters Plaza, Morristown, NJ 07960
Tel. 201/267–9100 or 800/225–1942 (800/225–1941 in NJ)

Administration
Manager, Richard Martinez; program director, Sheila Schwartz

Season
Year-round.

Accommodations
260 deluxe rooms in the Headquarters Plaza Hotel. Contemporary design and Art Deco.

Rates
Fitness weekend, 3 days/2 nights, $725 per person double occupancy, $940 single; total rejuvenation package, 7 days/6 nights, $1,755 per person double, $2,195 single. Rates may vary with the season. Programs include meals and lodging, treatments, and a hairstyling session. 50% payable in advance. Credit cards: AE, DC, MC, V.

Meal Plans
Dinner at the hotel on day of arrival, brunch on departure. Gourmet spa cuisine with calorie counts for all items in the formal dining room. Lunch at the Centrium Club.

Services and Facilities
Exercise Equipment: CamStar, Sprint, Nautilus, Keiser. **Swimming Facilities:** Indoor lap pool. **Recreation Facilities:** Racquetball and squash courts; shopping, horseback riding nearby. Shopping trip to New York City and exercise class at Spa Lady on Park Ave. with 7-day package. **Evening Programs:** Movie theater (free pass), dancing, sports at the Meadowlands complex.

Getting Here
Newark International Airport is 30 min away via Rte. 24. By car, Rtes. 80, 202, and 287. Free limousine service to and from the airport.

Special Notes
Children's nursery at the Centrium. No smoking in the Centrium Club.

Deerfield Manor

Weight management

Pennsylvania
East Stroudsburg
The program at Deerfield Manor, a former inn, takes an individualized approach to diet and nutrition and encourages you to achieve a healthy lifestyle. Participation is limited to 33 men and women who want to unwind and shape up. The daily activities include guided walks, exercise classes, aerobics, massage, yoga, and calisthenics.

The exercise regimen is complemented by calorie-controlled meals served in a bright, spacious dining room. Each guest selects a menu plan according to personal need and based on the consumption of no more than 600–800 calories per day. One alternative to this is a diet limited to freshly squeezed fruit and vegetable juices; a more severe option is fasting, in which only water from the manor's well is allowed.

The warm, supportive environment is nurtured by a 13-member staff, with occasional visits from lecturers and health professionals. A family-like feeling tends to develop among guests, some of whom return every summer—and some remain for the entire season.

Deerfield Manor
R.D. 1, Rte. 402N, East Stroudsburg, PA 18301
Tel. 717/223–0160

Administration Manager, Frieda Eisenkraft

Season May–Oct.

Accommodations 22 rooms with wicker furniture, antiques, private bath.

Rates 1-week program $460–$535 per person double occupancy, $575–$660 single. Personal services and massage not included. $150 payable in advance. Credit cards: AE, MC, V.

Meal Plans 3 meals daily; fish and chicken, locally grown produce, fresh fruit.

Services and Facilities **Swimming Facilities:** Heated outdoor pool. **Recreation Facilities:** 2 tennis courts and golf nearby; roller skating, ice skating, horseback riding, bike rental. **Evening Programs:** Guest lecturers on health-related topics.

In the Area Shopping tours, summer theater, antique markets, Indian Museum.

Getting Here By car, limousine service on alternate weekends from LaGuardia and Kennedy airports. I–80 from New York, I–84 from New England, I–83 from the Baltimore–Washington area connect with Rte. 402. By plane, major airlines serve Allentown, PA. By bus, Greyhound to Stroudsburg. Taxi, rental car available locally.

Special Notes No smoking indoors.

The Himalayan Institute

Stress control
Weight management
Spiritual awareness

Pennsylvania
Honesdale

Physicians and psychologists at the 422-acre international headquarters of the Himalayan Institute of Yoga Science and Philosophy use biofeedback, aerobic exercise, breathing, meditation, diet, and fasting to train people to live with stress. Their leader is Swami Rama, the Indian yogi who stopped his heart from pumping blood for 17 seconds in a Menninger Foundation clinic experiment in 1970, thereby reinforcing theories about the relationship between the body and the mind.

Biofeedback, a technique that uses machines to teach regulation of the nervous system, is linked with the practice of Eastern philosophy and yoga exercises to form the institute's holistic approach to living. Meditation and relaxation can enable one to gain control of the body and the mind, according to Swami Rama, and the serene atmosphere at this mountaintop retreat provides the appropriate setting for exploring the mind and exercising the body.

Weekday and weekend classes and seminars in stress management, inner growth, and health enhancement are scheduled throughout the year. Some weekend packages include transportation from the institute's branch in New York City.

Research into ancient healing and self-development techniques by the resident faculty is used as the basis for much of the program. Meditation is employed as a systematic method for developing every level of individual consciousness. Meals are eaten in silence to encourage efficient digestion, and guests are asked to abstain from emotional relationships and other distractions while at the institute.

The day begins at 7 AM with exercises of the joints and finishes with an after-dinner lecture. You are taught to assume responsibility for your own health. The people who come here are health professionals, families practicing yoga, and students working on degrees. Some guests come just for the weekend retreat in the mountains, the Indian food, and the walking and hiking in the woods that can be the best form of aerobics.

The Himalayan Institute
R.R. 1, Box 400, Honesdale, PA 18431
Tel. 717/253–5551

Administration
President, Rudolph Ballentine, M.D.

Season
Year-round.

Accommodations
100 guests are housed in the main building in austerely furnished rooms with communal toilet and showers. Each room has 2 beds, a sink, sheets and towels, no lock on the door.

Rates
Health, cooking, nutrition, and yoga weekend $125–$155, including room, meals, herbal tea throughout the day (discount for institute members). 2-week therapy program (Western medical sciences combined with Eastern concepts) $1,400. 4-week weight loss and self-awareness program $1,500. 10-day intensive retreat for purification and self-development $750. $9 per night additional for single room. $10–$50 nonrefundable

deposit on registration for seminars. Credit cards (limit $200): MC, V.

Meal Plans 3 vegetarian meals daily, buffet style. Dinner includes soup (butternut squash or potato), homemade bread, graham crackers, apples, or tofu and lentil casserole. Dairy products, no eggs. Vegetables from an organic garden.

Services and Facilities **Exercise Equipment:** Stationary bikes. **Services:** Biofeedback training (5 sessions $100), cooking classes, medical and psychological consultations, tennis lessons, breath tests. Massage and body therapies not available. **Swimming Facilities:** Lake on property, with sandy beach and bathhouse. **Recreation Facilities:** Tennis and basketball courts, handball court, nature walks, hiking trails; cross-country skiing, ice skating. **Evening Programs:** Lectures related to seminar topics.

In the Area Pocono Mountains sightseeing.

Getting Here *From New York City.* By bus, Short Line from Port Authority (3 hr) or weekend charters from 78 Fifth Ave. (13th St.) by reservation (tel. 212/243–5994). By car, via Lincoln Tunnel to I–80 West, Hwy. 6 through Milford and Honesdale to Rte. 670 (3 hr). By air, scheduled flights to Scranton. Taxi, rental car available.

Special Notes Preschool, kindergarten, and elementary school programs combine Eastern and Western educational concepts, Montessori methods, and yoga philosophies. No smoking indoors.

Kripalu Yoga Ashram

Life enhancement
Holistic health

Pennsylvania Re-creation, a yoga experience that taps inner sources of ener-
Sumneytown gy and peace, is the focus of four days with members of the holistic community of Kripalu Yoga Ashram, where life is enjoyed at a gentle pace. People from many backgrounds and age groups come here to learn and practice the tension-releasing movements of Kripalu Yoga, a series of postures and expanded breathing that has been called meditation in motion. In this peaceful place it becomes a vehicle for a change in lifestyle.

Between long stretches of practicing body awareness, participants have time to use the therapeutic facilities and share macrobiotic vegetarian meals. You can relax in a whirlpool and sauna or join groups in dance and on nature walks. Massage with the Kripalu meditative technique and a polarity energy balancing therapy are available (at additional cost).

Kripalu Yoga is based on theories of the balance and integration of body and mind. As taught by Yogi Amrit Desai, who is respectfully addressed as Gurudev ("honored teacher") when he lectures here and at the Kripalu Center in Massachusetts, it can be mastered readily without prior experience. Clearly demonstrated yoga postures help you to tone and relax every muscle, gland, and organ. Five-day yoga workshops as well as weekend and Sunday sessions are offered throughout the year.

The ashram has a weight-consciousness program that teaches nutritious eating habits; you follow a vegetarian diet while working on yoga routines and relaxation methods. Harakinetics, a system of physical movements and breathing patterns, stimulates energy and heightens an overall sense of well-being. Private counseling sessions on health or lifestyle issues can be scheduled for a $50 fee. An hour of reflexology therapy with acupressure point work on the feet costs $30.

Placed on a secluded hilltop overlooking some of Pennsylvania's most fertile farmland, the ashram abounds in idyllic spots for meditation and hiking. It is a safe, supportive environment for self-healing, relaxation, and rejuvenation.

Kripalu Yoga Ashram
Box 250, 7 Walters Rd., Sumneytown, PA 18084
Tel. 215/234-4568

Administration   Program director, Marcia Goldberg (Shantipriya)

Season   Year-round.

Accommodations   40 guests occupy 12 bedrooms with shared baths. Central living room has fireplace and tea nook. Some private rooms. Bedding, towels, linen provided for Re-creation vacations and retreats only.

Rates   4-day Re-creation vacation $220, week-long programs $285. $55 deposit for Re-creation vacation. Credit cards: MC, V.

Meal Plans   3 vegetarian meals daily, buffet style. Macrobiotic diet of whole grains, fresh vegetables, nuts and seeds, seasonal fruits. Tofu for protein.

Services and Facilities   **Swimming Facilities:** Indoor Olympic-size pool. **Recreation Facilities:** Tennis court, DansKinetics aerobic exercise class. **Evening Programs:** Satsanga (communal chanting and meditation); inspirational lectures.

Getting Here   The ashram is located in the Perkiomen Valley 35 miles northwest of Philadelphia. By car, Pennsylvania Turnpike Northeastern Extension, Quakertown and Lansdale exits. By train from Philadelphia, SEPTA's suburban Doylestown/Paoli-R5 Local leaves hourly for Lansdale, where pickup can be arranged with the ashram. From Philadelphia International Airport, Liberty Limousine to Kulpsville.

Special Notes   No smoking. Remember to bring a mat for exercise and a flashlight for evening walks.

Pritikin Longevity Center

Nutrition and diet
Weight management

Pennsylvania
Downingtown   A strict regimen of Pritikin-style meals, counseling, and medical testing is combined with exercise for 13-day and 26-day sessions at the Pritikin Longevity Center in the heart of Pennsylvania Dutch country. The Downingtown program is offered here as it is in the original center in California; it teaches the pleasures of a low-fat diet as you slim. The message of the company's founder, Nathan Pritikin, and his son Robert is that most major degenerative diseases of our time—heart disease, diabetes, hypertension—are caused largely by excessive levels of fat. If you're prepared to accept a new lifestyle, the Pritikin program teaches ways to protect yourself from diseases associated with obesity and aging.

The Pritikin diet consists of about 10% fat, 15% protein, and 75% complex carbohydrates. Meals are largely vegetarian, with lots of fresh fruit and whole grains; fish served several times a week. Oils, fats, salt, coffee, tea, and high-cholesterol foods (eggs, shellfish, animal organs, skin) are not served.

A treadmill stress test, full physical examination, and a complete blood chemistry panel are part of the program. A plan designed for home use is based on your personal history and fitness level. Exercise classes are supervised by professional physiologists.

Resort facilities are offered in the hotel that adjoins the Pritikin center. Program participants (up to 60 a week) have exclusive use of a large gymnasium, three racquetball courts, and a private dining room. Guided walks through the Amish countryside are a pleasant diversion.

Although some doctors and nutritionists consider the diet needlessly austere, the Pritikin program's serious approach to restoring health and prolonging life has devoted followers across the nation.

Pritikin Longevity Center
975 E. Lincoln Hwy., Downingtown, PA 19335
Tel. 215/873-0123 or 800/344-8243 (800/342-2080 in PA)
Fax 215/873-0169

Administration Executive director, Lawrence S. Berman; fitness director, Kim Alicknavitch

Season Year-round.

Accommodations Spacious rooms with private bath have modern amenities.

Rates Comprehensive medical management program, 13 days $5,045, $2,255 for spouse or companion; 26 days $8,713, $4,173 for spouse or companion. Cardiovascular fitness program, 26 days $8,433, $3,893 for spouse or companion; 6-day refresher, $2,349, $1,370 for spouse or companion. $500 advance payment for 13-day session, $1,000 for 26-day session. Credit cards: MC, V.

Meal Plans Buffet-style meals and snacks in daytime, table service at dinner. Fresh vegetables, whole grains, legumes, fruit, fish, lean meat.

Services and Facilities **Exercise Equipment:** Universal weight gym, 32 treadmills, stationary bikes, aquaerobics, a walking track. **Swimming Facilities:** Indoor and outdoor pools. **Recreation Facilities:** Tennis and racquetball courts; horseback riding and golf nearby; hiking trails. **Evening Programs:** Exercise classes, films.

In the Area Tours to farmer's markets; Philadelphia historical and cultural sites; Wyeth Brandywine Museum, Longwood Gardens, Valley Forge National Park.

Getting Here *From Philadelphia.* By car, Lancaster Pike (Rte. 30) or Pennsylvania Turnpike, I-76 (1 hr). By train, Amtrak to Downingtown (50 min). By plane, Philadelphia International Airport is served by major airlines. Free transfers to train station. Rental car available.

Special Notes No smoking in the center.

Weight Watchers Camp Colang

Youth camps for weight loss

Pennsylvania
Lackawaxen

The program at Weight Watchers Camp Colang, a coed summer camp for young people aged 10–21, focuses on education, exercise, and diet during an active vacation. Located in a wooded mountain range near the Delaware River, the camp has added a modern gymnasium and equestrian center to its traditional design. Campers have exclusive use of junior Universal equipment for bodybuilding and the specially designed cooking school.

Meals are prepared according to Weight Watchers International recipes; campers learn how to eat properly in classes on food preparation and lectures on nutrition. They get firsthand experience in the dining room, which is also a social hub.

Counselors supervise workouts, slimnastics and aerobics classes, and sports. Those who complete the course are guaranteed to lose weight, or they get a refund.

Weight Watchers Camp Colang
Lackawaxen, PA
Weight Watchers Camps
183 Madison Ave., New York, NY 10016
Tel. 212/889–9500 or 800/223–5600 (800/251–4141 in Canada)

Administration Program director, Anthony Sparber

Season Mid-June–late Aug.

Accommodations Dormlike rooms in modern cottages; limited maid service; separate areas for boys and girls.

Rates Sessions of 2–7 weeks from $1,450. $100 payable in advance. Credit cards: AE, MC, V.

Meal Plans 3 balanced meals a day in the dining hall, 2 snacks.

Services and Facilities **Exercise Equipment:** Complete junior-size Universal gym. **Swimming Facilities:** Olympic-size outdoor pool; beach and pier on river. **Recreation Facilities:** 8 tennis courts, team sports, tubing and canoeing; horseback riding. **Evening Programs:** Discos, talent shows, game nights, charm and poise courses, campfires.

Getting Here The mountain resort area is 100 mi by car from Philadelphia and New York. By bus, Greyhound from major cities. Van service to bus station.

Special Notes No smoking indoors.

Weight Watchers Camp Perkiomen

Youth camps for weight loss   *Girls only*

Pennsylvania
Pennsburg

Weight Watchers Camp Perkiomen, a summer camp for young women aged 10–21, offers the opportunity to lose weight in privacy on the wooded 100-acre Perkiomen School campus. The program balances diet, nutritional education, and exercise for an active vacation guaranteed to take off weight.

Campers have exclusive use of a new gymnasium (where dance and aerobics classes are held) and the Science Hall for lectures and demonstrations. The library, a fine arts center, and outdoor sports facilities broaden the range of activities available.

Meals are prepared following the menus of Weight Watchers International. Campers learn to eat properly in classes on food preparation and lectures on nutrition.

Weight Watchers Camp Perkiomen
Pennsburg, PA
Weight Watchers Camps
183 Madison Ave., New York, NY 10016
Tel. 212/889-9500 or 800/223-5600 (800/251-4141 in Canada)

Administration	Program director, Anthony Sparber
Season	July–mid-Aug.
Accommodations	Private double rooms and communal bath; 3 residence halls. Campers make their own beds. Limited maid service. No air conditioning.
Rates	Sessions of 2–7 weeks from $1,450. $100 advance payment. Credit cards: AE, DC, MC, V.
Meal Plans	3 balanced cafeteria meals and 2 snacks daily in the residence halls.
Services and Facilities	**Exercise Equipment:** Weights room with Universal gym; gymnastics and tumbling training. **Swimming Facilities:** Indoor Olympic-size pool. **Recreation Facilities:** Tennis, team sports, running track; drama and crafts instruction. **Evening Programs:** Talent shows and plays; movies, games, campfires, dances.
In the Area	Historic Valley Forge National Park, museums and shopping in Allentown.
Getting Here	Located an hour by car from Philadelphia, 25 mi from Allentown, the campus is close to the Pennsylvania Turnpike. By air, scheduled flights to Allentown. By bus, Greyhound. Pickup from airport and bus station.
Special Notes	No smoking indoors.

Berkeley Springs State Park

Taking the waters

West Virginia
Berkeley Springs

Berkeley Springs State Park has been called the K Mart of spas: An hour-long "tub and rub" treatment costs $20, and in the summer you can swim in the big outdoor pool at no extra charge. All the mineral water you care to drink or take home is free.

Taking the waters has been fashionable here since the time of George Washington. Yet even before he visited as a 16-year-old surveyor in 1748, Indian tribes had journeyed long distances to bathe in the warm waters. Afflicted by rheumatism, Native Americans established a tribal truce around the springs so that all might benefit.

General Washington returned many times, and the cottage he built in the town became the first presidential summer retreat. Grand hotels attracted crowds with gambling and horse racing, and the new railroad line carried visitors from Baltimore. Two of the bathhouses in use today were designed in 1784 by James Rumsey, who developed the first successful steamboat on the Potomac River nearby.

Spartan and a bit shabby by today's standards, the state-run facilities offer a down-home Blue Ridge brand of healing. In the original 18th-century Roman bath building, step-down tubs rent for $8 an hour. Filled with 750 gallons of spring water heated to 102 degrees, the 3½-foot-deep pools hold several people—coed company is fine—in privacy. No reservations are taken; the policy is first come, first served.

Both the main bathhouse and the Country Inn hotel across the street date to the Depression era. Men and women have separate Roman plunge pools; everything else is in one large rectangular room. Masseurs operate in open cubicles, steam cabinets line yellow brick walls, and old-fashioned bathtubs provide a relaxing soak. While there's little privacy here, reservations are taken up to two weeks in advance.

The tiny state park, no larger than a town square, wins high marks for cleanliness and no-frills treatments; bring your jeans and a sense of humor.

Berkeley Springs State Park
Washington St., Berkeley Springs, WV 25411
Tel. 304/258–2711

Season   Open daily 10 AM–6 PM, Fri. 10 AM–7 PM, year-round.

Accommodations   In the Country Inn adjoining the park and several bed-and-breakfast guest houses in town or nearby. The Highlawn Inn, a hilltop Victorian mansion, has rooms with full breakfast for $70–$85 (tel. 304/258–5700). Cabins and lodge rooms at Cacapon State Park (tel. 304/258–1022) 10 mi south of town.

Getting Here   By car, the park is located near the intersection of Rte. 522 and Hwy. 9, in the center of town.

Coolfont Resort

Life enhancement

West Virginia
Berkeley Springs
A relaxed, informal, budget-priced mountain retreat devoted to making you feel and look better, the rustic Coolfont Resort has weekend and five-day programs for health and fitness, a massage workshop, and a seven-day plan to stop smoking. And one mile away is the mineral springs where George Washington bathed.

Occupying 1,200 acres in the foothills of the Allegheny Mountains, Coolfont has the laid-back look of a summer camp for adults. The A-frame chalets and log cabins have built-in whirlpools, and some outdoor hot tubs overlook the lake. Meals are served in Treetop House, a wood and stone A-frame perched on a hillside surrounded by wildlife.

Members of the resident staff of health and fitness experts are certified in sports medicine, massage therapy, preventive medicine, yoga, and muscle-toning exercise. Both Martha Ashelman, the president of Coolfont Resort, Inc., and J. A. Kiefer, a registered nurse, took the Seventh-day Adventist Breathe-Free training before introducing the program here. Programs are limited to 20 participants.

The emphasis is on health awareness, yet there is a cultural dimension to the community. Folk singers, string quartets, and artists in residence perform on weekends. Those who want to lose weight will have to forgo the bountiful buffets and turn to the separate dining room where low-calorie meals are served.

Coolfont Resort
Cold Run Valley Rd., Berkeley Springs, WV 25411
Tel. 304/258–4500 or 202/424–1232

Administration   Managers, Martha and Sam Ashelman; program director, Jean Appold

Season   Year-round.

Accommodations   240 rooms (more under construction); the Woodland Lodge, Manor House, and 14 hillside chalets have a rustic look with modern furnishings inside.

Rates   2-night weekend package $195–$245; 5-night programs $475–$525 double occupancy, single $30 per night additional. Massage and personal services not included. 6-night/7-day smoking program, including 2 massages and a facial, $875 single. 50% payable in advance (refund when canceled at least 48 hr before start of program). Credit cards: MC, V.

Meal Plans   Breakfast, lunch, dinner buffet style. Choice of fish, chicken, meat, vegetarian dishes. Produce from local farms and orchards.

Services and Facilities   **Swimming Facilities:** Private beach on spring-fed lake, outdoor pool at state park (summer). **Spa Facilities:** Soak and rubdown at Berkeley Springs State Park, $20. **Recreation Facilities:** 4 tennis courts; boating, hiking, horseback riding; team sports; cross-country skiing, ice skating; golf course nearby. **Evening Programs:** Concerts, theme weekends, health lectures.

In the Area   Cacapon State Park, the Castle mansion (1886), Harper's Ferry National Historical Park, Charles Town racetrack.

Getting Here   By car, Rte. 522 from I–270 at Hancock, MD, or the Pennsylvania Turnpike (I–76) at the Breezewood exit. By air, Allegheny and Piedmont have scheduled service to Hagerstown, MD; private planes use Potomac Airport. By bus, Greyhound to Hancock. By train, Amtrak to Martinsburg, WV. Rental car, taxi available.

Special Notes   Special accommodations for the disabled. Supervised morning camp for children, summer only. No smoking in the spa dining room.

The Greenbrier

Luxury pampering

West Virginia
White Sulphur
Springs

The legendary resort of Greenbrier blends old-fashioned comfort with high-tech spa treatments. A new $6.5-million spa wing has separate soaking pools and therapy rooms for men and women, a mirrored aerobics studio, and interactive exercise equipment. Hydrotherapy comes with mineral water—your choice of sulfur soak or bubbly herbal foam. Sports, riding, and hiking in the foothills of the Allegheny Mountains are significant attractions in the neighborhood.

While the hotel is a busy scene of conferences and afternoon teas in vast halls filled with "oriental" decor, the spa is serene and small, awash in pinks and greens, with sprigs of rhododendron painted on tiles. The staff includes both old hands and university-trained physiology specialists; they make newcomers feel comfortable about trying some of the exotic-sounding treatments. One-on-one training is available for those who want an active regimen, and there's a complete beauty salon.

Seaweed body wraps, aromatherapy, and facials with European floral products are among the à la carte offerings. Package plans are available during the off-season. Anyone can join the water exercise group at 8 AM weekdays and the scheduled aerobics and yoga classes at no extra charge.

Taking the waters has been an attraction here for more than 200 years. The Greenbrier Clinic, established in 1948, occupies a separate building that is completely equipped for diagnostic and preventive medicine. Health examinations can now be combined with spa therapy.

The Greenbrier
White Sulphur Springs, WV 24986
Tel. 304/536–1110 or 800/624–6070

Administration Manager, Ted J. Kleisner; program director, Monica T. Brown

Season Year-round.

Accommodations 650 rooms in main building, deluxe cottages, and guest houses.

Rates Double room $128–$170 per day for 2 persons, suite from $198 per day for 2 persons, breakfast and dinner included, service charge ($11) additional. Rates lower in winter. Golf, tennis, spa packages. $250 per room payable in advance. Credit cards: AE, MC, V.

Meal Plans American fare plus low-calorie alternatives at breakfast and dinner in the main dining room. Entrees may include mountain trout, roast beef, game, pasta. Cafe service for lunch. Tea daily.

Services and Facilities **Exercise Equipment:** Treadmills, bicycle ergometers, rowing ergometer, arm ergometer, hydra-resistance weight units. **Swimming Facilities:** Indoor Olympic-size pool, outdoor pool. **Spa Facilities:** Private pools for mineral baths; hydrotherapy tubs for underwater massage; mud and seaweed treatments. **Recreation Facilities:** 15 outdoor and 5 indoor tennis courts, platform tennis, 3 golf courses, fishing, skeet- and trapshooting, bowling, horseback riding, carriage rides, jogging and hiking trails, parcourse, bicycle rental. **Evening Programs:** Feature films, food and wine weekends, dancing.

In the Area Presidents' Cottage Museum displays memorabilia of famous visitors; crafts studios; mineral water springhouse.

Getting Here Located just off I–64 and close to the Blue Ridge Parkway. By car, I–95 to Richmond. By plane, Lewisburg Airport has scheduled flights by Piedmont and its Henson subsidiary, USAir and its Allegheny commuter service via Pittsburgh. By train, Amtrak's Cardinal between New York City, Washington, and Cincinnati stops at the Greenbrier Fri., Sun., and Tues. Private limousine connects with flights at Lewisburg. Rental car, taxi available.

Special Notes Special accommodations provided for the disabled. Sports school for children June–Labor Day. No smoking in the spa and designated areas of the dining room.

The Spa at the Country Inn

Luxury pampering

West Virginia
Berkeley Springs
Taking the waters has been updated at the Renaissance Spa attached to a new wing of the Country Inn. Facials and massage for men and women and whirlpool baths are the main attractions. In contrast to the sterile white-tile facilities across the street in the state-run spa, the atmosphere here is comfortably contemporary. Mineral water from the historic springs is used in the whirlpool bath. The five contributory springs at Berkeley are nonsulfurous and naturally heated to 74.3 degrees.

Opened in 1932, the Country Inn retains the small-town charm of an earlier era in its public rooms. Spa guests are housed in the new wing, where smoking is not permitted. Located between mountain ranges and apple orchards, the inn can provide a cozy getaway or a convenient base for exploring the natural beauty of a historic area.

The Spa at the Country Inn
207 S. Washington St., Berkeley Springs, WV 25411
Tel. 304/258–2210 or 202/737–1071

Administration Manager, Alice Clark; spa manager, Angella Liner

Season Year-round.

Accommodations 32 rooms in the original Colonial-style building, furnished with brass beds, antiques, and flea-market finds; 40 larger rooms in the new wing, with handcrafted oak furniture, queen-size beds, floral wallpaper.

Rates Rooms without private bath $35 per night; single or double rooms in the new addition $75 per night. Spa package with 3 nights lodging and treatments $115 per person double occupancy, $125 single (Sun.–Thurs., Nov.–May 1 only). 1 night payable in advance. Credit cards: AE, DC, MC, V.

Meal Plans Standard American fare with salads, fish. A pub adjoins the main dining room, and meals are served on the terrace in summer.

Services and Facilities	**Swimming Facilities:** Outdoor pool in state park (May 30–Sept. 4). **Spa Facilities:** Whirlpool mineral-water baths ($15), Roman plunge pool in state park across the street. **Recreation Facilities:** 18-hole golf course in Cacapon State Park, mountain hiking, canoeing along the C & O Canal, tennis at municipal courts (limited availability).
In the Area	Harper's Ferry National Historical Park, Charles Town Races, antiques shop, Cacapon State Park 10 miles south of town.
Getting Here	Located in the Eastern Panhandle of West Virginia near the gateway to Maryland, the spa is a 2-hr drive from Washington, DC, or Baltimore, 3-hr from Pittsburgh. By car, Rte. 522 from I–270 at Hancock, MD, or the Pennsylvania Turnpike (I–76) at Breezewood. By air, Allegheny Airlines and Piedmont have flights to Hagerstown, MD; private planes use Potomac Airport. By bus, Greyhound to Hancock, MD. By train, Amtrak to Martinsburg, WV. Inn provides free car service. Rental car, taxi available in town.
Special Notes	Special accommodations available for the disabled. No smoking in the spa and in the new wing.

Sheraton Lakeview Resort

Non-program resort facilities

West Virginia
Morgantown

The fitness and sports center of the Sheraton Lakeview Resort complements an executive conference center and two championship golf courses. Surrounded by woodland and a scenic lake, it's a place for both rigorous workouts and simple relaxation.

The action is continuous in the free-standing fitness center, and registered guests enjoy unlimited free access to facilities. A personal fitness evaluation is offered when you arrive, and the only extra fees are for massage, use of the racquet-sport courts, and aerobics classes. A nursery will take charge of the kids while parents work out.

Sheraton Lakeview Resort
Rte. 6, Box 88A, Morgantown, WV 26505
Tel. 304/594–1111 or 800/624–8300

Administration	Manager, W. G. Menihan; fitness director, Greg Orner
Season	Year-round.
Accommodations	2-story inn with 187 well-appointed rooms and 79 condominium units with maid service.
Rates	Rooms $80–$95 per day during peak season; condominium apartments (up to 6 persons) $650 per day. Credit card guarantee for 1 night. Credit cards: AE, DC, MC, V.
Meal Plans	Light fare in the lakeview restaurant; juice bar and snacks in the fitness center.
Services and Facilities	**Exercise Equipment:** 10-station Nautilus circuit, Marcy weight-resistance gym and recumbent bike, StairMaster, Lifecycle, Liferower, free weights. **Swimming Facilities:** Indoor and outdoor pools, lake. **Spa Facilities:** Coed whirlpool, separate saunas. **Recreation Facilities:** Racquetball and wallyball courts, indoor and outdoor tennis courts; fishing,

boat rentals, 2 golf courses; cushioned indoor running track, aerobics room. **Evening Programs:** Dancing, cabaret.

Getting Here Located 75 mi south of Pittsburgh, the resort is accessible by interstate routes and commuter airlines. By car, Rtes. 48 and 79. By plane, Morgantown's Hart Field is served by USAir/ Allegheny. Sheraton courtesy car pickup to and from airport.

Special Notes No smoking in the fitness center, some guest rooms, designated areas of the dining room.

The Woods Fitness Institute

**Nutrition and diet
Weight management**

West Virginia
Hedgesville
Surrounded by forests of oak, maple, and poplar, the Woods Fitness Institute is located in a relatively new development of weekend homes. Programs of one to four weeks are offered in weight loss, fitness, and nutrition. Following a complete physical assessment, the resident staff of professionals will tailor activities to your fitness level. You set the pace for a prebreakfast hike into the mountains, swimnastics, and training in the completely equipped exercise room.

The mountain setting offers special benefits. The adjacent public hunting and fishing area has 70 miles of hiking trails, and the resort features a championship golf course. Appropriately woodsy accommodations are alongside a man-made fishing pond. Sauna and massage are available.

The Woods Fitness Institute
Box 5, Hedgesville, WV 25427
Tel. 304/754-7977 or 800/248-2222

Administration Manager, James Garvin; program director, Dee Blackstone

Season Year-round.

Accommodations Cottages with twin beds; deluxe rooms in the Lodge with whirlpool for 2; larger cottages sleep 4. Standard motel furnishings.

Rates 7-day program $650 standard room, $750 deluxe room. 28-day stays from $1,790. 50% payable in advance. Credit cards: AE, MC, V.

Meal Plans 3 meals daily, 1,200 calories per day. Special restaurant seating for program participants.

Services and Facilities **Exercise Equipment:** Universal gym, treadmill, free weights. **Swimming Facilities:** Indoor and outdoor pools. **Spa Facilities:** Mineral spring baths at Berkeley Springs. **Recreation Facilities:** 1 indoor and 5 outdoor tennis courts; hiking; racquetball and handball courts; gymnasium for basketball and volleyball; canoeing and cross-country skiing nearby. **Evening Programs:** Resort entertainment.

In the Area C & O Canal, Cacapon State Park, Harper's Ferry National Historical Park, Blue Ridge Outlet Center.

Getting Here By car, from Washington, DC, or Baltimore take I–270/70 west to Hagerstown, I–81 south to Martinsburg, WV: Exit 16W from the Pennsylvania Turnpike, Rte. 522 south. By air, Allegheny Airlines and Piedmont have flights to Hagerstown, MD, private planes use Potomac Airport. By train, Amtrak to Martinsburg. Rental car available.

Special Notes Supervised summer camp for children. No smoking in fitness cottages and dining area.

New England and New York

A return to elegance marks the end of a decade of intensive development throughout the northeastern states. Grand old estates have been rejuvenated, hotels have updated their fitness facilities and introduced European therapies. The result has been a broader range of vacation options for both luxury-minded and budget-conscious travelers.

In Saratoga, New York, where the mineral springs were a prime attraction during the age of Victorian health spas, a state park that encompasses 122 of the city's 163 springs has joined with the old Roosevelt Baths and the Gideon Putnam Hotel in a comprehensive health program. Among other vintage hotels now sporting state-of-the-art spa facilities are the Norwich Inn in Connecticut, the Equinox in Vermont, and the Sagamore Hotel at Lake George, New York.

In the Berkshires the newly built Foxhollow Wellness Spa and the first branch of Arizona's famed Canyon Ranch offer New Age retreats and the latest in health programs only minutes away from the Boston Symphony Orchestra's popular summer home at Tanglewood.

Grand Lake Spa Hotel

Weight management

Connecticut Shedding seven to 10 pounds a week is the goal of most guests
Lebanon at the Grand Lake Spa Hotel. The no-nonsense weight-loss program attracts both men and women, but don't expect resort amenities. The atmosphere is quaint and casual.

A physical examination by a registered nurse determines your level of fitness and nutritional needs and helps in designing your daily program. A computerized body composition analysis may be recommended (additional fee). The computer produces guidelines for daily caloric intake to help you reduce, and it calculates how many calories you need to expend to reach your goal.

There is no mandatory schedule; the choice of daily activities is broad enough to satisfy all but the hardiest fitness buff. Activities are geared to people who don't get much exercise at home, and the staff is supportive and sympathetic. No one should be intimidated by the array of classes.

Set on a lake surrounded by flowering gardens and rolling meadows in central Connecticut, the spa hotel has the feel of a country home. Simply furnished rooms are spacious and airy.

Most guests, women 18 and older, come for weekend or weeklong workouts. If you're single and on a budget, ask about sharing a room.

Grand Lake Spa Hotel
Rte. 207, Lebanon, CT 06249
Tel. 203/642–6696 or 800/232–2772

New England and New York

CANADA

ONTARIO

St. Lawrence River

N

Lake Ontario

NEW YORK

I-81

Syracuse

I-90

I-90

18

19

20

14 A

Lake Erie

I-81

Binghamton

I-88

28

17

17

29

30

32

I-84

PENNSYLVANIA

NEW JERSEY

Connecticut
Grand Lake Spa Hotel, **35**
Norwich Inn & Spa, **36**

Maine
Northern Pines Health Resort, **1**
Poland Spring Health Institute, **2**

Massachusetts
The Ann Wigmore Foundation, **10**
Canyon Ranch in the Berkshires, **18**

The Center of the Light, **24**
Evernew, **23**
Foxhollow Wellness Spa, **19**
Kripalu Center for Yoga and Health, **20**
The Kushi Macrobiotic Center, **22**
The Lenox Zone, **21**
Maharishi Ayur-Ved Health Center, **11**

The Option Institute, **25**
Rowe Conference Center, **17**
Weight Watchers Camp New England, **16**

New Hampshire
EarthStar, **4**
Waterville Valley Resort, **3**

New York
Aegis, **15**
International Health and Beauty Spa, **34**

Living Springs Lifestyle Center, **33**
Mohonk Mountain House, **31**
New Age Health Spa, **30**
Omega Institute for Holistic Studies, **26**
Pawling Health Manor, **27**
The Sagamore Hotel, **12**
Saratoga Spa State Park, **13**

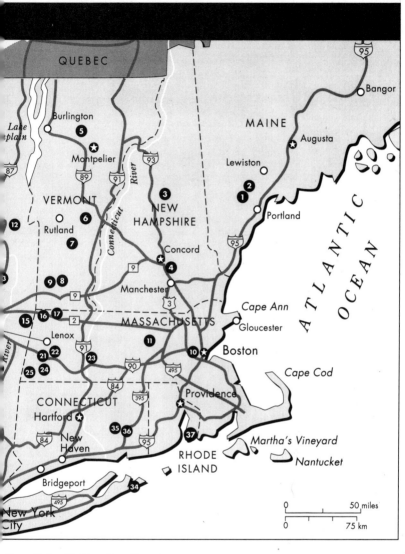

Sharon Springs Health
Spa, **14**

Sivananda Ashram
Yoga Ranch, **32**

Turnwood Organic
Gardens, **29**

Zen Mountain
Monastery, **28**

Green Mountain at
Fox Run, **7**

New Life Spa, **8**

Woodstock Inn &
Resort, **6**

Rhode Island

Castleview Camp, **37**

Vermont

The Equinox, **9**

Golden Eagle Resort, **5**

Administration   Director, Natalie Skolnik

Season   Year-round.

Accommodations   85 rooms in the main building and annexes, some singles, all with private bath.

Rates $150 a day per person double occupancy, $225 single. Packages available during spring and fall: 1 week (7 nights) $595–$695 double, $795–$895 single; weekend (3 nights) $345–$395 double, $465–$515 single. Tax additional. 1 night payable in advance. Credit cards: AE, MC, V.

Meal Plans   650-, 900-, or 1,200-calorie diets (per day). Optional juice fast for a minimum of 5 days. 3 meals daily, buffet style; entrees such as pasta primavera with artichoke, chicken breast, broiled shrimp, marinated mushroom salad.

Services and Facilities   **Exercise Equipment:** 3 stationary bikes, 3 rowing ergometers. **Services:** Complete blood chemistry analysis, body composition evaluation, stress-management consultation, daily massage. **Swimming Facilities:** Indoor and outdoor pools. **Recreation Facilities:** Tennis court. **Evening Programs:** Lectures on health-related topics, cooking demonstrations, dancing, movies.

In the Area   Antiques shops.

Getting Here   *From New York City.* By train, Amtrak from Penn Station to Hartford (90 min). By bus, Greyhound or Bonanza from Port Authority (2 hr). By air, scheduled flights to Bradley International Airport, Hartford/Springfield. By car, I–95 to Hwy. 91 (90 min). Courtesy pickup and return to airport or bus or train station.

Special Notes   Ramps and some ground-floor rooms afford access for the disabled. No smoking in some public areas.

Norwich Inn & Spa

Luxury pampering

Connecticut   Combine a 1920s country inn with a 1980s spa, and you have a
Norwich   perfect weekend escape for city dwellers. Located 1½ hours north of New York City, the imposing Georgian-style Norwich Inn & Spa took on a new life in 1987 with the addition of the spa wing. Today the inn blends sophisticated cuisine and beauty treatments with New England tradition.

The spa philosophy of the owner, Edward J. Safdie, is one of nurturing and unadulterated pampering, and this is evident throughout the inn's operation. From flowered chintz and hand-rubbed pine in the old-fashioned bedrooms to high-tech workouts in the gym, the regimen and comfort complement each other.

The 35-foot swimming pool under a soaring cathedral ceiling is the spa's centerpiece. An aerobics studio and an exercise room equipped with Keiser Cam II pneumatic resistance units flank the pool. You can sign up for massages, deep-cleansing facials, body scrubs, hydrotherapy, and a full range of skin and beauty treatments. Classes, scheduled throughout the day, are open to other guests at the inn as well as to program participants.

Because the inn caters to conferences, you may find yourself mingling with a large number of guests who aren't counting calories but have paid $10 for admission to the spa and may sign up for treatments and classes à la carte. For serious workouts, come on one of the Sunday–Friday packages. Accommodations are in the main building or new villas.

The range of treatments makes this spa special. Choices include guided imagery, acupressure, thalassotherapy body wraps with algae imported from France, and hydrotherapy in a deep tub with a 60-jet water massage.

Meals are served in a private dining room away from the bar and smoking areas. The author of a highly regarded book on spa food, Safdie has given the inn's menu a new look while retaining the classic New England flavor, high in complex carbohydrates —seafood, fresh fruits, local vegetables—and low on fat.

Charm and comfort came with the recent renovation. Antiques, four-poster beds, ceiling fans, handwoven rugs, and lace curtains enhance the bedrooms. A six-foot birdhouse in the lobby is home to a pair of fantail doves. Public areas include a taproom with a large stone fireplace and a quiet sun-room full of palms and wicker.

Surrounded by 37 acres of woodland and situated near a state park, the inn offers rural diversions after workouts.

Norwich Inn & Spa
607 W. Thames (Rte. 32), Norwich, CT 06360
Tel. 203/886–2401 or 800/892–5692

Administration Manager, Brian Donahue; program director, Vicki Bailey

Season Year-round.

Accommodations 65 rooms, 16 suites, all but two with private bath, furnished with antiques and reproductions. New villas with kitchen serviced by the inn.

Rates Rooms $95–$185 per day, suites $130 per person double occupancy. 5-day program $1,550–$1,900 single, $1,262.50–$1,437.50 per person double occupancy. 2-day program $575–$715 single, $460–$530 per person double occupancy. Tax and service charge additional. Lower rates in winter. $500 deposit for 5-day program, $250 for 2-day program. Credit cards: AE, MC, V.

Meal Plans New England specialties, spa cuisine; no salt, sugar, white flour, fatty oils. Lots of seafood, fresh fruit, vegetables. Menus of 1,200–1,500 calories per day for women, 1,800–2,000 calories for men.

Services and Facilities **Exercise Equipment:** 5 Keiser Cam II pneumatic resistance weight stations, Lifecycles, Trotter treadmill, StairMaster. **Services:** Facials, body massage, loofah scrub, hydrotherapy and thalassotherapy, aromatherapy massage; beauty and skin-care salon. **Swimming Facilities:** Indoor exercise pool, outdoor lap pool. **Spa Facilities:** Men's and women's sauna and steam room, coed whirlpool; aerobics classes, private workouts. Closed Sun. afternoon. **Recreation Facilities:** 2 tennis courts. Norwich Golf Course and Fort Shantok State Park adjoin the inn's 37 acres. Rental bicycles.

In the Area Mystic Seaport Maritime Museum, General Dynamics submarine base in Groton, Old Lyme art center and historic homes. Cathedral of St. Patrick in Old Norwich, Essex summer beach colony, Eugene O'Neill Theater Center, Goodspeed Opera House in Haddam.

Getting Here *From New York City.* By train, Amtrak from Grand Central Station to New London (90 min). By air, scheduled flights to New London by American Airlines and USAir. By car, I–95 to I–395, Rte. 32 to Norwich. Hotel limousine service to the airport and train station in New London ($12 each way). Taxi and rental car available in Norwich and New London. Ample free parking.

Special Notes No smoking in the spa and spa dining room.

Northern Pines Health Resort

Holistic health
Weight management
Stress control

Maine
Raymond Getting back to nature can be a healthy experience on the 80 acres of the Northern Pines Health Resort. The diet and fitness programs, based on a holistic approach, are designed to help participants develop a positive attitude toward weight loss and stress control; the transition is a gradual process, not a quick fix.

Essentially a self-help camp with a limited number of optional services, Northern Pines offers a program designed for men and women who want to take control of their lives. Campers range widely in age, a high percentage of them being over 40. The affordable rates make it popular with singles year-round. About 36 guests are resident in summer, 18 during the ski season, which makes for a friendly mix with lots of personal attention from the staff.

Each day begins with stretching exercises and a brisk walk through the woods, followed by a choice of focus sessions or aerobics. Morning and afternoon yoga are optional. Evenings offer more learning activities, from cooking classes to massage demonstrations. Fasting regimens are offered, and about 20% of the guests opt to go on a week-long juice fast.

The camp's lakeside log cabins date from the 1920s and provide total seclusion for couples. New lodge rooms and cabins with two bedrooms are on the hillside amid towering pines, spruce, and hemlock. There are also yurts (earth-covered cabins) for two that have carpeting and modern conveniences.

The informality and laid-back pace appeal to stressed-out professionals who come here to rejuvenate and relax. On a warm summer evening it's not unusual to see swimmers skinny-dipping in the lake after a rap session in the hot tub. Leave your resort clothes at home and bring your old sweatshirts and hiking boots.

Northern Pines Health Resort
Rte. 83, R.R. Box 279, Raymond, ME 04071
Tel. 207/655–7624

Administration	Managers, Pat and Marlee Coughlan; fitness director, Ann Maroeau
Season	Year-round except Nov.–mid-Dec., mid-March–May.
Accommodations	Private cabins and lodge rooms for 36. Some share a bathroom, others a communal facility; most have private toilet and shower. Well-worn wood furniture and buildings. Small laundry.
Rates	1-week summer program (Sun.–Sun.) $425–$695; weekend (2 nights) $135–$225. Rooms $70–$117 per day. $50 deposit per person for weekend, $100 for a week. Credit cards: AE, MC, V.
Meal Plans	Modified vegetarian diet, 800 calories per day. 3 meals daily include pasta, salads with home-grown sprouts, poached salmon. Supervised fasts begin with 2 days of raw fruit, vegetables, juices, and broth.
Services and Facilities	**Exercise Equipment:** NordicTrack cross-country ski machine, 2 stationary bikes, weight units, free weights. **Services:** Massage, reflexology, aromatherapy, facials, hair treatment, float-tank sessions. **Swimming Facilities:** Lake with sandy beach. **Recreation Facilities:** Hiking, canoeing, sailing; jogging trails. **Evening Programs:** Cooking demonstrations, massage techniques, sauna baths, salt rubs; videos, storytelling.
In the Area	L. L. Bean store, ocean beaches, White Mountain Range; Acadia National Park; ferry trips to Nova Scotia; Portland's restored Old Port, summer theater, Portland Museum of Art; factory outlets in Freeport.
Getting Here	*From Portland.* By car, I–95 to Exit 8, Rte. 302 northwest to Rte. 83 (45 min). By air, service to Portland International Airport. Bus station and airport van service for Sun. afternoon arrivals and departures $5 (other times $25–$40). Rental car, taxi available.
Special Notes	Summer camp for children, 3½ or 7 weeks. No smoking in public areas.

Poland Spring Health Institute

Preventive medicine

Maine
Poland Spring

An extended visit to Poland Spring Health Institute is more like taking a holiday in the country than being at a clinic. The program outlined for you by Dr. Richard A. Hansen is based on his experience at the Wildwood Lifestyle Center and Hospital in Georgia. Drinking the area's world-famous mineral water complements his philosophy of maintaining health through a vegetarian diet and rigorous outdoor exercise.

Just eight guests are accommodated in old-fashioned comfort in a big New England house; the average stay is two weeks. Because it is run on a nonprofit basis by Seventh-day Adventists, the cost is a surprisingly modest $75 a day for a semiprivate room.

Guests work closely with specialists on diabetes and stress-related ailments. A series of exercises and hydrotherapy treatments is prescribed that is appropriate to your physical condition. Testing by the medical office, when needed, is an additional charge; everything else is included in the weekly fee.

Poland Spring has been synonomous with healthy water for more than a century, largely due to a commercial bottling plant near the institute. Here you drink 8–10 glasses a day directly from the well and bathe in the mineral-laden water, which is piped into the steam room and used for body wraps during massage.

The institute's scenic surroundings compensate for a lack of recreational facilities. You can hike, jog, do the parcourse, borrow a bike. In winter there are cross-country skiing and ice skating. An aerobics studio is built into the house, as are the hydrotherapy facilities. After a full day, most guests seem to prefer relaxing on the sun porch and appreciating the view.

Poland Spring Health Institute
RFD 1, Box 433, Summit Spring Rd., Poland Spring, ME 04274
Tel. 207/998–2894

Administration Program director, R. A. Hansen, M.D.; manager, Ulla Hansen

Season Year-round.

Accommodations 6 large rooms, most sharing a bath.

Rates Semiprivate room $525 a week with meals, private room $745, tax and service charge included. $100 nonrefundable reservation fee. No credit cards.

Meal Plans Salads and steamed vegetables, lots of fresh fruit, and home-baked bread make up the Adventist diet of mostly complex carbohydrates. No butter, oils, sugar; high-fat foods such as nuts, avocados, and olives in modest amounts. No coffee, alcohol, irritating spices.

Services and Facilities **Exercise Equipment:** Stationary and outdoor bikes. **Swimming Facilities:** Private lake. **Recreation Facilities:** Rowboating, biking, horseback riding; nearby golf. **Evening Programs:** Lectures on health-related subjects.

In the Area Shopping and sightseeing trips into Portland; Shaker communal life and handmade goods at Sabbathday Lake.

Getting Here By air, Portland International Airport, 30 mi. By car, Boston, about 100 mi. No local transportation; arrangements can be made with staff.

Special Notes No smoking indoors. Remember to bring sturdy walking shoes, rain gear, and personal medical records as requested.

The Ann Wigmore Foundation

Nutrition and diet

Massachusetts **Boston** The Living Foods Lifestyle, a two-week course taught by Ann Wigmore, is devoted to practical experience in the planting, growing, and preparation of easy-to-digest natural foods. A holistic, New Age approach designed to strengthen the immune system and help avoid digestion problems, the program at the Ann Wigmore Foundation covers beauty care and longevity, as well. Participants are shown how to apply this knowledge in their daily life and to gather support through a network of community organizations.

The body's need for physical, mental, and emotional nourishment is central to the program. Wigmore's studies and experimentation with wheatgrass chlorophyll and other grasses and greens explain how the diet can increase energy.

Classes and demonstrations are conducted by resident staff members trained in the Living Foods Lifestyle. The foundation's homelike five-story building accommodates up to 10 guests and has a working kitchen and classrooms. Furnishings are simple and modern, with no frills.

The Ann Wigmore Foundation
196 Commonwealth Ave., Boston, MA 02116
Tel. 617/267-9424

Administration	Director, Ann Wigmore
Season	2-week periods scheduled year-round.
Accommodations	1 dormitory room with 6 beds, 1 double room, 2 single rooms, shared bath.
Rates	2-week residential tuition $500. 50% payable in advance. No credit cards.
Meal Plans	3 meals a day in the residence dining room. Soups made with fruits and vegetables, juices, salads, a baked loaf of seeds and vegetables.
Services and Facilities	**Exercise Equipment:** None; health club nearby. **Services:** Complete education program and menus. **Recreation Facilities:** Nearby beaches, parks. **Evening Programs:** Discussions on health-related topics.
In the Area	Health-food stores; Boston museums and institutions; historic sightseeing.
Getting Here	Centrally located in Boston's Back Bay area; easily reached by public transportation, taxi, or car from all parts of the city.
Special Notes	No smoking indoors.

Canyon Ranch in the Berkshires

Life enhancement
Weight management
Luxury pampering

Massachusetts
Lenox

Ten years after opening the first in a new generation of fitness vacation resorts, the developers of Arizona's wildly popular Canyon Ranch have come east. Scheduled to be in operation during 1989, Canyon Ranch in the Berkshires will be a four-season spa and a comprehensive medical center for prevention and treatment of stress-related illness.

The new Canyon Ranch has a mind-and-body approach to fitness. Focused on improving your lifestyle, the programs and facilities can be enjoyed for a weekend, a week, or longer. Skiers can get in shape before tackling cross-country trails, and executives can use the latest biofeedback systems to de-stress. A 100,000-square-foot fitness center includes racquetball, squash, and tennis courts; a running track; a 75-foot swimming pool; and separate spas for men and women with saunas, steam rooms, inhalation rooms, and Jacuzzis.

The Arizona Canyon Ranch's hiking and biking programs have been adapted to the Berkshire terrain, but don't expect to find Southwestern food and lodging. The Boston-based architectural firm of Jung/Brannen (designers of the Doral Saturnia Spa in Florida) has come up with an original design for bringing the outdoors inside. The centerpiece, a mansion that dates from 1897, and its formal gardens, in which it's now possible to dine elegantly on New American cuisine, is a replica of Louis XV's Petit Trianon. Wrapped around the structure are glass walkways that connect to the inn and fitness center.

Surrounded by majestic views of the Berkshires, the new Canyon Ranch will attempt to recreate the active, informal atmosphere that has been a hallmark of the original in Arizona.

Canyon Ranch in the Berkshires
Kemble St. (Rte. 7A), Lenox, MA 01240
Tel. 413/637–4100 or 800/621–9777

Administration Manager, Peter Campbell; program director, William Day

Season Year-round.

Accommodations 120 rooms, mostly garden units with private patios. New England–style functional furnishings.

Rates Weekend packages and special programs to be announced. 2 nights deposit in advance. Credit cards: MC, V.

Meal Plans 3 meals and snacks, plus nonalcoholic drinks. Low-cal menus include New England specialties cooked with a minimum of salt and fat. Recipes are 60–65% carbohydrate, 20% protein, and 15–20% fat. 1,000 calories per day recommended for women, 1,200 for men.

Services and Facilities **Exercise Equipment:** State-of-the-art treadmills, stair climbers, stationary bikes, rowing machines, free weights, and a full set of weight-resistance units. **Services:** Herbal wraps, massage, skin care, and beauty salon; holistic health counseling, MindFitness biofeedback training; medical checkup and fitness evaluation. **Swimming Facilities:** Indoor and 50-foot heated outdoor pool. **Recreation Facilities:** Cross-country skiing, hiking; bicycles for daily group outings; 3 tennis and 2 platform tennis courts; indoor racquet sports. **Evening Programs:** Visiting specialists speak on health and lifestyle topics.

In the Area Optional tours to local museums and festivals. Tanglewood Music Festival, Jacob's Pillow Dance Festival, The Sterling and Francine Clark Art Institute in Williamstown (25 mi), Williamstown summer theater.

Getting Here *From Boston and New York City.* By car, Massachusetts Turnpike (I–90). By train, daily Amtrak service to Pittsfield, with connections to Lenox by Bonanza Bus or Regional Transit. By air, scheduled flights to the nearest airport, Bradley International at Hartford/Springfield. Taxi, rental car, limousine for local travel.

Special Notes Ramp entry to all buildings and facilities. Some bedrooms specially equipped for the disabled. A combination of outdoor and supervised fitness training for teenagers called The Young and Restless, July–Aug. No smoking indoors.

The Center of the Light

Spiritual awareness

Massachusetts Healing and spiritual growth are brought together at the Cen-
New Marlborough ter of the Light's rustic retreat in a weathered wood barn and
large New England farmhouse surrounded by gardens, or-
chards, and distant mountains. Workshops lasting two to five
days offer instruction in massage therapies, herbal cures,
stress control, and a variety of practices from prayer to
personal transformation.

Vacationers who skip the workshops may still find that the center's spiritual environment sets the tone for a quiet holiday in
the Berkshires. Even an introduction to kayaking involves
yoga and tai chi chuan for balance and relaxation.

The Center of the Light
S. Sandisfield Rd., New Marlborough, MA
(Office) Box 540, Great Barrington, MA 01230
Tel. 413/229-2396

Season Mid-June–early Sept.

Accommodations 75 beds in dormitory, cabins, and the main house. Some single
and double rooms with bath. Cabins and dormitories sleep 4–8.
No bedding or linens.

Rates Room and board $35–$45 per day. Workshop tuition $90 week-
end, $150 5-day program. $50 deposit on registration. No credit
cards.

Meal Plans 3 meals daily, buffet style; a primarily ovo-lacto-vegetarian
diet; no refined flour, sugar, caffeine.

Services and **Swimming Facilities:** Outdoor pool, nearby lakes. **Recreation**
Facilities **Facilities:** Tennis court, hiking, kayaking. **Evening Programs:**
Sat. concerts, Sun. worship and healing services.

In the Area Tanglewood Music Festival, Jacob's Pillow Dance Festival,
Campbell's Falls.

Getting Here By car, Massachusetts Turnpike (I–90) to Lee Exit; Taconic
Parkway to Rte. 23 Great Barrington Exit. By air, nearest airport is Albany, NY.

Special Notes Remember to bring bedding.

Evernew

Life enhancement *Women only*

Massachusetts Creating a summer retreat for women was the dream of
South Hadley Barbara Slater, a Boston-based TV producer who wanted to
exercise and modify her appearance without going to a resort.
The 800-acre campus of Mt. Holyoke College in west central
Massachusetts has proved to be the perfect setting for the mod-
estly priced Evernew program.

Evernew combines elements of a health spa regimen with the
relaxed atmosphere of summer camp. There is no room service,
no roster of required classes, no dress code. For six days the

focus in the stress-free environment is fitness. Limited to 40 participants, the group typically consists of homemakers as well as professionals, women who want to lose weight and women who just want to tone up. Ages range from the early 20s to the middle 60s.

Seminars and workshops take full advantage of the college's sports facilities and the woodland campus. Having begun the day with yoga or power walking, you may choose aerobics classes (high or low impact), workouts in the pool, or relaxation exercise. Emphasis is put on proper body alignment and preventing injury. Afternoons can include a session on healthy backs or wardrobe planning. Beauty is on the agenda too: Massages and facials are $35. Then there is free time for tennis, squash, racquetball, golf, and bicycling.

Specialists, all women, from health clubs and schools in the Boston area make up the staff. There are two licensed massage therapists, a certified yoga instructor, and a dance-exercise teacher.

Evernew
South Hadley, MA;
Box 183, Milton Village, MA 02187
Tel. 617/265-7756 (413/538-2000 July–Aug.)

Administration	Program director, Barbara Slater
Season	7 sessions: full sessions Sun.–Fri., miniweeks Sun.–Tues., late June–mid-Aug. only.
Accommodations	Private rooms in a college dormitory. Bedding, towels, housekeeping provided; no maid service. Laundry facilities.
Rates	$650 per session (miniweek $400), single or double occupancy, includes meals, snacks, classes, use of facilities, and an hour-long massage. No tax or service charge. $150 deposit, balance due 30 days before arrival. Cancellation fee. No credit cards.
Meal Plans	1,200-calorie menu features local produce, recipes high in fiber and low in fat, sugar, salt, cholesterol.
Services and Facilities	**Exercise Equipment:** Exercise bicycles, rowing machines, weights room with hydra-fitness units, and sauna in the college fitness center. **Swimming Facilities:** Olympic-size indoor pool, private lake. **Recreation Facilities:** Tennis, squash, racquetball courts; bridle and bicycle paths; stable; 18-hole golf course; wildlife sanctuary. **Evening Programs:** Informal entertainment and lectures lakeside and in the community room.
In the Area	Boutiques in South Hadley, summer festivals.
Getting Here	By car, about 2 hr from Boston, 3 hr from New York City. By air, Bradley International Airport (45 min). By train, Amtrak to Springfield. Bicycles used locally.
Special Notes	Smoking discouraged.

Foxhollow Wellness Spa

Preventive medicine
Weight management
Life enhancement

Massachusetts
Lenox

Bringing together holistic health concepts and the latest psychological and medical treatments for stress-related illness, the new Foxhollow Wellness Spa is concerned with total well-being. Planned by Dr. Stephan Rechtschaffen, whose pioneering work in holistic health at the Omega Institute for Holistic Studies covers a broad spectrum of topics, the Foxhollow programs focus on behavioral change, degenerative diseases, the immune system, weight loss, and stress management.

Housed in a mansion that was built in a Berkshire summer colony during the Gilded Age by a wealthy industrialist, Foxhollow offers weekend and seven-day programs. Specific medical and cardiovascular problems will be addressed in week-long programs, with follow-up weekends throughout the year.

The fitness facilities are in a completely new free-standing building nearby. Here you can work out or be pampered, try flotation tanks or Japanese baths. Wholesome meals are served on a glass-enclosed terrace overlooking Laurel Lake. Two other dining rooms serve calorie-controlled gourmet cuisine, including one open to the public in the historic mansion.

Foxhollow Wellness Spa
Rte. 7, Lenox, MA 01240
Tel. 413/637-2000

Administration Director, Stephen Rechtschaffen, M.D.; program director, Liisa O'Maley

Season Year-round.

Accommodations 80-room guest lodge, new condos; all rooms and suites with fireplace, private terrace, full bath, air conditioning, color TV. Some kitchenettes.

Rates $100–$250 per person per day, with meals; $700–$1,500 weekly. Packages of 2, 3, 7 days from $350 per person double occupancy. Deposit of $100 or one-third of program cost. Credit cards: AE, CB, DC, MC, V.

Meal Plans 3 calorie-controlled meals daily in dining rooms. The public restaurant serves an à la carte gourmet menu.

Services and Facilities **Exercise Equipment:** 10-station Eagle weights gym, treadmills, Bally rowing ergometers, stationary bikes, free weights. **Swimming Facilities:** Indoor and outdoor pools, lake beach. **Spa Facilities:** Separate saunas and steam rooms for men and women. **Recreation Facilities:** 230-acre estate with hiking and horseback riding trails, 6 tennis courts, volleyball and basketball courts. Bicycles, sailboats, and cross-country skiing equipment. Downhill ski slopes nearby. **Evening Programs:** Lectures on health-related topics; videotapes.

In the Area Historical sites, summer theater, Jacob's Pillow Dance Festival. Tanglewood Music Festival, The Sterling and Francine Clark Art Institute in Williamstown (25 mi), Williams College Museum of Art.

Getting Here *From Boston and New York City.* By car, Massachusetts Turnpike (I–90), exit on Rte. 183 North (3½ hr). By train, Amtrak has daily service to Pittsfield, MA, with connections to Lenox by Bonanza Bus or Regional Transit. By air, scheduled flights to Bradley International Airport at Hartford/Springfield. Free car service to and from the airport and train station; taxi, rental car available.

Special Notes Some ramps and special rooms for the disabled. No smoking.

Kripalu Center for Yoga and Health

Spiritual awareness
Life enhancement
Preventive medicine

Massachusetts The ancient science of yoga has been synthesized with modern
Lenox approaches to holistic health and personal growth in a series of programs designed to fight stress and increase well-being. The enormous brick mansion, built for Andrew Carnegie and later enlarged, provides a suitably expansive setting.

On a typical day you have a choice of lectures, workshops, bodywork, and several yoga sessions. Mornings begin in a meditative mood at 5:20 in the main chapel, or with a 6:45 yoga session, followed by breakfast eaten in silence. Most of the guests, who can number to 350, start their day walking about the grounds.

In addition to the daily schedule, there are special programs with such names as Inner Quest Intensive, Relationships that Work, Self-Esteem, Transform Stress, and Getaway Health Holiday. These workshops, lasting four and five days or a weekend, are scheduled throughout the year.

Overseeing all activities is the center's founder, Amrit Desai, who developed the Kripalu style of yoga. By drawing on the slow performance of classic yoga positions, Kripalu creates a "meditation in movement." Even the aerobic dance class, called DansKinetics, mixes yoga stretches with energetic dance steps.

Classes are divided into beginner, intermediate, and advanced. After dinner, everyone is invited to *satsang*, an evening of meditation and chanting. The theme is not self-denial, but vibrant health.

Prevention and recovery from illness are the focus of an intensive, 20-day program that brings together several therapies. Health for Life emphasizes new ways of relaxing, eating, and exercising. Directed by Dr. Ronald Dushkin, a charter member of the American Holistic Medical Association, this program in self-healing involves progressive strengthening through aerobic exercise and yoga, daily sessions of therapeutic bodywork, and nutritional counseling.

Participants range in age from 18 to 80 and work together in problem-solving sessions, hiking, and skiing in the 300 acres of forest that surround the center. Some guests come for a few days of rest and renewal; others seek compassion and healing through private consultation. None of the programs are mandatory, and there's no effort to convert anyone to anything here.

Kripalu Center for Yoga and Health
Box 793, Lenox, MA 01240
Tel. 413/637-3280

Administration Program director, Yogi Amrit Desai

Season Year-round.

Accommodations Rooms and dormitory bunks for 350. Bedding, sheets, and towels not included. A few deluxe rooms with private or shared baths and a private lounge for breakfast. No maid service. Lakeview rooms (2 beds) at extra cost. Double beds in forest view rooms.

Rates $70 for a welcome weekend, dormitory accommodations; $330–$660 for 6-night workshops. $2,500–$2,800 (exclusive of medical fees) for 20-day Health for Life program in May, June, and Sept. with deluxe accommodations. 25% deposit in advance. No refunds, but deposit can be applied to future programs. Credit cards: MC, V.

Meal Plans 3 vegetarian meals daily, buffet style. Macrobiotic diet includes whole grains and vegetables, dairy products. Full salad bar, several entrees, fresh-baked bread, variety of condiments, and hot or cold tea served at noon. Food is low in fat and sweeteners. Special diets accommodated by advance request. Meals eaten in silence to maintain the spiritual atmosphere.

Services and Facilities **Services:** Massage therapies, including Kripalu bodywork, polarity, shiatsu; facial and foot care; medical tests. **Swimming Facilities:** Private lake. **Spa Facilities:** Saunas for men and women, whirlpool, flotation tank. **Recreation Facilities:** DansKinetic aerobic exercise class; skiing in winter. **Evening Programs:** Communal meditation and chanting; Indian dancing and concerts.

In the Area Tanglewood Music Festival (July–Aug.), summer theater and dance; the Sterling and Francine Clark Art Institute in Williamstown.

Getting Here By car, Massachusetts Turnpike (I–90) from Boston, New York City, and the west. Approaching Tanglewood and Stockbridge, look for Richmond Mountain Rd. By air, Bradley International Airport at Hartford/Springfield. By train, Amtrak has 1 train daily from Boston to Pittsfield, with connections to Lenox by Bonanza Bus or Regional Transit. Taxi and limousine service in Lenox.

Special Notes Facilities and rooms specially equipped for the disabled. Day camp for children 4–12, July–Aug., $25 per day. No smoking in or near the center. Remember to bring mat or cushion for meditation and yoga; bedding and towels for dormitory accommodations.

The Kushi Macrobiotic Center

Nutrition and diet
Spiritual awareness

Massachusetts At the Kushi Macrobiotic Center in the Berkshires, macro-
Becket biotics is taught and experienced as a way of life. The diet is so low in fat and high in antioxidant vitamins that its advocates be-

lieve it decreases the risk of heart disease and cancer, although some nutritionists find it restrictive, misleading, and perhaps even dangerous.

The macrobiotic diet, say its supporters, provides a unifying understanding of life. Since 1978, the Kushi Institute has been in the forefront of macrobiotics research and education. The center offers an intensive seminar in cooking, plus four or five days of instruction on preventing cancer and heart disease. For newcomers to macrobiotics, there is a week-long introductory course that includes exercise and massage.

Secluded on 600 acres of woodlands and meadows, the Berkshires Center provides a peaceful, natural environment for study and relaxation. In a former Franciscan abbey, the bedrooms and working kitchen accommodate up to 10 participants in year-round programs. Many of these seminars are taught personally by Aveline and Michio Kushi. In 1986, a spiritual dimension was added, focusing on personal health and transformation, issues of family and society, and global understanding.

The daily activities begin with a session of *do-in*, stretching exercises that are simple and easy to learn. Periods of meditation alternate with lectures and workshops in food preparation. Individuals, couples, and families often participate together.

The Kushi Macrobiotic Center
Box 7, Becket, MA 01223
Tel. 413/623–5742

Administration	Manager, Alex Jack; program director, Charles Millman
Season	Year-round. The residential seminar begins on the 1st and 3rd Sun. of the month, concludes the following Sat. with lunch. Cooking intensives and topical seminars run 4–5 days. 4-part spiritual training seminar scheduled at various times of the year.
Accommodations	5 guest rooms, simply furnished with 2 beds; 2 rooms have private bath or shower facility.
Rates	7-day residential seminars with meals and a shared bedroom, $800; $500 for room and board only. Private bath $17.50 additional per day. $100 advance deposit per person. Credit cards: MC, V.
Meal Plans	3 meals daily, family style. Brown rice, miso soup, and cooked vegetables with condiments. Specialties include *daikon* and *shiitake* mushroom casserole, *azuki* beans and squash, and mock lasagna with tofu and carrot sauce.
Services and Facilities	**Services:** Shiatsu massage. **Swimming Facilities:** Nearby lake. **Evening Programs:** Workshops and discussions on diet and nutrition; informal entertainment.
In the Area	Tanglewood Music Festival at Lenox (35 min); summer theater and the Sterling and Francine Clark Art Institute in Williamstown (90 min); Jacob's Pillow Dance Festival in Lee (15 min).
Getting Here	*From Boston.* By car, Massachusetts Turnpike (I–90), exit for Lee (2½ hr). By bus, Peter Pan Bus Lines or Bonanza Bus Lines to Lee (3 hr). By air, Bradley International Airport at

Hartford/Springfield. Free pickup at bus station in Lee; taxi, car rental available.

Special Notes No smoking.

The Lenox Zone

Spiritual awareness

Massachusetts Transformational experiences and the pleasures of summer
Lee camp blend at The Lenox Zone. The series of weekends planned by the spiritual director, Richard M. Moss, has involved members of the Sun Bear Tribe, drummers from several nations, and students of Avatar Meher Baba. All share a vision of health and spiritual development in modern society based on ancient philosophies.

Children have been coming to the camp for 70 summers, but these pre- and post-season weekend retreats are for adults. The experiences take some participants to the edge of their ordinary reality, uniting the spiritual and the mundane. Transformation reportedly occurs when the past is incorporated into the present, opening new possibilities for the future.

Campers have full run of the scenic, 250-acre site. The wooden cottages cluster on a hillside overlooking Lake Shaw, and there are 10 tennis courts, a weight training room, and a crafts center as well as water sports facilities. A lakefront dining room, an indoor theater, and newly designed community housing complete the villagelike atmosphere.

The Lenox Zone
Camp Lenox, Rte. 8, Lee, MA 01238
(Oct.–May 10) 345 Riverside Dr., New York, NY 10025
Tel. 413/243–2223 (212/662–3182 Oct.–May 10)

Administration Program director, Richard M. Moss, M.D.

Season June and Sept.

Accommodations Community houses and cottages for 8–14 persons, 8 private cottages with twin beds, tent area for 150. Limited bedding.

Rates Tuition $80–$220, meals included. Full payment in advance. No credit cards.

Meal Plans 6 vegetarian gourmet meals are served during the weekend, buffet style. Special diets accommodated with advance notice.

Services and **Exercise Equipment:** Fully equipped weight training room.
Facilities **Swimming Facilities:** Private lake. **Recreation Facilities:** Hiking, jogging, basketball, tennis, sailing, canoeing, kayaking. **Evening Programs:** Concerts, talent shows.

In the Area Summer theater and dance festivals; museums.

Getting Here *From Boston or Albany.* By car, Massachusetts Turnpike (I–90) to Lee (Exit 2), then Rte. 20 and 8. *From New York City and Connecticut.* By car, Rte. 8 North. By bus, daily scheduled service to Lee on Greyhound and Bonanza from Boston and New York. Taxi service in Lee.

Maharishi Ayur-Ved Health Center

Spiritual awareness
Preventive medicine
Nutrition and diet

Massachusetts
Lancaster

Ancient Indian healing techniques and modern biofeedback technology are the means to relaxation and good health in the elegant mansion of the Maharishi Ayur-Ved Health Center. Ayurvedic medical treatments are based on an analysis of one's *dosha*, or physical and emotional type. The therapy includes a special diet related to body type, massage with warm oil and herbal essences, and total relaxation.

The healing process of *panchakarma* begins with a physical examination, pulse measurement, and a thorough questionnaire to determine whether you are *vata* (quick, energetic, movement prone), *pitta* (enterprising and sharp), or *kapha* (tranquil and steady). Therapy and diet are prescribed accordingly.

While the system is based on Ayur-Veda, as practiced in Asia, the center's doctors and registered nurses are trained in both Eastern and Western medicine. Cancer and other disease sufferers frequently come for treatment.

A daily two-hour session to rid the body of impurities includes massage, heat application, and a gentle laxative. Neuromuscular training may be recommended through yoga exercises. Aromatherapy is also available, and a course in transcendental meditation is taught for an extra fee. Sound therapy is the focus of the stress-reduction program. Listening to primordial sounds re-created by musical instruments and the human voice, or to tapes of musical rhythms (called *gandharveda* sounds), induces relaxation.

Furnished with large beds and heavy but comfortable chairs, the high-ceiling rooms retain a look of luxury from the 1920s, when this was the country cottage of a shipping magnate involved with the *Titanic*.

Maharishi Ayur-Ved Health Center
679 George Hill Rd.;
Box 344, Lancaster, MA 01523
Tel. 617/365–4549

Administration Director, Ronald Pleasant

Season Year-round.

Accommodations 14 bedrooms with several suites. Some small single rooms share a bath. All rooms air-conditioned.

Rates 1-week program $2,200–$3,100 single or double occupancy. Week-long deluxe Royal Program with suite $4,000–$4,300. No credit cards.

Meal Plans 3 vegetarian meals daily in the formal dining room or guests' rooms. Indian rice and dal with cooked vegetables, herb seasoning, and cooked fruit. Specialties include vegetable pâté. Bland diet with few fats and no dairy products other than milk. Herbal teas as recommended by the doctor.

Services and Facilities Services: Transcendental meditation (TM) instruction in stress-management techniques, psychophysiological audio program, self-pulse diagnosis, aromatherapy. Most programs include massages, heat treatments, and internal cleansing. **Evening Programs:** Videotapes and lectures on health-related topics.

Getting Here *From Boston.* By car, Massachusetts Turnpike (I–90) west to Rte. 495 North, exit on Rte. 117 West to Rte. 70. Entrance is on George Hill Rd. (about 3 hr). Limousine, rental car for local use.

Special Notes No smoking.

The Option Institute

Life enhancement
Holistic health

Massachusetts The approach at the Option Institute, a mountain retreat, is to
Sheffield nurture healthy attitudes toward life rather than emphasize physical fitness. Personal attitudes, beliefs, and feelings are examined to develop a fuller understanding of how to improve one's physical and mental health. Working in group sessions and private consultations, participants are taught to be more accepting of themselves, to learn to find alternatives, and to form more loving relationships.

Founded in 1983 by Barry Neil Kaufman and Suzi Lyte Kaufman, who have written and lectured on interpersonal relationships, the Option Institute sets out to provide a stimulating environment for people from all walks of life. Young professionals as well as families of children with special needs come for weekends and intensive programs of up to eight weeks. The release of tensions here is expected to gain for individuals a profound sense of energy and vigor. The 85-acre campus set amid grassy meadows, forests, and streams provides the setting that can inspire a fresh attitude toward life.

The Option Institute
R.D. 1, Box 174A, Sheffield, MA 02157
Tel. 413/229–2100

Administration Manager, Anne Bianci; program director, Gita Wertz

Season Year-round.

Accommodations Cottages have 18 bedrooms, each with 2 beds, shared bath, and shower. The simply furnished, newly constructed cottages use natural wood and lots of windows for an open, rustic feeling.

Rates 3-day weekends (Thurs.–Sun.) $350 per person double occupancy, meals included. 1-week intensives exploring the impact of attitude on body and health $975. Specially designed programs, about $100 per day. Some kitchen-equipped cottages for families with autistic or learning-impaired children. 50% deposit. Credit cards: MC, V.

Meal Plans Vegetarian meals 3 times daily, buffet style. Specialties include vegetarian lasagna, whole-grain casseroles, legumes, seasonal vegetables, Greek salad, pasta. Limited amounts of eggs, cheese, milk.

Services and **Services:** Swedish massage; private counseling. **Swimming Fa-**
Facilities **cilities:** Pond. **Recreation Facilities:** Hiking the Appalachian

Trail; downhill skiing at Butternut and Catamount, cross-country skiing. **Evening Programs:** Workshops and group discussions on health, personal relationships, communication.

In the Area Tanglewood Music Festival at Lenox; summer theater; the Sterling and Francine Clark Art Institute in Williamstown; Jacob's Pillow Dance Festival in Lee.

Getting Here *From New York City.* By car, I–95 to the Massachusetts Turnpike, exit for Sheffield (3 hr). By bus, Bonanza Bus Line from Port Authority Terminal to Sheffield (3 hr). By air, Bradley International Airport at Hartford/Springfield. Free pickup at bus station in Sheffield; private limousine service from airport.

Special Notes Limited access for the disabled. Special training for children who are brain impaired, autistic, or have learning problems. No smoking indoors.

Rowe Conference Center

Spiritual awareness

Massachusetts Weekend programs to stimulate the mind on spiritual and
Rowe health topics are the specialty of the Rowe Conference Center, a mountain retreat affiliated with the Unitarian Universalist Association. The white clapboard farmhouse and two new buildings host a small, nondenominational community that offers a warm, uncompetitive atmosphere for personal and spiritual growth.

Surrounded by 1,400 acres of forest, Rowe provides a quiet place to discuss current health issues. Topics include clinical and spiritual healing, mastering the mind-body connection, and shamanism. The discussion leaders are on the leading edge of new ways to live full and productive lives.

Operated like a camp, the center offers no organized fitness program and lets visitors take advantage of natural attractions and a newly built sauna on their own schedule. Recently expanded guest accommodations provide basic comforts, but guests do their own housekeeping.

Rowe Conference Center
Kings Highway Rd., Rowe, MA 01367
Tel. 413/339–4216

Administration Director, the Reverend Douglas Wilson; program manager, Prudence Berry

Season Year-round.

Accommodations 10 private bedrooms, all with semiprivate bath and 2 beds (bedding at additional cost). Also dormitory rooms for 6–8 people.

Rates Weekend program $55–$95 (depending on guests' financial situation). Room and meals $95 double occupancy, $115 single, $75 dormitory. All require advance payment of $50. Credit cards: MC, V.

Meal Plans Meals from Fri. dinner to Sun. lunch. Vegetarian food served in ample quantities, family style. Seasonal specialties include lentil loaf, squash casserole, and pasta primavera. Eggs and dairy products served.

Services and Facilities **Services:** Swedish massage. **Swimming Facilities:** Lake. **Recreation Facilities:** Hiking, cross-country and downhill skiing. **Evening Programs:** Discussion groups.

Getting Here *From Boston.* By car, I–91 or Rte. 2 to Greenfield, MA, then west on Rte. 2 (the Mohawk Trail) 19 mi to Rowe (3 hr).

Special Notes Guest house accessible for wheelchairs. Summer camp for children; weeks for 4th graders to high school seniors. No smoking indoors. Remember to bring sheets and blanket or sleeping bag.

Weight Watchers Camp New England

Youth camps for weight loss

Massachusetts **North Adams** This coed summer camp for ages 10–25 focuses on fitness education, exercise, and diet for an active vacation. Located on the countrified campus of North Adams State College, with a lake for water sports, the Weight Watchers Camp is within minutes of hiking trails on Mt. Greylock (highest peak in the state) and close to the summer festivals for which the area is noted.

Meals are prepared following the menus of Weight Watchers International, Inc., and campers learn how to eat properly in classes on food preparation and nutrition.

Supervised by accredited counselors, guests participate in workouts, slimnastics and aerobics classes, and sports. Those who complete the course are guaranteed to lose weight or get a refund.

Weight Watchers Camp New England
North Adams, MA
Weight Watchers Camps
183 Madison Ave., New York, NY 10016
Tel. 212/889–9500 or 800/223–5600 (800/251–4141 in Canada)

Administration Program director, Anthony Sparber

Season July–mid-Aug.

Accommodations Private rooms for 2 in modern dormitories with communal bathroom facilities. Campers make their own beds.

Rates Sessions of 2–7 weeks from $1,450. $100 payable in advance. Credit cards: AE, MC, V.

Meal Plans 3 balanced meals a day, 2 snacks.

Services and Facilities **Exercise Equipment:** Weights room with Universal gym and free weights; gymnastic training. **Swimming Facilities:** Olympic-size indoor pool; private lake. **Recreation Facilities:** 6 tennis courts, team sports, boating, canoeing, hiking. **Evening Programs:** Discos, talent shows in campus theater, game nights, campfires.

In the Area Tanglewood Music Festival, Jacob's Pillow Dance Festival.

Getting Here *From Boston and New York City.* By car, Massachusetts Turnpike (I–90). By air, Bradley International Airport at Hartford/Springfield.

Special Notes No smoking indoors.

EarthStar

Spiritual awareness
Holistic health

New Hampshire The Alchemian Institute, a professional training center for
Hooksett bodyworkers, offers weekend retreats and single-day visits for
massage, meditation, and relaxation at EarthStar. Learning
who you are and how to make life more pleasurable and productive is the focus of the experience. Workshops and classes are
open to visitors, and individual sessions for instruction or
treatment can be scheduled.

Alchemia, the art of personal transformation, is practiced in
many ways. You can try rebirthing, creative visualization, and
tarot card readings; you can learn massage techniques. An in-
depth session of spiritual counseling looks at how you deal with
the issues in your life and offers a new perspective on personal
problems.

Getting a massage is perhaps the best part of the day. Powerful
yet gently energizing, it can release physical and emotional
tensions. Specialists in several techniques work on the areas of
your body that need energy balancing. For mental and physical
weariness, an Esalen full-body massage is advised; Reiki works
on the life-support system. The cost of an hour-long session is
$30–$40.

Refreshingly down to earth, this New Age outpost provides rejuvenation on a budget. Go for a day, stay in the dormitory, or
reserve one of the antique-filled bedrooms in the old farmhouse. This is a place where professionals in bodywork and
stress management come for a retreat of their own.

EarthStar
50 Whitehall Rd., Hooksett, NH 03106
Tel. 603/669–9497

Administration Manager, Kamala Renner

Season Year-round.

Accommodations 2 rooms with antique furniture or waterbed, large dormitory
(linens and towels provided). Shared bath.

Rates $35 per night single, $50 double. 50% payable in advance. No
credit cards.

Meal Plans No meals. Restaurants include the Swiss Cafe and Spatts,
which feature fresh seafood, salad bar, and such seasonal specialties as baked chicken, roast pheasant, duckling.

Services and **Services:** Alchemia bodywork combination, Reiki, Esalen mas-
Facilities sage, acupressure, foot reflexology, salt rub, colonics,
astrology, regressions, tarot reading, rebirthing. **Swimming
Facilities:** Outdoor, heated swimming pool. Naturists welcome. **Recreation Facilities:** Hiking, cross-country skiing, ice
skating. **Evening Programs:** New Age tapes and videos; meditation.

In the Area Manchester industrial area redevelopment (arts and crafts),
Currier Gallery (New England arts).

Getting Here *From Boston.* By car, north on I–93 to Manchester, Exit 7 onto Rte. 101 East to Bypass 28 for Hooksett, Rte. 27 to the Earth-Star Center (60 min). By bus, Vermont Transit to Manchester, NH (80 min). By air, major airlines serve Manchester. Complimentary transfers at Manchester.

Special Notes Limited access for the disabled. No smoking indoors.

Waterville Valley Resort

Non-program resort facilities

New Hampshire Surrounded by mountain peaks and forests of green fir and sil-
Waterville Valley ver birch, this 500-acre recreational complex became a four-season resort in 1987 with the opening of a $2-million sports center. The use of the facilities is a bonus for guests at the deluxe lodges and condominiums of the Waterville Valley Resort. In warm weather, you can play tennis on one of 18 clay courts (modest fee), golf, hike, or cycle. In winter, world-class downhill and cross-country skiing covers 225 acres.

At the foot of Mt. Tecumseh a full-service ski shop rents equipment and offers instruction. Thirty-five downhill trails are ranked for beginner, intermediate, and advanced skiers. Snowmaking equipment assures good snow conditions from mid-November through mid-April.

The Cross Country Ski Center at one end of the valley is another attraction. Fourteen trails lead into the heart of the forest. Inside the center are two restaurants and a barn where large, shaggy horses wait to be hitched to a wagon that treats children to an old-fashioned sleigh ride.

The Sports Center, open every day of the year, offers indoor and outdoor tennis and swimming, racquetball, squash, and a weights room. A coed sauna and Jacuzzi are available in addition to separate facilities and steam rooms for men and women.

The range of activities makes Waterville Valley a good choice for family vacations. A community bus service provides free transportation all day. While the kids are enjoying a fleet of boats on the pond or taking ski lessons, parents can exercise their options at the Sports Center.

Waterville Valley Resort
Box 417, Waterville Valley, NH 03215
Tel. 602/236–8303 (800/468–2553 for lodging)

Administration Sports center manager, Heidi Joyce

Season Year-round.

Accommodations 4,000 beds in quarters that range in variety from deluxe chalet-style inns to modest condominium apartments. Leading choices are Snowy Owl Inn, Black Bear Lodge, and fully equipped 2-story houses. Bookings through the lodging bureau.

Rates Rooms at the Snowy Owl Inn $75–$120 per day in summer for 1–2 persons, including Continental breakfast and unlimited use of sports and fitness facilities. 1-bedroom apartments at the Black Bear $80–$120 per day in a 5-night package ($5 weekend charge at Sports Center). 50% advance payment. Credit cards: AE, DC, MC, V.

Meal Plans   No meals in ski or spa packages. Spa food at 2 restaurants: O'Keefe's has vegetarian burgers, fitness salads; the Finish Line has light fare such as broiled fish, fruit plate with cottage cheese, roast chicken.

Services and Facilities   **Exercise Equipment:** 4 Nautilus weight training units, 2 Monark bikes, rowing machine, free weights. **Services:** Swedish massage, aerobics classes, aquacize. **Swimming Facilities:** Indoor and outdoor 25-meter pools, pond. **Recreation Facilities:** Tennis, golf, canoeing, horseback riding, skiing, ice skating, hiking, sailing, biking. **Evening Programs:** Seasonal entertainment.

In the Area   Mt. Washington cog railway.

Getting Here   *From Boston.* By car, Rte. 3 to I–93, exit for Waterville (28), then 11 miles on Rte. 49 (2½ hr). By bus, Greyhound to North Conway, NH (3 hr). By air, scheduled flights to Manchester, NH. Rental car, Valley shuttle bus available.

Special Notes   Ramps and elevator in Sports Center. Ski and tennis camps for children. No smoking in sports center.

Aegis

Spiritual awareness

New York
New Lebanon   A philosophy of the interrelatedness of all spiritual traditions is at the heart of the study programs offered by Aegis in historic Shaker buildings on the grounds of a 430-acre mountaintop compound. Life is celebrated here in all its diversity with topics ranging from Taoist healing to Zen dance, from crystal healing to shamanism, from Feldenkrais bodywork to acupuncture. A visit is an experience in living together harmoniously and learning how to share life's bounty.

Founded in 1975 as an esoteric school for the Sufi Order in the West, the permanent community here is known as the Abode of the Message. The teachings of their spiritual leaders, notably Pir Vilayat Khan, focus on the nature of healing. The Sufi path is explored at weekend retreats and in a summer series of five-day workshops.

Aegis brings together people from diverse walks of life in a common quest for self-fulfillment and inner growth. You can pitch a tent or work in the kitchen, join prayer sessions three times daily, or enter your own personal retreat.

Aegis
R.D. 1, Box 1030D, New Lebanon, NY 12125
Tel. 518/794–8095

Season   Year-round.

Accommodations   Log cabins with 2 beds, 1-person huts, and camping space in the woods; rooms and dormitory shared in the Abode community. Washhouses have hot showers and toilets for men and women. No bedding or towels.

Rates $20–$30 per night, including meals. Canadians receive 10% discount. 50% advance payment. Credit cards: MC, V.

Meal Plans 3 vegetarian meals a day, with dairy and nondairy choices.

Services and Facilities **Swimming Facilities:** Nearby lakes. **Recreation Facilities:** Hiking, cross-country skiing.

Getting Here Located between Albany, NY and Pittsfield, MA, the Abode provides pickup service at train and bus stations, and at Albany airport. *From New York City.* By car, Taconic Parkway north to Rte. 295, Rte. 22 to Rte. 20 in New Lebanon.

Special Notes No smoking in communal areas. Remember to bring sleeping bag or bedding, warm clothing, insect repellent. No children.

International Health and Beauty Spa

Luxury pampering

New York
Montauk

At the International Health and Beauty Spa the specialty is seawater therapy by the sea. Located on the tip of Long Island, with all the amenities of a big beach resort, the spa at Gurney's Inn draws on the ocean for inspiration. The sybarite can revel in seaweed baths, swim in a 60-foot indoor seawater pool, have a seaweed facial, and dine on seafood while enjoying a view of the sea.

Modeled after European spas where ocean water is an integral part of advanced hydrotherapy, Gurney's adds aerobics, stress control, diet programs, and beauty-salon services. Executives can join a longevity program based on a health and fitness assessment; exercise buffs can concentrate on conditioning. Five packages, all with thalassotherapy, last from three days to a week; or you can put together an à la carte program.

Sea air and miles of white sandy beach come with your room at the inn. Brisk morning walks along the shore start the daily program. Add to that a 14-station parcourse, with instruction twice daily, for exercise at your own pace. Invigorated by the natural effect of the ocean's negative ions, you can join an aquatics exercise class in the pool, relax in a sunken Roman bath, or swim in the surf.

The diversity of the seawater treatments makes Gurney's special among spas on this side of the Atlantic. Filtered and heated water from the ocean is pumped into whirlpools designed for underwater massage, mixed with volcanic mud from Italy, used in wraps with seaweed products from France, and added to body scrubs with salt from the Dead Sea. Treatments are scheduled in separate pavilions for men and women, 10 AM–10 PM.

Massage choices include thalassotherapy, Swedish-style massage, Trager rhythmic rocking, Rolfing, polarity, reflexology, and shiatsu. Lymph drainage and deep facial work are offered.

The spa building is a world apart from the convention and time-share vacation crowds that keep Gurney's Inn busy much of the year. The pool and classes are open to all guests, however, and this puts a strain on the facilities during the peak summer season. For peace and quiet, schedule your visit when the beach crowd goes home or during the winter, when you can take long walks, skate on the patio, and swim in the heated seawater pool while enjoying the seascape through the picture windows.

International Health and Beauty Spa
Gurney's Inn
Old Montauk Highway, Montauk, NY 11954
Tel. 516/668–2345

Administration	Managers, Gladys and Angelo Monte; program directors, Baroness von Mengersen, Vincent Preiss
Season	Year-round.
Accommodations	Time-share apartments, cottages, 109 motel-style rooms in 2-story buildings. None connect to the spa.
Rates	4-day Marine Renewal plan $339, Health and Beauty plan $495, 15% service charge additional. Rooms, suites, apartments available without spa packages; rates vary with season. 25% payable in advance. Credit cards: AE, MC, V.
Meal Plans	2 meals and snacks daily. Spa cuisine in a private room and the main dining room. Calorie-controlled meals (800–1,000 calories per day) low in salt and sugar. Dinner selections such as shrimp and scallops enbrochette with peppers and mushrooms, broiled lobster (no butter).
Services and Facilities	**Exercise Equipment:** Nautilus and Universal weight resistance units, free weights, stationary bicycles. **Swimming Facilities:** Indoor pool, ocean beach. **Recreation Facilities:** Hiking, jogging, disco dancing, yoga; tennis and horseback riding nearby; golf at Montauk Downs public course. **Evening Programs:** Lectures on health and nutrition; dancing and entertainment.
In the Area	Historic homes, art galleries, and boutiques in Montauk; summer theater; bird-watching.
Getting Here	*From Connecticut and New England.* By ferry, at New London and Bridgeport. *From New York City.* By car, Long Island Expressway to Sunrise Highway (Rte. 27). By train, from Grand Central Station, the Long Island Railroad has daily round-trip schedules (tel. 212/526–0900). By air, USAir has scheduled flights to MacArthur Airport at Islip, private planes land at Montauk and East Hampton airports. Courtesy car meets trains and private planes. Rental car, taxi available.
Special Notes	Children's swimming at midday and after 6 PM; under 18 not permitted in spa treatment areas. No smoking in the spa.

Living Springs Lifestyle Center

Preventive medicine

New York
Putnam Valley

A budget-priced alternative to health resorts, the Living Springs Lifestyle Center is a residential retreat where you can improve your life and tone your body with spa-quality treatments. The medically supervised educational and conditioning programs focus on disease prevention, stress control, nutrition, weight management, and quitting smoking. Nondenominational and open to persons of all faiths, Living Springs offers a holistic health program for people past the age of 50 who want to recharge their lives.

The homelike atmosphere can be conducive to establishing lasting new habits. Healthy cooking is taught, and methods for preventing heart and other diseases are discussed informally. Daily exercise is geared to your level of fitness and personal goals.

Following a consultation with a doctor, you can schedule hydrotherapy treatments to promote healing or focus on relaxation. Saunas, alternating hot and cold showers, and exercise are also prescribed.

Natural foods and lots of spring water are key nutritional features. A community health service of the Seventh-day Adventists, the retreat specializes in vegetarian meals that are high in complex carbohydrates and fiber and free of fats and oil. The kitchen is kosher.

Living Springs Lifestyle Center
Rte. 3, Box 357, Putnam Valley, NY 10579
Tel. 914/526–2800

Administration	Manager, Robert Willard; program director, William Murat
Season	Year-round.
Accommodations	2-level modern lodge with private, semiprivate rooms for 12.
Rates	7-day program $495, all-inclusive, Sept.–May; $595 in summer; couples $805–$875. Weekend programs and 21-day conditioning course available. One-third payable in advance. No credit cards.
Meal Plans	3 meals a day, buffet style. Lunch can include steamed vegetables, cashew chow mein, salad, fruit. No coffee or spices.
Services and Facilities	**Exercise Equipment:** Treadmill, rowing ergometer, 2 stationary bikes; outdoor parcourse. **Swimming Facilities:** Spring-fed lake. **Recreation Facilities:** Hiking and nature trail walks; boating; cross-country skiing; biking. **Evening Programs:** Lectures and films on health-related topics.
In the Area	West Point, Bear Mountain.
Getting Here	*From New York City.* By car, Taconic Parkway to Rte. 6 exit. By train, from Grand Central Station, Metro-North Commuter to Peekskill (free transfers). Pickup at airports on request. Courtesy car available.
Special Notes	No smoking.

Mohonk Mountain House

Sports conditioning
Life enhancement

New York
New Paltz

Nature walks have been a way of life at Mohonk Mountain House in the Hudson River Valley since 1875, and members of the founding family of Quakers are still active in organizing health and fitness weeks. Hikers, runners, and cross-country skiers choose from more than 100 miles of trails, paths, and carriage roads that link scenic sites within the 2,500 acres of private woodland. Others ride horseback or enjoy the crystal-clear lake.

What draws devoted guests back is an almost Zen-like detach-
ment from reality. One writer known to science fiction fans
calls it a private Shangri-la; time seems to stand still here.

In the hotel, a turreted and gabled Victorian structure that
rambles an eighth of a mile and accommodates up to 500 guests,
19th-century manners and ambience are preserved. Nooks and
crannies abound. There is no bar or smoking in public rooms,
and a dress code is in effect for dinner. A newly installed fitness
center, with a certified aerobics specialist teaching classes, is
the only break with the past.

Physiologists, sports trainers, and fitness buffs get together at
Mohonk for exercise workshops and lectures. Scheduled
throughout the year, they include weekend races, a five-day
hiker's holiday covering four grades of terrain, and a week devoted to walking. Your pathmate could be an editor of
American Health magazine or a professional boxer. Programs
range from designing a personal fitness plan to nutrition and
kinesiology. Weeks are devoted to quitting smoking, stress
management, and the holistic way, combining Mohonk's natural setting with practical tools to enhance the quality of one's
life.

Mohonk Mountain House
Lake Mohonk, New Paltz, NY 12561
Tel. 914/255-1000

Administration	Program director, Geri Owens
Season	Year-round.
Accommodations	300 rooms, many with balcony and working fireplace, some with washbasin only, some sharing an adjoining bath. Rooms and bed-sitting rooms with private bath.
Rates	Double rooms $204–$252 per day Full American Plan; tower room with fireplace $268–$307. Midweek sports packages $546 for 3 nights, $910 for 5 nights. 1 night payable in advance. Credit cards: MC, V.
Meal Plans	3 meals and afternoon tea included with room. The menu fol-lows the American resort tradition, with some light selections. Buffet-style lunch. Wine and alcoholic drinks available.
Services and Facilities	**Exercise Equipment:** 6-station Universal gym, 2 Schwinn Air-Dyne bikes, 2 Monark bikes, and hand weights. **Services:** Mas-sage. **Swimming Facilities:** Mohonk Lake, ½-mile-long 60-foot-deep freshwater lake with swimming and diving areas. **Spa Fa-cilities:** Sauna. **Recreation Facilities:** 6 tennis courts (4 clay, 2 Har-Tru), platform tennis courts; 9-hole golf course; ice skat-ing and downhill skiing; croquet. **Evening Programs:** Concerts, films, dancing; speakers on health and fitness.
In the Area	Carriage rides, trail rides, hayrides. Historic village of Rhinebeck.
Getting Here	By car, New York State Thruway (I-87) to New Paltz (Exit 18). By train, Amtrak to Poughkeepsie. By bus, New York City (Port Authority Terminal) and other cities served by Adirondack Trailways. Hotel transfer service to bus or train station for scheduled fee; limousine service for New York City and airports.

Special Notes Weekday outdoor adventures and walks for children. No smoking in public areas indoors.

New Age Health Spa

Weight management

New York
Neversink
Committed to a philosophy of fasting, the New Age Health Spa is a country retreat that offers a wide range of physical treatments to enhance your new appearance. The tranquil, 160-acre farm estate in the Catskill Mountains is an ideal setting in which to balance body, soul, and mind.

Having undergone a recent rejuvenation itself, the farm is now a full-fledged spa with new owners who supervised the redecoration of the pine-panelled guest rooms in five buildings surrounding the original farmhouse. They have added sophisticated pampering and astrological consultation to complement their serious weight-management program.

Determined dieters undertake water fasts with the approval of their doctor. Others may want to consider the choice of seven nutrition plans, from juice diets to light protein regimens, that provide 350–850 calories per day plus fish or chicken on alternate days. A full-time nurse on staff monitors your progress.

Beginning the day with a guided nature walk readies you for yoga before breakfast. Aquatic exercise in the 40-foot indoor swimming pool is a year-round feature; the larger outdoor pool is used in summer. Classes are scheduled throughout the day so you can match your activities to your energy level. Optional services include massage, paraffin and mud body treatments, herbal baths in the private Jacuzzi, and a complete beauty salon in the Annex. Exercise equipment is in the barn.

If you're not dieting and want to try a colonic cleansing, that can be arranged. When fasting, you're expected to do your own enema daily to detoxify and cleanse the system.

The guest rooms at New Age have no telephones, but they're all equipped with enema bags. Radios may be used with headphones in the privacy of your room. The program here, with its supportive environment, brings many guests back annually.

New Age Health Spa
Rte. 55, Neversink, NY 12765
Tel. 914/985–7601 or 800/682–4348

Administration Managers, Stephanie Paradise and Werner Mendel; program director, Sandra Lachaga

Season Year-round.

Accommodations 39 plainly furnished rooms, each with twin beds, private bath. Exercise facilities in the barn, bathing facilities in an annex.

Rates 1-week package, including diet and exercise program, $583 per person double occupancy. Single rooms, special diets additional. 25% payable in advance. Credit cards: AE, MC, V.

Meal Plans Fasting recommended but not required. 3 meals a day served in the farmhouse; mostly fresh vegetables, dairy products, fruit. Dinner choices include poached fish, baked chicken, and salads.

Sources of protein can be added to the 650-calorie (per-day) diet with a physician's recommendation.

Services and Facilities **Exercise Equipment:** Weight training circuit, free weights, stationary bikes, stair and treadmill machines, rebounders. **Swimming Facilities:** Indoor and outdoor pools. **Spa Facilities:** Sauna and steam room. **Recreation Facilities:** Volleyball; cross-country skiing and snowshoeing. **Evening Programs:** Talks on healthy living and personal growth; workshops in astrology, psychology, awareness; movies, disco.

In the Area Guided hiking into the mountains 3 times a week.

Getting Here *From New York City.* By train, Amtrak from Penn Station (40 min). By bus, Short Line from Port Authority (45 min). By car, New York State Thruway (I–87) to the Catskills, Rte. 17 to Liberty, Rte. 52 and 55E to Neversink (about 50 min). Local taxi available.

Special Notes Ground-level rooms for the disabled. No children. No smoking.

Omega Institute for Holistic Studies

Holistic health
Spiritual awareness
Life enhancement

New York *Rhinebeck* Call it a New Age mecca or a quest for higher consciousness; it's chiefly a summer camp where you can strive to develop physical and mental balance alongside people on the leading edge of preventive medicine and holistic health.

Sometimes referred to as Esalen East, the Omega Institute brings together people of different backgrounds—doctors, lawyers, housewives, college students—who want to function more positively as individuals and as members of society. More than 200 educational workshops, from Native American studies to wellness and stress control, last two to five days. The classes, including diet workshops and "Shamanic Journey, Power and Healing," are led by faculty and guest lecturers comprising a veritable *Who's Who* of the human potential movement.

Participants come away saying they achieved spiritual, emotional, and physical renewal. Even standard resort recreation is transformed: Tennis is choreographed with dance movements and music; archery becomes a Zen art.

Located about 100 miles north of Manhattan, the rustic, 80-acre campus features a massage center, sauna, pond, walking paths, theater, gift and bookshops, and cafe. Yet there's not a Nautilus gym in sight.

Two cross-training programs focus on wellness and fitness. A Wellness Week integrates study and practice of a healthy lifestyle. Omega's core faculty offers a sound medical understanding of the roles that diet, nutrition, exercise, and fitness play in the ongoing development of health. Through experiential sessions in massage, yoga, tai chi chuan, group support, and games, each participant forms a positive attitude toward wellness.

The annual Fitness Week is designed for peak performance through athletics. Classes are divided into levels of expertise, making them appropriate for beginners and advanced athletes alike. You can concentrate on cycling, yoga, running, or swimming. Special training for women includes body toning and the effect of exercise on pregnancy.

There are other classes in topics as diverse as clowning and mime, mask-making, socially responsible businesses, applying environmental awareness to politics, and exploring mother-daughter relationships.

On a typical morning, when as many as 600 people are camping out or living in the dormitories and cottages, groups assemble before breakfast for yoga and tai chi chuan sessions. The rolling Hudson Valley countryside provides an inspiring setting. Since it opened in 1977, Omega has nourished this environment, a safe place in which the concepts of transformation, New Age, and holism are rediscovered.

Omega Institute for Holistic Studies

Lake Drive, R.D. 2, Box 377, Rhinebeck, NY 12572
Tel. 914/266-4301 (May 15–Sept. 15), 914/338-6030 (Sept. 15–May 15), or 800/862-8890 (800/258-5353 in NY)

Administration Program director, Thomas Valente

Season June–early Sept. Winter programs sponsored off campus.

Accommodations Rooms in cottages, dormitory beds, camping facilities. Private rooms with shared bath.

Rates 5-day Omega Wellness Week $225 plus lodging. Dormitory $30 per day; cottage rooms $62 single, $40 per person double occupancy. 5-day Well-Tuned Body Workshop $210. Dormitory $150; cottage rooms $310 single, $200 double. Campsites $23 per day. Meals included in lodging fee. 50% payment in advance. Credit cards: MC, V.

Meal Plans Mainly vegetarian, with some fish and dairy products. Many locally grown fresh fruits and vegetables. Whole grains, beans, and bean products. No artificial sweeteners. 3 meals served daily, buffet style.

Services and Facilities **Swimming Facilities:** Private pond. **Spa Facilities:** Sauna. **Recreation Facilities:** Bicycle rental; canoeing, jogging, tennis. **Evening Programs:** Concerts, films, lectures.

In the Area The historic village of Rhinebeck, Old Rhinebeck Aerodrome.

Getting Here *From New York City.* By car, New York State Thruway (I–87) or the Saw Mill River Parkway north to the Taconic Parkway, to Rte. 199 and 308, which lead west into Rhinebeck (Rte. 9); By train, Amtrak from Grand Central Station stops at Rhinecliff, where Omega vans pick up guests (for train schedules, tel. 800/872-7245). By bus, Short Line from Port Authority Terminal to Rhinebeck (60 min). Omega vans pick up in Rhinebeck at Beekman Arms Hotel.

Special Notes Some cottages equipped for the disabled. Nature studies and creative games for children, Aug. only. No smoking in public buildings or dormitories.

Pawling Health Manor

Nutrition and diet

New York
Hyde Park

Vegetarianism is considered a pathway to healthful living at the Pawling Health Manor. Joy and Robert Gross, who have been health counselors here for more than 25 years, help you discover a sense of well-being through fasting and detoxification. Geared to your fitness level, it's a chance to give the body a break while you lose weight.

The imposing manor house sits on a hill overlooking the Hudson River region of grand estates once owned by the Astors and Vanderbilts. The surroundings lend a mood of serenity to long walks or, in summer, a swim in the big outdoor pool and sunbathing in a protected solarium. Aside from discussions and demonstrations, there's little else to do. Yoga and meditation are scheduled twice a week, massage can be arranged, but strenuous exercise is not encouraged.

Supervised fasting is a key ingredient in the manor's recipe of nutrition, relaxation, and education. If you qualify, Robert Gross advises beginning with a water fast. It can cause discomfort (a member of the medical staff is always on hand to help) and low energy, so it's suggested that you curl up with a book and get plenty of rest. Plan on staying at least a week. Rooms are comfortably furnished in contemporary style befitting a country home rather than a grand manor.

The educational program teaches how to adopt a vegetarian diet. Joy Gross has authored several books on the subject, and every meal is a demonstration of recipes you take home.

Pawling Health Manor
Box 401, Hyde Park, NY 12538
Tel. 914/889-4141

Administration Manager, Theresa Fariello; program directors, Joy and Robert R. Gross

Season Year-round.

Accommodations 30 bedrooms throughout the main house, annex, and motel units. Some single and deluxe rooms with private bath, others share a hall bathroom.

Rates $495–$800 per week, 1-week minimum. $100 advance payment. Canceled deposit can be applied to a future visit or returned. Credit cards: MC, V.

Meal Plans 3 meals daily, predominantly fresh fruits and vegetables in season. Some cheeses, steamed vegetables, soups, and seeds. Fish at the dinner buffet only. Meals can be delivered to your room or a small dining area during a fast.

Services and Facilities **Swimming Facilities:** Outdoor pool. **Evening Programs:** Talks on health and fitness; movies on big-screen TV.

In the Area Excursions to Colonial Rhinebeck twice weekly. The historic village of Rhinebeck, Old Rhinebeck Aerodrome, West Point Military Academy, Culinary Institute of America (calorie-controlled gourmet restaurant).

Getting Here *From New York City.* By car, New York State Thruway (I–87) or the Saw Mill River Parkway north to the Taconic Parkway, to Rte. 199 and 308, west into Rhinebeck on Rte. 9 (90 min). By train, Amtrak from Grand Central Station to Rhinecliff (1 hr). By bus, Short Line from the Port Authority Terminal to Rhinebeck (90 min). Taxi, rental car for local use.

Special Notes No smoking indoors.

The Sagamore Hotel

Luxury pampering

New York
Bolton Landing

Surrounded by the Adirondack Mountains and set on a 70-acre private island, the huge white clapboard Sagamore Hotel suggests an escape to the quiet pleasures of a bygone era. Rejuvenated recently by new owners, the resort now includes a modern health club, indoor swimming pool, and indoor tennis and racquetball courts. Fitness classes are scheduled throughout the day, from walks and low-impact aerobics to water exercise, at no charge to hotel guests who book one or more spa treatments and services.

The health club has separate sauna, whirlpool, and steam-room facilities for men and women. There is a coed exercise area, somewhat cramped for space to accommodate the equipment, and a wet area specially equipped for body scrubs. Appointments are made for treatments on an à la carte basis, which includes the daily charge for use of the club. If you simply want to swim and exercise with the equipment, a daily facilities charge is added to your account. Nonresident guests are also welcome.

In addition to massage, facials, and beauty makeovers, the specialty here is a full-body rubdown with a mixture of sea salt and massage oil that leaves your skin tingling. After the scrub with loofah sponges, the salt mixture is hosed off. Next, peppermint soap is applied, leaving you with a glowing feeling. The cost: $30. (A 17% gratuity is added to the cost of services.)

The Sagamore Hotel
Box 450, Bolton Landing, NY 12814
Tel. 518/644–9400 or 800/358–3585

Administration Manager, David Boyd; fitness director, Damian Alessi

Season Year-round.

Accommodations 350 rooms, suites, and cottages. The main hotel's 100 rooms embody history and contemporary comfort. Condominium-style suites in new lodges.

Rates Spa plan, with choice of services and exercise, $335–$467 single, $269–$335 per person double occupancy, 2-night minimum. In summer $356–$636 double, 4-night minimum. 5-day midweek spa package, $753. 1 night payable in advance. Credit cards: AE, MC, V.

Meal Plans Modified American Plan for all guests includes breakfast and dinner. Spa cuisine available on request. 6 restaurants provide varied menus, emphasizing fish and local produce.

Services and Facilities **Exercise Equipment:** 12-station Universal gym, stationary bikes, treadmill, rowing machine. **Swimming Facilities:** Indoor pool; lakeside docks. **Recreation Facilities:** 18-hole golf course, 4 outdoor lighted and 2 indoor tennis courts, jogging trails, hiking, boating, water sports; snowmobiling, ice skating, cross-country and downhill skiing, tobogganing; horseback riding and horse-drawn sleigh rides. **Evening Programs:** Dancing, jazz club, scheduled entertainment.

In the Area Cruises on Lake George aboard a classic wooden yacht; free transportation to golf course and ski areas; mineral baths at Saratoga Springs Spa by special arrangement. Saratoga Springs' Victorian area; summer season of concerts, ballet, and horse races; Colonial Fort William Henry; Lake George Village; hot-air balloon flights.

Getting Here Located about 65 miles north of Albany, NY. *From New York City.* By car, 4-hour drive on the New York State Thruway (I–87) to Exit 24 (Bolton Landing). By air, Albany is served by Eastern, Piedmont, and Continental airlines, among others. By train, Amtrak to Fort Edward, from Boston or New York City. A hotel car meets guests at Albany or the train station ($50 round-trip).

Special Notes No smoking in the spa.

Saratoga Spa State Park

Taking the waters
Luxury pampering

New York
Saratoga Springs

Once a rival of Europe's glamorous spas, Saratoga is better known today for Thoroughbred racing and the arts. But the mineral springs at Saratoga Spa State Park remain a major attraction, and plans are underway to develop a complete health and fitness center in some of the original buildings. Meanwhile, the Roosevelt Bath operates year-round, and the Lincoln Baths are open during July and August.

The mineral-rich water bubbles up all around the town, where it is bottled for drinking as well as bathing. Here, however, it's free. Pick up a map from the Old Drink Hall, downtown, or the spa visitor center operated by the State of New York. If you park at the Geyser Picnic Area lot and follow the path, you will encounter three of the best-known springs, all of the saline- alkaline variety. First is the Hayes Well, which has a breathing port at one side for inhaling carbon dioxide—said to be good for the lungs and sinuses. The gas also carbonates the water and powers geysers that spout up 10 feet or higher at this spot.

For a diuretic effect, try Hathorn Spring No. 1, a block east of Broadway on Spring Street. This water contains large amounts of sulfur, iron, lime, and other minerals. Dense, green-tinted, and faintly smelly, it has been prescribed for everything from sinus to complexion problems.

More palatable is the 90-minute relaxer offered spa visitors: a 15- to 25-minute mineral bath followed by a half-hour massage, then a 30-minute rest. Your float in the salty, effervescent warm mineral water induces relaxation by slowing breathing; studies have shown that some carbon dioxide is absorbed through the skin, where it dilates the blood vessels, improves circulation, and aids the flow of blood. Wrapped in warm sheets, you cool down after this treatment, which costs $15 during July and August.

To get a full taste of the town and its Victorian landmarks, stay at the venerable Adelphi Hotel on Broadway, built in 1870 and lovingly restored by the current owners. The elegant Gideon Putnam Hotel, a sprawling, neo-Georgian hotel with old-fashioned country club charm, was built during the New Deal era and now adjoins the spa buildings.

Saratoga Spa State Park
The Gideon Putnam
Box 476, Ave. of the Pines, Saratoga Springs, NY 12866
Tel. 518/584–3000

Administration	Manager, Kenneth Boyles
Season	Year-round.
Accommodations	Premium rates during the racing season in Aug. Meals included. Wellness program planned for 1989.
Rates	Double room $260 for 2 in Aug.; single room averages $84, double room $99 other times. Suites with sun porch $177–$410. 2-night package for 2, including dinner and breakfast, $218–$258. 1 night payable in advance. Credit cards: AE, MC, V.
Meal Plans	Salads and light cuisine on the spa menu.
Services and Facilities	**Exercise Equipment:** Weights room with Universal gym. **Swimming Facilities:** Victoria Pool in the spa park ($3); Great Scandaga Lake in nearby Adirondack State Park. **Spa Facilities:** Mineral-water baths in private tubs at the spartan facilities of Roosevelt Bath No. 1 (518/584–2011); semiprivate at Lincoln Baths (518/584–2010). Days and times of operation vary with season; call for reservation. **Recreation Facilities:** 8 free public tennis courts and 2 18-hole golf courses in the spa park; hiking trails at Spruce Mountain near town; guided history walks; jogging in Congress Park. **Evening Programs:** The Saratoga Performing Arts Center (tel. 518/587–3330) in Spa State Park presents the New York City Ballet in July, the Philadelphia Orchestra in Aug., and popular and jazz artists. Dance companies perform at the Little Theater (tel. 518/587–3330).
In the Area	900 buildings on the National Register of Historic Places; tours include the rose garden at the Yaddo artists' colony and the 1864 gable-roof clubhouse at the track. Polo matches and a harness-racing track nearby. Saratoga Battlefield National Historical Park has a scenic 9.5-mi drive open to bicyclists. Museums in former spa buildings are devoted to dance, racing, and local history.
Getting Here	Located close to Albany; about 3½ hours from New York City. By car, New York Thruway (I–87). By train, Amtrak from Montreal, Boston, and New York City. By air, USAir, Eastern, and Pan Am schedule flights to Albany. By bus, Adirondack Trailways. Rental car at airport; taxi in town. Park admission: $3 per car, free for Gideon Putnam hotel guests.
Special Notes	Specially equipped baths and rooms for the disabled. No smoking in the spa buildings. Remember to bring drinking cups.

Sharon Springs Health Spa

Weight management   *Women only*
Preventive medicine

New York
Sharon Springs

The holistic approach of the founder and director, Dolores J. Schneider, capitalizes on the mineral springs and natural beauty of an area that has attracted health seekers since the 1870s. Sharon Springs Health Spa offers a basic program of exercise, workshops, and vegetarian diet designed for weight loss and detoxification. The options are what's special here, from massage and sulfur water baths to Reiki therapy. The result is body sculpting and relaxation.

Joining a small sisterhood intent on shaping up, new arrivals are counseled on ways to maximize their activities. Weekends and miniweeks are offered as well as a single-day rejuvenator. For relief from arthritis, there is a special program that includes therapy for a week or a month.

Workouts are balanced by walks and lectures on health topics. The meals and freshly prepared fruit and vegetable juices exemplify how each woman can take control of her diet. The exercise program tones and firms with yoga, aerobics, dancercise, weight lifting, rebounding, and jogging. When you need a bit of pampering, there's hydrotherapy, herbal wraps, and facials.

The varied program introduces guests to new ways of relaxing; reflexology, shiatsu, and treatments with mud and salts from the Dead Sea are offered.

Sharon Springs Health Spa
Box 288A, Chestnut St., Sharon Springs, NY 13459
Tel. 518/284-2885

Administration Program director, Delores J. Schneider

Season Year-round.

Accommodations 27 cozy single and double rooms, shared baths.

Rates $63 a day per person double occupancy, $81 single. $405 a week per person double occupancy, $531 single. Meals, exercise programs, workshops included; treatments additional. 30% payable in advance. No credit cards.

Meal Plans 3 vegetarian meals daily. Home-baked bread, salads, steamed vegetables.

Services and Facilities **Exercise Equipment:** Weight training units, slant boards, rebounders, back swing units. **Swimming Facilities:** Nearby lakes and pools. **Spa Facilities:** Mineral springs within walking distance. Jacuzzi and sauna. **Recreation Facilities:** 2 tennis courts, bicycling, horseback riding, bowling; cross-country skiing, ice skating. **Evening Programs:** Lectures; optional trips to summer opera and theater.

In the Area Sightseeing at Cooperstown and Baseball Hall of Fame, horse racing, golfing, boating. 5 trips weekly.

Getting Here Located 185 mi from New York City and close to Albany. By car, New York State Thruway (I–87). By air and train, scheduled service to Albany. By bus, Greyhound and Trailways serve Albany. Complimentary pickup for afternoon arrivals and departures at train or bus station and airport.

Special Notes No smoking indoors.

Sivananda Ashram Yoga Ranch

Spiritual awareness

New York Yogic disciplines flourish in this country retreat two hours
Woodbourne north of New York City. When stressed-out urbanites join members of the farm community to exercise and meditate or to jog through 80 acres of woods and fields, the effect is spiritual as well as physical. Guests from diverse social and professional lives around the world meet at Sivananda Ashram Yoga Ranch to share their interest in yoga.

Morning and evening, everyone participates in classes devoted to traditional yogic exercise and breathing techniques. Teachings formulated by an Indian sage, Swami Sivananda, are revealed in practicing the *asana* positions; they range from a headstand to a spinal twist, a dozen in all, and each has specific benefits for the body. You will be taught that proper breathing, *pranayama*, is essential for energy control.

Meditation begins the 6 AM session, brunch is served at 10, and there's free time until 4 PM. Attendance at all classes and meditations is mandatory. The goal of yoga is to teach you to look and feel better, and the discipline of the ranch's intensive regimen promises psychological rewards in addition to getting you in shape.

Sivananda Ashram Yoga Ranch
Box 195, Woodbourne, NY 12788
Tel. 914/434-9242

Administration Manager, Lisa Brody; program director, Swami Sankarnanda

Season Year-round.

Accommodations 50 small rooms: singles, doubles, apartments in the farmhouse and cottages. Apartments have private bath. Tent space.

Rates Room $25 per day including meals, apartment $500 per month, 3-month work-study program $150. $25 payable in advance. Credit cards: V.

Meal Plans 2 meals daily, buffet style. Lacto-vegetarian diet with fresh vegetables grown on the ranch and dairy products. No coffee, eggs, alcohol.

Services and Facilities **Swimming Facilities:** Pond. **Spa Facilities:** Communal sweat lodge and sauna. **Recreation Facilities:** Woodland trail hiking. **Evening Programs:** Meditation, chanting, lectures.

Getting Here *From New York City.* By bus, Short Line (Port Authority Terminal) to Woodbourne, then arrange for pickup; during the summer, van service provided every weekend (W. 24th St. Sivananda Center, $20 round-trip). By car, Rte. 17N to Exit 105B.

Special Notes No smoking. Remember to bring towels and meditation mat.

Turnwood Organic Gardens

Holistic health
Weight management

New York
Livingston Manor

Fasting is the focus of the holistic approach to weight loss at Turnwood Organic Gardens. Supervised by an experienced staff, the daily diet of water or vegetable juice is complemented by training in yoga, meditation, and healthy habits. For the dedicated dieter who commits a minimum of one week to the program, the reward is quick and effective loss of unwanted pounds. Consult your personal physician before signing up if you are on medication or are under treatment.

The basic program consists of fasting, preparing to break the fast, and learning how to maintain the good effects. The belief is that as the body discards accumulated wastes, a sense of calm accompanied by clarity of mind grows. This program teaches natural hygiene principles by putting them into practice.

Sharing this experience with a small circle of supportive, like-minded people helps each participant achieve personal goals. The homelike atmosphere and chemical-free organic garden provide a natural environment for healing. Look at your stay as a self-help program, based on the teachings of Paavo Airola, rather than as a vacation.

Turnwood Organic Gardens
Star Route, Livingston Manor, NY 12758
Tel. 914/439–5702

Administration Director, Rose Robbins

Season May–Sept.

Accommodations 2-story country house housing 10–12 guests in 3 bedrooms with private bath, and dormitory-style rooms. Antiques and wood furniture.

Rates 1-week program $295–$395. 1-week health retreat $450 including meals. Additional weekly charge for single occupancy $70–$105. 1-week minimum stay for fasting. $50 confirmation fee. Credit cards: MC, V.

Meal Plans A 1-week stay requires at least 5 days of fasting on juice or water. Juice programs include broth and herbal teas. Meals of raw fruits and vegetables and whole grains and nuts are available daily. Dinner entrees include a baked casserole of tofu. No meat, fish, or eggs. Diets for allergies and other problems available.

Services and Facilities **Exercise Equipment:** Due to the large amount of rest required during fasting, no equipment other than a minitrampoline. **Services:** Yoga instruction, massage, reflexology, chiropractic adjustment. Learning experiences include why and how to fast, work in the garden, and sprouting demonstrations. **Swimming Facilities:** Nearby lake. **Recreation Facilities:** Hiking, lawn games, badminton, boating. **Evening Programs:** Library of records and tapes.

In the Area Zen monastery, cider mill, antiques shops, country craft shows and fairs. Summer stock and concerts at Sullivan County Community College. Movie theater nearby.

Getting Here *From New York City.* By bus, Short Line from Port Authority to Livingston Manor (2 hr). By car, New York State Thruway (I–87) to the Catskills, Rte. 17 to Livingston Manor, Rte. 28 and 30 to Lew Beach. Taxi available.

Special Notes No smoking.

Zen Mountain Monastery

Spiritual awareness

New York
Mt. Tremper
Joining a group of Buddhist monks as they work in silence, meditate, and celebrate Zen rituals and arts is the unique experience at the Zen Mountain Monastery. You can sip green tea at a Zen tea ceremony, hear the broken notes of a Shakuhachi bamboo flute, learn Sumi-e ink painting or traditional wood carving, and explore the subtleties of Ikenobo flower arranging. There are weekends devoted to Taoist martial arts, poetry, and Zen photography.

Founded in 1980 by Zen priest John Daido Loori, who is addressed as *sensei* (teacher), it is the only monastery in America that offers concerts and programs for visitors throughout the year. Daido Sensei, a first-generation American master, speaks directly to his students about the 2,500-year-old tradition of Buddhist practice.

Doing a retreat here seems to embrace almost every aspect of daily life. It blends monastic tradition with art and body practice, a characteristic of the golden ages in Japan and China. The hands-on experiences can include working in a Japanese Zen garden, or learning a body-focusing technique called still point.

The day's activities move to a measured cadence, sometimes with chanting, often in silence. Everyone does caretaking, an hour of giving back to the buildings and land some of the benefits received from them. Periods of *zazen* (meditation) provide concentration.

Located in a state forest preserve, a 10-minute drive from Woodstock, the monastery seems to be of another time and world. It was, in fact, built at the turn of the century by Catholic monks and Norwegian craftsmen. There are endless mountain trails, ponds, and streams for hiking and recreation, and the atmosphere of peace and solitude is conducive to re-creation and introspection.

Zen Mountain Monastery
Box 197PC, S. Plank Rd., Mt. Tremper, NY 12457
Tel. 914/688–2228

Administration Director, John Daido Loori; program director, Carol Walsh

Season Year-round; scheduled weekend programs in summer, retreats in fall and winter.

Accommodations 4-story stone monastery with 100-bed dormitory. Main hall, classrooms, dining hall, library. All facilities shared on a communal basis. Rustic cabins available for couples.

Rates	Weekend programs $125, retreats of 3–7 days $120–$195 per person, including 3 meals daily. Advance payment of $25. Credit cards: MC.

Meal Plans Vegetarian meals and some fish or meat, served buffet style 3 times a day. Weekends begin with Fri. dinner (steamed fish with rice and vegetables) and end with Sun. lunch. Dairy products served. Much of the food from the monastery garden.

Services and Facilities **Services:** Zen training, intensive meditation, artist retreats. **Swimming Facilities:** Nearby mountain lakes. **Recreation Facilities:** Hiking; tubing on creek; skiing at Hunter Mountain. **Evening Programs:** Occasional concerts of contemporary and oriental music; an introduction to Zen.

In the Area Woodstock artists' colony, Catskill Mountain Forest Preserve, Beaverkill River scenic area.

Getting Here *From New York City.* By bus, Adirondack Trailways from Port Authority via Kingston to Mt. Tremper (about 3 hr). By car, New York State Thruway (I–87) to the Catskills, Rte. 28 and 212 to Mt. Tremper (2½ hr).

Special Notes No smoking.

Castleview Camp

Youth camps for weight loss

As this book went to press, it was learned that the Diet Center Program introduced at Castleview Camp in 1988 had been discontinued here and would instead operate in the summer of 1989 at four other locations: El Cajon, California; Lake Forest, Illinois; New Lebanon, New York; and Greensboro, North Carolina. Complete information is available from the Diet Center office.

Rhode Island
Newport

The Diet Center Program at Castleview Camp teaches how to take off weight and keep it off. A daily weigh-in and private counseling help guests customize their exercise programs. Workouts in the weights room and aerobics class are offset by sailing trips and hiking along the waterfront.

The nutritional program, overseen by a licensed staff trained in the Diet Center's trademarked weight loss plan, helps campers change bad eating habits. Being part of a supportive group of about 100 boys and girls (ages 10–16) or young adults (ages 17–24) builds a new self-image.

Castleview Camp
Diet Center
708 Glen Cove Ave., Glen Head, NY 11545
Tel. 516/676–5300 or 800/782–3438

Administration Manager, Neal Nelson

Season Mid-June–late Aug.

Accommodations Spacious bedrooms for 6, doubles and small singles. Bathrooms either private or shared.

Rates 2-week sessions $1,000, 8-week sessions $3,750. 4-week and 6-week sessions available. $200 advance payment. Credit cards: MC, V.

Meal Plans 3 meals daily, plus snacks, served cafeteria style. The Diet Center's trademarked reducing program for young people is determined by the nutritional needs of each individual.

Services and Facilities **Exercise Equipment:** Universal gym, free weights, rowing machines, stationary bikes. **Swimming Facilities:** Olympic-size outdoor pool; nearby ocean beach. **Recreation Facilities:** Bicycling, sailing, bowling, roller skating, hiking. **Evening Programs:** Concerts and movies.

Special Notes No smoking.

The Equinox

Luxury pampering
Life enhancement

Vermont Rejuvenated in 1985, this 218-year-old hotel added a fitness
Manchester center called The Evolution Spa. The comprehensive health
Village and beauty facilities of the Equinox are open to all hotel guests on an à la carte basis. Three- and seven-night spa packages offer medical, nutritional, and beauty services.

An informal discussion of exercise physiology, nutrition, and stress management precedes a body composition analysis by the computer system to tailor your exercise schedule. Options include brisk walks and personalized training with weights.

European-style therapies are the spa's specialty, but they are not included in the package. A thalasso soak with sea algae at $55, or a facial for $50–$65, will quickly run up your bill. However, a herbal wrap, a loofah body scrub, and three calorie-controlled meals a day are part of the package.

The programs are limited to 16 participants, so early reservations and travel plans are suggested. Advance planning with the spa director will help you focus on weight loss, stress management, or behavior modification.

The Evolution facilities to which you have unlimited access include a coed Turkish steam bath, indoor and outdoor swimming pools, whirlpools, and a Swedish sauna. If you would rather explore the town or ski at Mt. Equinox, without a spa program, that's reason enough for visiting this historic resort.

The Equinox
Rte. 7A, Manchester Village, VT 05254
Tel. 802/362–4700 or 800/362–4787;
Fax 802/362–1595

Administration Manager, Thor G. Loberg; fitness director, Susan Thorne-Thomsen

Season Year-round.

Accommodations 154 bedrooms and 6 suites, furnished in classic New England style with pine beds and dressers, flowered chintz fabrics, modern conveniences. Beds turned down at night; *New York Times* delivered.

Rates 1-day spa package, with meals, $199 per person double occupancy; $254 single. Summer weekend (3 nights) $806 double,

$932 single. 1-week program $1,401–$1,795. Deposit of 50% of the package price. Credit cards: AE, DC, MC, V.

Meal Plans Full American Plan in both formal and informal dining rooms. Spa breakfast includes choice of fruit, buttermilk pancakes with blueberry coulis, hot oatmeal or bran cereal with skim milk; lunch can be ceviche of sole with cilantro, grilled medallion of beef with shallots, or chilled asparagus with seasoned wild rice; dinner choices include herbed pasta with mushrooms, poached salmon, or veal medallion.

Services and Facilities **Exercise Equipment:** 8-station Nautilus circuit, free weights, 2 Lifecycles, 3 AMF semirecumbent bikes, NordicTrack ski machine, computerized rowing machine. **Services:** Massage, herbal wrap, loofah body scrub, pedicure, paraffin treatments, hair and skin care. **Swimming Facilities:** Indoor and outdoor heated pools. **Recreation Facilities:** 3 tennis courts, golf course, hiking trails, bicycle rental, nearby downhill and cross-country skiing, horseback riding, canoeing, horse-drawn carriage rides. **Evening Programs:** Resort entertainment.

In the Area Antiques shops, shopping at factory outlets; summer theater, jazz concerts, Marlboro Music Festival; Brattleboro Museum, Norman Rockwell Museum, Bennington crafts center, Hildene (Robert Todd Lincoln's estate).

Getting Here *From New York City.* By car, New England Thruway (I–95) north to I–91, exit at second Brattleboro turnoff for Rte. 9 to Rte. 30 (4 hr). By bus, Greyhound from Port Authority Terminal (4½ hr). By air, scheduled flights to Albany, NY; bus service to Manchester by Vermont Transit. Taxis and rental cars available.

Special Notes No smoking in the spa.

Golden Eagle Resort

Life enhancement

Vermont A traditional mountain resort with winter and summer activi-
Stowe ties, the Golden Eagle sprouts spa wings from May through August. The five-night, all-inclusive program provides options for exercise, diet, and recreation to suit your personal needs. The health spa is open daily year-round 9 AM–9 PM, at no cost to guests at the resort.

Toning and body shaping are what the spa does best. Only six participants per week get the full treatment during the summer season. Schedules are planned individually when you arrive, and group outings are organized at your leisure.

You are free to order from menus in the resort's two dining rooms. Although there are temptations, the spa food is attractive enough to keep you on the set menu.

Popular with singles and families (most guests are between 30 and 60), this is a budget-priced alternative to luxury resorts. Serious workouts are geared to the fittest.

Golden Eagle Resort
Box 1110B, Mountain Rd. (Rte. 108), Stowe, VT 05672
Tel. 802/253–4811 or 800/626–1010

Administration Manager, Marc MacNamara; program director, Sandy Morningstar

Season Fitness weeks May–Aug.; 5-night program begins Sun. or Mon. Health spa open year-round.

Accommodations 80 rooms with private bath; suites, cottages, apartments with cooking facilities. Deluxe rooms for Fitness Week participants with color TV, air conditioning, oversize beds. Some rooms with Jacuzzi and fireplace. Also a Bavarian-style chalet.

Rates 5-night fitness program $625–$750 single, $500–$575 per person double occupancy. High season rates $110–$150 per night, including meals. $100 deposit per person on booking, nonrefundable unless space can be filled. Credit cards: AE, DC, MC, V.

Meal Plans Set menu totals 1,200–1,500 calories and includes veal marsala, fish rolled with vegetables, and broiled scrod. American plan menu available other times.

Services and Facilities **Exercise Equipment:** 8 Universal gym stations, Tunturi treadmills, stationary bikes, rowing machines, free weights. **Services:** Massage, nutritional and fitness counseling, physical examination and cholesterol test; facial; reflexology. **Swimming Facilities:** Indoor and outdoor 50-foot pools. **Recreation Facilities:** Tennis courts, bicycles, scenic path for jogging. **Evening Programs:** Seminars on health-related topics; resort activity.

In the Area Tours by van. Shelburne Museum, Cold Hollow Cider Mill, Trapp Family Lodge, Ben & Jerry's Ice Cream Factory.

Getting Here *From Boston or New York City.* By train, Amtrak to Waterbury, VT (10 mi from Stowe). By car, I–91, I–89 to Stowe exit (3 hr from Boston, 6½ hr from N.Y.C.). By air, scheduled flights to Burlington, VT. Hotel limousine arranged on request to meet trains and planes; taxi, rental car in area.

Special Notes Ground-floor rooms for the disabled. No smoking in the spa and areas of the dining rooms.

Green Mountain at Fox Run

Life enhancement   *Women only*
Weight management

Vermont For women with a serious weight problem, coming to Green
Ludlow Mountain at Fox Run is a commitment to change. The difference is not just a new diet or vigorous exercise, but a new lifestyle based on healthy habits.

The first lesson is that diets don't work. Instead of deprivation, moderation becomes the key. Eating three balanced meals a day is required, and you are encouraged to give in, ever so slightly, to an occasional yearning for sweets. Guests learn to cope with food fads and are shown that being more active can be as pleasant as taking a walk down a country lane.

Now in its 16th year of operation, Green Mountain at Fox Run is one of the country's best-documented educational programs for weight and health management. Designed exclusively for women, the intensive program of two or four weeks is devoted to taking charge of your life. The lodge, a long, barn-red wood building tucked into a mountain ridge, has the simple design of a ski lodge and views of the Okemo Mountain ski area.

Working with a team of nutritionists, exercise physiologists, and behavioral therapists helps each participant set personal goals. Other members of the group provide support in "going the extra mile." Guests range from 18 to 80, are from all parts of the world, and are united by a desire to shed bad habits and excess weight.

The facilities are homelike but spartan; there is no high-tech gym equipment or luxury pampering. Exercise classes, running, walking, hiking, biking, and cross-country skiing in winter fill most of the day. Aerobic dance and body-conditioning sessions teach that exercise can be fun, something that fits easily into everyday life.

Green Mountain at Fox Run
Fox Lane, Box 164, Ludlow, VT 05149
Tel. 802/228–8885

Administration	Program director, Alan H. Wayler
Season	Year-round.
Accommodations	26 rooms: singles, doubles, and duplexes (2–4 persons), all with modern bath. Lounge with fireplace; high-ceiling, raftered dining room.
Rates	2-week session $2,150–$2,500 per person double occupancy, $2,800 single. 4-week program $3,500–$4,200 double, $4,800 single. For 4 persons occupying a duplex unit, $1,900 per person for 2 weeks, $3,000 for 4 weeks. (Roommates matched on request.) $300 deposit with application. Credit cards: MC, V.
Meal Plans	1,100–1,200 calorie (per day) diet low in fat and sodium, high in carbohydrates. Menus include a salad plate, pasta, eggplant Parmesan, tortilla dishes, liver and onions, baked potato with trimmings, even ice cream. Coffee and tea available throughout the day.
Services and Facilities	**Exercise Equipment:** Stationary bikes, NordicTrack cross-country ski machine, free weights, mountain bikes. **Services:** Swedish massage; sports instruction. **Swimming Facilities:** Covered outdoor pool for all weather. **Spa Facilities:** Sauna. **Recreation Facilities:** 2 tennis courts, nearby golf course; downhill and cross-country skiing, snowshoeing. **Evening Programs:** Cooking classes, movies, group discussions, lectures.
In the Area	Trips into town for shopping, including antiques shops. Scenic mountain drives, summer stock theaters.
Getting Here	*From New York City.* By car, I–95 north to I–91, Exit 6 in Vermont (Rte. 103 North) to Ludlow (4½ hr). By bus, Greyhound from Port Authority Terminal to Ludlow. By air, scheduled flights to Rutland, VT, or Lebanon, NH. Complimentary pickup from airports and bus station. Transfers upon departure included in tuition.
Special Notes	Smoking only in specified areas. Remember to bring recent physical report, towels, walking and aerobics shoes.

New Life Spa

Nutrition and diet
Life enhancement
Holistic health

Vermont
Stratton
Mountain

Two vacations rolled into one is the concept of New Life Spa's resident fitness guru Jimmy LeSage. His spa attracts skiers in winter and hikers the rest of the year who want to get in shape and enjoy the outdoors at once. Set in a picturesque alpine valley full of ski chalets and maple syrup shops, the Liftline Lodge provides a healthy combination of nutritionally planned meals, fitness classes, and creature comforts. Days are filled with attractive options.

A former professional cook and hotel manager, LeSage caters to his guests' needs while exhorting them to learn ways to improve their habits. His philosophy on food and eating is published in a book given to each guest and experienced firsthand in a cheery dining room. Fresh fruit, herbal teas, decaffeinated coffee, and spring water are always on hand in the hospitality lounge.

Exercise classes are held in the Bavarian-style lodge and are scheduled around outdoor activities. Sivananda-style yogic movements gently stretch muscles and prepare the body for vigorous outdoor activity; the afternoon program relaxes the body and works off fatigue. Other options are offered at the Stratton Sports Center, an indoor complex with swimming, tennis, racquetball, steam room, and heated whirlpool that guests at the lodge can use at any time. Prebreakfast walks are also optional.

The winter ski program combines the daily workout schedule, fitness diet, and nutrition education with afternoons on the slopes or cross-country trails. Everything you need is included: lift tickets, lessons, and equipment—plus a massage and soak in the lodge's hot tub après-ski.

Hiking the lush valleys of the Green Mountain Range is a great way to strengthen your heart and muscles. Guided by New Life staff members, groups hike daily. The treks up Bromley and Stratton mountains become more challenging as your stamina increases. (If you're more than 20 pounds overweight, this is not recommended.)

The lodge's facilities include a tennis court, outdoor swimming pool (unheated), and sauna. In an area where big, noisy resorts or quaint inns are the norm, this is a happy compromise: small enough so that guests get to know each other, and supported by a youthful staff eager to help you enjoy the area's attractions.

New Life Spa
Liftline Lodge, R.R. 1, Box 144, Stratton Mountain, VT 05155 Tel. 802/297-2534

Administration Manager, Jimmy LeSage; fitness director, Carolyn Postel

Season Year-round with week-long programs Jan.–Sept., weekends (3 nights) late Oct.–Dec., and spring. Closed for year-end holidays and late Feb.

Accommodations	40 rooms with double beds, private baths, color TV, and phone. Pine-paneled lobby, lounge with fireplaces and comfy chairs.
Rates	Weekends $450–$495, 6-day and 7-day sessions $870–$970 Jan.–June, $970–$1,070 in summer. $150 advance payment per person. Credit cards: MC, V.
Meal Plans	3 meals served daily. Modified Pritikin diet (1,000 calories per day) low in fats and high in complex carbohydrates. Chicken, fish, vegetables, and fruit among the choices. Specialties include veal cacciatore, lentil loaf, chicken curry salad, pita sandwich with spicy tofu filling. Special diets accommodated.
Services and Facilities	**Exercise Equipment:** Cardiovascular power circuit with Lifecycle rowing ergometer, rebounders, NordicTrack ski machine, stair climber, and stationary bikes. **Swimming Facilities:** Indoor lap pool at Sports Center; private outdoor pool. **Recreation Facilities:** Indoor and outdoor tennis, racquetball courts; golf course and horseback riding nearby; mountain bike rentals. **Evening Programs:** Discussions on healthy living, talks on beauty, lectures on nutrition and stress.
In the Area	Antiques shops, factory outlets; summer theater, jazz concerts, Marlboro Music Festival; Brattleboro Museum, Bennington crafts center.
Getting Here	*From New York City.* By car, New England Thruway (I–95) north to I–91, exit at second Brattleboro turnoff for Rte. 9 to Rte. 30 into Bondville (4½ hr). By bus, Greyhound from Port Authority Terminal to Manchester, VT (5 hr). By air, scheduled flights to Albany, NY; bus service to Manchester by Vermont Transit. Complimentary pickup at Manchester bus station.
Special Notes	No smoking in public areas. Remember to bring warm clothing and hats both summer and winter, walking shoes, snow boots.

Woodstock Inn & Resort

Non-program resort facilities

Vermont
Woodstock

Picture the perfect New England town: the county courthouse and library facing an oval green, a covered bridge leading to immaculate farms, a cluster of fancy boutiques, and a Colonial inn. Add a $5-million sports center, 50 miles of cross-country ski trails, nearby mountains with more than 200 downhill trails, and you have the Woodstock Inn & Resort.

The current inn, the fourth on the site, spreads from the historic town center to the sports center. Included are a golf course and croquet lawn, outdoor and indoor swimming pools, tennis courts, and a 69-station parcourse. The weight equipment and aerobics studio are luxury-spa caliber, and they can be used for a nominal fee. Classes cost $4 each. A winter ski package includes lift tickets and equipment rental.

Traditions are alive at the inn from the dress code to the hearty New England menu. Under its new management, the complex has been expanded to include the nearby Billings Farm Museum with exhibits of early New England farm life, and offers visits to a prize-winning dairy barn. Phone and power lines were buried with a grant from a neighbor, Laurence Rockefeller, to preserve the view of the town green.

Woodstock Inn & Resort
14 The Green, Woodstock, VT 05091
Tel. 802/457–1100 or 800/223–7637 (800/442–8198 in NY)

Administration General manager, Chet Williamson; fitness director, Tom Avellino

Season Year-round.

Accommodations 121 bedrooms with patch quilts, cable TV, air conditioning, clock radio. Modern baths.

Rates In summer, $99–$170 per person double occupancy, $97–$168 single. Meals not included. Midweek sports package (3 days, 2 nights) $328–$558, includes golf, tennis, 2 meals daily. 2 nights deposit in advance. Credit cards: AE, CB, DC, MC, V.

Meal Plans Modified American plan (breakfast and dinner) $38 per person per day. Courtside Restaurant in Sports Center serves a chicken salad plate or assorted melon slices with cottage cheese, sherbet, or yogurt sauce for lunch. The main dining room offers poached chicken, roast young pheasant, and sea scallops for dinner.

Services and Facilities **Exercise Equipment:** 11 Nautilus units, 2 Concept II rowing ergometers, 2 Monark bikes, Trotter treadmill, incline station, hyperextension station, free weights. **Services:** Swedish and deep-tissue massage, sports instruction, yoga and aerobics classes, aquatics for arthritics. **Swimming Facilities:** Indoor and outdoor pools. **Spa Facilities:** Coed steam room, separate men's and women's saunas, whirlpools in the Sports Center. **Recreation Facilities:** 10 outdoor and 2 indoor tennis courts, 2 indoor racquetball courts, 2 indoor squash courts; cross-country skiing, downhill skiing at Suicide Six, Killington, Ascutney Mountain, Okemo Mountain; horseback-riding center nearby, sleigh rides and nature walks. **Evening Programs:** Resort entertainment.

In the Area Walking tours of historic Woodstock. Quechee Village (crafts), Dartmouth College Hopkins Center (performing arts), Saint-Gaudens Studio (sculpture), Marlboro Music Festival (chamber music).

Getting Here *From Boston.* By car, I–90 to I–91 (100 mi). By air, scheduled flights to Lebanon, NH. Taxi, rental car available.

Special Notes Ramps and specially equipped rooms for the disabled. Tennis camp for children June–Aug. only. No smoking in the sports center.

Hawaii

Polynesian culture has given new dimensions to the pursuit of fitness. On the volcanic island of Hawaii, guests at Kalani Honua live in traditional lodges made of cedar logs or camp out among the palm trees. On Maui you can join the Maui Challenge, a week-long trek in which participants encounter the natural features of the island. Pualani, terraced onto the slopes of Mt. Haleakala, offers privacy.

At the same time, developers of luxury resorts have competed for the distinction of having the most opulent health club on the island. On Oahu the Plantation Spa, staffed with health specialists from Sweden's Halsohem-Masegarden, marks the introduction of Scandinavian therapies and diet.

Halekulani Hotel

Non-program resort facilities

Hawaii
Honolulu (Oahu)

Starting your day with a run on Waikiki beach is reason enough to head for Diamond Head, but when you run with Max Telford, fitness consultant for the Halekulani Hotel, the experience becomes something more.

Three mornings a week, at 7:30, guests gather on the beach for stretching exercises and a morning jaunt. Telford, holder of numerous world records for distance running, offers fitness tips as you jog along his favorite route; he adds a special dimension to the Waikiki routine.

The Halekalani fitness room, open since November 1987, is the focal point for daily activities. Free weights, multiple-exercise Paramount weight training gym, computerized bicycles, rowing machines, and treadmill are available free of charge to all resort guests. For serious workouts, the hotel concierge arranges admission to the nearby Honolulu Club, where for a modest fee you can enjoy one of the best-equipped health clubs in the world.

The Halekulani is a small, private enclave, and the five-building complex and lush gardens have been meticulously restored and updated. Best moments: afternoon tea in a tropical garden and evening entertainment in the House Without a Key (Charlie Chan's favorite spot on the island).

Halekulani Hotel
2199 Kalia Rd., Honolulu, HI 96815
Tel. 808/923–2311 or 800/367–2343
Telex 8382 HALE HR, Fax 808/926–8004

Administration Manager, Urs Aeby; fitness program director, Max Telford

Season Year-round.

Accommodations 456-room luxury hotel, 5 wings (1930s building and new additions). Rated best hotel in Hawaii, 1986–87. Rooms have sitting area, full bathroom with deep-soaking tub, glassed-in shower, marble vanity. Most have views of the beach and Diamond Head. 3 telephones, nightly turn-down service, cable TV (CNN), work desk.

Rates Rooms $175–$300 daily, suites $350–$2,000 daily. Confirmation by credit card. Credit cards: AE, CB, DC, MC, V.

Meal Plans Award-winning La Mer Restaurant serves fish, veal, chicken, and beef with Continental flair. Orchids Restaurant specializes in Pacific seafood.

Services and Facilities **Exercise Equipment:** Paramount training gym, Ergo bike, Pritikin treadmill, free weights. **Services:** Shiatsu massage; aerobics class. **Swimming Facilities:** Outdoor pool, ocean. **Recreation Facilities:** At Honolulu Club: racquetball, volleyball, golf driving range; nearby tennis and golf. Water sports equipment on beach. **Evening Programs:** Resort entertainment.

In the Area 3 morning runs weekly; historic tours, Pearl Harbor, shopping.

Getting Here *From Honolulu International Airport.* Limousine, shuttle service, rental car, or taxi available (20 min).

Special Notes For the disabled, elevators, ground-floor lanai suites, and 14 specially equipped rooms are barrier free. Supervised activities and excursions for children. No smoking in designated dining areas; some nonsmoking rooms.

Hawaiian Fitness Holiday

Holistic health
Weight management
Life enhancement

Hawaii
Koloa (Kauai)
Combine a holistic approach to health and nutrition with a beach condominium resort, add chiropractic and physiotherapy treatments, and you have Dr. Grady Deal's prescription for a fitness holiday. Deal—a licensed massage therapist, gourmet cook, and practicing chiropractor—and his wife, Roberleigh, have created a warm, homelike atmosphere for their guests. Using facilities at the Lawai Beach Resort, the Hawaiian Fitness Holiday is tailored to individual needs and interests. By keeping the group small—an average of 10 per week—the Deals aim for a high level of success in meeting each person's goals.

Aquacize workouts in the swimming pool and stretching exercises (or yoga) are part of the daily program, but participation is not required, and pampering can be substituted at the request of guests. Included in the program cost is a massage or chiropractic therapy every afternoon except Sunday.

Weight loss and body toning are the primary objectives. Invigorating exercise and vegetarian meals are supplemented by naturopathic therapies, including herbs and colonics, to detoxify the body. Designed to clean out your digestive and eliminative tract and to reduce your appetite, the program can include such options as fasting on water or juice, and self-administered colonic cleansing.

Spending most of the day outdoors, on scenic hikes and walks as well as at aerobics classes, guests quickly discover the natural healing effect of the island. Excursions included in the basic fee take the group to such scenic places as Waimea Canyon, the

Hawaii

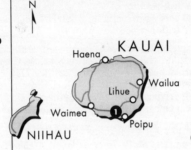

N

KAUAI

Haena

Wailua

Lihue

Waimea

Poipu

NIIHAU

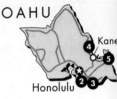

OAHU

Kane

Honolulu

0   50 miles

0   75 km

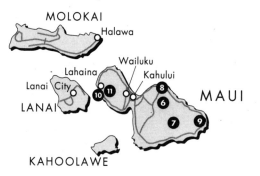

PACIFIC OCEAN

MOLOKAI
Halawa

Wailuku
Lahaina
Kahului
Lanai City
LANAI
MAUI
KAHOOLAWE

HAWAII
Kawaihae
Waimea
Mauna Kea
Hilo
Kailua-Kona
Mauna Loa
Honaunau
Kilauea
Kalapana
Naalehu

NaPali coast, and Lumahai beach, where *South Pacific* was filmed.

Kauai is said to have a rare energy vortex, a metaphysical natural beauty that relaxes the mind and body. Exploring the island with a like-minded group of health seekers adds a special quality to the fitness holiday. Each person is encouraged to search for inner energy.

Rounding out the program are cooking demonstrations based on the macrobiotic and vegetarian meals that are served, workshops on nutrition and health, meditation, and deep-breathing exercises for relaxation. At the end of the day, you can unwind in the steam room, sauna, or Jacuzzi while awaiting yet another memorable sunset.

On this quiet crescent at the southern tip of the island, colors become almost magically intense. Where the sand ends, the lava rocks begin, black and shiny as wet coal, grouted with red soil. Surf hisses and spits at you from hidden spout holes. Compared with Waikiki, Poipu Beach is like switching from rock music to Debussy.

The caring program here has inspired many guests to adopt a healthy lifestyle. Having a furnished apartment, with kitchen and laundry, is particularly attractive for older couples or those who are already fit and simply want to enjoy a few days or weeks in paradise.

Hawaiian Fitness Holiday
Box 279, Koloa, HI 96756
Tel. 808/332–9244

Administration	Program director, Roberleigh Deal; medical director, Grady A. Deal
Season	Year-round.
Accommodations	Furnished 1- or 2-bedroom condominium apartments at Lawai Beach Resort, shared. 2 oversize beds, rattan furniture, island fabrics as accents. Washer/dryer, fully equipped kitchen, full bath, living room, TV, telephone, air conditioning; choice of oceanfront or garden view. Maid service available at extra cost.
Rates	All-inclusive weekly program $1,895 single, $2,627 double occupancy in ocean view apartments; garden-view apartments $900 and up single, $1,600 double occupancy. Daily rate $271 single, $362 double. Taxes and service charge not included. $500 on booking, balance due 30 days prior to arrival. Credit cards (4.5% surcharge): AE, MC, V.
Meal Plans	Vegetarian, macrobiotic meals with whole grains, raw and cooked vegetables, fruit, juices, legumes, and fish. Breakfast can be wheatless waffles with berries; lunch, a vegetable stew or baked macaroni with cashew-pimiento cheeseless topping. Dinner includes green salad with oil-free dressing, brown rice cooked with sesame seeds, and herb tea. High in fiber and carbohydrates, meals include no dairy products, sugar additives, meat, free oils; eggs on request only. Optional diets: Fit for Life, full macrobiotic, low fat and cholesterol.
Services and Facilities	**Exercise Equipment:** Paramount variable resistance units (6 stations), 2 Lifecycles, rebounder, cable pulley machine, treadmill; Olympic free weights, dumbbells. **Services:** Massage (Swedish, shiatsu, deep tissue), reflexology, G-5 vibrator mas-

sage, chiropractic, physical therapy; skin, hair, nail care (added fee). Nutritional counseling, cooking classes. Detoxification/colonic program ($250 additional). **Swimming Facilities:** 2 outdoor pools, ocean beach. **Recreation Facilities:** 2 tennis courts, water sports, hiking. Golf, horseback riding, bicycle rental nearby. **Evening Programs:** Talks and slide shows on health-related topics; Hawaiian cultural performances.

In the Area Scheduled group hiking and sightseeing trips to various parts of the island; botanical garden, fern grotto, phosphorescent cave, Spouting Horn blowhole, Koloa (sugar plantation town), Kokee State Park, Waimea Canyon. Optional: helicopter tour, scuba dives, kayak river trip, day cruises.

Getting Here *From Koloa.* By car, Poipu Rd. to Poipu Beach, Lawai Rd. to beach villas (15 min). Transfers on arrival/departure at airport (and for all excursions) included in program fee. Taxi, rental car available.

Special Notes Ground-floor accommodations and special therapy program for the disabled. Full program for children over 12; resort activity available. No smoking in program areas. Remember to bring medical or chiropractic records.

Hawaiian Health Retreat

Stress control
Holistic health

Hawaii Acupressure, relaxation techniques, and bodywork are experi-
Hana–Kihei enced in settings of tropical splendor during this eight-day
(Maui) program sponsored by the Acupressure Institute of Berkeley, California. It is a movable retreat, from the beaches and waterfalls of old Hana to the coves and condominiums of Kihei. Completely programmed, each day includes exercises, massage, and hiking.

Led by author and acupressure specialist Michael Reed Gach, the retreat offers training as well as relaxation. Many of the participants are professional bodyworkers, therapists, and counselors. Demonstrations address specific stress-related problems.

Natural breathing exercises begin your day on the beach. Easy stretches are combined with yoga, alternately intensive and relaxing. After a light breakfast, there is an all-morning session devoted to Zen philosophy and the techniques of shiatsu massage. Working with finger pressure on nerve meridians, the participants learn new methods of self-healing.

Limited to 25 participants, this informal week (everyone pitches in to help with meals some evenings) offers maximum personal counseling in relaxation therapies. The island's lush, tropical forests and ocean sunsets provide an ideal setting. Maui, named for a demigod who guided early settlers across the South Pacific, is a heady mix of Hana-style seclusion and big-time resorts.

Hawaiian Health Retreat

Hana–Kihei (Maui), HI;
Acupressure Institute
1533 Shattuck Ave., Berkeley, CA 94709
Tel. 415/845–1059 or 800/442–2232

Administration Program director, Michael Reed Gach

Season Specific weeks, spring–Aug.

Accommodations Shared bedrooms in beach house at Hana, condominium apartments at Kihei resort. Private rooms for couples only. All have private bath, twin beds, simple modern furniture.

Rates All-inclusive program $795 per person ($150 extra for private accommodations). $100 advance payment, balance due 30 days prior to beginning of retreat. No credit cards.

Meal Plans Vegetarian meals featuring tropical fruits, salads, whole-grain dishes.

Services and Facilities **Services:** Acupressure massage, stress-control counseling, yoga therapy instruction. **Swimming Facilities:** Ocean beaches, swimming pool at resort. **Recreation Facilities:** Hiking, snorkeling. **Evening Programs:** Talks on Zen philosophy, yoga, stress control.

In the Area Guided hikes to beaches, waterfalls; the Seven Sacred Pools, Red Sands Beach, Makena Beach, historic sites.

Getting Here Local transportation provided during the retreat program.

Special Notes No smoking indoors.

Hawaii Health & Wellness Vacation

Life enhancement
Nutrition and diet
Stress control
Preventive medicine

Hawaii
Kailua (Oahu) The Castle Medical Center's unique five-day educational program includes medical tests, nutritional and lifestyle counseling, and the pleasure of a golf vacation at a Sheraton resort. Drawing on resources of its comprehensive health-care facility operated by Adventist Health System–West, the center created a cost-effective vacation with equal amounts of fitness and fun.

The program begins with a health-appraisal screening. Computerized evaluations of your blood test, fitness level, and health history form the basis for the Lifestyle Inventory and Fitness Evaluation (LIFE). Recommendations are then made in private counseling sessions with health professionals to help you develop a personal program that fits your lifestyle at home.

Limited to 20 participants per session, the program includes group exercises and beach walks, as well as an educational seminar. The lectures and films deal with nutrition and weight management, stress control, exercise, and developing good health habits. Free time is also provided for you to enjoy the swimming, tennis, and golf at the country club-style resort.

Being in a structured environment is a key element. Away from routine distractions, you can focus on making fitness a regular part of your life. In private sessions with health specialists at the center, there is an opportunity to discuss personal interests and concerns.

Long active in health education, Castle Medical Center created this program to help people stay well. Based on the Seventh-day Adventist philosophy of spiritual, mental, and physical health, with all meals included, it is a life-enhancing experience for people of all ages.

Hawaii Health & Wellness Vacation
Castle Medical Center
640 Ulukahiki St., Kailua, HI 96734
Tel. 808/263–5286 or 800/446–9522

Administration	Program director, John Westerdahl; fitness director, DeAnn Oertel
Season	Aug.–Mar.
Accommodations	Cottages at Sheraton Makaha Resort and Country Club (84–626 Makaha Valley Rd., Waianae 96792) provided for program participants. Clustered on emerald-green fairways, each cottage has 2 or more bedrooms, living room, Polynesian design, rattan furniture, full modern bath. Choice of twin oversize or king-size bed.
Rates	$1,195 enrollment fee single, $995 participating companion sharing room, $495 nonparticipating person sharing room (hotel only). $200 advance payment at time of booking. Credit cards: MC, V.
Meal Plans	Vegetarian meals high in complex carbohydrates, low fat, and salt (dairy products optional). Breakfast is tropical fruit, low-fat yogurt, whole-grain cereal with milk, whole-wheat bread. Lunch entrees include pizza made with whole-wheat crust and fresh vegetables or Mexican-style vegetarian enchilada. Dinner choices include vegetarian lasagna with mixed green salad, fruit plate, or baked eggplant Parmesan. No eggs, coffee, tea, or condiments served. (Resort's regular restaurants available to nonparticipants.)
Services and Facilities	**Exercise Equipment:** Outdoor paved jogging course with exercise stations. **Services:** Massage; tennis and golf instruction. **Swimming Facilities:** Olympic-size outdoor pool, nearby ocean beach. **Recreation Facilities:** 4 lighted tennis courts, 18-hole golf course, croquet, shuffleboard, hiking trails, horseback riding, bicycle rental, water sports.
In the Area	Local tours available; Waikiki Beach, Pearl Harbor, Pearlridge Shopping Center, Polynesian Cultural Center, Sea Life Park, Honolulu museums and historic buildings.
Getting Here	*From Honolulu.* By car, Hwy. SR-93 (Farrington Hwy.) to Waianae (60 min). Complimentary transfers on arrival/departure at Honolulu International Airport. Rental car, taxi, hotel van available.
Special Notes	Ground-floor accommodations are barrier-free. No smoking at Castle Medical Center and in dining room.

Hilton Hawaiian Village

Non-program resort facilities

Hawaii
Honolulu (Oahu)

Staying at the Ali'i Tower has its privileges for the fitness buff: a completely new health club exclusively for guests in the stylish, 15-floor hotel within a hotel. It has everything from aerobic exercise machines to a snack bar featuring a "spa menu" for weight-conscious guests.

Following a $100 million renovation, the Hilton Hawaiian Village made the Ali'i Tower its most extravagant guest accommodations. In addition to the health club, there is a private pool, sun deck, and lounge where complimentary breakfast and cocktails are served. Rooms are stocked with mineral water and designer robes, beds are triple-sheeted, and the shower has a massage head.

You can work out or get a massage at the fitness center. There are several specialists on staff offering sport massage, Trager, acupressure, and reflexology, as well as Swedish massage. Jacuzzi and sauna are coed.

Bursting with new tropical beauty, the giant resort—largest in the Pacific—has crashing waterfalls, placid *koi* ponds, and graceful jungle landscaping. Centerpieces are the grand central courtyard and a giant swimming pool ringed with lava rock. If you want action, there are more restaurants and casual dining spots on the 22-acre spread than most visitors can locate.

Hilton Hawaiian Village
2005 Kalia Rd., Honolulu, HI 96815
Tel. 808/949-4321 or 800/445-8667
Telex 8380

Administration Manager, Douglas C. Mattos

Season Year-round.

Accommodations 348-room Ali'i Tower has luxury suites and spacious rooms with balconies. Sitting area with wicker furniture, floor-to-ceiling views of beach and Diamond Head. Furnished with contemporary elegance, oversize beds, work desk (PC compatible), bath with separate dressing area. Cable TV, 3 telephones, in-room safe. Some rooms have furniture and accents of old Hawaii.

Rates $215–$310 single or double occupancy; suites $750–$2,000. First-night confirmation by credit card. Credit cards: AE, CB, DC, MC, V.

Meal Plans No special diet plan; all meals à la carte. Complimentary breakfast includes tropical fruit, fresh juices, granola, muffins, Kona or decaffeinated coffee. Lunch snacks at fitness center include salad or tofuburger. Lavish American/Continental dinner menu.

Services and Facilities **Exercise Equipment:** Universal weight training circuit (10 stations), 2 Lifecycle bicycles, Precor computerized treadmill, Avita rower, Apex butterfly and pullover machines, abdominal board. **Services:** Massage (Swedish, Trager, shiatsu, sports), acupressure, reflexology. **Swimming Facilities:** Outdoor pool, ocean beach. **Recreation Facilities:** Walks, jogging, water

sports, bicycle rental, tennis; golf, horseback riding nearby.
Evening Programs: Resort entertainment featuring the John
Rowles Show.

In the Area Local sightseeing tours; Honolulu museums and historic sites,
Pearl Harbor, shopping, Polynesian Cultural Center.

Getting Here Airport van shuttle service. Limousine, taxi, car rental available.

Special Notes Supervised beach activity for children. No smoking in fitness
center.

Hyatt Regency Maui

Non-program resort facilities

Hawaii
Lahaina (Maui)

Staying in shape while vacationing at the Hyatt Regency Maui
can be fun. In addition to all the usual resort facilities and programs, there is a complete health facility, including weights
room, steam room, sauna, and Jacuzzi. Scheduled daily are
aerobics classes, weight training clinics, and aqua-trim water
exercise.

Classes in high- and low-impact aerobics are complimentary to
hotel guests. There is also a large local membership working
out at the club. Located beneath a grotto and waterfalls, the
facility is open from 7 AM to 10 PM.

Bicycle rental is available for trips into nearby Lahaina, a colorful 19th-century whaling village recently gentrified with
boutiques and bars.

This fantasy island resort, set on 18 acres of lush beachfront,
comes complete with a private jungle lagoon and includes a museum of Asian and Pacific art, a collection of wildlife, and fine
restaurants. Joggers can enjoy a two-mile course on the beach.

"Fit-not-Fat" is the theme of the health club. The massage
therapists can introduce you to native Lomi-Lomi treatments,
shiatsu, and a wide range of bodywork techniques. Dining is
heart-healthy in several of the restaurants within the resort.

Hyatt Regency Maui
200 Nohea Kai Dr., Lahaina, HI 96761
Tel. 808/661–1234 or 800/228–9000

Administration Manager, Werner Neuteufel; recreation director, Christine
Aguilar

Season Year-round.

Accommodations 815-room resort has 3 towers, including concierge service
floors of the Regency Club. Spacious, contemporary rooms, full
bath, lanais, balconies; luxury amenities. Air conditioning,
TV, telephone.

Rates Singles and doubles $190–$320 a day, Regency Club $320–
$350, suites $275–$2,000. 2 nights advance payment or credit-
card confirmation. Credit cards: AE, CB, DC, MC, V.

Meal Plans No special meal plan. Selected low-calorie, low-fat items for
heart-healthy dining available daily.

Services and Facilities

Exercise Equipment: Nautilus weight training units (6 stations), Lifecycle, treadmill, free weights. **Services:** Massage (shiatsu, Lomi-Lomi, Swedish, Esalen), beauty salon, tennis clinics, private lessons, scuba course. **Swimming Facilities:** Free-form ½-acre pool, ocean beach. **Recreation Facilities:** 5 tennis courts, hiking; bicycle rental. **Evening Programs:** Resort entertainment.

In the Area

Catamaran sailing, whale watching, winery tour; Lahaina (old whaling port), Mt. Haleakala National Park, Sugar Cane Train, Maui Tropical Plantation (botanic gardens).

Getting Here

From Kapalua-West Airport. By car, Hwy. 30 (Honoapiilani Hwy.) via Lahaina (20 min). Rental car, taxi, airport shuttle van available.

Special Notes

Sports clinics and day-camp programs (seasonal) for children.

Kalani Honua

Holistic health
Life enhancement
Weight management
Taking the waters

Hawaii
Pahoa (Hawaii)

Suspended between fire and water, the Kalani Honua resort offers a full range of health-oriented activities. An intercultural program, with yoga and hula, complements workshops scheduled throughout the year. Visitors can participate or venture off to explore on their own.

The seaside ranch is surrounded by natural beauty. Lush jungle, black-sand beaches, and stark lava cliffs meet the ocean within the resort's 20 acres of seclusion. Nearby is the world's most active volcano, Kilauea, which provides spectacular scenery and areas of devastation and nurtures orchids and hot springs.

The resort attracts an interesting mix of robust, healthy men and women, families hiking the volcano trails, and professional bodyworkers attending seminars, but it has no fixed program. If you're lucky, Aunty Margaret may be presenting a demonstration of Hawaiian Lomi-Lomi massage. Her historical perspective on native cleansing programs has been recognized by the State of Hawaii.

In keeping with the spirit of old Hawaii, guests are housed in *hales*, wood lodges made of cedar logs. Each hexagonal lodge has its own kitchen and ocean-view studio space, with dormitory rooms and some private accommodations. Campers can sleep under the stars at 25 sites scattered among the palm trees.

Therapeutic services and exercise classes are the focus of a Japanese-style spa. The wooden bathhouse has a communal hot tub, sauna heated by wood-burning stove, and private massage rooms. Four pavilions with suspended wooden floors are used for yoga, aerobics, and dance performances. Nearby are a 75-foot swimming pool and a Jacuzzi.

Informal and laid-back, the days are totally unstructured. In addition to exploring craters and newly created beaches among the lava flows, you can soak at hot and warm springs, snorkel in a tidal pool, or join a scuba outing. Sunbathing on clothes-optional beaches is a major attraction, especially at nearby Kehana Beach.

The "Big Island" abounds with spiritual places, shrines to ancient gods, and mystical rain forests. Inner harmony and harmony with nature are qualities of ancient Hawaiian culture celebrated here.

Kalani Honua
Box 4500, Pahoa, HI 96778
Tel. 808/965–7828 or 808/965–8716

Administration Manager, Richard Koob

Season Year-round.

Accommodations 4 two-story lodges, 37 rooms double or multiple occupancy. Cedar walls and floors, minimal furniture, many windows; Hawaiian prints and fabrics, fresh flowers. Baths shared, except for private suite in each lodge. Maid service daily; communal kitchen. Also available: private cottage with cooking facility, 25 tent sites. Amenities: coin-operated laundry, rental of water sports gear. No air conditioning.

Rates $44 single with private bath, shared bath $33; $24 per person, double occupancy with private bath, shared bath $18; $15 per person, multiple occupancy (shared bath). Suites on request. Credit cards: AE, MC, V.

Meal Plans Primarily vegetarian, meals at Cafe Cashew are à la carte. Hawaiian-style breakfast includes papaya, passion fruit, banana smoothies, buffet of tropical fruits, brown rice, French toast. Lunch can be sautéed vegetables with *tempeh* and *tahini* sauce, broiled mahimahi, or spinach lasagna. Dinner choices from grilled chicken to mahimahi baked with mushrooms in lemon and garlic sauce; cream of curried papaya cashew soup, and a salad bar. Beer, wine, coffee, tea available. Special diet requests (Pritikin, macrobiotic) accommodated. Daily meal plan $19.

Services and Facilities **Exercise Equipment:** Weight lifting; bicycle rental. **Services:** Massage (shiatsu, Swedish, Esalen), acupressure, acupuncture, rolfing, chiropractic. Counseling on weight loss, diet, nutrition. **Swimming Facilities:** Outdoor pool (Olympic-size), ocean beaches. **Spa Facilities:** Natural pools at nearby springs and steam baths. **Recreation Facilities:** Tennis court, horseback riding, hiking, volleyball; golf course, ski slopes nearby. **Evening Programs:** Workshops on health and sports conditioning, yoga; cultural performances, traditional Hawaiian feasts.

In the Area Helicopter sightseeing tour of island; scuba trips (fee); Volcanoes National Park, Jaggar Museum (Volcanoes Park history), Kilauea caldera, lava tubes at Wahaula Visitor Center, Hawaii Tropical Botanical Garden, Parker Ranch resort area, Hawaii plantation town, King Kamehameha historic site, Mauna Kea observatory telescope, MacKenzie State Park (hiking, picnics, beach).

Getting Here *From Hilo.* By car, Rte. 11 to Keaau, Rte. 130 (45 min). Rental car, taxi available.

Special Notes No smoking in bathhouse area. Remember to bring sunscreen #15, mosquito repellent, and flashlight.

The Maui Challenge

Sports conditioning

Hawaii
Mt. Haleakala–
Lahaina (Maui)

An adventure in cross-training, the Maui Challenge is paradise found. Taking back roads, mountain trails, and sea routes, participants discover wonders not experienced by beach bathers at the luxury resorts—and get a better workout.

Led by naturalists, aerobics instructors, and wellness specialists, you make an eight-day trek that takes in the island's major attractions. A volcanologist interprets the awesome crater of Mt. Haleakala; then you hike right through the caldera. You view the majestic, 200-foot waterfalls of Hana; then you swim under them and even dive from the cliffs.

Hiking, mountain biking, and sailing are included in the challenge—a marathon of lava flows, rain forests, and tropical lagoons that challenge even fitness buffs.

Each day begins with yoga, and at trail's end there are stretch classes or relaxing massages. Sharing their love of the island and its ancient history, the guides explain every berry, mushroom, crater, and archaeological site along the way. The natural beauty becomes tangible and felt.

Limited to 12 participants, the program runs from Saturday to Saturday, airport to airport.

The Maui Challenge
Body & Mind, Inc.
Box 330820, Kahului, HI 96733
Tel. 808/878–6506

Administration Program director, Deborah R. Sturgess

Season Specific weeks, year-round except Jan.

Accommodations 6-bedroom beach houses across the island are shared; modern facilities have queen-size beds for couples, twins for singles.

Rates $2,000, one week, all-inclusive. $500 advance payment. No credit cards.

Meal Plans Vegetarian meals, with some fish and poultry, vary with season. Breakfasts of tropical fruit, granola; lunch picnics with salads, pita bread; dinner choices of grilled mahimahi, eggplant Parmesan. No coffee, tea, processed sugar.

Services and Facilities **Exercise Equipment:** Downhill bicycles. **Services:** Massage, seaweed wrap; hair, nail, skin care. **Swimming Facilities:** Lagoons, pools, beaches.

In the Area Sailing on a 50-foot sloop; aerial sightseeing tour.

Getting Here Local transportation provided throughout.

Special Notes No smoking indoors.

The Plantation Spa

Holistic health

Hawaii
Kaaawa (Oahu)

Combine the Swedish approach to health and natural living with a Polynesian plantation set between Pacific beaches and rugged mountains, and you have a new breed of health resort. An affiliation with a renowned Swedish spa, Halsohem-Masesgarden, adds a European flavor to the program as well. With a maximum of 14 participants per week, the Plantation Spa has the best of both worlds.

The resort was originally an old family estate where travelers watered horses. Now the old carriage house is a gymnasium, and wood cottages and an open-air aerobics pavilion are hidden in the lush foliage. Nearby gardens provide fresh fruits and vegetables for the kitchen, run by a Cordon Bleu chef.

Surrounded by natural beauty and scenic splendor, the program takes you on canoeing trips and hikes to waterfalls through primal palm groves. Classes in hula dancing, as well as aerobics and vegetarian cooking, are on the daily schedule. Beginning with a sunrise stretch and walk along the beach, the day is structured for exercise and relaxation.

An instructor leads a group through aquatic aerobics in the swimming pool. After lunch there is free time for a massage or herbal wrap (one of each is included in your package price for the week). A 45-minute session of low-impact aerobics and circuit training is followed by yoga and sunset serenity.

Although the days are well-balanced, you are not required to participate in all activities. The one-week program runs from Sunday afternoon through Saturday morning; extensions are possible if you fall in love with the place. It retains the peace and friendliness of old Hawaii and fosters positive thinking to rejuvenate you for today's world.

The Plantation Spa
51–550 Kamehameha Hwy., Kaaawa, HI 96730
Tel. 808/237–8685

Administration Manager, Bodil M. Anderson; program director, Judith A. Goldstone

Season Year-round.

Accommodations Rustic cottages with 8 guest rooms, private baths. Furnished with rattan chairs, double or king-size beds, decorative Polynesian arts and crafts. Cottages cluster around farm house where meals are served. No TV, air conditioning, or telephone in rooms.

Rates 1 week $1,250 per person double occupancy, $1,550 single. $500 advance payment per person, due within 14 days after reservation; nonrefundable. Credit cards: MC, V.

Meal Plans Vegetarian meals served from fixed menu. Breakfast is multigrain muesli with fresh fruit, raisins, apricots, papaya with lime juice, herbal teas. Lunch is chilled lettuce cardamom soup, home-baked Spanish tomato bread, carrot salad, tropical

fruit platter, vegetable juice. Dinner begins with slices of zucchini and tomato in pesto, an entree of ratatouille with fresh
herbs and crème fraîche, brown rice. Special diets accommodated.

Services and
Facilities
Exercise Equipment: 6 isometric and aerobic weights units,
rowing machine, stationary bike, parcourse. **Services:** Swedish massage, shiatsu, herbal wraps; fitness evaluation; arts
and crafts instruction. **Swimming Facilities:** 17-meter heated
outdoor pool; ocean beach. **Recreation Facilities:** Hiking, canoeing, croquet, badminton, volleyball. **Evening Programs:**
Lectures on health and fitness, cooking class, meditation class,
games.

In the Area
Scheduled group hikes and canoe trips; Polynesian Cultural
Center, Waimea Falls Park (botanical garden, nature trails),
Byodo-in Temple (Japanese shrine) and Haiku Gardens, Sea
World.

Getting Here
From Honolulu. By car, Hwy. 63 (Likelike Hwy.) to coastal
Hwy. 83 (Kamehameha Hwy.) via Kaneohe Bay (50 min). Ren-
tal car available. Transfers on request (fee).

Special Notes
No smoking on property. Remember to bring medical records
and hiking and exercise shoes.

Pualani Fitness Retreat

Life enhancement
Holistic health

Hawaii
Makawao (Maui)
Terraced into the Mt. Haleakala slopes, the fitness retreat
looks more like Aspen than Maui. Perhaps it is because the owners, Susan and William Linnemann, are part-time Aspenites.
But from its 3,000-foot elevation, the Pualani Fitness Retreat
commands a view that is pure Pacific.

Secluded and completely private, the mountainside home was
designed for a healthy lifestyle. There is a sauna, steam room,
outdoor Jacuzzi, 50-foot lap swimming pool, and an exercise
room where yoga, aerobics, and classes in stress management
are enhanced by the panoramic view of the island.

Susan often leads hikes. Raised in Hawaii, she treasures the
folklore of the Poli Poli rain forest, the vast volcanic crater atop
Mt. Haleakala, and the junglelike bamboo stands in Hana State
Park. Each day is different, balancing a walk or jog along the
beaches with exercise classes and massage.

Susan, with degrees in occupational therapy and clinical nutrition, is well qualified to work out a fitness program that is
tailored to her guests' interests. In addition to personal training in the weights room, her staff will organize aquatic exercise
in the pool or a cooking class to teach good nutrition. The program is limited to eight participants.

Pualani is the "heavenly flower" of Hawaiian myth, surrounded
by flowers (a protea farm is behind the house) and woodland.

Pualani Fitness Retreat
Box 1135, Makawao, HI 96768
Tel. 808/572–6773 or 800/782–5264

Administration	Director, Susan Linnemann
Season	Year-round; retreat weeks Apr.–Oct.
Accommodations	Main house has 5 bedrooms, 3 baths; 2 separate cottages can each be occupied by up to 4 persons. Built of native koa wood, with hand-painted tiles and stained-glass accents, main house has floor-to-ceiling glass windows. Interior designed in tropical colors and floral prints; custom-built carved koa wood furniture, and free-standing fireplace. Beds are king- or queen-size (1 room with double beds).
Rates	Bed-and-breakfast $55–$125 per day; 1-week fitness retreat, Sun.–Sat., $1,600 per person double occupancy, $1,800 single. Package includes all meals, activities, 3 massages. 25% of total fee due 30 days prior to arrival. Deposits are nonrefundable, may be applied to future visit. Credit cards: AE, MC, V.
Meal Plans	Vegetarian menu, plus fish. 3 meals daily. Specialties are mahimahi baked with herbs, sautéed papaya, organic rice, flower pancakes with blueberries.
Services and Facilities	**Exercise Equipment:** Paramount Universal gym and weights units. **Services:** Massage, exercise instruction, cooking class. **Swimming Facilities:** Outdoor lap pool; ocean beaches nearby. **Recreation Facilities:** Walks on garden paths; golf, tennis, water sports within 9 mi. **Evening Programs:** Guest speakers on fitness, nutrition, and stress management; demonstrations of meal planning and preparation; inspirational movies on well-being.
In the Area	Hiking to Mt. Haleakala crater, Hana's waterfalls and beaches; shopping in Lahaina. Interisland cruises, deep-sea fishing, helicopter sightseeing, sugarcane train ride.
Getting Here	*From the mainland.* Direct flights to Kahului airport from Chicago and West Coast on United Airlines, from California on American Airlines. Complimentary transfers on arrival/departure at Kahului. Local excursions provided during fitness retreats.
Special Notes	No smoking in house or cottages.

Strong, Stretched & Centered

Life enhancement
Holistic health
Sports conditioning

Hawaii *Paia (Maui)*	Working out with the instructors' instructor is a fitness buff's dream come true. Over 100 graduates of the professional certification course, an intensive six weeks, have spread the word of the body/mind training program originated here by Gloria Keeling. Now there are 2- and 4-week versions that incorporate aerobics, yoga, diet, nutrition, and psychological conditioning.

This is not a quick-fix, so you probably should be in shape before joining Gloria's beach gang. The techniques used synthesize several cultures, from tai chi chuan to aquacize, in an East-West experience. Weight-reduction methods employ the notion of muscle definition as well as the concept of *ki*, the centered self.

Formerly based at the Maui Inter-Continental Hotel, the program participants are now housed in condominium apartments at a private beach resort. The staff instructors and advisers from the Maui Holistic Health Center work with you on a one-to-one basis to develop and expand your potential. Training sites include spectacular Haleakala crater (the world's sixth largest dormant volcano), the lush jungles of Hana, with its waterfalls and bamboo forests, and the numerous white-sand beaches for which Maui is celebrated.

Orchestrated for maximum body movement, you'll learn "gestalt dance" and African jazz rhythms with your aerobics. It's a high-powered experience in interdisciplinary training, with people devoted to nurturing a balance of mind and body fitness.

Strong, Stretched & Centered
Box 758, Paia, HI 96779
Tel. 808/575–2178 or 800/367–8047

Administration Program director, Gloria Keeling

Season Scheduled sessions year-round.

Accommodations Lanai-style apartments shared by 2–4 persons. Twin beds, modern bath, ocean-view balcony or terrace. Furnished informally, with white rattan seating, lots of big cotton pillows, tropical fabrics; color TV, completely equipped kitchen. Beach area has shaded Jacuzzi and swimming pool. Maid service provided.

Rates 2-week program, including meals and bodywork, $1,150 per person, double occupancy; 4 weeks $2,300. $500 advance payment. Credit cards: MC, V.

Meal Plans 3 meals served family-style Mon.–Fri. Mostly vegetarian menu includes enchiladas with beans, choice of vegetables or chicken, eggplant Parmesan casserole, baked mahimahi fish, Thai satay noodles with oyster sauce, vegetables, and peanuts. On weekends, guests prepare their own meals.

Services and Facilities **Exercise Equipment:** Nautilus gym. **Services:** Sports conditioning, weight-lifting training, massage, video analysis, instructor certification. **Swimming Facilities:** Outdoor pool. **Recreation Facilities:** Water sports, hiking; nearby tennis courts, golf course, bike rental, horseback riding, scuba and water sports, all for extra fees. **Evening Programs:** Workshops on health and fitness.

In the Area Group outings for snorkeling, overnight hike in Hana State Park, sunrise hike on Haleakala crater. Interisland cruises, helicopter sightseeing, shopping and nightlife in Lahaina, sugarcane train ride.

Getting Here Direct flights to Maui's airport from Chicago and West Coast on United Airlines. *From Kahului.* About 20 min to Kihei by taxi or rental car. Rental car available for group use.

Special Notes No smoking in dining room. Guests are requested to smoke only on the beach.

The Westin Maui

Non-program resort facilities

Hawaii
Lahaina (Maui)

Breathtaking waterfalls, meandering streams, and a health club are among the attractions of this mega resort. The Westin Maui is set on 12 oceanfront acres and is bordered by two golf courses and a tennis complex; it has all the pleasures of paradise and none of the pain.

Take the wildlife and garden tour offered by Guest Services and you will learn that more than 650,000 gallons of water sustain the resort's aquatic needs. The pool area alone features five free-form swimming pools, two water slides, and a swim-up Jacuzzi hidden away in a grotto. Swans, flamingos, and other charming characters roam freely, adding their individual personalities to the tropical atmosphere.

Pool activities include water volleyball and aquacize classes. Scuba instructors are on hand to give beginner and refresher courses as well as guided ocean beach dives. For other water sports you can rent a Hobie cat, Windsurfer, or snorkeling equipment.

The coed health club offers weight training and an exercise room where aerobics classes are held daily, at no charge. There is a steam room, sauna, and Jacuzzi for relaxing stiff, sore muscles. Massage therapy is available by appointment.

Tennis and golf enthusiasts have easy access to the island's finest facilities: the Royal Kaanapali Golf Course with 36 holes, the Royal Lahaina Tennis Ranch with 11 courts, stadium seating, and a massage therapist. During the winter months, golfers get a bonus as humpback whales play offshore in the warm waters within view of the links.

Maui is only 48 miles long from its eastern to western tip, but it has more varied drives and hiking trails than any of the other islands. There is an isolated rain forest in the Iao Valley State Park and the imposing Mt. Haleakala, whose vast moonscape crater measures 21 miles around and is centerpiece of a national park. The most romantic road, however, heads for heavenly Hana, traversing lush jungle and deep ravines before reaching the ocean.

The Westin Maui
2365 Kaanapali Pkwy., Lahaina, HI 96761
Tel. 808/667–2525 or 800/228–3000
Fax 808/661–5831

Administration Manager, Bernard Agache; recreation director, Terry Albritton

Season Year-round.

Accommodations 762-room resort has two towers, each 11 floors. Luxury rooms and suites, including the exclusive Royal Beach Club. Air-conditioned, private lanais, king-size or double beds, views of ocean or golf course.

Rates	$185–$295 single or double occupancy, Royal Ocean Club rooms $350, suites from $500–$1,500. 2 nights advance payment or credit-card confirmation. Credit cards: AE, CB, DC, MC, V.
Meal Plans	No special dining plan. 3 restaurants, snacks to Continental fare. Best choice: Sound of the Falls.
Services and Facilities	**Exercise Facilities:** 10 Sprint weight training units. **Services:** Swedish massage, shiatsu, reflexology. **Swimming Facilities:** 5 outdoor pools, ocean beach. **Recreation Facilities:** 11 tennis courts (6 lighted), 2 18-hole golf courses, water sports. **Evening Programs:** Resort entertainment, Hawaiiana demonstrations.
In the Area	Guided tours of the resort, includes art collection and gardens. Lahaina (old whaling capital) shops, bars, restaurants; Mt. Haleakala; up-country ranches and rodeos; Sugar Cane Train Ride; winery tour; Maui Tropical Plantation (botanic gardens).
Getting Here	*From Kapalua-West Airport.* By car, Hwy. 30 (Honoapiilani Hwy.) via Lahaina (20 min). Complimentary transfers at airport. Rental car, taxi, shuttle van available.
Special Notes	10 barrier-free rooms specially appointed for the disabled. Children can enjoy Hawaiian arts and crafts classes and seasonal day camp (Easter, summer, Christmas). No smoking in designated areas of the dining room and in health club; two nonsmoking floors in Ocean Tower.

Canada

Scenic splendor is an essential part of the fitness vacation in many areas of Canada. Two resorts in Alberta are set in the mountains of Banff National Park, British Columbia's only holistic health retreat is on an island in the Strait of Georgia, and a thalassotherapy center and the Slim Inn are located on the Gaspé Peninsula of Quebec, facing the Atlantic Ocean.

Western Canada is endowed with a number of hot springs where outdoor activity is oriented toward tennis, hiking, skiing, and horseback riding.

The most significant new development for 1989–1990 may be the King Ranch in Ontario, a high-tech resort less than an hour from Toronto that aims to blend country elegance with preventive medicine programs using a combination of concepts from the Canyon Ranch in Arizona and the Four Seasons hotels of Ontario.

Banff Springs Hotel

Taking the waters

Alberta
Banff

Before the railroad and hotel builders arrived in 1885, the hot springs were sacred, shrouded in clouds of steam. Today the spring-fed pools are open again, rebuilt by Parks Canada for the public, and a high-tech health club, where you can get a shiatsu massage or dine on sushi, has been added to the venerable Banff Springs Hotel.

The turreted hotel—the largest in Canada west of Toronto—looks like a castle out of Camelot, and it is equally majestic inside. No four rooms are alike, and many are historically furnished. But instead of English lords and ladies, the baronial halls are filled with Japanese tour groups.

Golf and skiing are the main attractions. The park is at its best in summer when it's open to cyclers and horseback riders, backpackers and river rafters. Banff is a place to savor the scenery while bathing in the healthful, sulfurous waters.

Banff Springs Hotel
Box 960, Banff, Alta. T0L 0C0
Tel. 403/762-2211, 212/490-3900, or 800/828-7447
Telex 038-21705

Administration Manager, Ivor Petrak

Season Year-round.

Accommodations 246 new rooms in Banff Springs Manor; total of 835 rooms in hotel. Suites in several sizes with nooks and antiques. 3-story VIP suite with private glass elevator, sauna, whirlpool, and lap pool.

Rates High season, mid-May–Sept., $160–$195 (Can.); $215–$235 with Jacuzzi. Weeklong ski packages from $302. VIP suite

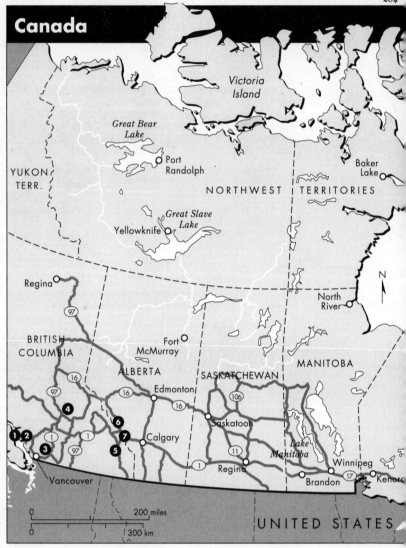

Canada

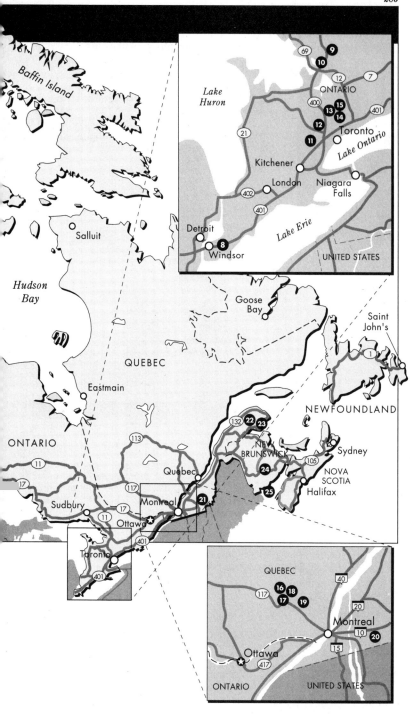

$2,500 per night. Confirmation with credit card. Credit cards: AE, MC, V.

Meal Plans 3 meals a day in main dining room. Japanese restaurant.

Services and Facilities **Exercise Equipment:** 10-station Universal gym weight training circuit, 2 Lifecycles, 2 stationary bikes, rowing machine. **Swimming Facilities:** Large indoor and outdoor pools at Banff Springs Hotel. **Spa Facilities:** Large outdoor swimming pool fed by mineral hot springs at Cave and Basin Centennial Centre. Upper Hot Springs Pool on Sulphur Mountain. Both 1.5 mi from downtown Banff. **Recreation Facilities:** 3 ski areas: Mt. Norquay with 17 runs on 123 acres is closest and open till 9 PM Wed.–Sat. Sunshine Village has a 3,514-ft vertical drop and cross-country skiing on 20 mi of groomed trails. Bicycle rentals in Banff. Trail maps at the park information center. Horseback riding and guided treks arranged through outfitters.

In the Area Nearby Cave and Basin Centennial Centre with interpretive displays, self-guided boardwalk trails. Columbia Icefield tours (May–Sept., weather permitting); Banff Festival of the Arts at the Banff Centre and School of Fine Arts (May–Aug.); art of the Canadian Rockies at the Whyte Museum in Banff.

Getting Here By air, Calgary International Airport, about 80 mi east of Banff, serviced by Brewster Transportation and Tours and Pacific Western Transportation Ltd. By bus, Greyhound from Calgary and Vancouver. By train, VIA Rail transcontinental service from Vancouver and Calgary (tel. 204/949–1830). By car, Trans-Canada Hwy. to park entrances, where a 1-year vehicle pass must be purchased. Local taxi, limousine, airport shuttle bus available.

Special Notes No smoking in health club.

Slimm In at Lake Louise Inn

Luxury pampering

Alberta Mountain hikes don't mean roughing it, nor do you have to give
Lake Louise up morning coffee to get fit at this alpine resort. In the spring and fall, the week-long Slimm In program replaces the usual tourist routine at Lake Louise Inn. The daily mix of classes, walks, exercise, and sensible eating takes full advantage of the invigorating Rockies for inspiration and is designed to introduce you to the benefits of a healthy lifestyle.

From the sunrise eye-opener walk to an afternoon stretch-and-tone session, the emphasis is personal development. A team of instructors works with you in small, compatible groups. Activities are geared to the general energy of the group rather than to peak performance.

Breathtaking surrounding peaks come in view on walks around Lake Louise. Snow-covered Victoria Glacier is mirrored in the green water. While one group does high-energy aerobics, another is in the pool for aquatic exercise. Two hour-long classes are scheduled each morning, and yoga is practiced before dinner. Massage and beauty services can be scheduled for an additional charge.

Slimm In at Lake Louise Inn

Box 209, Lake Louise, Alta. T0L 1E0
Tel. 403/522-3791 (800/661-9237 in western Canada)
Telex 03-824658/LK LSE INN LLU, Fax 403/522-2018

Administration	Program director, Larry Hoskin
Season	6-week sessions in both spring and fall.
Accommodations	91 motel-style rooms with double bed, private bath, and TV in a contemporary ski lodge hotel complex.
Rates	$545 (Can.) single, $440 double per person, including tax. $100 check with reservation. Credit cards: AE, MC, V.
Meal Plans	3 daily meals prepared with Slimm In recipes provided to guests on departure. 1,200-calorie diet (per day) includes between-meal refreshments. Nonalcoholic reception on Sun. evening.
Services and Facilities	**Exercise Equipment:** Exercycles, Universal gym unit. **Swimming Facilities:** Heated indoor pool. **Spa Facilities:** Whirlpool, sauna. **Recreation Facilities:** Bicycle rental, 3 outdoor tennis courts, nearby horseback riding. **Evening Programs:** Lifestyle lectures.
In the Area	Trail hikes, gondola rides at ski area, 2½-mi trail to Lake Agnes teahouse.
Getting Here	By car, 110 mi from Calgary on Trans-Canada Hwy. By bus, Greyhound and Brewster Transportation. By train, station within walking distance of the inn; daily VIA Rail service on the transcontinental *Canadian*.
Special Notes	Remember to bring hiking boots, warm clothing, gloves.

Chateau Whistler Resort

Sports conditioning

British Columbia
Whistler/Blackcomb Mountain

With year-round skiing on the greatest vertical rise in North America, alpine hiking in summer, horseback riding and water sports, the Whistler/Blackcomb vacation area continues to expand its fitness facilities. The new Chateau Whistler Resort, the largest hotel in Whistler Village, will open a complete health club during the winter of 1989-90. Plans call for nutrition seminars as well as ski conditioning.

There are aerobics classes, a 30-foot indoor-outdoor pool, and a Jacuzzi that overlooks the bubble-enclosed chair lift. The club offers massage and facials, a coed sauna, and separate steam rooms for men and women. There's also a juice bar where low-cal meals are served.

Designed around a pedestrian plaza, Whistler Village has dozens of boutiques and restaurants within a short walk of the hotel. There are more than 30 lodges—including one run by Nancy Greene, Canadian giant slalom gold medalist at the 1968 Olympics—and a high-rise Delta hotel. A therapy center for treatment of sport-related problems with hydrotherapy, massage, and a flotation tank is in the village.

The facilities and mountain climate attract crowds from Vancouver and Seattle on weekends, but it's easy to get away from the throngs to the mountain meadows and hiking trails behind the new golf course.

Chateau Whistler Resort
Whistler, B.C.
Canadian Pacific Hotels and Resorts
595 Howe St., Vancouver, B.C. V6C 2T5
Tel. 800/828–7447 in the USA, 800/268–9411 in Canada (800/268–9420 in Ontario and Quebec)
Fax 604/669–3607

Season Year-round.

Accommodations 400-room high rise with standard rooms and deluxe suites, concierge club floor services.

Rates Rate schedule to be announced. Confirmation by credit card. Credit cards: AE, MC, V.

Meal Plans Several restaurants for full meals and snacks. Pacific salmon specialty.

Services and Facilities **Exercise Equipment:** Complete circuit training. **Swimming Facilities:** Heated outdoor pool accessible from inside the health club. **Recreation Facilities:** Tennis courts and bike rental at the hotel; golf, canoeing, horseback riding nearby. 25 lifts and a gondola for skiing.

Getting Here *From Vancouver.* By car, Hwy. 99 past Horseshoe Bay, Squamish, and Howe Sound (70 mi; 90 min). By train or bus, daily service between Vancouver and Whistler.

Special Notes Specially equipped guest rooms for the disabled. No smoking in therapy center and designated dining areas. 1 floor of nonsmoking rooms.

Fairmont Hot Springs Resort

Taking the waters
Non-program resort facilities

British Columbia
Fairmont Hot Springs

Canada's largest hot mineral pools are an attraction of this family-oriented vacation complex in the Rocky Mountains. There's golf, skiing, and a deluxe Sports Center where spa treatments and exercise equipment make it possible to assemble your own spa program. The privately owned Fairmont Hot Springs Resort has large swimming pools for day visitors who come for sports and relaxation. The beautifully landscaped grounds are surrounded by mountain forests.

The recently completed fitness facilities and a private pool are for guests in the lodge and villas. Two international racquetball courts, one squash court, coed saunas and whirlpools, and hydra-fitness exercise equipment are available.

Fairmont Hot Springs Resort
Box 10, Fairmont Hot Springs, B.C. V0B 1L0
Tel. 604/345–6311 (800/663–4979 in western Canada)
Telex 041–45108

Administration	Manager, Bernard Gordon
Season	Year-round.
Accommodations	139 rooms with private baths in the main lodge. 75 deluxe villas near the golf course. 5 cottages and 48 suites with cooking facilities.
Rates	$55–$85 (Can.); ski-and-swim package also available. Meals and treatments optional. Credit cards: AE, MC, V.
Meal Plans	Standard items throughout the day in the public dining room.
Services and Facilities	**Swimming Facilities:** Outdoor pools open year-round; lakes and rivers nearby for summer water sports. **Spa Facilities:** Odorless mineral water for hot soaks and swimming pools, outdoor and indoor whirlpools. **Recreation Facilities:** Golf, tennis, racquetball, squash, water skiing, sailing, fishing, rafting; horseback riding; downhill and cross-country skiing; hiking.
Getting Here	Located on BC Hwy. 93, north of Cranbrook (64 mi) and south of Banff (100 mi). By air, private airstrip (1.5 mi). By car, west of Calgary (190 mi), north of Spokane, WA (260 mi). By bus, service from Calgary on Greyhound.

Harrison Hot Springs Hotel

Taking the waters
Non-program resort facilities

British Columbia
Harrison Hot
Springs

The introduction of a complete spa program and the planned wing of guest rooms at the Harrison Hot Springs Hotel will make this the largest and most complete health resort north of California. Japanese technology and management will be introduced early in 1990 when the new facilities are completed. Meanwhile, the lakefront resort offers hot mineral water soaks and therapeutic massage in the existing hydrotherapy pavilion.

A hot pool and a swimming pool are the main attractions. The pavilion is constructed of wood and brick and decorated with native carvings; it looks onto the garden where an Olympic-size swimming pool is filled with warm spring water year-round. The sulfurous, 140-degree spring water provides effective if temporary relief for aching muscles. The new owners, Itoman Canada, Inc., intend to introduce mud baths, Jacuzzis, herbal wraps, and oriental massage.

The pavilion has separate facilities for men and women, including private Roman baths with sunken seating. An exercise room is available but is not supervised. Joggers have the choice of running along the lake or on a Dynatrak paved circuit.

Lake Harrison looks scruffy when you arrive from the main road. The strip of rocky, gray beach is lined with parked cars and RVs, but beyond the tourist bars and souvenir stands are wilderness tracks for hiking and quiet country roads. The hotel, long popular with honeymooners and conventioneers, is being upgraded and refurbished, but afternoon tea is still served in front of the lobby fireplace.

Harrison Hot Springs Hotel
Harrison Hot Springs, B.C. V0M 1K0
Tel. 604/796-2244 (800/663-2266 in Seattle)
Telex 04-361551, Fax 604/796-9374

Administration	Manager, J. Hadway
Season	Year-round.
Accommodations	Motel-style rooms in main building, cottages in private garden area. Deluxe rooms in the new tower, some with lake view.
Rates	$83–$106 (Can.) daily, double occupancy; rate does not include meals. Credit cards: AE, MC, V.
Meal Plans	Cafeteria service for lunch.
Services and Facilities	**Exercise Equipment:** Hydra-resistance units and exercise bikes in weights room. **Swimming Facilities:** Indoor pavilion and outdoor pool open 24 hours, 104 degrees for soaking, 94 degrees for swimming; lake. **Recreation Facilities:** Tennis courts, horseback riding; golf nearby; curling and cross-country skiing. Bicycle rental. **Evening Programs:** Dinner dancing in the Copper Room.
In the Area	Boat trips and fishing on the lake in summer. Minter Gardens showpieces in bloom March–Oct.
Getting Here	*From Vancouver.* By car, Trans-Canada Hwy. (Rte. 1) east to exit for Rte. 9 at Minter Gardens; continue to Lake Harrison (65 mi).
Special Notes	Some specially equipped rooms for the disabled.

The Hills Health Ranch

Luxury pampering

British Columbia
100 Mile House

Saddle up for a Western-style workout at The Hills Health Ranch in caribou country, in the heart of British Columbia. Facials and skin treatments mix with hayrides and massage, and options include trail rides or cross-country skiing.

Woodsy A-frame chalets fan out from the main lodge where the spa and a pizza bar are located. Busy with skiiers in winter (several teams train here), the ranch is an all-season resort that offers special packages for weight management, beauty treatments, and an "Executive Renewal Week." Weekends and 11-day programs are available year-round; alternatively, you can schedule treatments and classes à la carte.

Trainers and beauticians cater to guests booked for the programs. After an initial fitness evaluation, you're scheduled for 3½ hours of guided brisk walks, classes (aerobics, aquacize, and stretch-and-flex), and training with weights each day. There's also yoga stretch, Jazzercise, and two-hour hikes.

Hearty fare is served in the dining room, but you can opt for low-cal meals. For a change of pace there is horseback riding or hayrides. Facilities are open 8 AM–10 PM.

The Hills Health Ranch
C–26, 108 Ranch, 100 Mile House, B.C. V0K 2E0
Tel. 604/791–5225

Administration	Program director, Juanita Corbett
Season	Year-round.
Accommodations	Private chalets with kitchen, bath, TV, and balcony for up to 6 guests; alpine cottages for couples and singles.
Rates	Chalet for 2 with the 7-day Executive Renewal package, $673 (Can.) per person, includes 6 massages, classes, and beauty treatments. Deposit of $50 or 25% of total cost 2 weeks prior to arrival. Cancellations within 2 weeks of reservation not refundable. Credit cards: V.
Meal Plans	3 calorie-counted meals a day with health packages. 1,000–1,200 calories a day diet recommended for weight loss.
Services and Facilities	**Exercise Equipment:** 2 Dynavit and 2 Monark bikes; 5-station hydra-pressure gym; Quinton running machine; rowing ergometer; free weights. **Swimming Facilities:** Indoor swimming pool. **Spa Facilities:** 2 whirlpools, 2 saunas. **Recreation Facilities:** Equestrian center with 28 horses; tennis courts, golf, and lake fishing nearby. **Evening Programs:** Western dancing with live local music; workshops on nutrition and wellness.
In the Area	Cowboy-led full- or half-day rides.
Getting Here	By air, Canadian Airlines International has daily flights to Williams Lake Airport. Complimentary transfers on arrival/departure. *From Vancouver.* By car, use main routes through the Rockies to the village of 100 Mile House. By train, BC Rail's Caribou Dayliner operates 3 times weekly on scenic route to 100 Mile House. Complimentary transfers on arrival/departure.
Special Notes	Riding and skiing instruction and tepee parties for children. No smoking in designated areas of dining room and spa. Remember to bring warm clothing and 2 pairs of running shoes.

Hollyhock Farm

Life enhancement

British Columbia *Cortes Island*	This secluded holistic community on an island in the Strait of Georgia, 100 miles north of Vancouver, welcomes summer visitors for weekend and five-day workshops in health and healing. Hollyhock Farm's wooden dormitories form an informal campus, surrounded by forest and beach, where discussion groups meet outdoors. You can jog, swim, or find the solitude to meditate.
	Since 1982, faculty members from the Victoria Centre for Complementary Medicine and specialists in alternative therapies and spiritual health have drawn inspiration from each other in the island setting. Andrew Weill, from Arizona's Canyon Ranch, leads a workshop in total wellness that discusses vegetarian diets and nutrition and practices massage, chanting, and visualization. Another week is devoted to practicing tai chi chuan movements for longevity and peace of mind.

Many summer courses focus on spiritual health. Several sessions are devoted to the healing philosophies of Buddhism, others are for chanting or bodywork. A herbology workshop uses the garden where vegetables and herbs are grown for communal meals.

Mornings begin with yoga and meditation. Arrangements can be made for bodywork—Swedish massage or oriental techniques like shiatsu and Reiki. Mostly, you are free to take advantage of the forest trails and beaches, the water, and the hot tub.

Hollyhock Farm
Box 127, Manson's Landing, Cortes Island, B.C. V0P 1K0
Tel. 604/935–6465

Administration	Manager, Shivon Robinsong
Season	Apr.–Oct.
Accommodations	Semiprivate or dormitory rooms, a few private double rooms. Heated buildings with communal showers and toilets.
Rates	5-day programs $225–$545 (Can.). $100 check must accompany application. $25 cancellation charge up to 2 weeks before reservation, full fee after that. Credit cards: MC, V.
Meal Plans	Buffet-style meals served 3 times a day. Organically grown vegetables, some seafood.
Services and Facilities	**Exercise Equipment:** Outdoor bicycles, canoes on lake. **Swimming Facilities:** Private lake, ocean beaches.
Getting Here	*From Seattle and Vancouver.* By car and ferries, via Vancouver Island. By air, Air BC has flights from Seattle and Vancouver to Campbell River for nearest ferry connection. Direct flights to Cortes Island from Seattle by float plane: book with Lake Union Air or Kenmore Air. Complimentary transfers on arrival/departure at Manson's Landing for 11-mi trip to Farm.
Special Notes	No smoking indoors. Remember to bring warm clothes, flashlight, rainwear, sturdy walking shoes, and footwear that slips on and off easily.

Manan Island Spa

Luxury pampering

New Brunswick
Grand Manan

This island retreat takes advantage of sea air, seafood, and solitude. You bathe in dulse, an edible seaweed harvested on the island's shores, and stay in an elegantly refurbished 1840s house. There's a body wrap and dulse scrub, even a taste of dulse in your salad or soup at lunch.

Dulse is a Grand Manan Island export, sought by connoisseurs in Japan and America for its salty, iodine flavor and nutrients. Only here and at the Aurora House Spa in Ohio is it used in the treatments developed by an island native, Joanne Liuzzo, Aurora's director.

The eight-bedroom inn looks like a New England summer cottage. Antiques in the parlor and bedrooms belie the sophisticated hydrotherapy equipment for facials and the steam baths in the treatment rooms.

Staffed by aestheticians and a chef from the Aurora House, the program here is tailored to the guests' wishes. Walks or jogs along the beach and the wooded cliffs can be made with or without an escort. Group exercise or yoga is organized on request.

Naturalists have come here ever since James Audubon visited in 1832 and recorded over 250 different species of birds, including the bald eagle, which still nests here. Whale watching, photography, painting, and rock collecting are popular pastimes. Willa Cather, a frequent visitor during the 1930s, wrote that the island was "tranquilizing to the spirit and seemed to open up great space for it to roam in."

Manan Island Spa

North Head, Grand Manan, N.B. E0G 2M0
Tel. 506/662–8624 or 216/562–9171

Administration Director, Joanne Liuzzo

Season July–Aug.; May, June, Sept. by request (groups only).

Accommodations 8 bedrooms with private baths. Some king-size brass beds, upstairs views.

Rates 3-day "Seaweed Soother" package $649 (Can.) double, $499 single. B&B or with 2 meals when space available. One-third advance payment. Cancellation charge for notification less than 48 hours in advance of arrival date. Credit cards: AE, MC, V.

Meal Plans Breakfast cooked to order: Entree choice at lunch and dinner. Fresh seafood, local salmon, and boiled lobster specialties.

Services and Facilities **Swimming Facilities:** Nearby ocean beaches and lakes. (Water tends to be cool.) **Recreation Facilities:** Bikes available to guests at the inn; canoeing by arrangement. 17 nature trails along the shore to landmarks such as Hole-in-the-Wall cave at Whale Cove, where dulse is harvested.

In the Area Whale-watching expeditions; museum of over 300 island birds, local geological exhibits at Grand Harbour.

Getting Here *From mainland.* By ferry, daily (2 hr). Reserve space in advance. Ferry lands at Blacks Harbour on the coastal road (Rte. 1) from St. John and the airport. Short walk from ferry dock to inn. *From Maine.* By car, border crossing at Calais/St. Stephen to Rte. 1. Free parking at both terminals.

Special Notes No smoking in the spa or dining room.

Mozart Chalets

Nutrition and diet

New Brunswick The lakeshore wilderness and the European-style natural
Cambridge cooking are the specialties here. The owners, Rosel and Hans Neumann, emphasize healthy eating and living. No treatments are offered, but the beauty of New Brunswick's heartland can be explored on nature trails. There's a Finnish sauna and whirlpool.

The home cooking at the Swiss chalet is a treat. The Continental menu is prepared with reduced salt and sugar, and without chemicals or preservatives. Dinner with a view of the lake is served by candlelight with classical music.

The Neumanns share their enthusiasm for the outdoors with guests who come for winter sports and with summer and weekend vacationers. Maps, literature, equipment, and advice on how to enjoy yourself are available on request.

Mozart Chalets
Lakeview Rd., Cambridge, N.B. E0E 1B0
Tel. 506/488-3071

Administration Manager, Hans Neumann

Season Year-round; best times are June–Oct., Jan.–Mar.

Accommodations Lakeview rooms in European-style chalets, various sleeping and living quarters, private baths. Additional beds available for families.

Rates 1 week package $209 (Can.) per person double occupancy includes breakfast, 2 sessions in the bathhouse. Midweek and weekend packages available. $100 deposit required. Credit cards: MC, V.

Meal Plans Breakfast and dinner served daily. Dinner menu features European specialties à la carte.

Services and Facilities **Exercise Equipment:** Bike, boat, and ski rentals. **Swimming Facilities:** Private beach on lake. **Recreation Facilities:** Hiking, boating, fishing, windsurfing, waterskiing, bicycle tours, deer- and bird-watching; cross-country skiing, snowshoeing, ice fishing, ice skating.

In the Area Car trips to the provincial capital, Fredericton; Beaverbrook Gallery's collection of Canadian art; Kings Landing historical village; the reversing falls, a tidal phenomenon at St. John seaport; restored Victorian landmarks; Gagetown riverside crafts community.

Getting Here By car, Trans-Canada Hwy. along the St. John River to Jemseg; Rte. 695 to Cambridge-Narrows. By air or train, to St. John and Fredericton. Car rentals available at both towns.

Special Notes No smoking in designated dining areas. Remember to bring bathrobe, hiking boots, and warm clothing.

Chestnut Hill

Weight management

Ontario
Gormley Juice fasts begin a week devoted to vegetarian diet and mild exercise at this getaway retreat close to Toronto. Set on a 50-acre estate, Chestnut Hill's main house and guest cottage provide privacy for a maximum of 16 guests. Organized activity is limited to two exercise classes daily, leaving you free for private workouts, professional facials and massages, and relaxation in the whirlpool and sauna.

Surrounded by woodlands, lakes, and a nature preserve, the atmosphere here is similar to that of a resort. You can sleep through the morning yoga class without interference or go for long walks on country roads and along the lakeshore, where boats and canoes invite your use.

Guests are encouraged to stay on the juice-and-soup diet for four of the seven days, but the program is flexible with low-cal solid food alternatives. Advance consultation with your personal physician is always advisable when considering a fast, and the folks here are experts on the subject. A nurse consults with you when you arrive and monitors your progress during the week.

Few spas of this size offer the services of registered and certified specialists in as wide a variety of body and beauty treatments. Stress reduction is accomplished through reflexology one day, Swedish massage another. Four treatments are included in the one-week package; shorter programs from Sunday to Friday and on weekends are available.

With the addition of an indoor swimming pool in 1988 and more service rooms, the year-round activities have expanded to appeal to both men and women.

Chestnut Hill
Box 454, R.R. 1, Gormley, Ont. L0H 1G0
Tel. 416/888–1231

Administration Manager, Katharine Kunz

Season Year-round.

Accommodations Main lodge with 10 bedrooms furnished in quiet good taste. All have twin beds, private bath.

Rates 1-week program $750 (Can.) includes 6 treatments or services, diet regimen. Sun. arrival and departure. Advance payment of $100; balance on arrival. No cancellation refund. Credit cards: V.

Meal Plans Liquid diet of juices and vegetable broth followed for 4 days; vegetarian meals total 800 calories other days.

Services and Facilities **Exercise Equipment:** Lifecycles. **Swimming Facilities:** Indoor pool; lakes in summer. **Recreation Facilities:** Tennis court, boating, horseback riding, cross-country skiing. **Evening Programs:** Talks on nutrition.

Getting Here *From Toronto.* By car, Don Valley Pkwy. (Hwy. 404) 17 mi north of Hwy. 401 at Bloomington Rd. By bus, service available to Gormley. Local taxis.

Special Notes No smoking indoors.

Eleanor Fulcher's Spa

Holistic health *Women only*

Ontario Developing a new sense of awareness about your mind and spir-
Gravenhurst it as well as your body is the goal of a week-long program for women only at Eleanor Fulcher's Spa. Strong on group dynamics, it includes plenty of personal pampering.

The program has the feel of a summer camp. It begins when the 10 or so participants are met in Toronto and shuttled to the lakeside retreat. Everyone is expected to join in aerobics, stretching, yoga, and hiking for 4½ hours every day. An indoor swimming pool is also used for exercise classes.

Eleanor Fulcher personalizes the program to suit her guests. Beauty treatments available include aromatherapy massage as well as facials, manicures, and pedicures. The exercise, diet, and stress-free environment are designed to help guests lose an average of five pounds each.

Eleanor Fulcher's Spa

Gravenhurst, Ont.;
791 St. Clair Ave. W., Toronto, Ont. M6C 1B8
Tel. 416/979-7577

Administration	Manager, Eleanor Fulcher
Season	June–Sept.
Accommodations	Country casual, with 5 bedrooms.
Rates	1 week $995 (Can.) per person, sharing room, all-inclusive. Confirmation by credit card. Credit cards: AE, MC, V.
Meal Plans	3 meals a day, total of 800 calories. Emphasis on vegetables and fish, some meat. Special dietary requests accommodated.
Services and Facilities	**Swimming Facilities:** Indoor pool, private beach on lake. **Recreation Facilities:** Boating, nearby tennis and golf. **Evening Programs:** Health lectures.
Getting Here	*From Toronto.* Complimentary transportation from the Royal York Hotel.
Special Notes	No smoking indoors.

King Ranch

Life enhancement
Preventive medicine
Nutrition and diet

Ontario
King

The comprehensive concept of this new fitness resort and spa, scheduled to open in the fall of 1989, is unprecedented in Canada. The integrated programs and facilities are in harmony both with the natural beauty of the setting and with the physical and emotional needs of the men and women who will come here to make informed lifestyle changes.

The luxury resort complex is the result of international teamwork by consultants from Arizona's Canyon Ranch. Headed by Mel Zuckerman, the Canadian architect Arthur Erikson, and the Toronto developers Tiana, Adam, and Murray Koffler, the resort's goal is to serve corporate executives and fitness buffs who want comfort while working out in a self-contained high-tech environment.

Arriving at this oasis of active rejuvenation, the first thing you notice among the trees is a glass and steel pyramid that houses the exercise areas. Spread across 3½ levels are four aerobics studios, a racquetball court, two squash courts, two indoor tennis courts, a circuit weights room, a swimming pool, and an elevated indoor-outdoor jogging track. There are separate men's and women's massage and body treatment rooms, with sauna, steam, and eucalyptus inhalation rooms and therapeutic whirlpool baths.

Residential buildings and a clubhouse hug a wooded escarpment overlooking a branch of the Humber River. Three interconnected low-rise buildings are sheathed in wood shingles. Rooms have balconies with views of rolling meadows and lush valleys. A forest of Canadian cedar, maple, and pine fills much of the 177-acre site.

The thrust of King Ranch programs is education and prevention. Drawing upon medical institutions in the Toronto area and its own staff of 350, special treatments will be offered for arthritis, pre- and post-natal conditions, and smoking. Courses in nutrition and cooking will complement natural cuisine served in the elegant dining room.

King Ranch
King Sideroad (E. of Hwy. 400), King, Ont.
(Office) 255 Yorkland Blvd., Suite 105, Toronto, Ont. M2J 1S3
Tel. 416/492–4330

Administration Director, Tiana Koffler Boyman

Season Year-round.

Accommodations Minisuites for approximately 180 guests, all with balcony or ground-level terrace.

Rates $200–$300 (Can.) daily per person. Weekend rates and package plans available. Full American Plan, with 3 meals daily and use of exercise facilities. Advance confirmation by credit card. Credit cards: AE, CB, DC, MC, V.

Meal Plans Calorie-controlled menu at 3 main meals in the Club House dining room. Specialties include poached salmon, seasonal green salad, and pasta with vegetables. Special diets accommodated; all food low in fat and sodium.

Services and Facilities **Exercise Equipment:** Lifecycles, stair climber, treadmills, rowing machines, circuit weights gym and free weights; outdoor parcourse. **Services:** Chiropractor, body therapy, hydrotherapy, biofeedback training, hypnotherapy, one-on-one exercise; beauty salon with aestheticians, cosmetic surgery consultant; stress management, body composition testing, fitness assessment, posture evaluation; food-habit management, nutrition counseling, smoking cessation. **Swimming Facilities:** Indoor pool. **Recreation Facilities:** Hiking, biking, tennis, and racquet sports; cross-country skiing, snowshoeing, ice skating. **Evening Programs:** Cineplex movie theater in Club House; lectures.

In the Area Museums and shopping in metropolitan Toronto.

Getting Here *From Toronto.* Complimentary limousine service on arrival/departure at area airports and downtown hotels. By car, Hwy. 400 north of Toronto City Hall, 55 mi (32 km), to King Sideroad east of the highway in King County (less than 1 hr). Local taxi, rental car, limousine available.

Special Notes Ground-floor accommodations and treatment areas designed for the disabled. No smoking in the spa building and dining room.

Portage Inn

Luxury pampering *Women only*

Ontario
Huntsville

Nestled in the heart of Ontario's cottage country, the gracious old Portage Inn hosts a maximum of 10 women who want to escape from tension and enjoy some first-rate pampering without the expense of going to a resort. Modest in all aspects, it's a vacation where you can have a good time while doing something good for yourself.

Mornings begin with brisk walks and after-breakfast exercise classes. Yoga is scheduled for three mornings, aerobics for two. Then you're on your own for afternoon walks along the lakeshore and country lanes, or to use sports facilities at the nearby Deerhurst Inn. A facial and manicure are included in the weekly package; massage and other services can be scheduled at an additional charge. Both bathrobe and spa wrap are supplied.

The inn's easygoing atmosphere reflects the philosophy of resident manager Cathy Sloan: Women need a pleasant and restful holiday rather than an excess of exercise. Weight loss is not a prime concern, although the low-calorie gourmet meals are prepared under the supervision of a nutritionist.

For relaxation, guests gather in the swirling water of a hot tub built into a second-floor solarium adjoining the bedrooms. The view of the lake and fields, where once a railroad portaged freight past the inn, adds to the sense of healthy living.

Portage Inn
R.R. 4, Huntsville, Ont. P0A 1K0
(Winter office) 248 Glengrove Ave. W., Toronto, Ont. M5N 1W1
Tel. 705/789–7602 or 416/488–5420

Administration Manager, Cathy Sloan

Season May–Oct.

Accommodations 6 single rooms, 2 doubles; guests share 2 baths. Pine furniture, feather duvets, and soothing colors for casual comfort.

Rates 1-week, Sun. afternoon–Sat. morning, $775 (Can.) single or shared room. Advance payment of $200. Refundable if canceled at least 2 weeks prior to scheduled arrival. No credit cards.

Meal Plans 3 meals daily, total of 1,200 calories. Limited menu with gourmet items such as veal piccata for dinner, vegetable frittata with orange and onion salad for lunch.

Services and Facilities **Exercise Equipment:** Stationary bicycle, rebounder. **Swimming Facilities:** Private beach on the lake. **Recreation Facilities:** Tennis and badminton courts; paddleboat and canoe.

In the Area Organized cruise on the lake.

Getting Here *From Toronto.* 142.6 mi (230 km) north, via Hwy. 400 and 11 North, then Hwy. 60 to Canal Rd.

Special Notes No smoking indoors.

Schomberg Manor

Weight management   *Women only*

Ontario A choice of vegetarian diet or fasting on fruit and vegetable
Schomberg juices is the focus of a nutrition program designed to restore
body balance while you enjoy a soothing getaway. The ambience of an English country manor, and the program of yoga,
deep breathing, stretching, and massage, will please women
who want to rejuvenate both body and mind.

With seven acres of forest and meadow surrounding the manor,
guests are encouraged to take brisk walks or to pedal on bikes
provided without charge. Morning and late afternoon exercise
sessions complete the day.

Pampering is a plus here, although most of the beauty and
health services are not included in the basic package price. For
relaxation try the solarium, take long walks on forested lanes,
participate in lawn sports, or read by the fireplace.

Schomberg Manor
Box 189, Schomberg, Ont. L0G 1G0
Tel. 416/936–2328 or 416/964–1742

Administration Manager, Susan Smith

Season Year-round.

Accommodations 6 double bedrooms with bath in country home of considerable
charm and style.

Rates 6-nights $750 (Can.) double occupancy; $820 single. Weekend
and 5-day packages include diet and exercise. Credit card confirmation. Credit cards: AE, MC, V.

Meal Plans Low-calorie vegetarian dishes supplement fruit and vegetable
juices 4 times during the day; vegetable broth at dinnertime.
Herbal tea only.

Services and **Exercise Equipment:** Free weights and videocassette programs
Facilities for individual workouts. **Services:** Aromatherapy, iridology,
reflexology, allergy therapy, all à la carte. **Spa Facilities:** Solarium with sauna, whirlpool. **Recreation Facilities:** Volleyball,
lawn darts, croquet; cross-country skiing and horseback riding
nearby.

In the Area McMichael Canadian Collection of paintings and native art, doll
museum, both in Kleinburg; Old Ontario House, makers of re-
production period furniture, in Schomberg.

Getting Here *From Toronto.* By car, Hwy. 400 or 27 northwest to Hwy. 9 (35
mi).

Special Notes No smoking indoors.

Weight Watchers Camp Canada

Youth camps for weight loss

Ontario Weight Watchers Camp Canada, a coed summer camp for young
Aurora adults and teenagers (ages 10–21), focuses on a balance of education, exercise, and diet for an active vacation. Located on a

wooded campus near Toronto, it affords campers full use of modern facilities leased from St. Andrews School.

The meals are prepared according to menus provided by Weight Watchers International, Inc., and feature their trademark recipes. Campers learn how to eat properly while attending classes on food preparation and lectures on nutrition, as well as socializing in the dining room.

Supervised by accredited counselors, campers enjoy full weeks of workouts with Universal gym equipment, slimnastics and aerobics classes, and team sports. Those who complete the course are guaranteed to lose weight or get a refund.

Weight Watchers Camp Canada
Aurora, Ont. L46 347
Tel. 416/727–3178
Weight Watchers Camps
183 Madison Ave., New York, NY 10016
Tel. 212/889–9500 or 800/223–5600 (800/251–4141 in Canada)

Administration	Program director, Anthony Sparber
Season	July–mid-Aug.
Accommodations	Complex of 3-story Old English-style buildings; single and double rooms, 12 persons per floor with lounge and tile bath with stall showers. Campers make their own beds.
Rates	Sessions of 2–7 weeks from $1,450; $100 payable in advance. Credit cards: AE, MC, V.
Meal Plans	Balanced meals served 3 times a day in the cafeteria, under supervision of a Weight Watcher–trained food adviser. 2 snacks daily in residence hall.
Services and Facilities	**Exercise Equipment:** Weights room with complete Universal gym; gymnasium apparatus; track and field training. **Swimming Facilities:** Indoor pool. **Recreation Facilities:** Hiking and jogging trails, tennis, racquetball, squash courts; team sports; arts and crafts center. **Evening Programs:** TV, trips to Shaw Festival theater (additional cost).
In the Area	Niagara Falls, the Welland Canal, historic towns, scenic parkland walks.
Getting Here	*From Buffalo and Toronto.* Easily accessible by car.
Special Notes	No smoking indoors.

Wheels Country Spa at Wheels Inn

Luxury pampering

Ontario
Chatham

Total fun and fitness is the concept for Wheels Inn, a motel that grew into an indoor resort with seven acres of sports and spa facilities under one roof. Cavort with the kids in the outdoor-indoor swimming pool and water slide or choose from 42 revitalizing services in the European-style Wheels Country Spa.

Taking a serious approach to shape-ups, staff members have credentials for cardiovascular and muscular testing. They do basic body measurements, a wellness profile, and the hour-long Canadian Standardized Tests of Fitness. Gym instruction and a weight-loss program are also available.

Runners and joggers can join organized outings of clubs based here, enjoying a tour of the town's Victorian mansions and modern marina along the way. There are 15 routes mapped out, ranging from 1.8 to 13.5 miles, and an indoor track where 22 laps equals one mile.

The variety of revitalizing body and skin treatments offered here, for men and women, is unique for Canada. Services are priced on an à la carte basis or on half-day or full-day packages. In this oasis of quiet luxury, stress melts away in the hands of certified masseurs and masseuses. There is also a fully equipped beauty salon. You can schedule a session of reflexology work on nerve centers or be cocooned in a fragrant herbal wrap. Therapeutic Swedish massage and invigorating body scrubs with a loofah sponge working sea salts and avocado oil into your skin are part of package offerings. There is a three-day deluxe spa program and a five-day "Super Tone-Up."

Aerobic exercise groups are scheduled according to your fitness level, from beginner to high-impact classes for the super-advanced, and run throughout the day, from 6:45 AM to 8 PM. A large number of club members from the community take advantage of the facilities and programs, so you'll never be at a loss for company, and the cushioned studio floor is easy on the feet.

All activities are coed, and you can join a group doing "aquabics" in the fitness pool, or the "renaissance" program for those with arthritis and circulatory problems. Then relax in the whirlpool and steam baths.

All this seems far removed from the family-oriented activity that fills the hotel atrium and dining room. Lunch is specially prepared and served in the privacy of the spa lounge for guests who want to avoid temptation. A supervised day-care center on the premises watches the children while parents are working out.

Wheels Country Spa at Wheels Inn
Best Western Wheels Inn
Box 637, Chatham, Ont. N7M 5K8
Tel. 519/351–1100
Telex 64–7110

Administration Manager, Roman Jaworowicz; program director, Diana Bos

Season Year-round.

Accommodations Spa program limited to 30 participants. The inn has 354 rooms, standard motel amenities, and "club class" rooms.

Rates 3-day package $635 (Can.) per person double occupancy, includes daily massage, herbal wrap, exercise periods, 3 spa meals, other services. Advance payment of $50. Refundable upon 5-day notice. Rooms-only reservations through Best Western. Credit cards: AE, MC, V.

Meal Plans 3 meals total 1,000 calories per day for spa program participants. Low in salt and fat; choices include meat, fish, salads.

Services and Facilities **Exercise Equipment:** Nautilus, Universal, and Olympic free-weight units. **Swimming Facilities:** 4-lane lap pool in the Fitness and Racquet Club; Olympic-size pool with indoor and outdoor sections in the atrium. **Spa Facilities:** Saunas, whirlpools. **Recreation Facilities:** Indoor courts: 6 tennis, 9 racquetball, 4 squash; maps of area running and jogging trails; sailing and fishing; bowling alley.

In the Area Walks through Colasanti's Greenhouses, acres of tropical plants; wine tastings in nearby Blenheim at the Charral Winery. The Guy Lombardo Museum in his hometown, London; Uncle Tom's Cabin, home of Rev. Josiah Henson in Dresden, used on the Underground Railroad.

Getting Here *From border crossing at Detroit/Windsor.* By car, Hwy. 401 to Exit 81 North, then turn right and left at traffic lights (1 hr). *From London and Toronto.* By car, Hwy. 401. By train, VIA Rail serves Chatham from Toronto with 4 trains daily (5 on Thurs.). By air, Windsor/London airport, 1 hr from inn. Local taxi and bus available.

Special Notes Children's programs include day-care center and Kent Kiddie Kollege, with daily activity and special summer outings for children 6–12. No smoking in designated areas.

Wyldrose Farm

Holistic health

Ontario
Acton
A weekend retreat close to Toronto, this 137-year-old farmhouse offers a peaceful combination of educational programs and vegetarian meals, treatments by specialists, and yogic exercise. Limited to 16 participants, weekends at Wyldrose Farm cover a wide range of holistic concepts, from crystals to Bach flower remedies, with both practical application and learning experiences. The opportunity to work with experts in a small, intimate group makes these weekends well focused and productive for those who are serious about learning new approaches to health and wellness.

A newly constructed guest house has country furnishings of old pine beds and dressers, antique lamps, and lace-curtained windows.

Wyldrose Farm
R.R. 1, Acton, Ont. L0N 1A0
Tel. 519/947–2472 (416/486–7472 for reservations)

Administration Director, Cristina Bardeyn

Season Year-round.

Accommodations 5 bedrooms with private baths: 3 double rooms, 2 with 4 beds.

Rates 2-night weekend program $190 (Can.) per person; week-long health and fitness programs $570. Rates based on double occupancy; single rates on request. Advance payment of $100. No credit cards.

Meal Plans 3 meals a day, family style. Vegetarian cuisine featuring stir-fried and baked items, rice, salad, and soup. Main courses can be a lentil burger, mock shepherd's pie, or tofu teriyaki. Limited use of eggs and dairy products; unlimited juice and tea.

Services and Facilities **Services:** Swedish massage, reflexology, Reiki, herbal healing, crystal healing, Bach flower remedy instruction, counseling in nutrition, stress management; juice fasts. **Swimming Facilities:** Pond. **Recreation Facilities:** Hiking. **Evening Programs:** Lectures and discussions on health-related topics; videotape movies.

Getting Here *From Toronto.* By car, Hwy. 10 to Hwy. 24, exit at Caledon onto Sith Line Rd. west for 5 mi (8 km)—60 min. By bus, Gray Coach to Orangeville (80 min). Complimentary pickup at bus stop. Pickup in Toronto on request.

Special Notes No smoking.

Aqua-Mer Center

Taking the waters

Quebec
Carleton The complete marine cure at this seaside auberge takes advantage of natural elements—seawater, algae, mud—and a mild Atlantic climate charged with iodine and negative ions. A combination of European and American therapies revitalize your body while you relax and enjoy the Gaspé food and scenery at Aqua-Mer Center.

The sequence of treatments prescribed for you after consultation with the professional staff involves bathing and exercising in the indoor swimming pool filled with comfortably heated seawater. There are no cold plunges into the ocean, but brisk walks along the beach and a massage under alternating showers of warm and cold water are encouraged. To stimulate blood circulation and lymph drainage you will be massaged in underwater-jet baths; this will enhance the effect of algae added to seawater that has been heated to a high temperature. Follow this with a toning shower that focuses high-powered jets on every muscle in your body for invigorating results.

The newly improved Marine Cure Center interconnects with a residential building that has the ambience of New England beach cottages. Facilities and equipment, while small-scale, are similar to European thalassotherapy centers. Guests and staff are mainly French-speaking.

Aqua-Mer Center
868 Boulevard Perron, Carleton, Que. G0C 1J0
(Winter Office) 7541 rue St. Hubert, Montreal, Que. H2R 2N7
Tel. 418/364–7055 (514/273–3300 in winter)

Administration Director, Yolande Dubois

Season May 15–Nov. 1.

Accommodations 27 rooms in 3-story auberge and adjoining building. Program participants also stay in nearby hotels and guest houses. Day visitors accommodated on a space-available basis.

Rates 6-day/7-night marine cure $805–$885 (Can.), double occupancy. Midsummer rates higher. Includes meals and thalassotherapy treatments. 5-day package without room under $400. Taxes included; gratuities extra. 25% deposit; balance on arrival. Refunds with notification 30 days prior to reserved dates. Credit cards: MC, V.

Meal Plans 3 meals a day in health cafe at the Marine Cure Center. Approximately 1,000 calories a day, including fish, chicken, fresh seasonal vegetables. Similar light cuisine at local inns.

Services and Facilities **Exercise Equipment:** Balneotherapy tubs, aerobics studio. **Swimming Facilities:** Indoor pool. **Recreation Facilities:** Nearby golf, tennis, sailing.

Getting Here Transfers on arrival/departure Sun. at Charlo airport and Carleton train station.

Special Notes Remember to bring bathing cap, slippers, 2 swim suits, beach towel, workout clothing, walking shoes.

Auberge du Parc Inn

Luxury pampering

Quebec
Paspebiac

Settle in for a relaxing week of seawater soaks and gourmet meals. This quiet retreat on the Baie des Chaleurs has a touch of Brittany and a style of its own.

Thalassotherapy is the main attraction. You are treated with mud, algae, and mineral-rich water pumped directly from the bay. Massage is part of the daily routine for guests on the one-week package.

Group activity is kept to a minimum. There are stretch-and-tone sessions, and in warm weather groups exercise in the outdoor swimming pool. But a large part of your day is occupied by treatments, a passive program that most of the men and women who come here regularly seem to prefer.

Small and self-contained, the 30-room inn books no more than 40 guests a week for treatments. French is spoken most of the time, though staff members are bilingual. Having some awareness of local customs helps, but with a sense of humor any problem can be solved.

After a walk in the countryside, appetite sharpened by the salty air, the low-calorie meals are a pleasant alternative to typical French-Canadian cooking.

Auberge du Parc Inn
C.P. 40, Paspebiac, Que. G0C 2K0
Tel. 418/752–3355 (800/463–0890 in Quebec)

Administration Manager, M. Le Marquand

Season Year-round.

Accommodations 30 modern bedrooms with private bath in a country manor house.

Rates Peak season rates July–Aug. 7-day package $985–$1,100 (Can.) per person double occupancy; $1,125–$1,250 single. 10% advance payment on booking. Credit cards: MC, V.

Meal Plans 3 meals a day included in package. Seafood and fresh produce of local farms featured.

Services and Facilities **Swimming Facilities:** Year-round heated outdoor pool; nearby beaches. **Recreation Facilities:** Hiking; golf, tennis, cross-country skiing nearby.

Getting Here *From Quebec City.* Located on the main approach to the Gaspé Peninsula. By car, Hwy. 20 to Rivière-du-Loup, then Hwy. 132 east via Mt. Jolie through Matapedia (5 hr).

Special Notes No smoking in spa.

Auberge Villa Bellevue

Non-program resort facilities

Quebec
Mont Tremblant Located on a natural lake close to the provincial park, the Auberge Villa Bellevue recently added an indoor swimming pool, exercise room, and sauna for year-round use by guests at no extra charge. Aerobics classes and water polo are scheduled daily. In addition, guests are teamed for volleyball and hockey. The Auberge, situated in one of Eastern Canada's most popular vacation playgrounds, is maintained and lived in by the owners and has the pleasant feeling of a country inn.

Open 8 AM–10 PM daily, the spa includes a coed whirlpool and a steam bath.

Auberge Villa Bellevue
Chemin Principal, Mont Tremblant, Que. J0T 2H0
Tel. 819/425–2734 or 800/567–6763

Season Year-round.

Accommodations 90 bedrooms including 14 deluxe rooms added in 1988.

Rates 1-week packages $335–$506 (Can.) per person double occupancy. Credit cards: AE, MC, V.

Meal Plans Breakfast and dinner daily included in the weekly package. Health salad bar in the dining room; special diets accommodated with advance request.

Services and Facilities **Exercise Equipment:** Circuit training with Global or Universal units in future; bicycles for country rambles. **Swimming Facilities:** Private beach on Lake Ouimet; heated indoor lap pool at the fitness center. **Recreation Facilities:** Windsurfing and sailing on the lake.

In the Area Mont Tremblant Provincial Park, about 15 mi from the villa, with full range of winter and summer activities. Shopping and antiques hunting in St. Jovite.

Getting Here *From Montreal and Quebec.* By bus, Voyageur lines from Montreal and Quebec City. By car, from Montreal airports and train station, about 1 hr drive on Route 117. Rental cars available at airport.

Special Notes No smoking in designated areas.

Centre Paulette Hiriart Spa Resort

Weight management

Quebec For the man or woman who wants to lose weight rapidly, this
Sutton supervised dietary program is combined with hikes or skiing and spa treatments. Run like a European pension for its eight to 11 guests, the Centre Paulette Hiriart Spa Resort offers active workouts as well as luxury pampering.

The detoxifying regimen begins with two days of eating only fresh fruit and vegetables, plus exercise and underwater massage to gently condition you for weight loss. A bilingual host introduces the philosophy behind the program and arranges special dietary needs for individual guests. (An advance consultation with your personal physician is advised.)

Unless you speak French, skip the lectures and concentrate on the treatments—a rare combination of thalassotherapy for the body and two-hour facials for good looks. Choices include body wraps with algae-enriched mud from the sea, or a coating of essential oils.

Alternating days of high-protein meals and vegetarian diet are programmed along with aquaerobics in the swimming pool, stretching, yoga, and country walks. This area of the Laurentian Mountains is known for ski resorts, and it has a well-equipped regional park with challenging downhill runs as well as hills for beginners. The Centre Paulette puts you conveniently close to the action yet offers quiet and seclusion for serious dieting.

Centre Paulette Hiriart Spa Resort
Box 927, McCullough Rd., Sutton, Que. J0E 2K0
Tel. 514/538-2903

Administration Manager, Paulette Hiriart

Season Year-round.

Accommodations 9 bedrooms in a country home, most with private bath.

Rates 6-day deluxe package $1,100 (Can.) double occupancy, $1,225 single. 10% advance payment. Credit cards: MC, V.

Meal Plans Alternating days of vegetarian diet and meat or poultry. 3 low-calorie meals daily.

Services and **Swimming Facilities:** Indoor pool; nearby lakes. **Recreation Fa-**
Facilities **cilities:** Organized hikes on mountain trails. **Evening Programs:** Informal fashion modeling.

Getting Here *From Montreal.* By car, Rte. 10 to the Eastern Townships. By bus, service to Sutton.

Special Notes No smoking in spa.

Domaine Saint-Laurent

Luxury pampering

Quebec
Compton

European-style thalassotherapy has been imported by the Centre de Santé-Détente at this country resort in the heart of French Canada. The treatments use seaweed, mud, and a variety of baths to complement massage in soothing muscular and skin problems. The emphasis at Domaine Saint-Laurent is on relaxation rather than on strenuous exercise.

Built around a 55-foot indoor swimming pool, the spa includes a coed sauna and whirlpool. Appointments for massage are scheduled Wednesday through Sunday with specialists in shiatsu, Swedish, and oriental-style therapies. Facials and beauty treatments are also available. Outdoor sports and recreation amid the scenic Eastern Townships is the main activity when you're not busy being pampered.

Originally built as a girls' school a century ago, the spacious lodge has been transformed and expanded in recent years by private owners who have combined the old-fashioned comforts of a country home with the latest in spa therapy. The resort, awarded four stars by the Tourism Ministry, caters to families and sales meetings as well as spa participants.

Domaine Saint-Laurent
C.P. 8180, 40 Chemin Cochrane, Compton, Que. J0B 1L0
Tel. 819/835–5464 or 800/567–2737
Fax 819/835–5290

Administration Manager, Gerard Saint-Laurent

Season Year-round.

Accommodations 50 standard rooms, 120 added in 1983–1984, plus 25 villas on a time-share basis.

Rates 3–5 day spa program from $383 (Can.) includes meals, treatments. Credit cards: AE, MC, V.

Meal Plans 3 meals per day; Sun. brunch. Diet menu reserved for spa guests.

Services and Facilities **Swimming Facilities:** Indoor pool open 10–5 daily. **Recreation Facilities:** 9 golf courses nearby, 4 tennis courts, woodland walking trails, horseback riding, cross-country skiing, sailing, bike rental. **Evening Programs:** Pub-style informal entertainment.

In the Area Organized outings in 3 minibuses to sailing on Lake Memphremagog, fruit picking, and antique hunting.

Getting Here *From Montreal and Quebec City.* By car only. Special arrangements for transportation in conjunction with Montreal's Le Nouvel Hotel owned by the same company.

Special Notes Some rooms are designed for the disabled.

Gray Rocks Inn

Sports conditioning

Quebec
St. Jovite

With the addition of Le Spa in 1987, this historic ski and summer sports resort gained a full-service fitness program. Classes and personal services are offered on an à la carte basis, although there is no charge to guests for use of the exercise equipment, coed sauna, or whirlpools. Along with an active social schedule, there are lean cuisine options for dining, making the Gray Rocks vacation package one of the best values in this part of Canada.

If you start with a fitness appraisal to help establish your goals, staff members, including an exercise physiologist, will test your cardiovascular capacity, body composition, and muscle flexibility. A computerized model provides an in-depth analysis of factors that affect your overall wellness. The spa has gained certification for customized exercise programs on their equipment. There are also aerobic dance sessions, stretch classes, and water-supported exercise in the pool. Charges are per session, discounted if you opt for a package.

Après-ski beach parties are a Wednesday-night feature at the spa. During the summer, activity at the 2,000-acre resort focuses on the marina and private beach, the championship 18-hole golf course, riding stables, and tennis complex. There are two dining rooms and social lounges at the Inn.

Gray Rocks Inn
Box 1000, St. Jovite, Que. J0T 2H0
Tel. 819/425–2771 (800/567–6767 in eastern Canada)

Administration Fitness director, Ross Andersen

Season Year-round. Spa open 7 AM–10 PM daily.

Accommodations 450 guests. Main bedrooms with ski-lodge comforts. 40-room private, upscale "Le Chateau" located a short distance around the lake. Villa rentals available.

Rates Budget and moderate-price package plans available, depending on season. Credit cards: AE, MC, V.

Services and Facilities **Exercise Equipment:** Lifecycles, Nautilus training equipment, complete Global gym, rowing ergometers, free weights, NordicTrack ski simulators. **Swimming Facilities:** Outdoor pools (not heated); lap pool in the spa. Private beach on Lake Ouimet. **Recreation Facilities:** 22 tennis courts, horseback riding, golf, jogging and walking trails. Ski school mid-Nov.–Apr. 30. **Evening Programs:** Dancing and theme parties.

In the Area Sleigh rides, shopping in nearby villages. Mont Tremblant Provincial Park (15 mi) for hiking and skiing.

Getting Here *From Montreal.* By air and train, Montreal stations about 2 hr from resort. By air, 4,200-ft landing strip for private aircraft. By bus, Voyageur service direct to inn. Local taxi and rental cars.

Special Notes No smoking in spa.

Sivananda Ashram

Spiritual awareness

Quebec
Val Morin
Living and practicing yoga from dawn to sunset, vacationers come here to relax the mind and revitalize the body. Located just an hour from Montreal, the yoga camp is an oasis of peace and harmony. Yet there is time for skiing and family fun within the daily schedule of meditation and vegetarian diet that you are required to follow.

Aside from the bare essentials of lodging, campers revel in the natural beauty of 350 acres of unspoiled woodland. At dawn, you are called to meditation, followed by yogic exercise or *asanas* that stretch and invigorate the body. A first meal comes at mid-morning, peak energy time; supper follows the 4 PM *asana* session. In between, you are free to enjoy the recreational facilities, to hike, or to get a massage. Sunset meditation and a concert of Indian music and dance conclude most days.

Based on five principles for a long and healthy life prescribed by Swami Vishnu Devananda, the program teaches how to breathe and exercise, and how to combine diet with positive thinking and meditation. The crisp mountain air and tranquil setting complement the quest for inner stillness.

The ashram attracts a diverse group of participants, college students as well as seniors, and has an introduction to yoga for youngsters while their parents meditate. Anyone is welcome, regardless of religion or age, and can stay for a weekend, a week, or longer. Many come for several weeks of advanced training, but you don't need to be an expert in any aspect of yoga to participate in the program. A special two-week "Total Health Intensive" focuses on yoga techniques for healthy and positive living.

The camp is also headquarters for an international nonprofit education organization that operates ashrams in New York State, California, and the Bahamas. Vacation opportunities at these retreats are detailed in chapters devoted to those areas.

Sivananda Ashram
Eighth Ave., Val Morin, Que. J0T 2R0
Tel. 819/322–3226

Administration Director, Swami Vishnu Devananda; manager, Claudine Asheey

Season Year-round.

Accommodations 2-story wood lodges with double and triple occupancy; private baths.

Rates Single-price all-inclusive policy for weekends or longer retreats; average $30 (Can.) per day. Reservations by mail, with deposit for $25 per person. Credit cards: V.

Meal Plans 2 vegetarian buffets daily. No meat, fish, eggs, alcohol, or coffee.

Services and Facilities **Swimming Facilities:** Large outdoor pool; lake. **Spa Facilities:** Sauna. **Recreation Facilities:** Hiking, biking, volleyball; downhill and cross-country skiing. **Evening programs:** Traditional music and dancing of India; bonfires and silent walks.

Getting Here *From Montreal.* By car, Laurentian Autoroute (Rte. 15), Exit 76. By bus, chartered service for special weekends and peak periods from Centre Sivananda (514/279–3545); Voyageur lines to Val Morin daily. Taxi service available in Val Morin. Airport pickup arranged for $50 (Can.).

Special Notes Kids' Yoga Camp, for ages 4–14, is a month-long combination of yogic exercises, swimming, and other activities. No smoking. Remember to bring an exercise mat or blanket, sandals or shoes that can be slipped on and off easily, and warm clothing.

Slim Inn

Weight management   *Women only*

Quebec
Lac-Supérieur Without exercise equipment or a staff of physiologists, Swedish-born Birgitta Stromberg-Parizot and her chef-husband Richard transform their cozy ski lodge into a summertime health retreat for women. The Slim Inn's daily routine consists simply of walking, swimming, and exercise, plus a 1,000-calorie-a-day diet. Some diversions are planned, and a beautician visits one afternoon each week.

A dozen guests share this rustic lakeside retreat, walking along the shore and working out in a studio under the watchful eye of their hostess. They also travel together, visiting crafts studios in St. Jovite and hiking Mont Tremblant. At meal times, the chef shares tips on cooking with herbs instead of salt or seasonings. Evenings are spent in conversation by the big fieldstone fireplace. Group support is an important but intangible part of the experience.

Some women may simply come to tone and slim, others are escaping from pressures of family and job for serious weight loss. Guests come from a wide variety of professional and educational backgrounds, and they range in age from 22 to the mid-60s. Most live in the Montreal area, 75 miles south of the lodge.

Since 1977 the Slim Inn has built a loyal following with this common-sense approach to healthy living. Enhanced by the undemanding atmosphere of Caribou Lodge-on-the-Lake, therapy comes naturally.

Slim Inn
Caribou Lodge-on-the-Lake
Lac-Supérieur, Que. J0T 1P0
Tel. 819/688–5201

Administration Program director, Birgitta Stromberg-Parizot

Season June–Sept.

Accommodations 12 single bedrooms share 2 large baths on the 2nd floor of the lodge. Modestly furnished with pine bed, wardrobe, sink with mirror, bathrobes.

Rates Single, all-inclusive price policy for lodging, program, and meals for 6 days (Sun.–Sat.). 1988 cost was $475 (Can.) including tax. No gratuities. $100 deposit accompanied by a physical evaluation from your personal physician. No credit cards.

Meal Plans 3 meals a day, family style. European-trained chef. Nouvelle cuisine with no fat, small portions of meat, lobster, and fish. 1,000-calorie (per day) low-carbohydrate, high-protein diet.

Services and Facilities **Swimming Facilities:** Private beach on the lake. **Recreation Facilities:** Mountain hikes and walking trails in Laurentians. Other facilities at nearby resorts by arrangement.

In the Area Shopping for antiques and handicrafts in nearby towns; scenic drives.

Getting Here *From Montreal.* By car, Autoroute 15 to St. Faustin. By bus, connections via Voyageur.

Mexico

Mexican fitness resorts are a well-kept secret, perhaps because so few of them match the standards of the facilities north of the border. Yet the traditional *balnearios* (spa resorts) and *baños termales* (hot-spring baths) are a bargain, offering mud baths, thermal waters, and warm hospitality. The largest and most luxurious of them is in Ixtapan de la Sal, an hour's drive southeast of Mexico City.

A very different experience, and a success since it opened 50 years ago, is the Rancho La Puerta in Baja California, founded by Deborah Szekely and her late husband. This is the action-oriented counterpart to the Golden Door in California; its holistic health program, vegetarian meals, and the stress-free environment of the Sierra Madres blend into a seamless vacation experience.

Balneario San Bartolo

Taking the waters

Querétaro
Querétaro The Hospital de San Bartolomé, a rustic spa built in 1599, is close to Querétaro, one of Mexico's most historic cities and capital of the state of the same name. The rudimentary *balneario* (baths) can be enjoyed in an ancient stone building or in the open air. The facilities include private cubicles and a swimming pool.

Brought by aqueduct from the springs, the sulfurous water has to cool before circulating in the baths. An ingenious cooling system cut into the rock has been in use for almost 300 years.

No services are available at the baths, but the nearby city has a variety of attractions and accommodations. Local hotels can recommend you for admission to the Querétaro Country Club, which offers horseback riding, tennis courts, swimming pool, and an 18-hole golf course.

The Mesón de Santa Rosa (Plaza de Armas, Pasteur Sur 18; tel. 4–5781 or 800/372–1323), a historical colonial landmark, is the city's best hotel. Run by Peter Wirth, the fifth generation of a Swiss hotelier family, this elegant inn has 21 rooms, an excellent restaurant, and a swimming pool. Rates per day range from $60 to $70, single or double occupancy. Dinner costs $20 to $25 per person.

In colonial times, the city played a role similar to that of Boston and Philadelphia in the American independence movement. Plans for what became the big break with Spain were first made in Querétaro. Half a century later, the monarchy of Emperor Maximilian ended with his execution at the Hill of Bells, the site now marked by a chapel and statue of Benito Juárez. And in 1917, the Mexican Constitution was drafted and approved in the city.

Among the notable churches are Santa Clara (1797), with its Neptune fountain, and Santa Rosa (1752), filled with exotic gold-leaf *retablos* and murals. The regional museum exhibits cover the prehistoric, colonial, independence, imperial, revolution, and post-revolution periods. Fine examples of colonial architecture include the palace of the Counts of Escala, and the baroque home of Francisco Antonio de Alday, now a restaurant.

Located about 130 miles from Mexico City, this can be a pleasant stopover on your way to San Miguel de Allende. There are mariachi band concerts Sunday and Thursday evenings in the Jardín Obregón, and the Plaza de Toros, an 18,000-seat landmark, has bullfights in November, December, January, and February. There is a vegetarian restaurant, Vegetariano Natura, at Vegara Sur 7.

Getting Here   *From Mexico City.* By car, Hwy. 57 north (2 hr). By bus, from Terminal Norte, Tres Estrella de Oro, Omnibús de Mexico, and Flecha Amarilla provide frequent departures (4 hr). By train, from Buenavista Station (4–5 hr).

Hacienda Spa Penafiel

Taking the waters

Puebla   Drinking at the source of Mexico's most popular bottled water
Tehuacán   is a bonus when you come to the gracious old resort of Hacienda Spa Penafiel. The hacienda stands regally on a mile-high plateau, surrounded by fragrant pines, literally atop crystal springs that gush forth the purest drinking water in Mexico.

This same mineral water shimmers in three swimming pools—one larger than half an acre—and fills whirlpools in the richly tiled spa. Here guests relax in Turkish baths and work out in a fully equipped gymnasium. For outdoor sports, arrangements are made for visitors at the Tehuacán Golf and Country Club.

Said to be especially good for kidney and liver disorders, the Peñafiel mineral water and the clear, scented air are a welcome change of pace for travelers in this historic part of Mexico.

Hacienda Spa Penafiel
Tehuacán, Puebla 75700
Tel. 238/20190 (800/421–0767 in the USA)

Accommodations   200 spacious rooms in the colonnaded hacienda-style hotel. Furnished with colonial-era antiques, Spanish tiles and hand-carved woods in rooms and public halls, all with private baths, air conditioning, TV, telephone.

Rates   Single room $25; 2 persons $29. Credit cards: AE, MC, V.

Meal Plans   Diet requests can be accommodated.

Services and   **Exercise Equipment:** Weights room, stationary bike, treadmill,
Facilities   free weights. **Services:** Swedish massage. **Bathing Facilities:** Jacuzzi pools. **Swimming Facilities:** Outdoor pools. **Recreation Facilities:** Tennis courts, golf, horseback riding, bowling alley, billiards, Ping-Pong, card rooms. **Evening Programs:** Mariachi concerts.

In the Area   Cholula archaeological site (Aztec pyramid, Church of Our Lady of the Remedies), Puebla museums and marketplaces, tile and ceramic art galleries; The Principal Theater (1756) presents opera, concerts, and folkloric shows.

Mexico

ARIZONA

NEW MEXICO

Tijuana

Ciudad
Juarez

Hermosillo

Thihuahua

Gulf of California

Cidad
Obregon

Torreon

Culiacan

P A C I F I C

Guadalajara

O C E A N

Acapulco

N

| 0 | | 200 miles |
| 0 | | 300 km |

Balneario
San Bartolo, **4**

Hacienda Spa
Penafiel, **7**

Hotel Balneario
San José Purua, **3**

Hotel Ixtapan, **5**

Rancho La Puerta, **1**

Rancho Rio Caliente, **2**

Villa Vegetariana, **6**

Getting Here *From Mexico City.* By car, Hwy. 150 south (3 hr). By bus, from Terminal del Sur (3 hr). Local transportation by taxi, rental car available.

Special Notes Limited access for the disabled. No smoking in health club.

Hotel Balneario San José Purua

Taking the waters

Michoacán Set on the edge of a small canyon, with spectacular views of
San José Purua the mountains and a nearby waterfall, the Hotel Balneario San José Purua has been a popular watering place since the times of the Tarascan Empire (AD 1200). Lush gardens and giant trees bearing orchids surround the bathhouse where thermal waters from several springs on the hillside are piped into private bathing pools. Dipping into the fizzy water, which is highly carbonated, is a daily ritual that relaxes travelers' aches and pains.

Mud packs are a specialty here. Facials using a mixture of the thermal water and highly mineralized mud are said to be beneficial to the complexion. Gently applied, the mud mask dries as you relax, and it is followed by a massage with herbal and fruit-based creams.

Treatments are booked on an à la carte basis. While there is no planned fitness program, the costs for a facial or massage are quite modest. And the resort offers a full complement of diversions, from golf and tennis to bowling and horseback riding.

Secluded and quiet, the hotel has the atmosphere of a colonial hacienda. Guest rooms with red-tile roofs, private terraces, and garden walks line the canyon to a small lake filled with ducks.

Situated in the highlands between Guadalajara and Mexico City, the resort is near the town of Zitcuaro. Nearby attractions include stately old Morelia, a city richly endowed with museums, cultural and educational institutions, and crafts shops, and Lake Patzcuaro, where descendants of the Tarascan Indians still fish with butterfly nets and worship at the Virgin of Health statue in the town basilica.

Hotel Balneario San José Purua
San José Purua, Michoacán
(Office) Calle Colón 27, Mexico D.F.
Tel. 905/510–4949

Season Year-round.

Accommodations 225 rooms in the hacienda-style hotel; heavy wood furniture, handwoven bedspreads, colorful decorations; all rooms with large private baths, modern facilities; no TV. Some small private terraces; 1 suite comes with private swimming pool. No air conditioning.

Rates Several plans available. Double room with 3 meals $60 per day for 2, $38 single. European and modified American plan rates lower. Credit cards: AE, MC, V.

Meal Plans Trained under German and Spanish master chefs, the restaurant staff takes a light approach to traditionally spicy Mexican cuisine. Fresh fish grilled over wood, without butter on request. Chicken, lamb, and beef usually well done. Fruits and salads from local farms.

Services and Facilities **Services:** Massage, facials, mud packs. **Bathing Facilities:** Indoor pool, private baths. **Swimming Facilities:** Outdoor pool. **Recreation Facilities:** Golf, tennis, bowling, riding, games rooms for billiards, Ping-Pong, cards. **Evening Programs:** Folkloric groups.

In the Area Michoacán Museum (Museo Michoacano) in an 18th-century palace on Morelia's main plaza houses Indian artifacts, a puppet collection, colonial furniture and paintings; Museum of Contemporary Art (Museo de Arte Contemporaneo) in Morelia has changing exhibitions, as does the Casa de la Cultura; Church of the Christ of Health (Iglesia del Niño de la Salud) on Rte. 15 near Morelia, has an image of the Christ Child said to have healing powers.

Getting Here *From Mexico City.* By car, Rte. 15 northwest (3½ hr). By bus, from the Northern Bus Terminal, Transportes Norte de Sonora (tel. 567–9221, 567–9664, 587–5633), 4½ hr. By van, service costs $16 per person, one way. Rental car available.

Special Notes Limited access for the disabled. Organized games for children. No smoking in the bathhouse.

Hotel Ixtapan

Luxury pampering
Taking the waters

Mexico
Ixtapan de la Sal
Hotel Ixtapan, largest and most luxurious thermal springs health resort in Mexico, is located in Ixtapan de la Sal, which has been a popular center for cures since the 16th-century Aztec emperor Móctezuma came to bathe. It is 70 miles southeast of Mexico City, easily accessible from the capital by car or limousine service.

Its health and beauty programs are designed to revitalize, rejuvenate, and refresh the total person. A typical day can include breakfast in bed, a nature walk, rhythmic gymnastics, aquatic exercises, and some pampering bodywork. Among the specialties are a facial with fresh fruit and vegetable oils, and a scalp massage.

The hydrotherapy facilities include 20 private Roman baths. Elegantly tiled and mirrored, the sunken whirlpools are filled with warm mineral water, ideal for a late-afternoon soak.

Treatments are gentle and relaxing, and exercises are not strenuous. The masseuses work muscles by hand and utilize electric vibrators as well.

There are numerous hotels and 13 lakes in the area. Among recreational facilities are train rides, horse-drawn carriages, water slides, and a bowling alley. Avoid weekend crowds if possible.

Hotel Ixtapan
Ixtapan de la Sal, Mexico
(Office) 132 Paseo de la Reforma, Mexico 06600 D.F.
Tel. 905/566–2855 (800/223–9832 in the USA)
Telex 17–71–413 Hotime

Administration	Manager, Barbara F. De Margalef
Season	Year-round.
Accommodations	250 minisuites plus 58 private chalets; pre-Hispanic motifs, colorful native fabrics; rooms comfortable but not modern; king-size bed plus sofa bed standard; all suites with private baths and air conditioning.
Rates	Full spa program, 1 week $600 per person double occupancy, $770 single. Tax and 15% service charge additional. Daily rate $97–$123 double, $73–$99 single. 50% at time of booking, plus 1-way transfer if requested. No credit cards.
Meal Plans	800-calorie diet plan is available with approval from nutritionist, served daily in a private dining room. Fresh fruits and juices for breakfast, grilled fish or veal at lunch, vegetarian tortilla for dinner among the selections.
Services and Facilities	**Services:** Massage, reflexology, mud packs, spot reducing; hair, skin, and nail treatments. **Bathing Facilities:** Private whirlpools. **Swimming Facilities:** Outdoor pools. **Recreation Facilities:** Tennis courts, 9-hole golf course, horseback riding, volleyball, badminton. **Evening Programs:** Resort entertainment, movies, folkloric ballet.
In the Area	Taxco (artisan center), archaeological sites.
Getting Here	*From Mexico City.* By car, Hwy. 2 via Toluca (Constituyentes) (60 min). Transfers on arrival/departure at airport or downtown hotels on request. Taxi, rental car available.
Special Notes	Elevators and ground-floor rooms provide access for the disabled. Minicamp and play areas for children. No smoking in the baths. Remember to bring Mexican Tourist Card.

Rancho La Puerta

Life enhancement
Weight management

Baja California Norte
Tecate

The Rancho La Puerta regimen can be easy or challenging. Hiking in the Cuyamacha foothills, a broad range of exercise classes (more than 30 daily), meatless meals spiced with Mexican specialties, and spa pampering are among your options.

The original formula for fitness has expanded since the resort opened nearly 50 years ago, but the basic attractions endure: a nearly perfect year-round climate (an average of 341 sunny days) that's dry and pollen-free, the natural beauty of purple foothills ringed by impressive mountains, and the lacto-vegetarian diet. "The Ranch," as old hands call it, has had a high percentage of repeaters. Newcomers quickly get into the swing of things. The day's most strenuous activity is "killer" volleyball, open to all comers.

Encouraged by instructors who use innovative techniques in workouts, and soothed or stimulated by music—say a flutist playing New Age tunes—you focus on recharging body and mind. Some classes are intense, others relaxing; counselors are on hand to help with your schedule.

Designed in the style of a Mexican village, there is a central complex of swimming pools and men's and women's health centers linked by brick-paved walkways to casitas and villas that accommodate 148 guests. Gyms dot the landscape like airy ramadas, some open-air, others enclosed for chilly or rainy days. You can play tennis on one of six courts or simply sunbathe.

This flowering oasis, set amid 300 acres of seclusion, also gives you a taste of Mexican resort life. Accommodations vary from studiolike rancheras to luxury haciendas and villas decorated with native handmade furniture and rugs. Many feature tiled floors, fireplaces, and kitchenettes. (Large units can be shared by single guests on request.) Although the decor leans toward Mexican kitsch, the Ranch has its own style and personality thanks to the smiling staff who look after the rooms and run the kitchen.

Meals in the Spanish-colonial dining room become a communal exercise in stamina building. The 1,000-calorie, low-fat, high-carbohydrate diet provides ample energy. Fish, dairy products, and eggs are included. Breakfast and lunch are buffet style, dinner a sit-down menu of four courses. Potatoes require advance tickets, issued during the morning, but you can have coffee, tea, homemade bread, and plenty of salads and vegetables grown organically on the Ranch.

After two or three days on this diet, without distractions from TV, newspapers or telephone, guests usually discover that their appetite for food has decreased remarkably, while they look and feel healthier. Some do go "over the hill," tempted by Tecate's shops and burrito bars.

Learning the psychology of healthy living, pioneered here by Deborah and Edmond B. Szekely, is the real benefit of visiting the hemisphere's original fitness resort.

Rancho La Puerta
Tecate, Baja California Norte
Tel. 706/654–1005 or 706/654–1155
(Office) Box 2548, Escondido, CA 92025
Tel. 619/744–4222, 619/295–3144, or 800/443–7565

Administration Manager, Jose Manuel Jasso; fitness director, Phyllis Pilgrim

Season Year-round; special weeks for couples only during March and October.

Accommodations Single-level studios and suites (65) with bath in adobe haciendas and villas. Some large units with 2 bedrooms, 2 baths, Southwestern-style beamed ceilings, fireplace, and dining-living area. The maximum number of guests is 150, cared for by a staff of 250.

Rates The weeklong program, Sat.–Sat., includes all sports, use of facilities, 3 meals a day. Rate varies according to accommodation. Treatments and personal services charged on an individual basis. Single accommodations $1,000–$1,650 plus tax, double $1,039–$1,402.65. $250 on confirmation of accommodations; balance payable 30 days prior to arrival. No credit cards.

Meal Plans The lacto-ovo-vegetarian diet includes fish 2–3 times a week; wine on Friday optional. Breakfast and lunch buffets offer lavish selections of fruit, vegetable salads, eggs, plus whole-wheat pizza. Dinner entrees include lasagna, enchiladas, and fish fillets spiced with cilantro-based salsa. Fasting on juices supervised Mondays.

Services and Facilities **Exercise Equipment:** Weight training gym located between the men's therapy center and women's spa has 6 Trotter treadmills, 15 CamStar weight units, Paramount gym, 9 Monark bikes, PTS recumbent bike, 2 StairMasters, Bosch computerized bikes, dumbbells, incline benches. **Services:** Massage, herbal wraps, facials, beauty-salon services available daily by appointment. Charges will be added to your account. Golden Door hypoallergenic cosmetics used exclusively. **Swimming Facilities:** 5 outdoor pools, 1 heated, used primarily for aquatic exercise classes. **Recreation Facilities:** Tennis on 6 lighted courts, a putting green, volleyball and basketball courts. Hiking ranges from "moderate" to a challenging climb up Mt. Cuchuma. **Evening Programs:** Movies and lectures scheduled nightly. Recreation hall is open for Ping-Pong and other games. Conversation after dinner is the main activity, with an early bedtime.

In the Area Tecate is 3 mi (5 km) west of the ranch. Tijuana, close to the border, bustles with curio shops, a cultural center, and, on summer Sundays, bullfights.

Getting Here *From San Diego airport.* Complimentary transfers on arrival/departure. Taxi service available for 40-mi (64-km) trip to ranch. Local transportation by taxi or rental car.

Special Notes Most facilities are barrier-free and ground-level for the disabled. Those with difficulty walking or seeing, or whose weight is 35% above normal for their height, are not accepted. Families are welcome, though no special activity for young guests is organized. No smoking in the health center or dining room.

Rancho Río Caliente

Taking the waters
Nutrition and diet

Jalisco
Guadalajara For thousands of years, Indians used the meandering river of hot mineral water for curative purposes. Now the fertile valley around the tiny village of La Primavera is a national forest. And the Rancho Río Caliente offers nature-oriented cures, including vegetarian meals.

The synthesis of therapies, diet, and bathing is the key to enjoying this unique health resort. Entering the bathhouse, you encounter a 20-foot wall of volcanic rock, in front of which are wooden benches where guests relax while enjoying a sweat. A stream of hot thermal water snakes through the room, emitting occasional puffs of steam. Welcome to the Aztec steam room.

After about 10 minutes in this superheated room (130 degrees), you begin to sweat out the body's toxins. Then you can cool down in a plunge pool (separate facilities for men and women) and enjoy a 60-minute massage. In addition, there are pampering services at very reasonable rates.

Classes in yoga, tai chi chuan, and body awareness are scheduled for all guests who want to participate.

The therapeutic water used in the pools and baths contains 10 major elements. Odorless, the water is used for drinking as well as bathing. There is a special diet of papaya for internal cleansing.

Rancho Río Caliente
APDO 1-1187, Guadalajara, Jalisco

Administration Director, Caroline Durston

Season Year-round.

Accommodations Cabanas and rooms for 50 guests in the main buildings; hand-crafted beds and chairs; colorful fabrics by local artisans; small and simple rooms, all with private baths; no phones, TV, or air conditioning.

Rates Daily rate $35 per person, double occupancy, $39 single. Taxes and gratuity added. $100 deposit. No credit cards.

Meal Plans Vegetarian meals served buffet style 3 times daily. Tropical foods in season include guavas, jícama, zapote, and guanabana. Organically grown raw greens, raw and cooked vegetables, soups and home-baked whole-wheat bread supplement vegetarian platters.

Services and Facilities **Services:** Massage, reflexology, facials, manicures, pedicures, waxing. **Bathing Facilities:** Private pools, swimming pool; waterfall for nude bathing. **Swimming Facilities:** Indoor and outdoor pools. **Recreation Facilities:** Tennis courts, hiking, bicycling. Horseback riding and golf are nearby. **Evening Programs:** Nightly lectures on health-related subjects.

In the Area Group trips into Guadalajara for shopping and cultural events. Other attractions include Lake Chapala, Cabanas Institute (center for arts), and Plaza of the Mariachis in Guadalajara.

Getting Here *From Guadalajara.* By car, Hwy. 80 to La Primavera (20 min). Shuttle service from airport; taxi, rental car available.

Special Notes Limited access for the disabled. No smoking indoors.

Villa Vegetariana

**Weight management
Nutrition and diet**

Morelos
Cuernavaca Emphasizing weight reduction and fasting cures, Villa Vegetariana health school was established by David and Marlene Stry as a center for nutrition and exercise. They serve tropical fruits and juices, vegetables raw and cooked. Low in cholesterol, and often grown organically on the property, the meals are included with consultation on diet and nutrition.

For recreation, there is a swimming pool, bicycles, a basketball court, and wall tennis. Walks and hikes in the countryside are arranged for groups of guests on request.

Yoga, Spanish classes, and organic gardening are among the activities scheduled. Surrounded by lush, tropical terrain, the villa is three miles from the center of one of the most interesting and colorful cities in Mexico.

Cuernavaca glitters in the sun, its plazas surrounded by baroque churches and palaces. One building, planned as a fortress by Hernán Cortés, is now a museum, exhibiting a collection of murals by Diego Rivera. There is also an herb museum (Museo de la Herbologia, Matamoros 200) with gardens and a small show.

Places to swim include rustic thermal springs and the recreation area at Oaxtepec, formerly the site of Móctezuma's botanical gardens.

The warm, dry climate and caring staff at the villa add up to a healthy vacation. (For reservations: Apdo. 1228, Pino 114, Sta. Maria Ahuacatilan, Cuernavaca, Morelos 62058; tel. 73–13–1044).

The Caribbean, the Bahamas, Bermuda

The current trend in the Caribbean is to import European thalassotherapy and American fitness programs. At a seaside estate on St. Lucia, the body holiday at Le Sport provides the fitness buff's counterpart to Club Med. On the seafront malecón of the Dominican Republic's capital city, a high-tech European spa adjoins the casino at the Jaragua Resort. And in the vicinity of Puerto Rico's Loquillo Beach, the newly opened Instituto de Vida Natural offers mud baths and holistic health programs.

Jamaica has the widest range of options, among them the luxurious Charlie's Spa at the Sans Souci resort, the vegetarian and holistic health program at the Lady Diane Hotel, and the equestrian center at Chukka Cova, all outstanding opportunities for combining a Caribbean holiday with a health regime.

St. James's Club

Luxury pampering
Non-program resort facilities

Antigua
St. Johns

St. James's Club, an outpost of a London private club, is a laid-back playground for the luxury-minded set on a crescent-shaped beach at the ruggedly beautiful east end of Antigua. After breakfast in bed or a run on the beach, participants amble down to the Body Shop for the aerobics classes, private massage rooms, and beauty treatments available exclusively for resort guests. The well-equipped weights room is staffed by an exercise specialist.

Among the recreational facilities are seven tennis courts lighted for night play and stables for trail rides. Swimmers can choose from a lap pool with outdoor Jacuzzi and smaller pools for dipping and sunning. For privacy there are hillside homes complete with pool and panoramic views.

Antiguans claim to have a beach for every day of the year, 365 of them in shades of white, pink, and tan. The powdery sand, turquoise waters, vibrant blue sky, and balmy temperature are an ideal combination.

No visit to the island would be complete without a call at English Harbour. Ever since Admiral Lord Nelson sailed in as commander in chief of the Royal Navy's Leeward Islands Squadron in 1784, this has been a haven for sailors and yachtsmen. Fishing trips and longer charters can be booked through some of the Caribbean's finest outfitters. Within the old fort walls is a museum of Nelson memorabilia; whether Nelson lived here is a matter of dispute, but the museum is well worth visiting for a taste of 18th-century maritime lore.

An independent nation since 1981, Antigua still calls cricket its national game. Matches are played at the Recreation Ground near the island's main town, St. Johns, from February to July.

The Caribbean, the Bahamas,

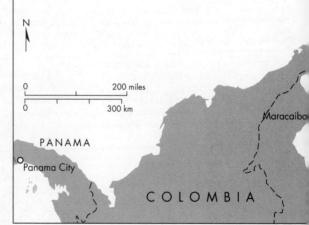

Bermuda

Bermuda

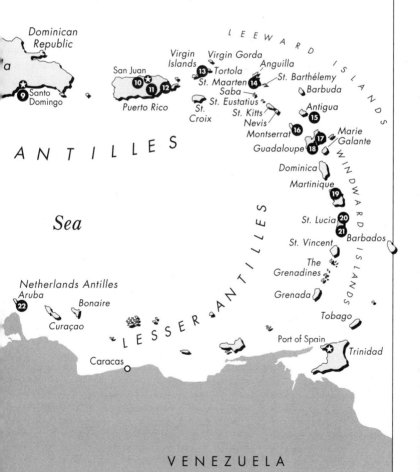

ATLANTIC OCEAN

Dominican
Republic

Virgin
Islands

Virgin Gorda

Anguilla

St. Barthélemy

San Juan

13 Tortola

St. Maarten **14**

Barbuda

9 Santo
Domingo

10
11 **12**

St. Eustatius

Saba

Antigua

Puerto Rico

St.
Croix

St. Kitts

15

Nevis

16

Montserrat

Marie
Galante

17

Guadaloupe

18

A N T I L L E S

Dominica

Martinique

19

Sea

St. Lucia **20**
21

St. Vincent

Barbados

The
Grenadines

L E E W A R D   I S L A N D S

W I N D W A R D   I S L A N D S

Netherlands Antilles

Aruba

Bonaire

Grenada

22

Curaçao

Tobago

L E S S E R   A N T I L L E S

Port of Spain

Trinidad

Caracas

VENEZUELA

Race meetings are scheduled during holiday weeks throughout the year at Cassada Garden Race Track east of St. Johns, on the road to the airport.

Tennis draws pros for weeklong matches in January (men), April (women), and November (mixed doubles). Serious runners can participate in the Antigua Half-Marathon held during the celebration of Independence Day (Nov. 1), which attracts an international field. There is also a fun run during the multiday celebration.

The St. James's beach and marina is equipped for waterskiing, aqua biking, sailing, and snorkeling; it's a perfect place to take the children. Would-be scuba divers can get international certification in just three days. And there's a casino for late-night action.

St. James's Club
Box 63, St. Johns, Antigua
Tel. 809/463–1113, 212/486–2575, or 800/274–0008

Season Year-round.

Accommodations Main buildings offer 105 large rooms with air conditioning, full bath, modern amenities. 73 spacious villas on the beach; hillside homes available.

Rates Package with complimentary sports and exercise programs and 2 meals daily, 8 days, 7 nights, from $750 per person. 3 nights payable in advance. Credit cards: AE, MC, V.

Meal Plans Modified American Plan includes breakfast and dinner daily. Tropical fruits and fresh fish are staples of island dining, abundantly available here. Continental breakfast is standard, with omelets and croissants favored. Dinner is sometimes innovative, as chefs introduce new versions of Caribbean favorites: spinachy callaloo in quiche or blended with crab soup, fricassee of red snapper, lobster with island spices. Ice cream and pies made with soursop fruit are local specialties.

Services and Facilities **Exercise Equipment:** Weight training room with Universal gym, Nautilus-type units, treadmill, stationary bikes. **Services:** Massage, facials, hair and skin care. **Swimming Facilities:** Outdoor pools, ocean beach. **Recreation Facilities:** 7 tennis courts, croquet, water sports, horseback riding; golf course nearby.

In the Area Scuba (extra fee), sailing, sightseeing boats. Nelson's Dockyard and Museum, Clarence House (prime minister's residence), botanical gardens, Dow Hill Museum (Arawak Indian artifacts), University of the West Indies (art exhibits, concerts).

Getting Here *From Coolidge Airport.* By car, the main cross-island road via Nonesuch Bay (25 min). Rental car, taxi available.

Special Notes Programs for children include tennis clinics and swimming instruction.

I Love Myself Wellness Center

Holistic health

Aruba Jane Fonda workout aficionados rejoice: In the middle of a
Palm Beach glitzy casino hotel is an oasis where you can work out to her exercise tapes! (And others, from Raquel Welch to Lillas Yoga, even a self-guided aquaerobics routine for exercise in the swimming pool.) The VCR library complements a circuit of Hydro-Fitness exercise equipment. Geared to injury-proof muscle toning, the program emphasizes wellness and natural healing. But the main attractions are bodywork and skin care: Massage therapy, chiropractic treatments, and facials are available à la carte. A complete salon offers manicures, pedicures, and hairstyling for men and women.

The I Love Myself Wellness Center is privately operated (separate from the hotel) and has local members. Guests from other hotels and cruise-ship passengers can drop in for a day or take advantage of package plans for three to five days.

It's the only place on Aruba where you can go straight from the sauna into placid Caribbean waters and back to the juice bar stocked with protein drinks.

Training programs are planned with the aid of a computerized analysis. Based on data that you feed into a questionnaire, the printout provides guidelines. Standard measurements include your training heart rate, body composition, ideal weight.

Aerobics classes for beginners and advanced workouts are scheduled on certain days. Equally good for fun and fitness are the Caribbean dance classes, three times a week, a mix of exercise and merengue, salsa, soco, and calypso. Classes will be offered on stress management for executives, holistic wellness, and relaxation. Members of the staff have developed sunburn-prevention therapy, a treatment with the aloe plant that grows wild along the island roads.

Arubans are naturally friendly and welcome visitors with suggestions for hiking, water sports, and golf. Drive to the old capital, San Nicolas, to play the oiled-sand links of the Aruba Golf Club. Along the way, stop at the fish market in Savaneta, the island's first settlement, and later dine on Dutch Creole dishes at the Brisas del Mar restaurant. Charlie's Bar, a tavern on Main Street in San Nicolas, provides local color.

Beaches are public throughout the island. Hike from the natural bridge (carved by the sea), on the rugged coast near Boca Prins, to Andicouri for a romantic picnic on a secluded beach surrounded by a coconut plantation.

Aruba's volcanic origins are revealed at Casi Bari, a rock garden of giants, and at tall, unusual rock formations called *Ayo*. Hikers can enjoy panoramic, breezy views from paths cut into the rock.

I Love Myself Wellness Center
King Holiday Inn
230 L. G. Smith Blvd. Box 408, Aruba
Tel. 599/23600 or 800/465–4329 (Spa: 599/34870)

Administration Manager, Constance Talisesky

Season Year-round.

Accommodations Modern twin towers with 390 rooms and suites recently refurbished, spacious, with balcony and full modern bath, queensize beds. Air conditioned, TV, telephone, maid service.

Rates $75–$110 double occupancy, $70–$105 single. Credit card confirmation. Credit cards: AE, CB, DC, MC, V.

Meal Plans New heart-healthy options are being added to main dining room menu. No special meal plan is available. Vegetarian dishes, fruit salad, grilled fish among daily selections. Empress of China restaurant serves stir-fried specialties to order. Snack bar in health spa has herbal teas, protein drinks, fruit.

Services and Facilities **Exercise Equipment:** 8 Hydro-Fitness pneumatic muscle toning units. **Services:** Massage (myotherapy, shiatsu, acupressure, reflexology), chiropractic therapy, sunburn treatment, skin care, facials. Beauty salon for hairstyling, manicures, pedicures. **Swimming Facilities:** Outdoor pool, ocean beach. **Recreation Facilities:** 4 tennis courts, water sports. **Evening Programs:** Carnival costume show and barbecue; casino.

In the Area Boats to underwater gardens; scuba and snorkeling. Marlab marine biology tour (3 hr) booked through DePalm Tours. Trail riding at Rancho El Paso (tel. 23310). Boca Prins (sand dunes, secluded beach), Chapel of Alto Vista (1750), Fort Zoutman (history museum) and Olde School Straat (colonial architecture) in Oranjestad, DePalm Island (recreation), Santa Anna Church (carved altar) in Noord, Cas di Cultura (concerts, art exhibits).

Getting Here *From airport.* By car, coastal road to L. G. Smith Blvd. (20 min). Bus, taxi, rental car, moped available.

Special Notes Ground-floor accommodations and elevators for the disabled. Children can enjoy beach play equipment area and body toning instruction with Hydro-Fitness equipment. Children under 12 stay with parents free. No smoking in spa.

Sivananda Ashram Yoga Retreat

Spiritual awareness

The Bahamas
Paradise Island,
Nassau

A few steps from one of the best-known beaches in the Bahamas, secluded in a grove of pines and palm trees, is a unique combination of spiritual retreat and tropical holiday. Based on the teachings of Swami Vishnu Devananda, the yogic discipline and vegetarian diet at the Sivananda Ashram Yoga Retreat are identical to Sivananda ashrams in Canada, New York, and California, but the sunny climate and beach make this one of the best bargains anywhere.

The regimen is intensive; attendance at classes and meditations is mandatory for all guests. Mornings begin at 6 with a session of yogic exercises, or *asanas*, to stretch and invigorate the body. Brunch is served at 10, then you are free to enjoy the beach or a relaxing massage until the 4 PM yoga session.

The retreat attracts an international eclectic group of vacationers and yoga disciples. New students are given personal coaching in the 12 basic asanas, from headstands to spinal twists. Children are encouraged to join in.

Although there are glitzy hotels and casinos a short walk away, the environment here is totally suffused with a mystical quality—partly due to the quaint appearance of the buildings, some on stilts and topped with fake domes, some on houseboats. The main house, once the retreat of a wealthy family and leased since 1967 to the Sivananda group in appreciation for healing services, might have sunk into the sand long ago without the volunteer labor of the retreat members. Plans for additional improvements in the wooden structures call for modest comfort in the form of new beds. Many guests prefer to bring their own tent and camp among the tropical shrubbery. Arrival can be any day; average stay is two weeks.

The retreat's informal atmosphere sharply contrasts with the structured schedule of classes. Based on five principles for a long and healthy life, the program focuses on proper exercise, breathing, diet, relaxation, and meditation techniques. The regimen demands total self-discipline and is designed to develop a better understanding of the mind-body connection.

The daily routine is gentle and, once you get accustomed to rising at 5:30 AM, can be quite stimulating. In a sense, it is preventive medicine, a way of warding off psychological and physical problems through rigorous training. People come here to recuperate from job burnout or to heal after surgery.

To provide the proper nutritional balance, there is an organic garden in which herbs and vegetables are grown. Coconuts come gratis from the palm trees that shelter the 4½-acre compound. For snacks and sweets, a canteen is tucked into a building near the communal laundry and shower facilities. The retreat is a quiet place, far removed from the resort life that surrounds its gardens.

Sivananda Ashram Yoga Retreat
Box N7550, Paradise Island, Nassau, Bahamas
Tel. 809/362-2902

Administration Program director, Swami Shanmug Ananda

Season Year-round.

Accommodations Wooden huts on the beach, dormitory rooms, and cottages provide 103 beds. Furnished with 2–6 beds and table; linens and towels provided. Communal shower and toilet facilities, laundry equipment. Tent space: 50 sites.

Rates $40–$55 daily, rooms shared by 2–6 persons. Beachfront meditation huts are preferred location. Tent space $30 per night. $200 advance payment. Credit cards: MC, V.

Meal Plans The lacto-vegetarian diet includes midmorning meal of wholegrain cereal, fresh fruit, homemade yogurt and wheat bread. Dinner dishes include stir-fried tofu and rice, steamed vegetables, green salad. No fish, meat, fowl, eggs, coffee are served.

Services and Facilities **Services:** Massage (shiatsu, reflexology), personal counseling. **Swimming Facilities:** Ocean beach. **Recreation Facilities:** Tennis court, volleyball, walks. **Evening Programs:** Workshops in Hindu culture, philosophy. Concerts.

In the Area   Boat trips; botanical gardens, Colonial and Victorian architecture.

Getting Here   *From Nassau airport.* Shared taxi van (fixed fee) to Mermaid Marina, Bay, and Deveaux Sts. Shuttle service by Ashram boat operates on daily schedule.

Special Notes   Yoga training for children. No smoking on premises. Remember to bring beach towel, blankets during winter months.

The Royal Bahamian Hotel & Villas

Luxury pampering
Non-program resort facilities

The Bahamas   This grand manor, reeking of Colonial decadence, is one of the
Cable Beach,   best little spas in the Bahamas. Created as part of a $9 million
Nassau   renovation in 1985, the Royal Bahamian Hotel & Villas facilities include mud baths and a large whirlpool, sauna and steam rooms, and an aerobics studio with exercise equipment.

The resort was originally a private reserve for the rich and titled and is still an oasis for those who seek peace and quiet. A modest strip of powdery sand, manicured gardens abloom with bougainvillea, and a parlor where tea is served with cucumber sandwiches are among the attractions enjoyed by its international clientele. Formerly a Wyndham resort, the Royal Bahamian is now managed by Le Meridien.

Tarted up but showing its age, the six-story hotel offers more spacious rooms than any of the fancier neighbors down the road. And for those with a taste for privacy (and the means) there are 10 villas, all pink with sugar-white roofs. Three are individual townhouses—each boasting three bedrooms, a private pool, sun room, and a whirlpool in the master suite.

The spa can be reached by elevator in the main building or by a private entrance alongside the swimming pool terrace. Chrome and mirrors add a sleek, modern look to the smallish spaces where you can work out at leisure or book private treatments. Services are offered à la carte, billed to your account, or payable with credit card.

Try a luxurious mud bath for the ultimate in body-stimulating treatments. The ancient therapy of soaking in herbs and algae has been re-created here with a mixture of peat mud taken from deposits in the Neydharting Valley Basin of northern Austria. The therapeutic effect soothes nerves, eliminates sleeplessness, improves circulation, and rejuvenates the skin.

Soaking in the mud bath is like stepping into a tub of yogurt. Dark in color—almost black—the formula leaves no stain while opening and closing the pores. Mixed with tap water, the odorless liquid easily showers off, leaving a visible sheen on the skin.

The mud treatment should be followed with a brief nap. An early dinner and full night's rest enhance the effect, as the body reacts to the healing substances absorbed during the bath.

The physiotherapy specialist Charles Bowleg is both manager and head masseur; a graduate of Dr. Swanson's School of Swedish Massage in Chicago, he returned to the Bahamas more than 30 years ago to work on the muscles of such notables as the Duke of Windsor, the prime minister of the Bahamas, and the screen star Sidney Poitier.

The facilities are designed to pamper and relax rather than give a serious workout. Outside guests can drop in for a day by making advance reservations for treatments. With one of the classiest restaurants on the island, the spa is the kind of place that makes you yearn for an extra day in which to do nothing.

For more active pursuits, try the sports center at the Cable Beach Hotel and Casino complex. Just a few minutes' walk from the Royal Bahamian, the indoor, air-conditioned facilities include squash and racquetball/handball courts. Nearby is a championship 18-hole (par 72) golf course. Guests at both hotels get special rates.

The Royal Bahamian Hotel & Villas
Box N 10422, Cable Beach, Nassau, Bahamas
Tel. 809/327–6400 or 800/543–4300
Telex 20317

Administration	Physiotherapy director, Charles Bowleg
Season	Year-round.
Accommodations	Beachfront main building has 145 rooms; villas and townhouses offer suites with 25 bedrooms. Ocean view, twin queen-size beds, dressing room, twin baths with shower or bathtub, balcony. Cable TV, air conditioning, bathrobes.
Rates	In winter, $145–$215 daily, single or double occupancy. Tariffs for suites/townhouses depend on length of stay and include butler or maid service. First-night confirmation by credit card. Credit cards: AE, DC, MC, V.
Meal Plans	Buffet breakfast and dinner in Cafe Royale, dinner only (jacket and tie required) in Baccarat pavilion. Dinner offers innovative crossovers of Continental and island fare: Gâteau de Conch et Saint-Jacques au Safron is a mousse of Bahamian conch and scallops baked in delicate saffron sauce. Other specialties include grouper baked in pastry shell with saboyan sauce and rack of lamb dusted with herbs, roasted and broiled.
Services and Facilities	**Exercise Equipment:** Universal weight system (6 stations), stationary bikes, treadmill. **Services:** Swedish massage, mud bath, facial, manicure, pedicure, waxing. **Swimming Facilities:** Outdoor freshwater pool, ocean beach. **Recreation Facilities:** 2 tennis courts, chess tables. Nearby bicycle rental, golf course, indoor sports center. **Evening Programs:** Casino and theater nearby, with complimentary transportation.
In the Area	Island tours, interisland flights, charter boats for fishing and scuba; Seafloor Aquarium (performing dolphins and sea lions), Fort Charlotte, botanic garden, Adastra Gardens (performing flamingos), Junkanoo Art Gallery.
Getting Here	*From airport.* By car, coastal road (10 min). Jitney minibus for trips into town. Taxi, rental car available.
Special Notes	Elevator to all floors of main building. No smoking in spa or designated dining areas.

Sonesta Beach Hotel & Spa

Luxury pampering
Weight management
Non-program resort facilities

Bermuda
Southampton

Weight maintenance is the principle at the Sonesta Beach Hotel & Spa. You can drop in between business meetings or after a round of golf or plan a comprehensive schedule of treatments and exercise classes for three to seven days. Package plans can begin any day of the week.

The flexibility of planning your own program is a plus, but only if you are prepared to work with the spa staff. They will do a preliminary fitness assessment; don't expect counseling. The emphasis is on relaxation and beauty treatments, not strenuous exercise. Even the diet plan is optional.

Aerobics are moderate or vigorous, plotted over 30- or 40-minute periods, alternating active and passive exercise with relaxing stretches. You can select from early morning walks (moderate), circuit training (vigorous), workouts in the water, and yoga. And don't miss the loofah body scrub.

If you simply want to be pampered and left alone to swim or shop, there is a three-day "spa refresher break." For women who want to learn nutrition, exercise, and beauty skills, an exclusive eight-day program is offered. Spouses get a discount when they aren't participating in a spa program.

Variety makes the options attractive. For a person who wants to try many different activities and treatments, there are dance exercise routines and easy aerobics, hiking and walking on the beach, and clinics devoted to awareness of proper posture for exercise and running. All can be included in a spa package, or you can simply pay a daily facility charge ($15) and use the whirlpool baths, Finnish sauna, Turkish steam bath, and Universal equipment room.

Separate facilities for men and women offer privacy when you want to soak and relax. Workout clothing is provided daily: a leotard, warm-up suit, gym shorts, shirt, robe, and slippers.

Sonesta Beach Hotel & Spa
Southampton, Bermuda
Tel. 809/298–8122 or 800/343–7170
Deepdene Spas Ltd.
Flatts Village, Bermuda
Tel. 809/292–8570
Telex 380 3462

Administration Manager, Michael J. Ternent

Season Year-round.

Accommodations 25-acre peninsula setting. 6-story hotel and Bay Wing suites with 403 guest rooms, ocean or bay view. Spacious split-level units have sitting area and dressing room, full bath, modern rattan furniture, floor-to-ceiling windows, balcony or patio (all rooms). Queen- or king-size beds, full carpeting, air conditioning, color TV, telephone.

Rates 3-night Spa Refresher package $405–$525 per person, double occupancy; $540–$780 single. Minivacation 7-day plan from $1,001 per person, double occupancy; $1,421 single. Additional options: 7-day concentrated program and 8-day women-only program up to $2,597 single, $1,792 double. Two-night payment at booking. Credit cards: AE, DC, MC, V.

Meal Plans Breakfast and dinner daily included in Refresher and Mini vacation plans, 3 meals daily in concentrated programs. Optional diet plan, 800–1,000 calories per day, can be developed by staff nutritionist after a personal consultation. Spa meals in separate section of the main dining room. Breakfast may be a whole-grain cereal with fruit; lunch, a garden salad or cold seafood platter. Dinner entrees include grilled swordfish, vegetarian lasagna, and skewers of vegetables broiled with sea scallops. 2 juice breaks are included in the daily program.

Services and Facilities **Exercise Equipment:** Universal weight training gym (8 stations), aerobicycle, computerized bicycle, Total Hip machine. **Services:** Massage (Swedish, aromatherapy, reflexology, G-5 mechanical), facials for men and women, loofah body scrub, herbal wrap, manicure, pedicure, cellulite control treatments, European facial treatments. Hairstyling and beauty-salon services. Consultation on fitness, nutrition, and makeup; skin-fold test, facial skin analysis. Passive reducing treatments with Vivatone; Therabath treatments for hands and feet; depilatory treatments. **Swimming Facilities:** Outdoor fresh water pool, indoor pool, 3 ocean beaches. **Recreation Facilities:** 6 lighted tennis courts, volleyball, badminton, croquet, shuffleboard, table tennis. Golf and bicycle rental nearby. Water sports include helmet and scuba diving, windsurfing. Horseback riding available at Spicelands Riding Centre, Warwick. **Evening Programs:** Resort entertainment.

In the Area Island tours; St. George's (replica of colonists' ship *Deliverance*), Blue Grotto (dolphin show), Verdmont House (Georgian antiques), Hamilton (shopping, museums), Maritime Museum (ship replicas).

Getting Here *From airport.* By taxi, North Shore Rd. to South Rd. (45 min). Public bus for trips to town. Frequent ferry service to points on the island. Moped available.

Special Notes Play area in gardens for children; under 18 not permitted in spa. No smoking in spa or designated sections of the dining room.

The Jaragua Resort

Luxury Pampering

Dominican Republic *Santo Domingo* An impressive new entry in the Caribbean casino-cum-spa scene is the Jaragua Resort in the center of the hemisphere's oldest capital city. A few minutes' drive from the flashy ocean boulevard is the colonial capital founded by Bartholomew Columbus, the brother of the Discoverer. Vacationers can combine culture and fitness with casino action.

The new and the old meet on Avenida George Washington, a lively strip of hotels, restaurants, and shops fronting the ocean. There is no beach here, but spa goers hardly notice; with an oversize swimming pool surrounded by tropical gardens, Scandinavian saunas, Turkish steam bath, Roman whirlpool, and cold plunge, the resort complex has an ample supply of water sports. Daily beach trips are complimentary.

The freestanding fitness facility is a world unto itself. All marble and glass, it is an oasis of aerobics and bodywork. You work out on the latest in exercise equipment or join a calisthenics class. Exercise is scheduled in the Olympic-size swimming pool, as well as the air-conditioned gym.

Pampering services come in several packages or à la carte. The staff has been trained by a consultant well known at Florida's Palm-Aire resort, and you can get a herbal wrap, a body scrub, a facial, or a massage. Grandly titled the European Spa, the facilities include no thalassotherapy tubs or seawater treatments, but you may bliss out in a private Jacuzzi, then get a surge of energy from the cold plunge.

The daily entrance fee of $10 is waived when you book a Jaragua Energizer, with massage, for $25 or a 4-day/3-night Tropical Tone-Up. With this come robe and slippers, and snacks of fresh fruit and juices throughout the day.

Secluded on 14½ palm-fringed acres, the resort has a tennis stadium with four clay courts and spectator seating. During the day this facility can be used by spa guests free of charge. From your room it's a pleasant walk or jog along a specially designed track through the garden and alongside the lagoon to the spa.

The Jaragua Resort

367 George Washington Ave., Santo Domingo
Tel. 809/686-2222 or 800/331-3642
Telex 3460758 TRANSAM

Administration Manager, Anthony Bayarri

Season Year-round.

Accommodations New 10-story Jaragua Tower and an older 2-level wing of garden suites provide 355 luxury rooms. 6 suites with butler, marble baths. All rooms with modern rattan furniture, large bath with magnified makeup mirror, hair dryer. Air conditioned, carpeted; 3 telephones with direct dial, color cable TV, decorative works by Dominican artists.

Rates Daily $65–$110, single or double occupancy. 3-night Jaragua Energizer package $240–$375.50 single, $143–$210 per person double occupancy; additional options with a tone-up package are $83. 8-day/7-night Tone-Up $583–$898 single; $355.50–$513 per person, double. Taxes and service charge are added. Payment for 1 night at time of booking. Credit cards: AE, CB, DC, MC, V.

Meal Plans No diet plan available. Modified American Plan (2 meals) $35 daily, offers a choice of four restaurants: Latin American Cafe for meats char-broiled, grilled, or cooked on a spit; Oriental Cafe for stir-fry specialties; fresh homemade pasta in the Italian Cafe; New York deli.

Services and Facilities **Exercise Equipment:** Nautilus gym (10 stations), stationary bicycles, treadmills, rowing machine, free weights. **Services:** Swedish massage, loofah body scrub, herbal wrap, facial. Fitness evaluation. Beauty salon for hair, skin, and nail care. **Swimming Facilities:** Olympic-size outdoor pool. **Recreation Facilities:** 4 lighted tennis courts, jogging track; golf nearby. **Evening Programs:** Casino theater; National Theater for concerts and opera.

In the Area Daily beach trip (complimentary), walking tour of the colonial area, full-day tour to Casa de Campo and Altos de Chavon (golf, polo, fishing; fantasy architecture, crafts center). Cathedral of Santa Maria la Menor (oldest in the Hemisphere, Columbus monument), Museum of the Royal Houses in the colonial quarter; Gallery of Modern Art and Natural History Museum downtown; National Botanical Gardens (train ride) in northern section of the city; Altos de Chavon (artisans, museum of Taino Indian artifacts) near La Romana. Baseball (Oct.–Feb.), Merengue Festival (July), Polo (Casa de Campo).

Getting Here *From airport.* By taxi (25 min). Public bus, rental car available.

Special Notes Elevators and ramps to all levels for the disabled. No smoking in the spa.

Centre Thermal Harry Hamousin

Taking the waters
Non-program resort facilities

Guadeloupe Christopher Columbus saw the volcano La Soufrière erupting
Saint-Claude when he stepped ashore November 4, 1493, at Sainte-Marie, a fishing village along the road to the island's present-day capital, Basse-Terre. The native Caribs were not hospitable to the Discoverer. All that's left of that time are primitive drawings scratched into black rocks at Trois-Rivières, where the road branches toward a nature preserve around La Soufrière.

The new discovery is Centre Thermal Harry Hamousin, a therapy center that taps the natural healing power of the mineral springs. French hydrotherapy equipment and therapists trained at leading French spas provide treatments for rheumatism, asthma, and dermatology problems. The classic "cure" has come to the Caribbean.

As an overseas department of France (not a colony or an independent country), Guadeloupe offers its citizens all the benefits of the mother country, including health coverage for the cost of spa therapy. Thus the Centre Thermal Harry Hamousin, a private institution, enjoys a steady stream of visitors from Europe and other islands in the French Antilles. Opened in 1978 with state-of-the-art facilities, the center now welcomes any visitors needing massage or special therapy.

Physical training to aid recovery from injuries includes exercise in shallow pools of mineral water and on special equipment in the gymnasium. Respiratory problems are treated with aerosol-like inhalations of mineral water. There are douches with high-powered jets of water and sulfur baths.

The thermal center is open every morning except Sunday and accepts reservations for one-time treatments. Serious problems require consultation with a doctor at the nearby clinic Les Eaux Vives. Arrangements can be made by your hotel or directly with the clinic, and medical records should be brought along for the interview with *le médecin thermal*. Several doctors speak English if your French isn't sufficient.

Hotel arrangements are not provided by the center. One of the most interesting places to stay is the Hotel Bleus de la Soufrière. Located at the base of the volcano, it reflects the old-world charm of the banana plantations that cover nearby fields. Once a government-owned *relais*, or country inn, the hotel is now under private management. The dining room is popular with local families and businessmen who escape from the city for lunch.

The attractions of the island include the Nature Park; the spectacular three-tiered Carbet Falls near Capesterre, reached by a moderately difficult hike that starts at the end of Habituée Road; the Grand Etang (Great Pond), surrounded by luxuriant vegetation; and La Grivelière, an atmospheric old coffee plantation near Vieux Habitants.

Guadeloupe cuisine is a fascinating mixture of Gallic and African flavors. Among the best places to sample this spicy food is La Canne a Sucre (tel. 83–58–48), near the fashionable Point-à-Pitre shops, and La Plantation (tel. 90–84–83), overlooking the marina at Bas du Fort. Wherever you go on this butterfly-shaped island there are wonderful native cooks offering inexpensive homemade meals.

On market days the stalls are filled with herb sellers hawking natural seasonings and medicines: *matriquin*, Marie-Perrine, *zhèbe-gras*, *fleupapillon*, *bois-de l'homme*, *bonnet-carré*, and the like. All the tastes and stimulations of the old Carib Indian flavorings and remedies are still on sale, alongside modern pharmacies and boutiques laden with Parisian fashions.

Centre Thermal Harry Hamousin
97120 Saint-Claude, Guadeloupe
Tel. 590/80–13–23
Hotel Bleus de la Soufrière
97120 Saint-Claude, Guadeloupe
Tel. 590/80–01–27

Administration Director, Dr. Guy Beaubois

Season Year-round.

Accommodations 22-room plantation great house decorated with fine antiques. Spacious and airy rooms have no air conditioning, telephone, or TV. All have private bath.

Rates In winter, daily tariff is 300–500 French francs, single or double occupancy. Meals à la carte. 1 night advance payment. Credit cards: AE.

Meal Plans No diet plan available. Creole cooking specialties include spicy fritters, *accras de morue* (salt cod; stuffed land crab, called crabs *farcis;* goat stew; classic *boudin* sausage).

Services and Facilities **Exercise Equipment:** Weight training units, treadmills. **Services:** Massage, underwater massage, steam cabinet, loofah body scrub, Scotch douche, skin peeling, acupuncture, physical therapy. **Swimming Facilities:** Outdoor pool. **Spa Facilities:** Therapy pool, hydrotherapy tubs. **Recreation Facilities:** Hiking, nearby beaches.

In the Area Ferry to Les Saintes (natural bathing), organized hiking with Friends of the Nature Park, scuba at Club Med.; Basse-Terre gardens and Prefecture, botanical garden and zoo, Fête des Cuisinères (mid-Aug.), Neuf Château (experimental orchard).

Getting Here *From airport.* By car, coastal road to Trois Rivières, Allée Dumanoir, Route de la Traversée (50 min). Rental car, taxi, public bus available.

Special Notes No smoking in the center. Remember to bring passport and medical certificate.

Hotel PLM Azur-Marissol

Luxury pampering

Guadeloupe French and American fitness regimes merge at the large and
Gosier popular Hotel PLM Azur-Marissol beach resort. Set in a tropical garden perfumed by blossoms, the facilities include a "hammam" steam room and private rooms for massage and thalassotherapy. Light gymnastics on the beach and stretching exercises in the swimming pool are offered at no extra charge for all guests.

The Gym Tropique is open daily, except Sunday, 8 AM–8 PM. There is a coed steam room, aerobics studio, and hydrotherapy tubs but no exercise equipment.

European spa treatments included in the week-long fitness package are a plus: underwater massage, steam baths, a facial, and whirlpool treatment with seaweed and oils. Classes are scheduled for yoga and aerobics, all optional.

The program, which can begin any day of the week, includes group outings for hikes in the Parc Natural. Most of the guests are French, with an interesting mix of Canadians and Americans. Designed for fun and fitness, the program rejuvenates strung-out bodies and souls with a blend of Gallic style and disco routines.

Hotel PLM Azur-Marissol
Bas-du-Fort, 97190 Gosier, Guadeloupe
Tel. 590/908444 or 800/223–9862 (800/255–3393 in Canada)
Telex 91950 GL, Fax 590/908332

Administration Manager, Nicole Duval

Season Year-round.

Accommodations 200 air-conditioned rooms (50 bungalows) with terrace or loggia. Modern furniture accented with island fabrics and prints. All rooms have private bath, radio, direct-dial telephone. Superior rooms have color TV.

Rates 7-night package $807 per person double occupancy, $1,005 single. 25% payment at time of booking. Credit cards: AE, DC, MC, V.

Meal Plans Fitness package includes breakfast and dinner. Breakfast buffet includes yogurt, croissants, granola, fresh fruit. Selections from the dinner menu include steamed vegetables, fresh grilled fish, salads. Grilled specialties: veal scallops, entrecote steak, seafood brochette.

Services and Facilities

Services: Massage, body wrap with seaweed, underwater massage, whirlpool bath with seaweed, skin and nail care. **Swimming Facilities:** Outdoor freshwater pool, ocean beach. **Recreation Facilities:** Tennis, hiking, water sports.

In the Area

Scuba, mountain hiking; thermal mineral-water treatments at Centre Harry Hamousin, Nature Park, La Soufrière (volcano).

Getting Here

From airport. Complimentary transfers on arrival and departure. Taxi, rental car available.

Special Notes

No smoking in fitness center.

Charlie's Spa at the Sans Souci

Luxury pampering

Jamaica
Ocho Rios

Charlie's Spa takes a fresh approach to island holidays. More hedonistic than health-oriented, the resort atmosphere up on the hill complements vigorous workouts on the beach. It's a pleasant combination if you're interested in toning up or taking off a few pounds.

With the sea on one side and a cascade of mineral water on the other, it provides instant stress reduction. The waters, however, are not used for therapy or beauty treatments; you can soak or swim at leisure, and you may join an exercise class in the pool.

Long noted as a luxurious hideaway, Sans Souci came under new management a few years ago and revamped the facilities—and its image. Aided by experts from the Phoenix Fitness Center in Houston, new cottages and an open-air aerobics pavilion were designed to blend with the old-world ambience of the hotel. Introduced for the first time in the Caribbean were beauty treatments and a nutritious diet that work together. The result is a program that offers more than the sum of its parts.

Begin with a fast-paced walk through the terraced gardens and along the curve of beach where tennis courts and water sports await your pleasure. After Blue Mountain coffee, freshly squeezed orange juice, and a muffin or banana porridge, you have a wide variety of options to fill your day—within the program at Charlie's Spa or on your own. Anyone staying at the resort can join in the group activities and take treatments à la carte.

Appointments are scheduled in the tiny spa office alongside a pool that's home to mascot Charlie, a huge sea turtle who thrives in the mineral water. The Hideaway is a charming gazebo on the rocks, just big enough for a private massage. Facials and other treatments are given inside a tiny wooden cottage.

The grotto conceals a dry sauna next to steps entering the sea. The shallow water here is a mix of saltiness and refreshingly cool mineral water from the springs. It's ideal for washing off oils and salts used for body scrubs (depending on your skin type, it can be aloe, peppermint, or coconut, plus cornmeal).

Sybarites can enjoy a secluded soak, free of charge, by climbing down a wooden ladder at a second grotto where the springwater seeps into a sand-bottom pool; or sunbathing on an upper-floor terrace among the treetops.

Charlie's Spa at the Sans Souci
Box 103, Ocho Rios, Jamaica
Tel. 809/974–2353 or 800/237–3237
Telex 7496

Administration	General manager, Werner Dietel; fitness director, Susan Brewer
Season	Year-round.
Accommodations	72 suites and rooms in villa-style buildings overlooking gardens and the sea. All are air conditioned, with private balcony. Main building nearby houses the Casanova Restaurant and bar/lounge (pianist nightly).
Rates	Charlie's Spa Program, 7 days/6 nights, $1,600–$1,733 per person double occupancy; other all-inclusive plans available mid-Apr.–mid-Dec. Tax and service charge added to accounts. 3-night deposit due within 2 weeks after reservation; cancellation must be received 30 days prior to scheduled arrival to avoid charges. Credit cards: AE, V, MC.
Meal Plans	Breakfast and lunch are specially planned or ordered from regular menu. Dinner in main dining room or under the stars features fresh local seafood, pasta, vegetarian dishes.
Services and Facilities	**Exercise Equipment:** 2 Monark bikes, free weights, 4-station Universal unit on the beach beneath the aerobics studio. **Swimming Facilities:** Two pools and a private beach. **Spa Facilities:** Mineral springwater swimming and soaking pools. **Recreation Facilities:** Guest membership at Upton Country Club (18-hole golf course) and St. Ann Polo Club; horseback riding at Chukka Cove Farm; tennis and instruction on Sans Souci's 4 courts (2 lighted); croquet lawn; snorkeling and scuba equipment. **Evening Programs:** Folkloric groups, combo for dancing on terrace.
In the Area	Tour operators in Ocho Rios offer group and private car trips to area attractions. The Gardens of Cariñosa cover 20 acres of hillside overlooking Ocho Rios; guided tours are included with the admission fee. 14 waterfalls, aquarium, walk-through aviary (200 tropical birds), open-air restaurant serving traditional Jamaican food for lunch and dinner. Horses are available for trail rides at Prospect Plantation.
Getting Here	*From Montego Bay Airport.* Transfers to and from (about 2 hr) are included in some package plans. Air Jamaica has frequent nonstop flights from U.S. cities and Canada. Taxi or limousine available at all times.
Special Notes	For the disabled, elevator connects guest rooms with spa facilities on the beach. (Hillside location of the hotel requires considerable stair climbing.)

Chukka Cove

Sports conditioning

Jamaica	More than horseback riding, a holiday at Chukka Cove intro-
Ocho Rios	duces you to parts of Jamaican life rarely glimpsed or experienced by tourists: For non-riders (and on non-riding Wednesdays), a full range of resort activity is available, includ-

ing the spa at nearby Sans Souci; for budding equestrians, there is expert training by a gentle and patient staff of instructors and grooms.

The rides, however—through working plantations, into mountain villages, and along coral cliffs at the beaches—are the focus of an all-inclusive one-week program. Visitors may book horses by the hour or by the day(s). There are polo ponies and horses for jumping and dressage—35 in all—with full English tack. Guided rides, clinics, and individual instruction are scheduled daily.

Staying overnight in a historic home is the highlight of a two-day trail ride at midweek. Lilyfield, a restored 18th-century great house currently occupied by a former Jamaican minister of culture, provides gracious hospitality. This six-hour ride through the mountainous interior of the island features spectacular views of the coast, a picnic stop at a waterfall, and hiking on the coffee plantation. Guests who prefer to make the trip by car arrive with the luggage, if space is available.

Ensconced in your private villa at Chukka Cove, with cook and staff to take care of personal needs and diet, you will find that the exhilaration of riding gives way to restful relaxation. Six identical villas share the compound and swimming pool, and each villa has a private terrace and fully stocked bar. A ceiling fan cools and keeps mosquitoes at bay.

Chukka Cove

Chukka Cove Farm Ltd.
Box 160, Ocho Rios, Jamaica
Tel. 809/974–2593 or 800/223–7296
(Reservations) Enid Lee, 7028 N.W. 169th St., Hialeah, FL 33015.

Administration	Manager, Danny Melville; program director, Yvonne Whittingham
Season	Year-round.
Accommodations	Villas with 2 bedrooms and open veranda, private dining room on ground floor; ceiling fans.
Rates	1-week all-inclusive program $1,125 per person double occupancy; for polo clinic, $1,500 per person. Nonrider companions $800 per week. 25% advance payment. Maximum of 6 rider participants. 15% tax and service added. No credit cards.
Meal Plans	Breakfast and dinner prepared by your cook in villa; lunches are mostly picnics. 1 night out for lobster dinner.
Services and Facilities	**Services:** Beginner and intermediate level clinics in dressage, show jumping, cross-country riding; polo clinic. **Swimming Facilities:** Private cove for ocean swimming and snorkeling (equipment provided); freshwater pool for laps. **Spa Facilities:** Spa treatments at Sans Souci can be reserved; mineral springwater-filled soaking pool. **Recreation Facilities:** Jogging and countryside hiking, 18-hole golf course in nearby Runaway Bay. All water sports can be arranged in Ocho Rios (20 min drive). **Evening Programs:** Starlit barbecues, reggae dancing. **Polo Matches:** Chukka Cove's arena features international teams throughout season. Local riders compete Sat. afternoon at nearby Drax Hall.

In the Area Excursions: Half-day tour of Ocho Rios includes admission to Dunn's River Falls, rock climbing, dinner show at Little Pub.

Getting Here *From Montego Bay International Airport.* Transportation to and from provided. Taxi, rental car available.

Special Notes Horseback riders should remember to bring high boots, caps, and plenty of sunblock (#15 or stronger).

Jamaican Mineral Springs

Taking the waters

Jamaica
Milk River and Bath

Getting off the beaten track is easy, but you need a car to explore some of the most scenic areas of the hilly island of Jamaica. In addition to breathtaking vistas there are botanical gardens, a bird sanctuary, and two spas built around mineral springs that have been attracting cure seekers for nearly two centuries.

Legend holds that an African slave, wounded in an uprising, was healed by bathing in pools of water fed by hot springs located high in the lush valleys between Kingston and Port Antonio. English plantation owners seeking respite from the coastal heat spread the word. By the beginning of the 18th century there was a spa hotel, church, and botanical garden for cultivation of medicinal herbs in the town of Bath. What remains today is primitive, nothing like its Georgian namesake in England. The waters, however, still gush forth in a setting of tropical splendor enjoyed by hill people and an occasional visitor.

From the town, a narrow road cuts through fern gulleys alongside the Sulphur River to reach Bath Fountain Hotel. Cut into rocks beneath the hotel are private chambers where you can soak in the sulfurous warm water. European spa experts have confirmed high levels of radioactivity, equal to the best springs on the continent.

The hotel's 19 guest rooms are airy, simply furnished. Meals are prepared to order in the public dining room (no credit cards). *Bath Fountain Hotel, Bath, St. Thomas Parish. Rooms cost $20 per night, without private bath.*

West of Kingston's high-rise government center, past agricultural and industrial developments, is the former capital city, Spanish Town, and from there you can reach the Milk River spa in about two hours. Stop to admire the main square, surrounded by Georgian buildings that date from 1762. One now houses the Jamaican People's Museum of Craft and Technology. A classical statue of Admiral George Rodney commemorates his 1792 naval victory over the French that saved the British colony.

Continuing westward on Route B12 past the market town of May Pen, you reach the Milk River near a crossroads called Toll Gate. Built on a hillside, the spa hotel has private cubicles hewn from stone that are filled directly from the springs. Here, too, an analysis of the water in 1952 confirmed a high degree of radioactivity and minerals, similar to that of the best European spa waters.

Although there are no special treatments or exercise equipment, the hotel has a large outdoor swimming pool filled with the cool mineral water. Ocean beaches and citrus groves are a few miles away. Trout Hall, which produces *ugli* fruit, can be visited on request.

Most of the guests at Milk River come to soak three times a day, reserving cubicles with the receptionist. Bottles of mineral water are on the tables in the dining room. The hotel has seen better days (and may again); the 24 guest rooms are simple, clean and inexpensive, with two meals included in the daily tariff.

Milk River Spa and Hotel
Middlesex, Jamaica
Tel. 809/924–9544

Rates Double room with private bath $39 per person, single room with private bath $23.64. Tax and service charge added. No credit cards.

Lady Diane Hotel

Holistic health
Stress control

Jamaica An informal blend of yoga, pampering, and macrobiotic meals
Montego Bay is Lady Diane's formula for stress reduction. Located a few steps from a placid beach, far from the frenetic tourist areas of Montego Bay, this quiet little hotel offers a taste of Jamaica the way it used to be.

Color and light set the mood for relaxation in the main house. The furniture might have come from a plantation home in the hills: simple wooden cabinets, straw carpets, and wicker chairs. The owners, Beva and Richard Cherkiss, created and manage the program for people like themselves who want to enjoy island life without frills.

Nothing is programmed except for twice-daily sessions of yoga and meditation in an open-air garden pavilion. Long walks on the beach, swimming, perhaps a volleyball game, are the main forms of recreation.

Naturalness comes through most appealingly in the food served at large communal tables in a dining room cooled by sea breezes. Jamaicans use the island's vast bounty of tropical fruits and vegetables with ingenious variety; large dishes of legumes and rice are served family-style; dolphin or snapper are bought directly from the fishermen. Springwater is used for cooking and drinking.

Total cleansing of your system in the first few days is recommended by Beva Cherkiss, who is a native Jamaican. Detoxification is aided by a loofah body scrub, followed by a massage with essential oils to slough off dead skin. During a week-long visit you are treated to two shiatsu massages.

Lady Diane's staff makes you feel like a member of the family. Box lunches are offered for the beach, baby-sitters arranged, bicycles rented. The modest cost of staying here is balanced by the airport runway just beyond the garden. Although noise from jet aircraft is rarely heard at night (most international flights are scheduled during the day), it could be a problem for those who seek total seclusion. Meditators don't seem to notice.

Lady Diane Hotel

5 Kent Ave., Montego Bay, Jamaica
Tel. 809/952–4415
Telex Cherjam 915

Administration	Manager, Richard Cherkiss; program director, Beva Cherkiss
Season	Year-round.
Accommodations	17 large, airy rooms in main house, plus motellike garden unit for families, all with air conditioning, ceiling fan, private bath. Simply furnished, with touches of tropical decor, they have queen- or king-size beds. Only upper-floor rooms have a view.
Rates	From $85 per person double occupancy, $110 single, including 3 meals, bottled water, yoga instruction. 50% advance payment. 15% tax and service added. Credit cards: AE, MC, V.
Meal Plans	Macrobiotic meals: choice of fish, locally grown fruits, vegetables. No dairy products. Jamaican specialties include ackee and fish (breakfast), banana fritters, "apple" pie made with a vegetable called cho-cho instead of apples. One night is all-Italian. Kosher kitchen.
Services and Facilities	**Exercise Equipment:** Free weights, bicycles. **Services:** Aromatherapy and shiatsu massage, skin care with ginger compress, loofah body scrub. **Swimming Facilities:** Small freshwater pool on hotel terrace beach. **Recreation Facilities:** Sailing, waterskiing, scuba diving. Spectator sports include cricket and polo matches, soccer, basketball. Half Moon Hotel golf course open to the public. **Evening Programs:** Occasional informal talks by yoga masters and physiologists; on request, a clairvoyant will hold group sessions.
In the Area	Hiking through nearby bird sanctuary, botanical garden; farmers' market; train rides in restored "Governor's Coach" to visit plantations and rum distillery; ballooning.
Getting Here	By air, Air Jamaica and other international carriers offer excursion fares in conjunction with the hotel. Montego Bay airport is less than 2 mi away. Taxi or rental car available.
Special Notes	No smoking in dining area.

Pine Grove Hotel

Non-program resort facilities

Jamaica **The Blue** **Mountains**	Hiking the mist-shrouded vales and jungle-lined rivers that crisscross the rugged Blue Mountains is an adventure for backpackers and experienced walkers. The Pine Grove Hotel is a convenient base, easily reached by car from Kingston. The chalets and dining room command breathtaking views of the mountains and the city far below. Outings can be arranged to the Mavis Bank Coffee Factory, where beans are sorted by hand before roasting, and to Charlottenburg House, an antiques-filled example of a coffee plantation Great House. Naturalists will discover rare specimens of Asam tea plants and

the cinchona tree (whose bark is a source of quinine) cultivated since 1868 at the Cinchona Botanical Gardens.

The hotel owners, Marcia and Ronald Thwaites, will arrange for guides if you want to see the sun rise above the island's tallest peak. This difficult trek reaches 5,402 feet and requires proper personal gear.

Pine Grove Hotel
Blue Mountains, Jamaica
Tel. 809/922–8705

Rates In winter $22.50 per person double occupancy, $35 single. Meals à la carte. No credit cards.

Plantation Leyritz

Luxury pampering
Weight management

Martinique An oasis of tranquillity in a sea of pineapple and banana planta-
Basse Pointe tions, the legendary Plantation Leyritz is for lovers of seclusion. The old workers' cottages house guests with simple comfort, and the main mansion preserves all the gracious aspects of 18th-century Creole life. Antique marble dolphins guard a swimming pool in the formal gardens, and a floodlighted tennis court is nearby. Dinner is served by candlelight in the stone-walled remnant of a sugar mill and distillery, an impressive setting with a backdrop of vines from ceiling to floor.

Amid all this natural beauty sits the health spa. What was once a chapel has become a place to restore the body and your inner self.

Directed by a doctor trained in European spa therapies, the program includes massages and loofah body scrubs worthy of the most contemporary health resort. Dieters have a choice of four meal plans, for shedding pounds or maintenance. And for relaxation, the rooftop solarium features an alfresco Jacuzzi whirlpool, where you can take in the view while soaking au naturel.

Adding to the revitalization process are hair, nail, and facial treatments. Herbal products and natural creams imported from France are featured. Optional therapy with a type of Gerovital developed in Romania is available under the doctor's supervision. Exercise classes are held Monday and Friday.

Located in the breezy, lush hills of northern Martinique, the resort is 30 minutes' drive from beaches and colorful villages. Guests staying for the full- or half-week spa program are treated to a beach excursion and several outings. The program can begin any day of the week, and because your transportation from the airport and back is included, there is no need to rent a car unless you want to explore other parts of the island.

While there may be occasional intrusions into your private paradise from group tours coming to lunch, the gracious hosts at Plantation Leyritz are adept at scheduling outings for their guests on those days. Tranquil days begin with a breakfast of tropical fruits and strong French coffee or health drinks, served on the stone-paved terrace of the old mill. Nothing is planned or mandatory; guests set their own schedule.

What makes this island such a favorite of Francophiles is the Creole history and culture. Much of it is documented in the library of Chevalier Michel de Leyritz, who built and developed the plantation for his family. Across the island is the town of St. Pierre, once called the Paris of the West Indies. It was a gay, cultivated seaport of 30,000 inhabitants when Gauguin visited. Then, on May 8, 1902, the town was obliterated by an eruption of Mt. Pelée. Today's visitors see remnants in a museum on the waterfront of a reborn St. Pierre and head up into the rain forest for a closeup view of the towering, cloud-shrouded volcano.

Plantation Leyritz
97218 Basse Pointe, Martinique
Tel. 596/75-53-92, 800/223-9815, or 800/223-1510
Telex 912 462 MR

Administration Managers, Charles and Yveline de Lucy de Fossarieu; program manager, Will Fenton

Season Year-round.

Accommodations 53 rooms, some in main mansion (antiques, mahogany 4-poster beds, carved wooden armoires, kerosene lamps), most in stone bungalows spread along road between pineapple fields. Bungalows have tile floors, mix of modern and period furniture, tiny bath. Air conditioning, telephone; some kitchenettes.

Rates Daily in winter $89–$144 single, $112–$168 per person double occupancy. 3-night spa package $675 single, $1,230 double; full week with spa treatments and meals $1,434–$1,650 single, $2,626–$3,000 double. 3 nights advance payment (in summer 2 nights). Credit cards: AE, DC, MC, V.

Meal Plans French and Creole cuisine. Spa program special diets include all-vegetarian, with some fish and dairy products; calorie-controlled selections are low in fat and salt, high in natural fiber. Breakfast fruits and yogurt, fresh green salads, and grilled fish and chicken are among choices. Spa program includes 3 meals daily.

Services and Facilities **Services:** Massage, herbal bath, facial, loofah body scrub; hair, nail, and skin care. **Swimming Facilities:** Outdoor pool. **Recreation Facilities:** Tennis court; horseback riding nearby. **Evening Programs:** Folkloric show once weekly.

In the Area Beach trip, island tours included in program. Paille Caraïbe Crafts Center (basket and straw weaving) and Restaurant Le Colibri in Morne des Esses; St. Pierre (volcano museum); Fond-St. Denis (restored monastery); Balata Church (replica of Sacre Coeur), Balata Garden (botanical garden), archaeological museum in Fort-de-France (Arawak and Carib Indian artifacts); Museum de la Pagerie (Napoleon and Empress Josephine mementos at her family home), Museum of Manioc (cassava or tapioca) at Trois Islets Empress Josephine Golf Course.

Getting Here *From Fort-de-France.* By car, expressway to La Trinité, coastal road to Basse-terre (2 hr). Transfers provided on arrival and departure at Lamentin Airport. Rental car, taxi available.

Special Notes Remember to bring passport and medical certificate.

The Hard & the Soft

Sports conditioning

Montserrat
Isles Bay Beach

When the New York Road Runners Club searched for a fitness vacation site, it found an ideal combination of challenges in a tiny British Crown Colony. On Montserrat there are clean and sparkling dove-gray obsidian beaches for running and a stark volcanic island marine ecosystem for hiking. Add workshops on health and nutrition, yoga, and a special diet, and you have a daily regimen for total fitness training.

Developed as a cross-training system for athletes by Beryl Bender Birch, wellness director for the NYRRC, the program is designed for people of all ages and fitness levels. Included is training in Ashtanga yoga, an ancient therapeutic form of exercise for health, strength, and personal growth. Daily workouts on the beach are precise and vigorous. The Ashtanga system builds intense heat and energy in the body through static muscular contraction, increased circulation, and concentration on a powerful breathing technique.

Daily options are hiking, swimming, snorkeling, sailing, tennis, and golf. Nearby are natural pools fed by hot springs where mineral waters soak away muscular pain.

Limited to 35 participants, the week-long program is designed to balance exercise and practice with a fun-filled vacation. The focus is on increasing your knowledge of the positive effects of exercise, good nutrition, and stress management in your life while enhancing your competitive ability in sports.

Your reward for hiking in the lofty green mountains only 30 minutes from the island's capital, Plymouth, is the Great Alps Waterfall, a lush setting for picnics. Also nearby is the 15-acre Foxes Bay Bird Sanctuary, a protected wildlife area of the Montserrat National Trust. The ultimate challenge is a 5K road race, held at the end of the second week's program.

Far from the beaten path of Caribbean holidays, the colony traces its Emerald Isle character to 17th-century settlers fleeing religious persecution in Ireland. Today it is a mélange of African, Irish, and other European influences that contribute to an overriding sense of peace and tranquility.

The Hard & the Soft
Isles Bay Beach, Montserrat
New York Road Runners Club
9 E. 89th St., New York, NY 10128
Tel. 212/860–4455
Telex 238093 NYRR UR

Administration   Program director, Beryl Bender Birch

Season   Jan.–Feb. only.

Accommodations   Modern villas with 3–4 bedrooms shared by program participants; cottages at the Vue Pointe Hotel. Villas and cottages overlook Old Towne beach; modern furniture, twin or king-size beds, private bath, living room with balcony. Air conditioning, VCR and cassette player, TV. Maid service daily.

Rates 1-week program $1,295 per person in villa, $1,395 per person in cottage. 50% payment with registration. Credit cards: AE, MC, V.

Meal Plans 2 meals daily included in program. Hotel caters breakfast buffet of blue-corn muffins or blue-corn pancakes, oatmeal; fresh fruit is accompanied by "smoothies" made of whipped juices from banana, papaya, mango, coconut. Eggs, low-fat homemade yogurt, freshly baked whole-grain breads available. Dinner (at hotel) includes steamed vegetables, green salad, choice of grilled fish or chicken; vegetarian meals and West Indian barbecue are other options.

Services and Facilities **Services:** Lectures and workshops on health, fitness, nutrition; personal consultation on nutrition, fitness; analysis of body biomechanics, posture. **Swimming Facilities:** Outdoor freshwater pool, ocean beaches. **Spa Facilities:** Hot springs at Soufrière Hills. **Recreation Facilities:** Tennis courts, horseback riding, hiking. **Evening Programs:** Workshops alternate with reggae and disco nights; Calypso steel band.

In the Area Group hiking (optional).

Getting Here *From airport.* Transfers provided. Taxi, car rental, bicycle rental available.

Special Notes No smoking in the villas.

Instituto de Vida Natural

Holistic health
Preventive medicine

Puerto Rico Secluded in the foothills of the Caribbean National Forest, *Luquillo* practically in the shadow of towering El Yunque, the highest peak on the island, the Instituto de Vida Natural has carved out a 10-acre center for natural health. Vegetarian meals, mud treatments, and psychological counseling are offered.

With one of the island's best ocean beaches just down the hill at Luquillo, and hiking trails leading into the lush rain forest of El Yunque, the institute is an ideal getaway, winter and summer. The informal accommodations consist of an old farmhouse and cottages with private apartments.

The health center offers nonintrusive diagnostic procedures as well as kinesiology and massage. Workshops on physical and mental health are scheduled periodically, and individual counseling is available by appointment. The focus may be on building a psychological immune system, love and hate in health, or organic farming.

Taking a psychological approach to prevention and cure of disease, the center's services are geared to serve a wide range of interests. Therapies such as cleansing the body with burial in sand and immersion in mud can be combined with colonics and urine analysis. And there are some pieces of exercise equipment not found elsewhere in the islands—gravity inversion, for instance.

The program developed by New York–based psychoanalyst Jane G. Goldberg was introduced in 1988. At present, only 16 guests can be accommodated, and plans are to keep the center small, emphasizing personal attention to each guest.

Surrounded by natural beauty, panoramic views of the ocean, and the mountains, the pristine air and water are in natural harmony with the earth. Luquillo Beach, once a thriving coconut plantation, is protected by barrier reefs. The crescent-shaped, white-sand beach is perfect for swimming but gets crowded and noisy on weekends when families picnic under the palms. Numerous roadside stands offer slices of whole roasted pig and sweet *pastillas*.

El Yunque, protected by the U.S. National Park Service, encompasses 28,000 acres. Reaching an elevation of 3,526 feet, its rain forest includes 240 different tree species, as well as orchids and wildflowers. Brief tropical showers keep things lush, moist, and cool.

Hot sulfur springs, known to the earliest Taino Indians, are an hour's drive from the center. At the Parador Baños de Coamo you can bathe in the same pool where Franklin D. Roosevelt, Thomas Edison, Alexander Graham Bell, and Frank Lloyd Wright took the waters. Now a modern mountain inn, the Parador offers Puerto Rican meals to visitors as well as overnight lodging. (Rte. 546; tel. 825–2186)

Instituto de Vida Natural
Rio Grande, Luquillo, Puerto Rico 00673
(Reservations) 222 Park Ave. S, New York, NY 10003
Tel. 809/887–4359 or 212/260–5823.

Administration Director, Jane Goldberg; program director, Jo Anne White

Season Year-round.

Accommodations Recently renovated farm house has 8 rooms, simply furnished with 2 beds each; shared baths.

Rates $75 daily; 5-day workshop $500. Advance payment $200 for workshops or 2 nights' lodging. No credit cards.

Meal Plans 3 meals daily included in program fee. Vegetarian diet emphasizes raw fruits and vegetables grown on the property; whole-grain home-baked bread, sprouts, juices, salads. Special diets are accommodated. No coffee is served; herbal teas available.

Services and Facilities **Exercise Equipment:** Stationary bicycle, trampoline, slant board, gravity inversion machine. **Services:** Massage (full body, $25), colonics, mud pack, sand burial. Holistic medical counseling, nutritional and psychological consultation. **Swimming Facilities:** Outdoor pool; ocean beaches nearby. **Spa Facilities:** Banos de Coamo (60-min drive). **Recreation Facilities:** Hiking, river boating. **Evening Programs:** Informal workshops.

In the Area Fajardo (marina, ferry to Vieques); National Park Service interpretive program at El Yunque.

Getting Here *From San Juan.* By car, Rte. 3 east to Luquillo Beach, Carr. 186 to El Verde (60 min). Rental car, taxi, public car *(publico)* available.

Special Notes No smoking on property.

Palmas del Mar

Non-program resort facilities

Puerto Rico
Humacao
Sports and fitness go together at this spacious resort complex of Mediterranean-style villas, hotels, marina, golf course, and equestrian center in Humacao. The basic exercise program includes training on the exercise equipment. Set out in a "super circuit," the variable resistance units firm and tone muscles faster than conventional exercises. Recommended is a 30-minute circuit, at fitness levels for the exercise novice or professional athlete.

The resort has one of the finest tennis centers in the Caribbean, with 20 courts for day and night play. A canal encloses the development, leading to lagoons on the golf course and through 2,700 acres of coconut grove. There is also a parcourse for a combination of jogging and exercise, and marked walking trails.

Set amid flowering bougainvillea and oleander, the inn and villas slope toward the sea, evoking visions of hill towns in Italy and southern France. The impression grows with the sight of fountains one comes upon suddenly, of steps and paths that twist and turn past doorways and passages, and of a sign in a tiny square that reads simply "Cafe de la Plaza."

Palmas del Mar
Box 2020, Humacao, Puerto Rico 00661
Tel. 809/852-6000 or 800/221-4874
(Reservations) 600 Third Ave., New York, NY 10016
Tel. 212/983-0393 or 800/221-4874

Administration General manager, Arnold Benitez

Season Year-round.

Accommodations 102 rooms in Candelera Hotel. Handcrafted furnishings, colorful Mediterranean decor; tile floors, rattan furniture, flowered bedspreads. Some rooms have patios opening on to golf course, others face swimming pool and gardens. All have private bath, TV, telephone, king- or queen-size beds, air conditioning.

Rates Daily $85–$190, single or double occupancy. Basic 4-day/3-night Palmas Package (May–Dec. 18 only) $255 single, $170 per person double occupancy. Winter–spring 7-day/6-night package $553 single, $1,066 double. Optional packages for golf, tennis, water sports, riding. 1-night credit-card guarantee. Credit cards: AE, DC, MC, V.

Meal Plans Modified American Plan (breakfast and dinner) $40 per person. Light options for diet maintenance on the menu at Las Garzas restaurant, which features fish, fresh salads, vegetables, Puerto Rican specialties.

Services and Facilities **Exercise Equipment:** Hydra-Fitness Circuit (12 machines), Bally Lifecycles, Body Guard ergometer, free weights. **Swimming Facilities:** Outdoor pools, ocean beaches. **Recreation Facilities:** Horseback riding, water sports, tennis, golf, miniature golf, game room. Bicycle rental on property. **Evening Programs:** Resort entertainment.

In the Area Trail ride, scuba trips, deep-sea fishing, sailing; Ponce (Museum of Modern Art), El Yunque rain forest, Baños de Coamo hot-sulfur springs.

Getting Here *From San Juan.* By car, Hwy. 52 (Las Americas) to Caguas, Hwy. 30 to Humacao (90 min). Transfers included in package rates for arrival/departure at San Juan International Airport. Taxi, rental car, scheduled van service available.

Special Notes Supervised day camp for children July–Aug.

Spa Caribe at the Hyatt Resorts

Non-program resort facilities

Puerto Rico
Dorado Beach Talking back to the exercise machines might improve your fitness rating during a workout at the new health clubs in Hyatt's sports-oriented resorts. Like a personal coach, the computerized system monitors your progress. Powercise machines converse not only with the users but with each other. Their composite rating is handed to you at the end of the exercise circuit, with suggestions for additional improvement.

These high-tech shape-ups are the latest feature at both the Hyatt Regency Cerromar Beach and the Hyatt Dorado Beach, sister resorts two miles apart, on the north shore of the island, 22 miles west of San Juan. In addition to computerized equipment, they offer aerobics classes and aquaerobics, jogging trails, sauna, and a parcourse. Plus some professional pampering.

Lifestyle-management prescriptions that you can take home are also computer-generated. Based on medically approved models, the programs evaluate your body composition, diet, exercise profile, and general fitness level. The spa's fitness specialist can then work up an exercise program tailored to your needs and schedule.

Geared to serve large groups at conferences and conventions in the resort, the spa also caters to the health club regular. A full day of exercise and bodywork, with facial as well as computerized evaluation, is available for $160. Groups meeting at both resorts are offered corporate games, seminars, workshops, and spouse programs, all supervised by experts.

Spa services are available daily on an à la carte basis. In addition to the usual body and skin care, the specialties include neuromuscular therapy, sports massage, herbal wraps, and loofah body scrub.

Spa Caribe
Hyatt Resorts in Puerto Rico, Dorado, P.R. 00646
Tel. 809/796–1010, ext. 3011, or 800/228–9000
Telex 3859758

Administration Director, Marietta Fridjohn; program manager, Patricia Lach

Season Year-round.

Accommodations Low-rise construction, luxurious landscaping, and vast swimming pools are hallmarks of these resorts. Hyatt Regency Cerromar Beach has 506 rooms on 7 floors, the Dorado Beach has 300 rooms on 2 floors. Both hotels feature sleek new tropical looks: rattan furniture, pastel fabrics, island prints on bedcovers and window drapery; baths have marble-top counters, tile floors, contemporary lighting.

Rates $110–$250 daily, single or double occupancy. Suites and Regency Club rooms higher. Guarantee by credit card. Credit cards: AE, MC, V.

Meal Plans No special diet available. Modified American Plan (breakfast and dinner) $45 per person.

Services and Facilities **Exercise Equipment:** Powercise system (8 machines), 2 Lifecycles, Liferower, Hydra-Fitness muscular and cardiovascular training units. Outdoor parcourse with Dynacourt equipment. **Services:** Massage (Swedish, reflexology, sports, neck and shoulder), herbal wrap, loofah body scrub, facial cleansing treatments, aromatherapy. Hair, nail, skin care. **Swimming Facilities:** Outdoor freshwater pools, ocean beaches. **Recreation Facilities:** Tennis courts, golf courses, bicycling, volleyball, pool volleyball, water sports. **Evening Programs:** Resort entertainment; casino.

In the Area Scuba, deep-sea fishing, sightseeing tours; Old San Juan (colonial architecture, art galleries, boutiques, museums), El Yunque rain forest, Camuy caves, Aricebo Observatory, San German (architecture, university).

Getting Here *From San Juan.* By car, Hwy. 22 (De Diego Expwy.), Rte. 693 to Dorado (30 min). By air, Dorado Airport. By public car *(publico)* from Old San Juan (60 min). Airport transfers ($45) by Dorado Transport Van. Rental car, taxi available. Shuttle service between hotels.

Special Notes Specially equipped rooms by advance request for the disabled. Elevators to all levels. Supervised day camp for children June 1–Labor Day. No smoking in spa and designated dining areas; nonsmoking rooms available. Remember to bring a medical certificate of fitness.

Cunard La Toc Hotel & Suites

Non-program resort facilities
Taking the waters

St. Lucia Hiking across a sulfurous volcano crater, bathing in hot mineral
Castries springs, and working out in a brand-new fitness center is the unique combination offered by the island's leading hotel. The baths at La Soufrière, built in 1786 to "fortify" troops of Louis XVI, have been restored for public use. La Toc's array of exercise equipment, massage therapy, and spa cuisine is designed for shape-ups with a contemporary beat.

Verdant and steeply terraced, La Toc is both a traditional hotel and a cottage colony. Premium-price suites come with a private plunge pool on the terrace. There are two large swimming pools and a lovely beach, but stepping from your bedroom into a pool just big enough for two is the ultimate in sybaritic delight.

Aerobics classes (twice daily) and use of the exercise facilities are complimentary to resort guests. The fitness center also has a juice bar, with veggies and snacks charged to your account along with massage. A beauty salon is on the premises.

Framed by a tropical rain forest and twin peaks called Les Pitons, the volcanic crater of La Soufrière is a 45-minute drive from La Toc. You walk into a seven-acre wilderness of bubbling black water and yellow-green sulfur deposits baking in the steamy atmosphere. Government guides point to the baths where you can soak for a small fee. The water is said to cure whatever ails you, including sunburn and mosquito bites.

Cundard La Toc Hotel & Suites
Box 399, Castries, St. Lucia, W.I.
Tel. 809/45–23081 or 800/222–0939
Telex 0398-6320

Administration Manager, Michael Marko

Season Year-round.

Accommodations Hotel has 154 standard rooms: twin beds, balcony, air conditioning; 54 suites cluster on the beach and cliffs, 30 with private plunge pool on terrace. Furnished in quiet fashion of older island resorts. All rooms have VCR.

Rates Summer rates are about 30% lower than winter. In winter: $155–$185 single, $175–$205 for 2 persons; 4-night package $325–$425 per person, European Plan, double occupancy. 3 nights advance payment. Credit cards: AE, MC, V.

Meal Plans 2 restaurants serve standard American and Continental fare, with recently added selections of spa cuisine. No meals included in room rate, but Modified American Plan is available on request.

Services and Facilities **Exercise Equipment:** Nautilus and Universal gym units, exercise bicycles, treadmills. **Swimming Facilities:** 2 pools, private ocean beach. **Spa Facilities:** Hot springs. **Recreation Facilities:** 5 tennis courts, 9-hole golf course, water sports; nature walks, 3-hour hike through rain forest. **Evening Programs:** Videocassette library.

In the Area Plantation and volcano tours; picnics on nearby islands; sailing to La Soufrière (wooden brig *Unicorn);* yacht charters.

Getting Here By air, the island's two airports are served by American Airlines, Eastern, BWIA, British Airways, and interisland LIAT. By sea, Cunard and other cruise ships. Taxi, van, rental car available.

Special Notes Supervised beach and water sports for children. No smoking in fitness center.

Le Sport

Sports conditioning
Luxury pampering
Taking the waters
Weight management

St. Lucia Thalassotherapy has come to the tiny nation of St. Lucia in a big
Cariblue Beach way. After searching all of Europe for the finest body treatments at leading spas, the new owners of the Cariblue Hotel embarked on a vacation program completely devoted to health and fitness. They call it the Body Holiday.

The beneficial properties of seawater used to massage joints and muscles and the culinary pleasures of a diet based on meals created by famed chef Michel Guerard are the main features of the Body Holiday; its tonic part is complemented by the friendly nature of the St. Lucians and the balmy seaside resort.

Thermal-jet baths and seaweed wraps beautify the body. Image-enhancing treatments for men and women—facials, loofah body scrubs, and skin care—are included in the basic program price. Tipping is not permitted. The daily schedule offers aerobics classes, toning, and physical culture workshops, and an array of land and water sports. All come with expert instruction, at no additional charge.

The food part of the Body Holiday is called "cuisine legère," which simply means that calories don't count. In emulating the renowned Michel Guerard, the chefs provide meals balanced in complex carbohydrates, low in sodium and sugar, and full of options if you want to indulge. They even include wine with lunch and dinner, an open bar stocked with premium brands, fresh fruit juices, and mineral waters.

Before any treatments, a checkup is scheduled with the staff physician. Stress-linked fatigue and muscle tension, poor circulation, and lymphatic drainage are noted, and measurements are taken for blood pressure, heart rate, and weight. A prescribed course of treatments can include the "hydrator," a bubbling bath with herbs and sea algae, in which underwater jets needle away at the fatty tissue found on the upper arms, thighs, and calves. Another pool fitted with underwater jets is for exercise in seawater, which is denser than fresh water and thus gives greater support for the body. And the therapeutic nutrients of seaweed act as catalysts to create changes in the skin as you are wrapped, cocoonlike, in a coating of algae and sea mud.

St. Lucia's natural resources also include sulfur baths. Twin volcanic peaks called Petit Piton and Gros Piton rise dramatically above the tiny village of Soufrière on the southwest coast where signs point to the baths. From bubbling, underground springs, the sulfurous water flows into natural pools. Bathing here is said to cure whatever ails you.

A short jaunt up into the hills, across the ridge, brings you into the rain forest. Located between Soufrière and Fond St. Jacques, it's a three-hour trek through a tropical wonderland of dense foliage, flowering plants, and colorful birds.

Situated on a 1,500-acre estate, the new thalassotherapy center complements a hotel and golf course that were formerly part of the Steigenberger chain. Now unified as Le Sport, it is an oasis of restorative treatments, luxurious privacy, fine food, and lazy days at the beach. Like the local Creole patois, liberally sprinkled with French, this is a resort that blends the best of many worlds.

Le Sport
Cap Estate, Cariblue Beach, St. Lucia
Tel. 809/452-8551 (800/221-1831 in USA)
Telex LC6330, Fax 809/452-0368

Administration	Manager, Craig Barnard
Season	Year-round.
Accommodations	120-room hotel is a series of beach pavilions linked to dining room and lounge. Newly decorated rooms have tropical contemporary look, rattan furniture. Air conditioning, private balconies or patios, full modern bath.
Rates	Winter–spring $190–$235 single, $170–$215 per person double occupancy. Credit-card guarantee for first night. Credit cards: AE, DC, MC, V.
Meal Plans	3 meals daily included in program price. Breakfast: fresh fruits and juices, bran and meusli cereals, omelets, smoked salmon, pastries, coffee, milk, tea. Lunch selections include fresh salads, stuffed chicken legs in leek-and-cream sauce, boiled wild rice, julienne of carrots and zucchini. Dinner options broccoli soufflé, scallop of veal with champagne sabayon, fresh asparagus. Desert offerings include homemade pear sherbet. Selected wines with lunch and dinner at no additional charge.
Services and Facilities	**Exercise Equipment:** Nautilus-type units, bicycles, fencing outfits. **Services:** Massage, hydrotherapy, facials, beauty and rejuvenation treatments. **Swimming Facilities:** Outdoor freshwater pool, seawater pool, ocean beach. **Spa Facilities:** Therapy tubs in private rooms. **Recreation Facilities:** Tennis courts, golf course, horseback riding, bicycling, archery, volleyball, scuba diving, windsurfing, waterskiing. **Evening Programs:** Live entertainment nightly, disco.
In the Area	Shopping tour to duty-free Point Serephin. Pigeon Island National Park (museum), Rodney Bay marina, Castries market (built 1894), Government House.
Getting Here	*From Castries.* By car, coastal road to Gros Ilet (15 min). Complimentary transfers on arrival/departure. Taxi, rental car available.
Special Notes	No smoking in thalassotherapy center.

L'Aqualigne

Life enhancement
Preventive medicine

St. Maarten At L'Aqualigne, European beauty and rejuvenation therapies
Simpson Bay can be combined with aerobic exercise and a weight-loss diet in
programs designed and developed by the cosmetologists Claire
and Marc Van Thielen, who researched natural healing and cosmetic products used at leading spas throughout the world. The
focus ranges from anticellulite French body-sculpting massage
and injections to the antiaging cell therapies created in Romania by Dr. Ana Aslan. For relaxation, a week of fitness training
is interspersed with body peeling, postural reeducation, and
soothing massage. The tranquillity of the island beach setting,
in addition to the sophisticated equipment for beauty treatments, can produce a total experience of revitalization.

Located within a large time-share resort on the Dutch side of
the half-French, half-Dutch island of St. Maarten, the therapy
center adjoins La Vista Hotel, a breezy, intimate combination
of traditional Antillean charm and European flair. Guests from
many nations mix with local residents who come for special one-
day programs. Treatments can be scheduled over one or two
weeks.

The medically oriented programs are structured to achieve serious results even though facials and massage are included. A
thorough examination, including blood analysis, precedes some
therapies. Plastic and reconstructive surgery, sclerosis injections, liposuction, collagen implant for facial scars and
wrinkles, and injections of Gerovital H3 are offered here. The
advanced equipment for aesthetic treatments is based on techniques created by plastic surgeons and dermatologists.
L'Aqualigne technicians are joined by specialists who participate in the scheduled programs.

Dieters are treated to foods that satisfy the appetite and appeal
to a sense of being well fed. Planned individually by a nutritionist who works with guests throughout the week, the weight-
loss program is geared to taking off inches and pounds. Daily
anticellulite massages and the metabolism-balancing oligo
therapy are intended to enhance your new look.

Refreshing breezes, gentle surf, and the relaxed atmosphere of
island life complete the stress-reduction process, and naturalist beaches and a casino are nearby.

L'Aqualigne
Pelican Resort, Simpson Bay, St. Maarten
Tel. 011/599–5–42426

Administration Program director, Marc Van Thielen

Season Year-round.

Accommodations 24 units in suites and cottages with air conditioning, king-size
beds, spacious closets, kitchenette, cable TV, direct-dial telephone, large balcony. Cool white walls, tile floors, rattan
furniture, island fabrics, prints by native artists.

Rates 1-week beauty and fitness program $2,545; 1-week weight-loss
program $3,605; 2-week anticellulite program (with special

diet and therapies) $5,630; 2-week electroridopuncture program $5,816; 1-week rejuvenation program (with Gerovital therapy) $3,582. All prices per person, single occupancy, including hotel, all meals, transfers, daily robe and juices. 1-day revitalizer (includes lunch) $180. Use of facilities (only) $30 day, $60 week, $100 week for a couple. 50% payable in advance. Credit cards: AE, CB, DC, MC, V.

Meal Plans Fresh fish and fruit salads on the calorie-controlled menu at the hotel restaurant. Grilled snapper, sautéed aubergine, other island specialties at lunch and dinner. Breakfast selections include cereal, yogurt, home-baked whole-wheat bread. Diets of 800–1,500 calories a day. Juice bar.

Services and Facilities **Exercise Equipment:** 16 stations Weider circuit weights, 2 Tunturi bicycles, free weights and bench; aerobics exercise area with special flooring. **Swimming Facilities:** Outdoor freshwater pool, ocean beach. **Spa Facilities:** Coed sauna, steam room, hot and cold whirlpools. **Recreation Facilities:** Marina, 2 tennis courts (1 lighted). **Evening Programs:** Resort entertainment, casino.

In the Area Duty-free shopping in Philipsburg, French boutiques in Marigot, boat trips to St. Bart, water sports, horseback riding.

Getting Here *From Juliana Airport.* By car, Union Road to Simpson Bay (15 min). Taxi, rental car available.

Special Notes Limited access for the disabled. No smoking in the therapy center; some nonsmoking cottages.

Omega Journeys at Maho Bay

Holistic health
Spiritual awareness

U.S. Virgin Islands
Maho Bay, St. John

Workshops in health, music, movement, and personal growth are mixed with fun in the sun during three week-long programs planned by the New York–based Omega Institute for Holistic Studies. The annual migration to the sunny beaches of St. John is joined by faculty members who lead explorations into the body, mind, and spirit. Living close to nature in a tent village, the workshop participants experience many dimensions of natural healing.

Early birds can start the day with sunrise meditation, tai chi chuan, or yoga. Workshops run two hours each morning and afternoon, allowing a choice of several subjects. Informal and experiential, the group sessions are devoted to bringing health, aliveness, and peace into the many dimensions of contemporary life.

Drawn from a variety of professions, ages, and backgrounds, the participants find common ground in the open-minded, natural atmosphere. Maho Bay Camp Resort is a unique tent-cottage community dedicated to the concept of simple comforts and life in harmony with nature. Perched in thickly wooded hillsides, the canvas-walled cottages are set on plank decks that cantilever over the forest. The 16-by-16-foot units blend in so naturally that they seem to be part of the environment.

Located within the Virgin Islands National Park, the campground has unrestricted access to miles of pristine beaches and well-marked hiking trails, where you may pursue both ecological and historical interests. The National Park Service conducts free tours and lectures on island flora, fauna, and marine biology, as well as on St. John's colorful history and culture.

St. John remains the sleepiest and most tranquil of the three islands (with St. Thomas and St. Croix) the United States bought from Denmark for $25 million. Its main town, Cruz Bay, isn't very sophisticated, but it is delightful just for that reason and is much loved by Virgin Island visitors.

A good place to begin an island tour is the National Park Service visitor center next to the pier where ferries carry passengers and cargo from St. Thomas. Scheduled hikes are posted, brochures on trails are free for the asking. Panoramic views and lush foliage reward hikers and photographers. For those who prefer to ride, open-sided vans pick up passengers along the main Northshore Road to Caneel Bay and a string of public beaches around Maho Bay.

Thanks to the efforts of preservationists, about two-thirds of the island was designated a national park in 1956. Although the Caneel Bay Resort developed by Laurence Rockefeller is still extremely popular with those who like to experience some luxury with their wilderness, Maho Bay welcomes those who are serious about exploring the natural wonders of St. John.

A must, if time permits, is a drive over Bordeaux Mountain, with its rain forest and spectacular views, to Coral Bay and East End, where descendents of the Danish settlers still farm in the old style. En route you will have to be patient with the wildlife, especially the prolific mongooses. Imported to deal with rats on the sugar plantations, they consider the road to be their own playground.

Surrounded by mahogany and bay trees (from which bay rum is derived), the campground is alive with large and small birds and with brilliant flowers including tamarind and flamboyant. Underwater at Trunk Bay, snorkelers can explore a marked trail of sealife: flora, coral, and brilliantly colored fish.

Omega Journeys at Maho Bay
Maho Bay, St. John
Tel. 809/776–6240 or 800/392–9004
(Reservations) Omega Institute, RD 2, Box 377, Rhinebeck,
NY 12572
Tel. 914/338–6030

Administration	Director, Stephan Rechtschaffen
Season	Jan. only.
Accommodations	96 tent/cottages tucked into foliage on 14 acres overlooking white-sand beach. Wooden floors, 2 beds, living/dining area

(equipped with 2-burner propane stove), lounge chairs, sofa. Linens and bedding supplied, no maid service. Boardwalks connect to toilets, showers, dining pavilion, commissary.

Rates 1-week workshop, with lodging, meals, and round-trip airfare from New York, $1,080 per person double occupancy. Lodging for single persons and children available. 50% payment at time of booking. Credit cards: MC, V.

Meal Plans Vegetarian meals 3 times daily. Omega's natural-food chefs prepare sumptuous buffets of vegetables and tropical fruits. Some fish and dairy products are available. Lunch includes salads, home-baked whole-wheat bread. Dinner menus offer vegetarian lasagna, baked eggplant Parmesan, tofu casserole.

Services and Facilities **Services:** Personal consultation on nutrition, body movement, energy training. Yoga instruction. **Swimming Facilities:** Ocean beaches. **Recreation Facilities:** Tennis, hiking, volleyball. **Evening Programs:** Informal workshops, concerts.

In the Area National Park Service interpretive tours, ferry to Tortola, catamaran trips. Annaberg Plantation (Danish-era ruins, special programs), Trunk Bay (underwater trail), Caneel Bay Plantation, Virgin Grand Beach Hotel (water sports).

Getting Here *From Cruz Bay.* By bus, shuttle service from ferry landing or along Northshore Rd. (15 min). Car rental, taxi, minimoke, bicycle rental available.

Special Notes No smoking indoors. Remember to bring flashlight, insect repellent, hiking shoes.

3 Health & Fitness Cruises

Staying fit at sea is no longer a matter of doing 10 laps around the promenade deck. Today's luxury liners feature fitness facilities and programs that are the equal of anything ashore. And cruises add a new dimension to a fitness vacation, combining workouts and pampering for a taste of the good life with healthy options.

Seagoing spas were an innovation of the 1970s. Since water is the basic ingredient in many spa cures, it was argued, a spa on the high seas should only make the experience more enjoyable. With abundant fresh air and sunshine, swimming pools filled with filtered sea water, and aerobics classes on deck, the cruise would be an invigorating escape from health club routines at home.

For cruise connoisseurs, however, diet was a dirty word. And the gourmet meals and lavish buffets aboard ship have been the downfall of many calorie counters. Then came the American Heart Association's "Eating Away From Home" program adapted for shipboard dining by Royal Cruise Line, followed by the Golden Door menu selections offered on Cunard cruises. Today the Chandris Fantasy Cruises liner *The Azur* has an optional completely vegetarian menu plan in addition to a superb gymnasium and squash court.

The rich buffets and gala meals commonly associated with the cruise have not been eliminated; rather, the lines are enhancing their menus and promoting a commitment to satisfying travelers who want to maintain a healthy lifestyle away from home. According to Duncan Beardsley, the Royal Cruise Line senior vice president responsible for introducing "Dine to Your Heart's Content" menu selections, passenger reaction has been positive and enthusiastic. While special dietary requests have always been accommodated, Beardsley says, it is considerably easier now for passengers to enjoy special menus without scrimping on flavor or presentation.

Advance planning is important for those on a special diet. Specific foods and general preferences can be discussed with a travel agent, who can then secure a confirmation of your meal plan from the cruise line. All the leading lines offer such services at no extra charge.

As a further aid to passengers, Royal Cruise Line distributes a comprehensive guide by the nutritionist Ruth Johnson; it provides nutrient analyses, with calorie counts, for each of the new menu items. In addition, the booklet offers suggestions for maintaining a diet when making selections from standard shipboard menus—such as substituting yogurt for cream and ordering an omelet made without egg yolk.

For the truly committed fitness buff, cruising can provide the best of both worlds. Norwegian Cruise Line has turned the new *Seaward* into a floating sports palace for their annual Fitness and Beauty cruises at the end of October. Guest lecturers on nutrition, sports medicine, hairstyling, and makeup make the trip along with football, golf, and tennis stars. Basketball cruises, baseball cruises, and football cruises allow passengers to team up for fun and fitness aboard the *Seaward* and its sister ship the *Norway*.

Shore excursions on these cruises offer more than shopping and sightseeing. Several lines, including Norwegian Cruise Line and Chandris, provide entree to local racquet clubs, golf courses, and fitness centers. Some ships have access to private ports of call, islands where passengers may swim, snorkel, and sunbathe on their own "deserted island." Others have scheduled nature walks and bicycle tours.

While the Caribbean and the Bahamas account for 60% of all cruise destinations, a steadily growing fleet of ships sails from California and Canadian ports. Alaska, the Mexican Riviera, and the Hawaiian islands offer exciting variations on the cruise theme. And there is little problem in maintaining a reduced fat and cholesterol diet while traveling when your meals are planned and scheduled aboard ship.

The latest in seagoing spa programs teams Holland America Line with the Bonaventure resort in Florida. Passengers can work out before or after a Caribbean cruise; during the cruise, specialists from the Bonaventure are on board ship to lead aerobics classes and provide expert massage and beauty care. The program is also available during the summer season of Alaskan cruises.

For newcomers to fitness programs, the cruise may be a good way to inaugurate a personal fitness routine that can then be continued effectively at home. Staff instructors offer one-on-one workouts that teach proper exercise routines—perhaps the best bargain in fitness education. And there's a healthy bonus from mother nature: The bracing effect of the fresh air generated by seawater and sun may be just what the doctor ordered for our high-pressure society.

The Azur

Sports-oriented facilities, shipboard sports programs, and shore excursions to golf courses, tennis courts, and a fitness center are among the options offered on *The Azur*'s seven-day Caribbean cruises. Indoor activity focuses on a duplex gymnasium and squash court, a two-story fitness center where passengers participate in aerobics classes, badminton, and volleyball and work out with weights and exercise machines. The squash court and equipment can be reserved by the hour without fee. Unfortunately, there is no sauna, steam room, or Jacuzzi. Dieters choose between a full vegetarian menu and the regular menu with highlighted items that are low in sodium and cholesterol.

Chandris Fantasy Cruises. *900 Third Ave., New York, NY 10022, tel. 212/223–3003, 800/621–3446, or 800/423–2100 (800/ 432–4132 in FL).* Built in 1971, rebuilt and renamed in 1976, extensively renovated in 1980. Deluxe staterooms and outside cabins; most cabins are compact, located inside without view; all have private shower and toilet. 700 passengers. Panamanian registry, European officers, Caribbean staff.

Fitness facilities: Stationary bikes, rowing machines, windsurfing simulator, free weights; indoor and outdoor swimming pools. **Sports:** Squash, scuba, and snorkeling demonstrations and lectures, table tennis clinics, windsurfing instruction, parasailing.

Cruises weekly from San Juan; fares $899–$1,399 per person double occupancy.

Crown Odyssey

The newest and largest addition to Royal Cruise Line, the 40,000-ton *Crown Odyssey* sports a lavish health center complemented by a healthful alternative dining program approved by the American Heart Association. Principal attractions are an indoor swimming pool, whirlpools, gymnasium, saunas, and a health bar. Reminiscent of a sumptuous Roman bath with its tile walls and floors in shades of green, coral, and white, the health center offers the latest in exercise equipment and programs. Choices include classes in yoga, aerobics, dancercise, aquafit water workouts, Body Shop for strengthening and tightening muscles, and Sit and Be Fit, which incorporates exercises that can be done while sitting in a chair. In addition, there are two outdoor whirlpools, parcourse walking track, and two golf-driving ranges. Programs include lectures and workshops with guest experts on subjects ranging from stress management to nutrition and self-esteem. Offered on 25 select cruises aboard the *Crown Odyssey* (and her sister ship the *Golden Odyssey*) is an expanded New Beginnings program that has included a pain clinic and workshops on retirement adjustment. A special tennis cruise arranges courts in every port of call.

Royal Cruise Line. *Maritime Plaza, San Francisco, CA 94111, tel. 415/956–7200 or 800/227–4534.* Launched in 1988. 1,000 passengers (most have outside staterooms with picture windows). Exclusive suites have private Jacuzzis, balconies, butler service. Greek registry and crew.

Fitness facilities: Universal 8-station gym, Bally Lifecycles, Precor rowers, parcourse, aquacourse, free weights, ballet barre; outdoor swimming pool, indoor pool. **Services:** Massage, herbal wraps, facials; hair, nail, and skin care. **Sports:** Golf driving instruction; tennis and golf ashore.

Cruises to Canada, New England, the Panama Canal, the Mexican Riviera, the Caribbean, Hawaii. Fares for 7-day cruises $1,698–$4,078 per person double occupancy.

Nieuw Amsterdam and Noordam

With a new Bonaventure Spa at Sea program aboard their twin luxury liners the *Nieuw Amsterdam* and the *Noordam*, Holland America Line offers one of the best values in health and fitness cruises year-round. A special package includes four one-hour Swedish massages, complete salon makeover, manicure and pedicure, special Kerstin facial, invigorating loofah body scrub treatment, and souvenir exercise outfit. Aerobics classes and aquatic workouts led by specialists from the Florida resort are available to all passengers. A newly introduced spa menu has such healthful selections as Thai chicken salad and fresh Pacific snapper. Tennis and golf programs and a scuba certification course are offered on shore excursions. An optional package at the Bonaventure Resort & Spa in Fort Lauderdale, $215 per person in conjunction with Caribbean cruises, includes a rental car for two days. The twin luxury liners, immaculately maintained and decorated with an extensive collection of art and antiques, offer services and amenities in the grand tradition of transatlantic travel.

Holland America Line. *300 Elliott Ave. W, Seattle, WA 98119, tel. 206/281-3535. Nieuw Amsterdam* built 1983, *Noordam* built 1984. 1,214 passengers each. Netherlands Antilles registry, Dutch officers, Indonesian and Filipino staff.

Fitness facilities: Gymnasium with Ultra Mac multipurpose 9-way muscular exercise unit, stationary bicycles, rowing machines, free and pully weights, slant boards, treadmills; 2 outdoor swimming pools (1 has whirlpool jets), 2 saunas. **Services:** Massage, loofah body scrub, facials, manicure, pedicure, hairstyling, makeup consultation. **Sports:** Tennis courts, shuffleboard, scuba instruction.

Fare for the spa package, with deluxe outside stateroom, from $2,335 per person double occupancy.

Norway

Fun and fitness are the objectives of the theme cruises with sports celebrities, fitness experts, and beauty specialists that depart weekly from Miami on the *Norway*. A dynamic "Fit With Fun" program is tailored to individual needs and fitness levels, so passengers do as much or as little as they want. Classes offer aerobics, swimnastics, calisthenics, and instruction in golf putting and driving. Team games are organized in the "*Norway* Olympics," and there's snorkeling at a beach party on NCL's private, uninhabited island in the Bahamas. The Fitness and Beauty Cruises scheduled at the end of October (alternate years on the *Seaward*, beginning 1989) include guest appearances by aerobics instructors from leading health resorts. Exercises under the Caribbean sky and lectures on nutrition, sports medicine, fitness, beauty, skin care, and makeup are included in the cruise fare. Running clinics help passengers get their sealegs by jogging on deck, and workouts with sports personalities are offered. Golf and tennis Pro Am cruises have four or five well-known professionals who will offer hints on improving your game, and there are opportunities for play ashore.

Norwegian Cruise Line. *2 Alhambra Plaza, Coral Gables, FL 33134, tel. 305/447-9660.* Launched in 1960 as the *France*, rebuilt in 1980. 1,864 passengers. Norwegian registry and officers, international staff.

Fitness facilities: Gymnasium with Universal equipment, stationary bicycles, rowing machines, free weights; 2 outdoor swimming pools, 1 indoor pool, sauna; no whirlpool or steam room. **Services:** Massage; hair, nail, and skin care. **Sports:** Racquetball, basketball, volleyball courts, golf putting and driving areas, skeet shooting.

Cruise fares $1,245–$2,950 per person depending on season.

Queen Elizabeth 2

The oceangoing teamwork of The Golden Door in California and the Cunard Line is best experienced on board the *Queen Eliza-*

beth 2. Introduced with instant success in 1982, the facilities have since been expanded to include a solarium and a massage center. Available at no extra charge to all passengers are a spacious exercise area with ballet barre, Jacuzzi whirlpool baths, and a hydrocalisthenics pool. The refurbished gymnasium, featuring state-of-the-art equipment, is open daily 7:30 AM–7 PM (7:30 AM–11 PM in port). The daily program begins with a wake-up stretch and a brisk walk on deck, gentle aerobics, and water exercises. One aerobics class is tailored to the special needs of men. Aerobic circuit training with weight equipment, exercise in chairs, and water volleyball are scheduled daily. The mirrored exercise area has glass doors that lead to a teak deck surrounding a swimming pool that has heated seawater at an ideal depth for doing laps or aquatic workouts. A library of videocassettes permits self-guided exercise. Special menu selections from the Golden Door spa cuisine are available in all dining rooms. The union is an unlikely one: the world's largest server of caviar joined with a spa where every pound lost costs more than a pound of caviar. Your reward for sticking to the program is a fitness cocktail party and certificate at the end of the cruise.

Cunard Line. *555 Fifth Ave., New York, NY 10017, tel. 212/661–7777 or 800/221–4770.* Launched in 1969; refurbished 1982, 1986. 1,815 passengers. British registry and crew.

Fitness facilities: Gymnasium with exercise weight equipment, stationary bicycles, treadmill, dumbbells; 4 swimming pools (2 indoors), sauna. Services: Massage, facials, manicure, pedicure, hairstyling. **Sports:** Optional shore excursions for scuba diving, windsurfing, nature walks.

Fares for 9-day Caribbean cruise $1,645–$5,600 per person double occupancy.

Royal Princess

Located high atop the *Royal Princess* on the Sun Deck, a well-equipped gymnasium affords panoramic views of the sea and excursion scenery to those working out. A quarter-mile cushioned jogging track circles the Promenade Deck. The dining room menu offers heart-healthy items that are low in sodium and cholesterol, prepared according to American Heart Association guidelines.

Princess Cruises. *2029 Century Park E, Los Angeles, CA 90067, tel. 213/553–1770 or 800/421–0522.* Commissioned in 1984. 1,200 passengers. British registry and officers, Italian dining room staff, British stewards.

Fitness facilities: Gymnasium with Hydrofitness 10-station multipurpose weights unit, rowing machines, treadmill, Lifecycles, slant boards, free weights; aerobics studio with classes at all levels scheduled daily; 4 outdoor swimming pools (with a 33-foot pool for laps), 2 whirlpools, sauna. **Services:** Massage, facials; hair, skin, and nail care.

Cruises include Alaska, Trans-Panama Canal, Caribbean. Fares for 10-night cruise, Acapulco–San Juan, from $2,370 including round-trip air connections.

Royal Viking Sun

A new addition to the parade of cruise ships in the Caribbean and around the world, the *Royal Viking Sun* upholds Royal Viking Line's reputation for luxury. Among its features are a computerized indoor golf simulator that enables passengers to play some of the world's most challenging courses and—breaking new ground—the first croquet court on a cruise ship. The elaborate Viking Spa overlooks the ship's pool area, where a swim-up bar permits you to combine exercise and socializing. One of the most spacious cruise ships afloat, offering more deck space and cabin room per passenger than most new ships, this newcomer has a library with working fireplace and butlers for the penthouse suites.

Royal Viking Line. *1 Embarcadero Center, San Francisco, CA 94111, tel. 415/398–8000 or 800/634–8000.* Debut season 1988–89. 740 passengers. Norwegian registry, Norwegian officers, European crew.

Fitness facilities: Gymnasium with equipment for toning muscles and building endurance; 2 heated outdoor saltwater swimming pools, saunas for men and women; aerobics studio with scheduled classes at all levels. **Services:** Massage, manicure, pedicure, facials, hairstyling. **Sports:** Badminton, tennis practice court, Ping-Pong, quoits, darts.

Fares for 19-day trans–Panama Canal cruise, New York–San Francisco via the Caribbean, $8,430–$14,610 per person double occupancy including air connections (shorter segments available).

Seabourn Pride

With almost an entire upper deck devoted to a seagoing spa, the *Seabourn Pride*—the creation of an experienced team of Norwegian and American designers—takes aim at the upscale cruiser who demands service and spaciousness. The all-suites ship has six passenger decks, an open-seating dining room where meals are prepared to order, and many attractive features. The spa program directed by Susan Harmsworth, formerly associated with England's Grayshott Hall Spa, includes a full range of aerobics and activities. Passengers may request a personalized fitness evaluation and dietary guidance. Treatments include body firming and silhouette refining with marine algae body wraps and baths, herbal massages, and facials. A staff of five specialists serves passengers daily. Shore excursions include ports rarely visited by large cruise ships, such as Soufrière Bay in St. Lucia, where a visit to the thermal baths can be arranged.

Seabourn Cruises. *55 Francisco St., San Francisco, CA 94133, tel. 415/391–7444.* Debut season 1988–1989. 212 passengers. Norwegian registry and officers, European staff.

Fitness facilities: Gymnasium with Nautilus exercise units, computerized exercycles, rowing machines, isotonic exercisers, free weights; outdoor swimming pool and twin whirlpool baths, sauna, steam room, aerobics studio. **Services:** Massage, body wraps, facial care, hairdressing, personal fitness consultation. **Sports:** Swimming from the ship's marina deck.

Fares for 14-day Caribbean cruise from Fort Lauderdale $7,610–$10,410 per person double occupancy.

Seaward

The *Seaward*, a Finnish-built addition to the Norwegian Cruise Line fleet, is a 42,000-ton beauty complete with cascading waterfall, cushioned running track, and basketball court. Although smaller than her big sister the *Norway*, she has a quarter-mile promenade deck that encircles the ship—a detail missing on many new liners. The top-deck spa, all glass and gleaming chrome, affords panoramic views of the sea to those working out. Separate saunas and showers are provided for men and women, and massage is performed by experts using Decleor organic and herbal products made in France. Afloat and ashore, the accent is on sports. The ship's two swimming pools and adjacent whirlpools have splash areas surrounded by Astroturf, where a "dive-in" center offers snorkeling equipment and instruction. Excursions in port take in some of the finest golf courses and tennis courts in the islands. Pro-Am cruises team passengers with golf and tennis pros on designated weeks throughout the year. Racquet Club cruises and Tee-Up golf cruises offer clinics and workshops at sea and special games and matches ashore. As host to the annual NCL Fitness and Beauty cruise in October 1989, the ship will become a seagoing spa with lectures and classes on nutrition, sports medicine, fitness, exercise, and personal image, jogging and running clinics, and a nature walk on a Bahamian out island. Dining alternatives include a choice of lighter meals at an informal cafe and an à la carte restaurant where meals are prepared to order.

Norwegian Cruise Line. *2 Alhambra Plaza, Coral Gables, FL 33134, tel. 305/447–9660 or 800/327–7030.* Inaugurated in 1988. 1,534 passengers. Bahamian registry, Norwegian officers, international crew.

Fitness facilities: Health spa with Universal equipment, stationary bicycles, aerobics studio with daily scheduled classes, Vita exercise course, rowing machines, free weights; 2 outdoor swimming pools, whirlpools, sauna, no steam room. **Services:** Massage, herbal wrap, waxing, manicure, pedicure, facials, hairstyling. **Sports:** Basketball, volleyball, snorkeling, skeet shooting, golf driving.

Cruises on Sun. from Miami, calling at Great Stirrup Cay, Ocho Rios in Jamaica, Grand Cayman, and Cozumel. Cruise fares $975–$2,145 per person double occupancy.

Sovereign of the Seas

Sovereign of the Seas, the world's largest ship, regal in every way, sports a central lobby area, the Centrum, that spans five decks where glass elevators whisk you to the ShipShape exercise center. Located one step down from the Sports Deck, this exercise and relaxation facility features the latest in weight training equipment, sauna, massage, and whirlpool. Passengers earn "ShipShape Dollars" by participating in activities that range from yoga and aerobics classes to shooting basketball free throws. The program offers 12 activities, beginning with a morning Walkathon of timed laps; other choices include aquacize in the swimming pools and team sports. Muscle tension can be soothed away with a cleansing sauna followed by a relaxing massage by qualified therapists. Dining options include a selection of light items that are highlighted on the regular menu as being low in sodium and cholesterol, in line with the American Heart Association guidelines. At the end of the cruise, passengers have an extra incentive to cash in fitness points for "ShipShape" T-shirts and visors.

Royal Caribbean Cruise Line. *903 South American Way, Miami, FL 33132, tel. 305/379-4731 or 800/327-6700 (800/245-7225 in Canada).* Commissioned in 1988. 2,690 passengers. Norwegian registry and officers, international staff.

Fitness facilities: Gymnasium with David pneumatic pressure exercise units, abdominal board, 5 Lifecycles, 6 Liferowers, StairMaster, Boland dumbbells; two outdoor swimming pools. **Services:** Massage, facials; hair, nail, and skin care; personalized exercise program. **Sports:** PGA sanctioned "Golf Ahoy" program aboard and ashore, tennis clinics, basketball, golf putting, shuffleboard, skeet shooting.

Cruises from Miami on Sat., calling at San Juan, St. Thomas, and a beach resort. Fares $1,365–$2,495 per person double occupancy.

Windjammer Figaro

The *Windjammer Figaro* provides an unusual opportunity for vegetarians and yoga devotees to sail among the islands of Maine and the Bahamas aboard a 51-foot yawl that offers programs in nutrition, nature studies, and seamanship. With accommodations for just six passengers, this ocean racing ship cruises from the storybook harbor of Camden, Maine, to secluded coves of Acadia National Park. Meals are based on whole grains, fresh garden vegetables, and fruit, in the macrobiotic tradition, with dairy products and coffee as desired. Dulse and mineral-rich seaweed are harvested at the source. There are opportunities for taking nature walks with resident naturalists, and passengers can participate in sailing the ship. Yoga for all levels, with a week for intermediate students of the Iyengar style, is taught on scheduled cruises during the summer and by request in winter. Journal writing and autobiography are examined as tools for personal growth. Life aboard is informal; smoking is not permitted.

Figaro Cruises. *Box 5035, Camden, ME 04843, tel. 207/236-8962.* Built in 1965, rebuilt in 1987. 6 passengers (2 double-berth cabins, 2 semiprivate berths). U.S. registry, Coast Guard inspected. Crew of 4.

Cruises on Mon. for 5 days, fares $400–$475 per person double occupancy; weekenders depart Sat. morning, with sleep-aboard privilege the night before sailing.

Wind Spirit

A blend of modern technology and the romance of cruising under sail, the yachtlike *Wind Spirit* offers a fitness center and a full program of water sports. While under sail, a computerized system raises the six sails automatically in less than two minutes. While anchored in secluded coves, away from the routes of the large cruise ships, the vessel's crew members organize waterskiing and snorkeling expeditions. For certified divers there is scuba equipment aboard. Shore excursions to golf and tennis resorts can be arranged through the ship's purser. Special menus will be provided on request in the dining room, where all passengers are seated at their convenience.

Windstar Sail Cruises. *7415 N.W. 19th St., Miami, FL 33126, tel. 305/592–8008 or 800/258–7245 (800/341–7245 in FL).* Commissioned in 1988. 150 passengers. Bahamian registry, international crew.

Fitness facilities: Exercise room with Apollo exercise units, stationary bikes, treadmill; outdoor swimming pool, sauna. **Services:** Massage. **Sports:** Water sports program, shore excursions for golf and tennis.

Cruises from St. Thomas on Sat., calling throughout the Virgin Islands. (A sister ship, the *Wind Star*, departs Antigua on Sun. for 7-day cruises of the Leeward islands.) Fares for 7-day cruise $2,195–$2,495 per person double occupancy.

Glossary

A **Acupressure.** Finger massage intended to release muscle tension by applying pressure to the nerves.

Acupuncture. A Chinese system that inserts pressure-point needles at key points of the body in order to relieve muscular, neurological, and arthritic problems.

Aerobics. Exercise routines orchestrated to enhance cardiovascular and muscular strength.

Aerobics studio. A gymnasium used strictly for floor exercise; a cushioned or suspended floor aids in avoiding injury.

Air-Dyne Bicycle. See *Schwinn Air-Dyne Bicycle.*

Alexander Technique. A massage system created in the 1890s by the Australian actor F. M. Alexander to correct physical habits that cause stress.

Aquaerobics. Aerobics workouts in a swimming pool: stretch, strength, and stamina exercises that combine water resistance and body movements. Also *aquafit.*

Aquafit. See *aquaerobics.*

Aromabath. See *herbal wrap.*

Aromatherapy. Massage with oils from essences of plants and flowers intended to relax the skin's connective tissues and stimulate the natural flow of lymph.

B **Bach Cures.** Healing with flowers.

Balneology. Traditional study and practice of water-based treatments using geothermal hot springs, mineral water, or seawater.

Barre. Balance bar or rail used during exercise.

Behavior modification. Change in personal habits brought about through counseling and psychological conditioning.

Biofeedback. Monitoring and control of physical functions such as blood pressure, pulse rate, digestion, and muscle tension with an electronic sensing device.

Body composition test. Evaluation of lean body mass and percentage of body fat, using standard weight charts; a computerized system compares personal data with standard percentages to determine whether an individual is overweight.

C **Calipers.** Measuring device used in determining the percentage of fat in the body.

Cardiovascular endurance. Oxygen utilization by the body.

Cathartic. Laxative compound of natural or organic substances.

Chiropractic. Realignment of the spine and bone/body mechanics.

Circuit training. The combination of aerobics and high-energy workout with weight-resistance equipment. Also *Circuit weight work*.

Circuit weight work. See *Circuit training*.

Cold plunge. Deep pool for the rapid contraction of the capillaries.

Colonic irrigation. Enema to cleanse high into the colon with water.

Contour. Calisthenics for deep toning of muscle groups.

Coordination. Connection and integration of parts of the body during movement.

Cross-country ski machine. A device that simulates the motions of cross-country skiing.

Cross-training. Alternative high-stress and low-stress exercise or sports to enhance physical and mental conditioning.

Cybex. Patented equipment for computer-aided isokinetic strength testing and training.

D **David System.** Pneumatic weight training units in which air is pumped. See *Circuit training*.

Drinking cure. Medically prescribed regime of mineral water consumption.

E **Ergometer.** Exercise machine designed for muscular contraction.

F **Facial.** Deep-cleansing massage.

Fango. A mud pack or body coating intended to promote the release of toxins and relieve muscular and arthritic pain.

Fast. Supervised diet of water, juice, nuts, seeds; intended to produce significant weight loss.

Feldenkrais. System of bodywork developed by Moshe Feldenkrais that attempts to reprogram the nervous system through movement augmented by physical pressure and manipulation.

Flex and stretch. Continuous movement exercises intended to increase endurance, flexibility, and muscular strength.

Flexibility. Muscular elasticity; the ability to stretch over joints.

Free weights. Hand-held dumbbells or barbells.

G **Gestalt.** Sensory awareness; the inner experience of being.

H **Haysack wrap.** Kniepp treatment with steamed hay intended to detoxify the body.

Hellerwork. A system of deep tissue bodywork, stress reduction, and movement reeducation developed by Joseph Heller.

Herbal bath. See *herbal wrap.*

Herbal wrap. A treatment in which moisture, heat, and herbal essences penetrate the skin while the body is wrapped in hot linens, plastic sheets, and blankets; it is intended to promote muscle relaxation and the elimination of toxins. Also *aromabath, herbal bath.*

Herbology. The therapeutic use of herbs in treatments and diet.

Holistic health. A nonmedical approach to the healing and health of the whole person that seeks to integrate physical and mental well-being.

Hot plunge. Deep pool for the rapid dilation of the capillaries.

Hot tub. A wooden soaking pool.

Hydromassage. See *hydrotub.*

Hydrotherapy. Underwater massage; alternating hot and cold showers; and other water-oriented treatments.

Hydrotub. Underwater massage in deep tubs equipped with high-pressure jets and hand-manipulated hose. Also *hydromassage.*

I Inhalations. Hot vapors, or steam mixed with eucalyptus oil, inhaled to decongest the respiratory system; breathed through inhalation equipment or in a special steam room.

Interval training. A combination of high-energy exercise followed by a period of low-intensity activity.

Iridology. A theory that links markings in the iris of the eye to the condition of organs of the body.

J Jacuzzi. A patented design of a whirlpool bath with underwater jets.

K Keiser Cam II. A patented system of pneumatic weight training units. Keiser Cam III is the new version.

Kinesiology. The testing and strengthening of muscles through exercise and diet, intended to achieve better balance in the body.

Kniepp cures. Treatments combining hydrotherapy, herbology, and a diet of natural foods, developed in Germany in the mid-1800s by Pastor Sebastian Kniepp.

L Lap pool. A shallow swimming pool with exercise lanes; the standard lap length is 50 feet.

Lifecycle. A computer-programmed exercise bike, made by Bally.

Liferower. A computer-programmed exercise machine that simulates rowing, made by Bally.

Loofah body scrub. Cleansing of the body with a mixture of sea salt, warm almond or avocado oil, and a loofah sponge.

Low-impact aerobics. A dancelike exercise in which one foot is always on the floor; intended to avoid muscle fatigue and to enhance cardiovascular fitness.

M **Macrobiotics.** A vegetarian diet low in fat and high in antioxidant vitamins.

Manicure. Nail care.

Massage. Soothing, energizing deep-muscle manipulation, usually by hand, intended to reduce stress and fatigue while improving circulation. Various methods.

Maximal heart rate. An individual's highest attainable heart rate (the number of heartbeats per minute). It is best determined by means of a graded maximal exercise test, but an estimate can be made by subtracting one's age from 220. See *target heart rate*.

Mineral bath. A soaking in hot or cool water from thermal springs that contains mineral salts, natural elements, and gases.

N **Naturopathy.** Natural healing prescriptions that use plants and flowers.

Nautilus. Patented strength training equipment designed to isolate one muscle group for each exercise movement that contracts and lengthens against gravity.

NordicTrack. A patented design of cross-country ski machine.

Nutrition counseling. The analysis of an individual's eating habits and dietary needs.

O **One-on-one training.** Personal instruction on exercise equipment from a professional exercise therapist.

Ovo-lacto diet. A regime that includes eggs and dairy products.

P **Parafango.** See *fango*.

Parcourse. A trail, usually outdoors, equipped with exercise stations. Also *parcours*, *vitacourse*.

Pedicure. Nail care and treatment of the feet to remove dead skin with a pumice stone or razor; involves soaking feet, scraping, and massage.

Polarity therapy. Balancing the energy within the body through a combination of massage, meditation, exercise, and diet; created by Dr. Randolph Stone.

Power. Anaerobic force exerted by a muscle.

R **Radiance technique.** See *Reiki*.

Rebirthing. A yoga breathing technique combined with guided meditation to relax and clear the mind. Also, reliving the experience of birth.

Rebounder. A miniature trampoline.

Reiki. An ancient healing method that teaches universal life energy through the laying on of hands and mental and spiritual balancing. Intended to relieve acute emotional and physical conditions. Also *Radiance technique.*

Reflexology. Massage of the pressure points on the feet, hands, and ears; intended to relax the parts of the body.

Rolfing. A bodywork system developed by Ida Rolf that improves balance and flexibility through manipulation of rigid muscles, bones, and joints. It is intended to improve energy flow and relieve stress (often related to emotional trauma).

Roman pool. A step-down whirlpool bath, for one or two persons.

Rowing machine. An exercise machine that simulates rowing; it can include computer graphics.

Rubenfeld Synergy. A method of integrating body and mind through verbal expression and gentle touch, developed by Ilana Rubenfeld.

S **Salt glow.** A cleansing treatment similar to the loofah body scrub. Also *salt rub.*

Salt rub. See *salt glow.*

Sauna. A wood-lined room with dry heat generated at temperatures of 160–210 degrees, intended to induce sweating to cleanse the body of impurities. In the Finnish tradition, which seeks even higher temperatures, heat is generated by a stove containing a heap of stones (*kiuas*) over which water is thrown to produce vapor (*löyly*).

Schwinn Air-Dyne Bicycle. A stationary exercise bike that works the upper and lower body simultaneously.

Scotch douche. A treatment with high-pressure hoses that alternate hot and cold water, intended to improve circulation through rapid contraction and dilation of the capillaries.

Shamanism. Spiritual and natural healing performed by medicine men.

Shiatsu. A massage technique developed by Tokujiro Namikoshi that uses finger (*shi*) pressure (*atsu*) to stimulate the body's inner powers of balance and healing.

Sitz bath. Immersion of the hips and lower body in herbal hot water, followed by cold water, to stimulate the immune system. Also a Kniepp treatment for constipation, hemorrhoids, prostate problems, menstrual problems, and digestive upsets.

Spa cuisine. Fresh, natural foods low in saturated fats and cholesterol, with an emphasis on whole grains, low-fat dairy products, lean protein, fresh fruit, fish, and vegetables and an avoidance of added salt and products containing sodium and artificial colorings, flavorings, and preservatives.

StairMaster. A patented exercise machine that simulates climbing stairs.

Steam room. A ceramic-tiled room with wet heat generated at temperatures of 110–130 degrees, intended to soften the skin, cleanse the pores, and calm the nervous system.

Stress management. A program of meditation and deep relaxation intended to reduce the ill effects of stress on the system.

Swedish massage. A treatment that duplicates gymnastics movements with stroking, kneading, friction, vibration, and tapping to relax muscles gently; devised at the University of Stockholm early in the 19th century by Henri Peter Ling.

Swiss shower. A multijet bath that alternates hot and cold water.

T Tai chi chuan. Physical movements intended to unite body and mind; an ancient oriental discipline for exercise and meditation.

Target heart rate. The number of heartbeats per minute an individual tries to attain during exercise; the figure is 60% to 90% of one's maximal heart rate. The American College of Sports Medicine recommends maintaining this rate for 20–30 minutes during exercise three to five days a week. See *maximal heart rate.*

Thalassotherapy. Water-based treatments that use seawater, seaweed, algae, and sea air; an ancient Greek therapy.

Trager massage. A technique developed by Milton Trager that employs a gentle, rhythmic shaking of the body to release tension from the joints. Intended for sensory repatterning.

Treadmill. An exercise machine that simulates walking.

U Universal Gym. A patented weight training system.

V Vegetarian diet. A regime of raw or cooked vegetables and fruit, grains, sprouts, and seeds; natural foods with no additives.

VersaClimber. A patented exercise machine that simulates the climbing of stairs.

W Water volleyball. The net game played in a pool.

Whirlpool. A hot pool with water rushing from jets on the sides at temperatures of 105–115 degrees, used to stimulate the system and relax sore muscles.

Y Yoga. A discipline of stretching and toning the body through movements or asana postures, controlled deep breathing, relaxation techniques, and diet. A school of Hindu philosophy that advocates physical and mental discipline for the unity of mind, body, and spirit.

Z Zen shiatsu. A Japanese acupressure art intended to relieve tension and balance the body.

Fodor's Travel Guides

U.S. Guides

Alaska
American Cities
The American South
Arizona
Atlantic City & the
  New Jersey Shore
Boston
California
Cape Cod
Carolinas & the
  Georgia Coast
Chesapeake
Chicago
Colorado
Dallas & Fort Worth
Disney World & the
  Orlando Area

The Far West
Florida
Greater Miami,
  Fort Lauderdale,
  Palm Beach
Hawaii
Hawaii *(Great Travel
  Values)*
Houston & Galveston
I-10: California to
  Florida
I-55: Chicago to New
  Orleans
I-75: Michigan to
  Florida
I-80: San Francisco to
  New York

I-95: Maine to Miami
Las Vegas
Los Angeles, Orange
  County, Palm Springs
Maui
New England
New Mexico
New Orleans
New Orleans *(Pocket
  Guide)*
New York City
New York City *(Pocket
  Guide)*
New York State
Pacific North Coast
Philadelphia
Puerto Rico *(Fun in)*

Rockies
San Diego
San Francisco
San Francisco *(Pock
  Guide)*
Texas
United States of
  America
Virgin Islands
  (U.S. & British)
Virginia
Waikiki
Washington, DC
Williamsburg,
  Jamestown &
  Yorktown

Foreign Guides

Acapulco
Amsterdam
Australia, New Zealand
  & the South Pacific
Austria
The Bahamas
The Bahamas *(Pocket
  Guide)*
Barbados *(Fun in)*
Beijing, Guangzhou &
  Shanghai
Belgium & Luxembourg
Bermuda
Brazil
Britain *(Great Travel
  Values)*
Canada
Canada *(Great Travel
  Values)*
Canada's Maritime
  Provinces
Cancún, Cozumel,
  Mérida, The
  Yucatán
Caribbean
Caribbean *(Great
  Travel Values)*

Central America
Copenhagen,
  Stockholm, Oslo,
  Helsinki, Reykjavik
Eastern Europe
Egypt
Europe
Europe *(Budget)*
Florence & Venice
France
France *(Great Travel
  Values)*
Germany
Germany *(Great Travel
  Values)*
Great Britain
Greece
Holland
Hong Kong & Macau
Hungary
India
Ireland
Israel
Italy
Italy *(Great Travel
  Values)*
Jamaica *(Fun in)*

Japan
Japan *(Great Travel
  Values)*
Jordan & the Holy Land
Kenya
Korea
Lisbon
Loire Valley
London
London *(Pocket Guide)*
London *(Great Travel
  Values)*
Madrid
Mexico
Mexico *(Great Travel
  Values)*
Mexico City & Acapulco
Mexico's Baja & Puerto
  Vallarta, Mazatlán,
  Manzanillo, Copper
  Canyon
Montreal
Munich
New Zealand
North Africa
Paris
Paris *(Pocket Guide)*

People's Republic of
  China
Portugal
Province of Quebec
Rio de Janeiro
The Riviera *(Fun or*
Rome
St. Martin/St. Maa
Scandinavia
Scotland
Singapore
South America
South Pacific
Southeast Asia
Soviet Union
Spain
Spain *(Great Trave
  Values)*
Sweden
Switzerland
Sydney
Tokyo
Toronto
Turkey
Vienna
Yugoslavia

Special-Interest Guides

Bed & Breakfast
  Guide: North America
1936...On the
  Continent

Royalty Watching
Selected Hotels of
  Europe

Selected Resorts
  and Hotels of the U.S.
Ski Resorts of North
  America

Views to Dine by
  around the World

Reader's Survey

Join us in updating the next edition of your Fodor's Guide

Title of Guide:

1 Hotel □ Restaurant □ Shop □ Other □ *(check one)*

Name

Number/Street

City/State/Country

Comments

2 Hotel □ Restaurant □ Shop □ Other □ *(check one)*

Name

Number/Street

City/State/Country

Comments

3 Hotel □ Restaurant □ Shop □ Other □ *(check one)*

Name

Number/Street

City/State/Country

Comments

Your Name *(optional)*

Address

General Comments

Business Reply Mail

First Class   Permit Nº 7775   New York, NY

Postage will be paid by addressee

Fodor's Travel Publications

201 East 50th Street
New York, NY 10022